United States History:

SINCE 1865
Fifth Edition

Nelson Klose
Professor Emeritus, American History
San Jose State University

Curt Lader
Formerly President,
Columbia Scholastic Press Advisor's Association
Columbia University, New York

BARRON'S

All inquiries should be addressed to:
Barron's Educational Series, Inc.
250 Wireless Boulevard
Hauppauge, New York 11788

International Standard Book No. 0-8120-1835-4

Library of Congress Catalog Card No. 93-50952

Library of Congress Cataloging-in-Publication Data

Klose, Nelson, 1914–
 United States history, since 1865 / Nelson Klose, Curt
Lader. — 5th ed.
  p.   cm.
 Rev. ed. of v. 2 of: United States history. 4th ed. ©1983.
 Includes bibliographical references and index.
 ISBN 0-8120-1835-4
 1. United States—History—1865–1898—Outlines, syllabi,
etc. 2. United States—History—20th century—Outlines, syl-
labi, etc. I. Lader, Curt. II. Klose, Nelson, 1914–   United
States history. III. Title.
E661.K62   1994   93-50952
973—dc20   CIP

PRINTED IN THE UNITED STATES OF AMERICA

4567   9770   987654321

TO THE STUDENT

This book has been written to simplify and present the essentials of American history in unified topics to help college students understand and remember subject-matter. The authors have specialized for many years in teaching American history and understand the explanations they need. A controlling aim has been to avoid personal, original interpretations that are unavoidably controversial and confusing to students. Such originality of treatment reflecting individual interpretations and choice of subject-matter and emphasis limits the usefulness of the usual study aid. The author has avoided the enlargement of his favorite subjects and has sought to explain American history rather than "reinterpret" it. A student aid should not attempt to be encyclopedic; accordingly, the selective approach used here has avoided the fault of citing unimportant persons and a multitude of official names of agencies and of less significant legislation.

How To Use this Book—Special features have been provided to make this book especially helpful. The topical treatment of subject-matter arranges significant facts and the explanation of each topic in a unified discussion that is easy to follow. This avoids the choppiness and fragmentation of "outlines" and makes it unnecessary to artificially force bits of information under headings where they may not belong. The relative importance of subjects, as determined by the consensus of leading history textbooks, is indicated at the beginning of each topic by stars (✪). This more significant information will be emphasized in well-balanced college examinations; some examination questions, however, will probe, quite properly, the thoroughness of the student's preparation by questions over less significant material.

Dates carried at the top of each page guide the student in locating events by chronology; attention to developmental chronological arrangement of topics has made this possible. Anachronistic organization of topics under large-subject headings in literary treatments confuse history students, who think chronologically, as they should. A chronological arrangement is more likely to parallel any given textbook than an arrangement of subject-matter under broad headings.

Students should underline for themselves important names, dates, and facts as indicated by the instructor in the classroom; this underscoring is an important learning exercise in itself. It is assumed the student will probably be assigned a traditional textbook with its detailed treatment. Bibliographies are provided here to guide the student in selecting additional reading and sources for doing assigned written projects. A large number of review questions have been provided after each chapter, and essay questions for midterm and final examination review are given in the back of the book.

Use of Stars—This guide offers a useful feature to assist the student and teacher in concentrating attention on the relatively more significant subjects in the great mass of materials presented in American history courses and textbooks. The authors have inserted stars (✪) before headings to indicate the importance of each topic. The determination of the relative importance of topics represents a consensus based upon a study of widely used textbooks, books of selected readings and documents, and subjects covered by prepared examination questions offered for the use of students and teachers.

Three stars (✪✪✪) indicate topics of great significance, two stars (✪✪) indicate important topics, one star (✪) indicates topics of secondary importance, and topics not marked are of least relative significance but too important to omit. This use of stars should help the student gain perspective, but since opinions vary, students should be alert to the individual instructor's judgment of the significance of topics covered in his or her lectures. To be well prepared for examinations, students should "overlearn" the more important topics and study the others as time permits.

How To Use the Review Questions—Review questions of several types follow each chapter. The student should know that these questions have been carefully prepared to give the types of questions at the level of difficulty the student is likely to encounter in college objective examinations. They have been prepared for use as study exercises and by themselves, will give the student a substantial review of important subject matter. For good reasons college teachers much prefer to use the multiple-choice items; therefore, more space has been given to this type of question. The name "best-answer" is actually a better description of this type of question. If these questions are ideally framed, the student will often find that there are two or more alternate responses that seem to be correct; therefore, the student needs to consider each response carefully and select the response that seems to be the "best answer"—rather than throwing down the first answer that appears to be satisfactory. In using these exercises for review, remember that it is just as helpful to understand why a statement is untrue as to know that it is true.

Dictionary of Important and Difficult Terms—A full dictionary and glossary has been added to provide definitions conveniently for difficult, confusing, and more important terms. It is suggested the student mark those that are difficult and concentrate all study upon them. If a term is not found here, use the index to locate it in the main body of the book.

TO THE INSTRUCTOR

The instructor who wishes to replace the traditional textbook with supplementary, selected readings of sources, documents, and interpretative articles should find this ample summary sufficient to supply the basic, factual subject-matter of his course. Classroom time can then be used for lectures on special subjects, discussion, and the use of other teaching devices instead of dictating essential subject-matter to students. This condensed treatment could be used also in conjunction with an inexpensive paperback United States history (not necessarily a standard textbook) with literary and interpretive features. This plan would still leave the student enough time and textbook budget to afford a book of "readings" or documents. Or, still better, a selection of fine paperback histories, of which so many are now available, could be substituted for the traditional textbook. Lists of currently available paperbacks are provided here after each chapter, but many new titles are constantly being issued. For these see Bowker's guide to *Paperbound Books in Print*.

The *Chronology* at the beginning of each chapter is intended to give the student a summary of leading events and to satisfy his queries regarding important dates. The *Review Questions* following each chapter and essay questions in the Appendix may be used by the student in lieu of a workbook or other guide to provide study exercises. They also might be suggested for the student's use as review exercises for examinations and to illustrate the type of questions to be expected in both objective and essay examinations.

The emphasis in this concise guide has been placed upon the traditional subject-matter of political, diplomatic, military, and economic history. Cultural and intellectual developments are selected mainly when there is a consensus of opinion as to their significance and to their relevance to traditional subjects.

CONTENTS

(Stars are used to indicate the relative importance of topics. See instructions "To the Student" for "Use of Stars.")

THE CONSERVATIVE PERIOD, 1877–1900   61

6. POLITICAL DEVELOPMENTS, 1877–1889   64

THE RECONSTRUCTION PERIOD, 1865–1877

CHRONOLOGY / CHAPTER 1

1863 Lincoln's plan of easy reconstruction announced.

1864 Wade-Davis Bill vetoed by Lincoln, a defeat for policy of harsh reconstruction.

1865 Andrew Johnson succeeded to Presidency after Lincoln's assassination.

Johnson proceeded to reconstruct South along lines of Lincoln's plan.

Black Codes passed by Southern states.

Sumner and Stevens control Joint Committee on Reconstruction and thwart Johnson's plan to reconstruct the South.

1866 Napoleon III's withdrawal of troops from Mexico vindicates Monroe Doctrine.

Johnson vetoed Freedmen's Bureau Bill.

Race riots in the South.

Civil Rights Bill passed over Johnson's veto.

Ku Klux Klan organized in the South.

1867 Alaska purchased from Russia.

✪✪✪   GREAT SIGNIFICANCE
✪✪   IMPORTANT TOPICS
✪   SECONDARY IMPORTANCE

1
EARLY RECONSTRUCTION, 1865–1866

> The term "Reconstruction Period" designates the years following the surrender of Confederate military forces in April 1865 to the final withdrawal of Union occupation troops in the early part of 1877. During this time the North attempted to reshape Southern government and society according to goals determined by the victorious North.

THE PROBLEM OF RECONSTRUCTION

The word "Reconstruction" was applied to Northern endeavors to restore the Southern states to the Union under certain stipulations set forth by the presidents and Congress. In its broader meaning the term takes in the whole process of attempting to rebuild and change the South along lines suitable to the North. Reconstruction ended without achieving its far-reaching goals of social and political reform.

✪ **Physical and Economic Ruin in the South After the War—** The South, as the battlefield of the war, suffered much destruction. South Carolina, Georgia, and Virginia suffered most from the destruction of the campaigns and from the scorched earth policy of Sherman in Georgia and of Sheridan in the Shenandoah Valley of Virginia.

Cities were shelled and burned and farmhouses destroyed as the invading Union armies sought to destroy the war potential of the South. Systematic destruction of railroads and bridges and wartime wear and neglect left transportation severely crippled. River shipping, seaports, and country roads were destroyed or left in sad disrepair.

Much private property in the South had been confiscated during the war. Confederate government property, including cotton in storage, naturally became property of the victors. Many dishonest individuals, either actual Treasury agents or thieves posing as Treasury agents, wrongfully confiscated private holdings of livestock, cotton, and other farm commodities from intimidated Southerners.

Individuals in the South suffered disastrous economic losses. Banks all closed their doors and individual accounts were lost. Confederate currency became only a collectors' item. Holders of war bonds lost their investment; the emancipation of slaves meant the loss of valuable property to their owners. Farm land lost most of its value as the result of the loss of the slaves and other economic disruption, and many plantations were foreclosed for taxes. The whole country faced the problem of physical rebuilding, and of devising a new economic system under which the African American might work. The South is the only part of the United States that has experienced the disaster of losing a war.

Social Losses and Upheaval—About 250,000 Southern men died in uniform and others returned crippled, while many civilians lost their lives as a consequence of the war. The emancipation of the slaves uprooted hundreds of thousands of them and brought sudden freedom, for which they were unprepared. Their labor was lost and they created a social problem for themselves and for the South as they wandered about looking for food and trying, like children, to enjoy their new freedom.

✪✪✪ **Lincoln's Plan of Reconstruction**—As the armies of the North occupied Southern territory, the North faced the problem of organizing loyal state governments. Lincoln assumed control and appointed as provisional governors Northern military commanders. Late in 1863 Lincoln formulated a simple and generous plan to achieve a speedy return of the conquered states. 1) Pardons were offered all residents of the South, except for higher political and military leaders, on condition they take an oath of allegiance to the United States. 2) As soon as ten percent of those who had voted in 1860 had taken the oath of allegiance to the federal government and to support the Thirteenth Amendment, a state government could be organized and recognized by the President. Some Congressional leaders thought this plan was too lenient and spoke of it derisively as the "ten percent plan." Under this plan governments in Tennessee, Louisiana, Arkansas, and Virginia were recognized by Lincoln.

✪✪ **Bases of Opposition to Moderate Reconstruction Policy**— From the beginning of the Lincoln administration there was a division of opinion within the Republican Party towards the South. While the moderate Republicans, like Lincoln, favored a lenient and understanding policy, the Radical Republicans favored harsh policies and more extreme reforms in the South.

Differences between the Presidential and Radical plans may be explained as follows: 1) The Radicals feared that the supremacy of the Republican party, a newcomer to the political scene, might prove to be temporary if Northern and Southern Democrats should become united, as they had been before the war. 2) Conflict over the authority of the President was another cause of the opposition of Congress to Lincoln. Many congressmen were convinced that the President had exceeded his proper authority during the war and afterwards in assuming control over reconstruction of the Southern states. 3) There was disagreement with

Lincoln regarding the legal status of the South. Lincoln held that the states of the South had never ceased to exist, nor had they left the Union; they could not legally secede. This theory would limit the power of Congress to freely govern and reorganize the South as it might choose. 4) A strong desire among Northerners to punish the South asserted itself because of the sacrifice made to fight a long and costly war.

5) Behind most of the measures of political reconstruction in the South was the desire of Northern business interests to preserve and strengthen the Republican Party as the advocate of business interests. It was planned to keep the South impotent politically until the Republican Party had consolidated its gains and carried out its program. The control of the African American vote was a part of this plan. 6) Reformers in the North wished to promote social changes to humble and weaken the planter aristocracy of the South. They unwisely and revengefully sought to give full and immediate equality to the former slaves. The drastic measures they took were to embitter the South and cause hardship to the freedmen, and make more difficult their adjustment to freedom and responsibility.

○ The Wade-Davis Bill (July 1864)—The Radical Republicans, the advocates of extreme reforms and punitive measures in the South, early challenged Lincoln's moderate measures. Under their leadership Congress passed the Wade-Davis Bill to give the Radicals control over the South. Lincoln gave the bill a pocket veto. Nevertheless, it demonstrated that Lincoln would have to deal with determined opposition in Congress from members of his own party. But Lincoln hoped to restore the Southern states to their former place in the Union before Congress could act.

○○ Johnson's Plan of Reconstruction—The assassination of Lincoln on April 15, 1865 threw the problem of reconstruction into the hands of the new President, Andrew Johnson. The Radicals assumed that Johnson would go along with their plans, since he had often railed against the planter aristocrats in favor of more political power for the common whites of the South. Johnson had remained in the Senate when his own state, Tennessee, seceded. However, as a Democrat and a Southerner, Johnson favored a moderate policy. He wished to leave the Southern states free from federal intervention in what he considered internal affairs. He proceeded, therefore, to carry out a policy very similar to Lincoln's. Johnson's plan 1) called for the appointment of Southern civilians as provisional governors. 2) Next, constitutional conventions were to be called by the states and to be made up of delegates who had taken the oath of allegiance to the United States. 3) The conventions would next be expected to a) withdraw the ordinances of secession, b) abolish slavery, and c) cancel all Confederate war debts.

Having completed these steps, the states could resume their former places in the Union. The Southern states carried out this plan or were on their way to doing so when Congress convened in December 1865. None of the states made provision to permit the freedmen to vote; Congress resented this and soon showed their unwillingness to recognize Johnson's plan. Congress refused to seat senators and representatives chosen by state governments under Johnson's plan.

POSTWAR DIPLOMACY UNDER JOHNSON

To President Johnson fell the task of expelling the French from Mexico, thereby upholding the Monroe Doctrine. Johnson and Seward handled this problem tactfully and secured French withdrawal during the time of the conflict with Congress over reconstruction policy. The purchase of Alaska originated with friendly wartime relations with Russia.

✪✪✪ **The French in Mexico**—French intervention began in 1862 when Archduke Maximilian of Austria, with the support of the French forces in collaboration with reactionary landowners and churchmen in Mexico, was enthroned as Emperor of Mexico. In back of the French intervention was the Emperor Napoleon III and his ambitions for an empire. Mexico was only one of a half-dozen instances of Napoleon's aggression. The ambitious young couple, Maximilian and Carlota, were the unwitting dupes of Napoleon's scheme. Secretary of State Seward demanded the withdrawal of the French troops that upheld the French puppets against the will of the people of Mexico, but the Civil War precluded the use of American troops. In the fall of 1865 General Sheridan was sent to the Texas border at the Rio Grande by Johnson and Seward, and quiet demands invoking the Monroe Doctrine were made again for withdrawal; at the same time Benito Juarez, the revolutionary leader, was tacitly recognized. With growing problems of his own in Europe, Napoleon had no alternative and withdrew his troops in May 1866. Without foreign military support, Maximilian was captured and shot by a Mexican firing squad. The American course of action further reinforced the Monroe Doctrine.

✪✪ **Territorial Expansion, 1867**—Secretary of State Seward, an eager expansionist, was approached in December 1866 by the Russian minister in a move that resulted in the purchase of Alaska by the United States. The friendliness of the Russians in sending their fleet to New York during the Civil War opened the way for these negotiations. The Russians wished to sell Alaska because its fur resources had now been well exhausted. Expecting that friction with Great Britain might lead to war and the capture of defenseless Alaska by the British, the Russians preferred to see it in American hands.

The United States bought "Seward's Folly" in 1867 chiefly through the energetic efforts of the Secretary of State. It was urged that the purchase would repay the Russians for their show of friendship during the Civil

War. Rumors of its wealth of furs, fish, and gold, along with a propaganda campaign, helped to convince Congress of the wisdom of the purchase. It proved to be a profitable acquisition at a cost of $7,200,000.

In 1867 the United States also occupied the Midway Islands west of Hawaii; the United States had discovered them in 1859. Seward negotiated a treaty with Denmark for the purchase of the Virgin Islands, but it failed to pass the Senate.

THE BEGINNINGS OF CONGRESSIONAL RECONSTRUCTION

In order to control and delay reconstruction of the conquered states, the Radicals of both houses of Congress appointed a Joint Committee on Reconstruction.

✪✪✪ **Leaders of Congressional Reconstruction**—The outstanding Radical congressional leader was Thaddeus Stevens, a Representative from Pennsylvania long noted for his advocacy of popular reforms, his hatred of the ruling class of the South, and his sincere sympathy for the African American. His theory of reconstruction held that the Southern states had become "conquered provinces," completely at the disposal of Congress. He maintained his domineering and vindictive leadership in Congress until 1868.

Charles Sumner, from Massachusetts, became the Senate Radical leader on the Joint Committee on Reconstruction. In bad health, avowedly due to the beating by Preston Brooks, his mind was obsessed with the single question of the African American. As an idealist and reformer, he wished to enforce immediate racial equality. From cynical, selfish motives, the other Radicals permitted these misguided idealists to dominate Congress. Sumner reasoned, under his theory of "state suicide," that the Southern states had destroyed themselves by secession and were now as completely at the disposal of Congress as any territory.

✪ **Mistakes of the South**—The Southern states chose many former high-ranking Confederate leaders to represent them in Congress upon the restoration of their state governments under Johnson's plan; this greatly irritated the North.

The "Black Codes" were passed by the Southern legislatures to settle the future status of the freedmen. These laws were meant to protect the freedmen from their own helplessness, to make sure they would go back to work, and to severely restrict their legal, social, and economic rights.

Race riots occurred in the early part of 1866 in certain parts of the South with considerable loss of life, especially among the freedmen.

These events in the South played into the hands of the Radicals, who now contended that the South was unwilling to accept the verdict of the war and that strong measures were necessary.

○ **The Freedmen's Bureau Bill**—The first direct clash between the President and Congress occurred in February 1866, when Congress passed a bill to renew the Freedmen's Bureau. This agency, though basically a wartime relief organization of the national government, came to be used as a political device for making the African Americans loyal to the Republican Party. Because it represented federal action in an area which Johnson, with his states' rights views, believed should be left to the states, he vetoed the bill. The Radicals were unable to command enough votes to override the veto. As a consequence Johnson became overconfident and tactlessly denounced the Radicals and strongly criticized their leaders.

○ **The Civil Rights Bill**—Soon afterwards, in March, Congress passed the Civil Rights Bill. This law gave the African Americans citizenship and equal civil rights. The bill was vetoed by Johnson but now repassed over his veto. The Radicals next passed a slightly modified Freedmen's Bureau Bill over the President's veto and thereby demonstrated that they now had the upper hand.

CHAPTER BOOK LIST

Current, R.N., *Lincoln Nobody Knows* (American Century).

Degler, Carl, *The Other South* (1974).

Donald, Hendersen H., *The Negro Freedman: The Early Years After Emancipation* (1952).

Foner, Eric, *Reconstruction: America's Unfinished Revolution* (1988). Good one-volume account.

Franklin, John Hope, *Reconstruction After the Civil War* (University of Chicago).

Litwack, Leon F., *Been in the Storm So Long: The Aftermath of Slavery* (1979). The African American experience of emancipation.

McKitrick, Eric L., *Andrew Johnson and Reconstruction* (1960) (University of Chicago).

Patrick, Rembert W., *The Reconstruction of the Nation* (1967).

Randall, J.G., *Lincoln: The Liberal Statesman* (Apollo).

Randall, J.G., *The Civil War and Reconstruction* (1961). Scholarly and readable.

Williams, T.H., *Lincoln and the Radicals* (University of Wisconsin).

Woodward, C. Wann, *The Strange Career of Jim Crow* (1953).

REVIEW QUESTIONS

MULTIPLE CHOICE

1. Lincoln's and Johnson's reconstruction policies agreed in which way? (1) Both appointed military men as governors in the South (2) neither favored cancellation of Confederate war debts (3) both held that the Southern states had never been out of the Union (4) neither favored compensated emancipation.

2. Which necessitated the greatest economic readjustment in the South after the war? (1) Emancipation of slaves (2) confiscatory taxes (3) disruption of export markets (4) property damage.

3. Which motive was least apparent in Radical reconstruction plans for the South? (1) Consolidation of the Republican Party in the South (2) equality for the African American (3) hasty reconciliation of North and South (4) humiliation of ex-Confederates.

4. The Radicals hoped Johnson would acquiesce in their reconstruction plans because Johnson (1) had always been a Republican (2) favored equality for the African American (3) believed in states' rights (4) disliked the Southern aristocrats.

5. Congress early killed Johnson's reconstruction plans by (1) impeachment proceedings against him (2) refusing to seat congressmen from the South (3) early military occupation of the South (4) emancipation of all slaves.

6. The French intervention in Mexico was undertaken to (1) enlarge the French empire (2) aid the Confederacy (3) sustain the upper class in Mexico (4) forestall British intervention.

7. The negotiations for the purchase of Alaska began with an offer by (1) President Johnson (2) Secretary Seward (3) Russia (4) President Grant.

8. Which of these events did not occur in the South and convince the North that stronger measures were needed to reconstruct the South? (1) Refusal to ratify the Thirteenth Amendment (2) the "Black Codes" (3) race riots (4) election of former Confederates to Congress.

9. The Freedmen's Bureau was organized primarily to (1) provide relief and aid to freed slaves (2) organize the African American vote for the Republican Party (3) confiscate and redistribute plantation lands (4) intimidate Southern voters.

10. Which did *not* occur during the Reconstruction Period? (1) Congress dominated the Supreme Court (2) systematic, widespread redistribution of plantation lands was realized (3) the Radicals defied the office of the President (4) corruption in government was widespread.

TRUE-FALSE

11. Reconstruction was notably successful in achieving its goals.

12. Treasury agents rightfully confiscated cotton and other property belonging to the defeated Confederate government.

13. Individuals in the South escaped serious economic loss in the war.

14. Lincoln appointed Southern civilians as governors in the states under Reconstruction.

15. Lincoln accepted several states as being "reconstructed" under his plan.

16. One of the strongest motives behind the harsh reconstruction policy of the Radicals was the desire to entrench the Republican Party in the South and to remain powerful as the spokesman of the victorious Northern business interests.

17. Many Congressmen sincerely believed the presidents had exceeded their rightful authority in assuming control of Reconstruction.

18. The policy of the Radicals was first proposed in the extremist Wade-Davis Bill.

19. Under his reconstruction plan Johnson appointed military commanders over the Southern states.

20. The Southern states all made plans to give the vote to the freedmen under Johnson's reconstruction plan.

21. Johnson vetoed the Freedmen's Bureau Bill because he felt it dealt with a type of activity that should be left to the states.

COMPLETION

22. The Reconstruction Period extended from _____ to _____ .

23. Lincoln's reconstruction plan was called the _____ .

24. President Johnson asserted the right of the United States under the _____ to expel the French from Mexico.

25. It was the emperor of France _____ who intervened in Mexico during the Civil War and made _____ emperor of Mexico.

26. Alaska was purchased in the year _____ ; about the same time a treaty with _____ for the purchase of the Virgin Islands failed to pass the Senate.

27. The leader of the Radical Republicans in the House was _____ and in the Senate was _____ . Their theories of reconstruction were called respectively the _____ theory and the _____ theory.

28. After the Civil War the South passed the _____ to regulate the behavior of the freedmen.

CHRONOLOGY / CHAPTER 2

1866   After February, Radicals gained enough adherents in Congress to override Johnson's vetoes.

Johnson's supporters in Congress reduced by congressional elections.

In December, Radicals began to enact harsh measures to reconstruct the South.

1867   Reconstruction Act of 1867 applied main features of Congressional Reconstruction.

Fourteenth Amendment passed by Congress.

Tenure of Office Act passed over Johnson's veto.

Impeachment proceedings against President Johnson begun.

1868   Attempt to remove Johnson from office failed by one vote.

Fourteenth Amendment ratified.

Grant (Rep.) elected President.

1869   Grant began first term as President.

1870   Fifteenth Amendment ratified.

Reconstruction governments ended in most Southern states.

First Enforcement Act passed to suppress Ku Klux Klan.

1872   Amnesty Act restored political rights to most former Confederates.

1876   Election results disputed but settled in 1877 in favor of Hayes (Rep.). Party leaders agree to withdraw federal troops from last of the Southern states.

1877   Reconstruction governments ended in all Southern states.

Rule of the "Solid South" began.

Chapter

2
THE CONGRESSIONAL RECONSTRUCTION PERIOD, 1866–1877

After the Radicals in Congress had gained sufficient votes to carry their program against the President, they permitted few restraints to block their program. The authority of both the President and the Supreme Court were disregarded. After a few years Northern opinion revolted against the arbitrary policies and untimely reforms of the Radicals. Social and political reconstruction substantially failed to achieve its long-range goals in the South.

THE STRUGGLE BETWEEN CONGRESS AND THE PRESIDENT

Congress refused to seat members elected by the Southern states under Johnson's plan. After February 1866, the Radicals had enough adherents in Congress to override presidential vetoes. Congress next sought to nullify all interference by Johnson, even going so far as to attempt a political impeachment.

✪ **Johnson and the Elections of 1866**—The congressional elections of 1866 provided a popular referendum by which the North could endorse either Johnson's policies or those of Congress.

President Johnson entered the campaign vigorously to win election of his supporters to Congress. He made the typical tour of campaign speeches to Chicago and back to Washington, the "swing around the circle." His enemies campaigned more effectively; the President was heckled and angered into undignified retorts to his enemies among his audiences. The Radicals argued that a victory for Johnson would bring low tariffs and repudiation of the national war debt. Such events in the South as the election of ex-Confederates, the race riots, and the black codes convinced many Northern voters that the more strenuous program of the Radicals was needed. In the same election ten Southern states angered the North by rejecting the Fourteenth Amendment.

13

The Radicals won overwhelming control of both the Senate and the House and now proceeded without hindrance in the enactment of their program.

✪✪✪ The Congressional Plan of Reconstruction—When Congress reconvened in December 1866, the Radicals enacted a series of laws that were vindictive and intended to assure the perpetuation of Radical Republican rule.

1) The Tenure of Office Act forbade the President from removing civil officers without the consent of the Senate; the purpose was to prevent Johnson from removing Radicals from office. 2) The Army Act was passed to make the military establishment almost free of presidential control.

3) The Reconstruction Act of March 2, 1867 a) rejected the new state governments in all the South except in Tennessee; b) the South was divided into five military districts, each under a high-ranking Northern army officer; c) in each district all voters were to be registered so as to enfranchise the freedmen and deny the vote to large numbers of white voters for disloyalty. This provision ensured Radical control of state governments. d) Another provision required the states to provide for African American suffrage under newly drafted constitutions. e) The Fourteenth Amendment had to be ratified by state legislatures. f) Newly elected senators and representatives must be able to take the "ironclad oath" that they had never voluntarily aided the Confederacy. 4) Another act required that Congress convene on March 4, 1867. This was done to insure that they would remain in session to dominate reconstruction policies.

✪✪✪ The Fourteenth Amendment—In the summer of 1866, the Radicals passed the Fourteenth Amendment to fix into law more firmly the provisions of the Civil Rights Bill. It was not ratified until 1868. This "Omnibus Amendment" carried several other provisions to put the Radical program into effect and ensure its success.

1) It gave citizenship with full rights to all persons born or naturalized in the country and forbade the states to pass any law to restrict such rights or deny equal protection. This same section forbade any state to deprive any person of life, liberty, or property without due process of law.

2) The next section, which was to become a dead letter, provided that to the extent that any state denied the vote to any of its male inhabitants, it would have its representation proportionately reduced in Congress and in the Electoral College.

3) The third section took from the President the traditional pardoning power by which ex-Confederates might be permitted to hold any state or federal offices.

4) The fourth section guaranteed the payment of the United States Civil War debt, but prohibited the payment of any debt or obligation incurred by the Confederacy and precluded any compensation for loss of slave property.

5) The power of enforcement of its provisions was vested in Congress, although traditionally the executive is the law-enforcing branch of government. The Radicals would not entrust its enforcement to President Johnson.

The Fourteenth Amendment went into effect in July 1868, after ratification by the Southern states while under carpetbag control.

✪✪✪ The Impeachment of Johnson—Although the Radicals had enough votes to override any presidential veto, they were determined to consolidate their strength further by removing Johnson from office by impeachment. Johnson ordinarily was careful to abide by the laws enacted by Congress. However, in August 1867, he asked for the resignation of Edwin M. Stanton, the two-faced Secretary of War, who acted as a spy for the Radicals in cabinet meetings. Johnson correctly believed the Tenure of Office Act to be unconstitutional and wished to bring a test case to the Supreme Court. But the Radicals in Congress welcomed Johnson's action, since they could use his violation of an act of Congress as the basis for impeachment.

In February 1868, the House of Representatives voted overwhelmingly to impeach Johnson; most of the charges were based on violations of the Tenure of Office Act. The Senate sat as a court to hear the case and judge the guilt of the accused. The President was ably defended, and the evidence against him was weak; but the Radicals, desperate to remove him, used all kinds of pressure on individual senators to force them to vote a verdict of guilty. Yet they could not muster the one additional vote needed to make good the charges by the necessary two-thirds vote. Seven independent Republican senators refused to join their colleagues in voting for removal. The trial demonstrated the extremes to which the Radical Congress would go to override the executive branch and dominate the government.

✪✪✪ Radical Reconstruction in Effect in the South—After the Radicals won control of the government, they proceeded in 1867 to enforce their extreme measures in the South. The South was organized into five military districts, each under a Union general whose authority was enforced by federal troops. The state governments were supplanted by military government—an unconstitutional peacetime military rule.

The control of the African American vote was the key to Republican political control of the Southern states. The African Americans were assured the vote by the Fourteenth Amendment and the presence of federal troops. The Union League, the Radical propaganda arm in the South, worked to cement the loyalty of the freedmen to the Republican Party and provided the effective Republican leadership in the South during Reconstruction. "Carpetbaggers," a term applied to Northerners who came to the South during Reconstruction, supplied leadership and encouragement to the Freedmen and voted Republican themselves. The carpetbaggers were government officials, missionaries, politicians, and businessmen who came to work or to take advantage of the various opportunities in the South after the war.

Another Southern group supporting Radical reconstruction was the "Scalawags," Southern whites who hoped to win office or realize private advantage by collaborating with the Northerners. African American leaders among the freedmen also helped indoctrinate their fellows to loyalty to the Republican Party. These groups comprised the main elements of government in the South as long as federal troops were present to support them against the mass of Southern whites. The program of the Reconstruction governments called for enforcing civil, political, and social equality of African Americans with Southern whites. Many Southerners were denied the vote to enable the carpetbag governments to obtain power and keep it.

✪✪✪ **Reconstruction Governments in the South**—The Reconstruction "Carpetbag" governments in the states have been strongly condemned for several features. 1) They rejected the educated and politically experienced Southern white leaders and placed many ignorant and illiterate freedmen in office. 2) There was widespread graft and corruption. Cynical politicians and businessmen in both the North and the South were responsible during this period for the many flagrant instances of dishonesty in public life. 3) The carpetbag legislatures levied burdensome taxes upon property holders, indulged in wild spending, and saddled the states with heavy debts.

Certain constructive results followed from the reforms instituted by the Reconstruction governments. 1) The new constitutions provided for more democracy by guaranteeing civil liberties and universal male suffrage. 2) Public works projects provided necessary roads, bridges, and public buildings. 3) A system of compulsory, free public education was started. Not only were the African Americans helped by the schools, but the submerged whites benefited. 4) Taxes were redistributed in such a way as to levy the burden more equitably among different classes.

✪ **Radical Defiance of the Supreme Court**—After the Radicals had gained enough votes in Congress, they carried out their drastic program against both the executive and judicial branches of the federal government. Only the Supreme Court stood in the way of complete congressional domination after Johnson was outvoted in Congress. When Grant succeeded Johnson to the Presidency, that office offered no resistance to the Radicals.

Congress manipulated the Court first by raising the number of justices to ten during the war. In the decision *Ex Parte Milligan* (1866) the Court ruled that military trials were illegal where civilian courts were in operation. In retaliation for this decision Congress passed a law that new vacancies in the Court should not be filled until the number of justices should be reduced to seven. When Congress felt that new appointees under Grant would be friendly, the number was increased to nine. The Court lost much of its prestige in 1871 when, apparently under pressure from the Radicals, it reversed an earlier decision against the greenbacks. Thus, in the case of *Hepburn v. Griswold* the two new appointees of Grant joined in ruling that the greenbacks were legal tender for payment of all debts. The Supreme Court went out of the way to avoid giving offense to the Radical Congress. Not until national opinion had turned against the extremism of the Radicals did the Court assert itself to declare unconstitutional a number of the Reconstruction measures.

✪ **The Election of 1868**—In 1868 the Republicans were practically assured of victory by their control of Southern state governments made effective by the presence of federal troops and the control over the registration of voters. The military hero Grant became the Republican nominee; he was completely acceptable to the Radicals and the business interests that had come to dominate the party. The Democrats passed up Johnson for renomination and chose Horatio Seymour of New York. The Democrats supported the "Ohio Idea" for the payment of the national debt in greenbacks; this inflationary proposal frightened conservatives in the North. In spite of the factors favoring a Republican victory, Grant won by a lead of only 300,000 votes—a lead clearly due to Union League manipulation of the African American vote and army disenfranchisement of Southern whites.

✪ **The Fifteenth Amendment**—The slim victory of the Radicals in 1868, even in the South, convinced them of the need to be sure that the African American would not be denied the vote. The danger existed that the Southern states would amend their constitutions to deprive the African American of suffrage. Some Northern states were taking such steps also. The result was the passage of the Fifteenth Amendment by Congress in 1869 and its ratification in 1870. This amendment simply provided that no one could be denied the vote on account of race, color, or having been a slave.

THE LAST YEARS OF RECONSTRUCTION

By 1868 the states of the South except Mississippi, Texas, Virginia, and Georgia had adopted new constitutions and otherwise had complied with provisions of the Reconstruction acts and were readmitted to the Union. These four states were required to ratify the Fifteenth Amendment as a further condition for readmission; they ratified it by 1870.

✪✪ **Restoration of Southern Control**—After readmission the Southern whites gradually regained the upper hand. Northern opinion softened towards the South as the public turned against the more extreme Radical measures. The Reconstruction governments lost popularity because of high taxation, increases in indebtedness, and corruption. The native Southern whites united against outside control; the African Americans stopped voting. Opinion in the North, reacting against dishonesty among the Radicals and Northern Democrats, helped to soften the extremism of the Radicals.

In 1872 Congress passed the Amnesty Act, which restored political rights to most of the former Confederates. The election of 1876, in reality a defeat for the Republicans, brought an end to the Reconstruction period in the next year. After this the reforms of Reconstruction were almost completely undone.

✪ **The Ku Klux Klan**—The Klan was a secret vigilante organization in the South that had many imitators. The motive of these societies was to maintain native white rule and frustrate the program of political and social equality for the African American. The South faced a perplexing social problem in that many of the freedmen were pitifully misled by Union League agitators who encouraged them to assert themselves irresponsibly. The Klansmen resorted to the worst forms of intimidation and violence, especially against the African Americans. Unscrupulous and lawless elements joined or imitated the Klan to achieve their own selfish purposes. They all operated at night under masks and robes.

Congress and President Grant took drastic measures to suppress the Klan. The Enforcement Acts were passed in 1870 and 1871. The writ of *habeas corpus* was suspended and troops used to protect federal courts; these efforts sharply decreased Klan effectiveness. A Ku Klux Klan Committee in Congress investigated and exposed both the evils of the extralegal Klansmen and the problems the South faced. The Klan has been revived since then in both the North and the South.

✪✪ **Factors in the Economic Recovery of the South**—Of the various agencies and forces working for Southern economic recovery 1) the Freedmen's Bureau was one of the first to become effective. The national economic philosophy of rugged individualism prevalent in nineteenth-century America did not call for government measures to revive the Southern economy. Yet the destitute condition of the freedmen called for a minimum of relief in the form of food, clothing, fuel, and medicine. Whites as well as African Americans were cared for by the Bureau's agents. 2) The federal troops stationed in the South after the war shared their food, clothing, and supplies with Southerners. Many African American troops stationed there shared with their own race. Money spent by the army and the troops indirectly helped bring recovery. 3) The War Department rebuilt Southern railroads where it needed them. 4) Northern churches carried on missionary activities among the African Americans and built churches, schools, and gave relief to the needy. 5) Private philanthropy, such as that of George Peabody, provided some funds for schools. 6) The South promoted its own recovery by establishing new, small businesses in such industries as cotton milling, tobacco processing, and lumbering. 7) Cotton production was revived after a few years against the greatest handicaps.

✪✪✪ EFFECTS OF RECONSTRUCTION IN THE SOUTH

In the eyes of many Southerners and competent historians, too, Reconstruction has been judged as more destructive to the South and more harmful in its long-lasting consequences than the war itself. Lincoln's generous and moderate policy would most likely have healed quickly the wounds of the war. But it was replaced by a vindictive ten-year policy of trying to force the South into a mold that it was bound to reject. The racial problem in the South was aggravated by an attempt to turn society upside down and accomplish a social revolution in a day. Southern whites all felt compelled to unite to preserve white supremacy. The attempt to create a Republican party in the South backfired and created instead a deplorable one-party system under the Democrats. The African Americans became Republicans but were kept from the polls by various means so that effective party rivalry that might have brought better government to the South never developed. The term "Solid South" came to be applied to the unbroken loyalty to the Democratic Party that lasted until 1928.

CHAPTER BOOK LIST

Bentley, G.R., *A History of the Freedmen's Bureau* (1970).
Bowers, C.G., *The Tragic Era* (Sentry). Moving account critical of Radicals.
Buck, P.H., *Road to Reunion, 1865–1900* (Vintage). Mainly about the South.
Cash, W.J., *The Mind of the South* (Vintage). Literary interpretation of the South.
Cruden, Robert, *The Negro in Reconstruction* (1969).
Current, Richard N., *Those Terrible Carpetbaggers: A Reinterpretation* (1989). A good word for them.
DuBois, W.E.B., *Black Reconstruction in America* (Collier). By the African American leader: favors Radicals.
Dunning, W.A., *Reconstruction, Political and Economic, 1865–1877* (Torchbooks). Takes conservative position; a standard one-volume history.
James, J.B., *The Framing of the Fourteenth Amendment* (1956).
Les Benedict, Michael, *The Impeachment and Trial of Andrew Johnson* (1973). The best treatment of a very tangled episode.

McFeeley, Michael, *Yankee Stepfather: General O. O. Howard and the Freedmen* (1968). Study of the director of the Freedmen's Bureau.

Nevins, Allan, *The Emergence of Modern America, 1865–1878* (1927). Best account of the nation for this period.

Nieman, Donald G., *To Set the Law in Motion: The Freedmen's Bureau and Legal Rights for Blacks, 1865–1869* (1979).

Quarles, Benjamin, *Frederick Douglass* (Associated Publishers).

Randall, J.G., and Donald, David, *The Civil War and Reconstruction* (1961).

Sharkey, Robert P., *Money, Class, and Party* (1959).

Stampp, Kenneth M., *The Era of Reconstruction 1865–1877* (Knopf).

Washington, Booker T., *Up From Slavery* (Bantam). Autobiography.

Woodward, C. Vann, *Reunion and Reaction* (rev. ed., 1956) *and Origins of the New South, 1877–1913* (1951). Both treat the end of Reconstruction.

REVIEW QUESTIONS

MULTIPLE CHOICE

1. Johnson's influence while President   (1) steadily increased (2) increased after 1866 (3) declined further after 1866 (4) greatly hindered the Radicals.

2. The Fourteenth Amendment did all *except* (1) give citizenship to the freedmen (2) cancel Confederate war debts (3) free the slaves (4) guarantee payment of the Union war debt.

3. The Fifteenth Amendment   (1) denied the president power to pardon ex-Confederates (2) gave citizenship to African Americans (3) freed the slaves (4) sought to assure the African Americans' right to vote.

4. Johnson was impeached mainly on charges that he had (1) become an habitual drunkard   (2) violated the Tenure of Office Act (3) opposed the vote for the freedmen (4) was a Democrat and not elected to his office.

5. The Union League   (1) kept the African Americans from voting (2) worked to make the African Americans loyal to the Republican Party (3) provided food and clothing to the destitute in the South (4) elected Lincoln and Johnson in 1864.

6. Which was *not* a group supporting Radical reconstruction in the South? (1) Freedmen (2) "Carpetbaggers" (3) "Scalawags" (4) Liberal Republicans.

7. A desirable outcome of Reconstruction was the (1) introduction of honesty in the Southern state governments (2) practice of economy in state government (3) restoration of educated leaders to public office (4) beginnings of free public schools.

8. Grant was elected in 1868 because (1) the Democratic Party had just split (2) the African American vote in the South was under the control of the Radicals (3) the Democratic candidate was unpopular in the South (4) the Democrats in the North had dissolved their party.

9. The Ku Klux Klan activities sharply declined after (1) Southern public opinion rejected the Klan (2) passage of the federal Enforcement Acts by Congress (3) their leaders were found guilty of misappropriation of funds (4) Cleveland became President.

10. An important proposal supported by the Democrats in the election of 1868 was (1) the "Ohio Idea" (2) termination of Reconstruction (3) the acquisition of Alaska (4) a transcontinental railroad.

TRUE-FALSE

11. President Johnson was formerly a Democrat and remained one, as can be seen from his political policies during Reconstruction.

12. The Reconstruction Act of 1867 embodied the most important essentials of the Radical Reconstruction program; it divided the South into five military districts.

13. The Radicals required the Southern states to grant suffrage to African Americans.

14. The Fourteenth Amendment guaranteed the payment of both the Union and Confederate war debts.

15. Johnson's impeachment trial was heard before the Supreme Court.

16. Several Republican senators voted "not guilty" in the impeachment charges against Johnson.

17. Many Southerners were denied the vote in order to keep carpetbag governments in power.

18. Grant resisted the application of the vengeful Radical policies in the South.

19. The Supreme Court suffered considerable loss of prestige before and after the Civil War.

20. The "Ohio Idea" called for the payment of the Civil War debt in gold.

21. The Fifteenth Amendment provides that on no account may the African American be denied the right to vote.

22. After a time public opinion in the North rebelled at many of the extremist policies of the Radicals.

23. Grant's administration successfully suppressed the Klansmen in the South.

24. Southern economic recovery came about mainly from efforts within the South and from economic developments, unaided by government.

25. Southern social and political reconstruction by the North failed both because of a certain lack of sincerity and misguided idealism.

COMPLETION

26. To keep Johnson from removing Radicals from office Congress passed the _____ .

27. The _____ Amendment is the civil rights amendment.

28. Johnson was impeached in the year _____ ; presiding over the trial was _____ . One of the main charges against Johnson is that he had removed his Secretary of _____ named _____ from office. The impeachment failed by _____ vote(s) .

29. In 1868, instead of renominating Johnson, the Democrats chose _____ as their presidential candidate.

30. Political rights were restored to most of the former Confederates by the _____ Act in 1872.

31. The one-party politics of the South is referred to by the term _____ .

CHRONOLOGY / CHAPTER 3

1867   Farmers' Grange organized.

1868   "Ohio Idea" made a campaign issue, called for redemption of federal bonds with greenbacks.

Cubans began ten-year war of revolt against Spain.

Burlingame Treaty drawn up with China.

1869   Grant inaugurated as President.

"Black Friday" gold conspiracy.

Attempt to annex Santo Domingo failed.

1870   Second Fenian invasion of Canada.

1871   Tweed Ring exposed in New York City.

Treaty of Washington signed and ended disputes with Great Britain, particularly the Alabama claims.

1872   Credit Mobilier scandal exposed in Congress.

Liberal Republicans revolted against Republican Party and nominated Horace Greeley as President, but he was defeated by Grant.

1873   "Salary Grab" Act.

Panic of 1873.

"Crime of '73" demonetized silver.

1874   Sanborn Contract fraud revealed.

1875   Resumption Act provided for return to gold standard in 1879.

Greenback Party organized.

1876   Hayes-Tilden disputed election.

Chapter

3

THE ADMINISTRATION OF GRANT, 1869–1877

> The moral climate of the times was more responsible for the scandals of his administration than Grant himself. Most of the scandals would have occurred no matter who was President. The conservative policies of the administration resulted from business control of the national government. The foreign policy of the administration was largely well-managed and constructive.

THE PRESIDENCY OF GRANT

Although Grant was popular and had been successful in his military career, his qualities of character and lack of political experience were not equal to the demands of the presidency.

● **The Rise of Grant**—Grant's rise from a typical Western family farm background to become the nation's leading military hero of the Civil War made him a logical candidate for the American presidency. His career began when he graduated from West Point in 1843. He served creditably in the Mexican War and after that served in military outposts in California and Oregon. Bored with army life, he resigned in 1854, and in Missouri and Illinois engaged unsuccessfully in farming, real estate, and clerking in his father's store. With the opening of the Civil War, he volunteered for the Illinois infantry and was later commissioned colonel. His notable victories at Forts Henry and Donelson, at Shiloh, Vicksburg, and Chattanooga brought him rapid promotion until he became supreme commander of the Union army. At the conclusion of the Civil War, his magnanimous attitude towards the Confederate forces and his moderation but willingness to cooperate with the Radical Republicans made him attractive to various political elements. In personality he was quiet and unassuming, but determined.

●● **Grant's Imperfections**—His military experience in some ways proved a handicap in public office. He expected his political appointees to carry out orders as his military subordinates had done, but his trust was proven misplaced. His lack of experience in public affairs often led to absurd decisions, and the appointment of poorly qualified persons.

Among numerous friends and relatives he appointed, there were several dozen of his wife's relatives. Grant was often petty and vindictive in his decisions and favored those who had contributed funds to purchase three expensive houses and the wealthy and grateful who bestowed upon him large money contributions. Having himself failed in business matters, he held high regard for those who succeeded in piling up fortunes. He admired and listened to aggressive, selfish, and tricky businessmen who became his close friends. Not until Eisenhower did the nation choose another *professional* military man for the presidency.

⊙ **The Moral Climate of the Postwar Period**—Grant's administration with its scandals reflects the low moral climate of his time. The spending of vast amounts of money during the war had conditioned those responsible to a large degree of carelessness in handling public funds. The widespread corruption may be explained by the lust for power of cynical politicians, the aggressive greed for money by wartime profiteers, and the war-caused letdown in public morals. Both the North and the South suffered from cynicism and corruption during the Reconstruction period. A dog-eat-dog attitude prevailed in business life. It was as if businessmen were being guided by the new Darwinian idea of "the survival of the fittest." Businessmen survived and grew fat because they were ruthless, tricky, and by corruption gained special favors from government. In this environment Grant appeared as a callous, obtuse individual; unlike some of the reformers of the time, he was insensitive to what was going on around him. Although he received great contributions of wealth in the form of cash and property, he did not accept gifts as recompense for specific favors.

⊙⊙ **Grant's Favoritism Toward Big Business**—Under Grant big business interests of various sorts enjoyed more freedom from government interference and a more positively favorable political climate than ever before. The Civil War itself represented a victory for business interests centered in the Northeast, and the Radical Republicans saw to it that the gains they had won in war would not be lost in the political forums. Grant's administration favored business by maintaining high protective tariffs. The railroads received federal subsidies in land grants, loans, and exemption from tariff duties on imported steel. The creditor classes benefited from the deflationary return to the gold standard and a limited currency supply. Financiers and speculators benefited from inside information and from the favorable refinancing of the national bond issues.

SCANDALS OF GRANT'S ADMINISTRATION

Several prominent scandals occurring in Grant's administration illustrate the moral laxity of the times.

✪ **The "Black Friday" Gold Conspiracy**—Two notorious and unscrupulous speculators, Jim Fisk and Jay Gould, in September 1869, engineered a plot to make millions in quick profit by cornering the nation's gold supply. Through a brother-in-law the President was convinced by a seemingly logical argument that a stoppage of the sale of gold by the Treasury would help farmers by causing a rise in the price of wheat. Grant's innocent complicity enabled these two speculators to buy much of the small supply of gold in the country and drive the price up fantastically. Businessmen who needed gold in legitimate transactions were driven to bankruptcy on "Black Friday" when the price was bid up madly. When Grant realized what was happening, he ordered the Treasury to sell gold and thereby broke the speculative bubble, but great harm had already been done to thousands of persons.

✪ **The Tweed Ring**—For several years prior to 1871, "Boss" Tweed at the head of an organization of political crooks in New York City plundered the city's treasury of approximately $200,000,000. The gang operated through faked payments and graft. *The New York Times* had the courage to publish evidence in 1871, and Samuel J. Tilden led the prosecution that finally convicted Tweed. Thomas Nast, the famous cartoonist, publicized the scandals and helped end the rule of the grafters.

✪ **The Credit Mobilier Scandal**—This scandal reflected badly upon the Republican majority in Congress in Grant's first term. The Credit Mobilier was the construction company organized by the insiders of the Union Pacific Railroad to skim off millions in profits paid to themselves for building the railroad. Oakes Ames, acting as the agent of the Credit Mobilier Company, bribed members of Congress to prevent any action to halt the profiteering made possible by the congressional subsidies for railroad building. Most of the wrong doing occurred before Grant became President. The scandal, exposed in 1872 by congressional investigation, injured the reputation of many prominent members of Congress.

The Salary Grab Act—In 1873 Congress doubled the salary of the President and voted themselves a salary increase of 50 percent. The worst part of the act was that it made the increase retroactive two years back. Public reaction gave the Democrats control of the next Congress, and the law was repealed.

Sanborn Contract and Other Scandals—In the Sanborn Contract fraud, it was revealed in 1874 that a politician named Sanborn had been given a contract by the Treasury Department to collect $427,000 in unpaid taxes. He was allowed a commission of 50 percent; the commission was used to finance Republican political activities.

The Whiskey Ring fraud was a conspiracy between distillers and treasury officials to defraud the federal government of revenue from the excise tax on liquor. Grant's personal secretary accepted favors in the plot, and the President himself accepted gifts he should have suspected. Grant defended his secretary against the investigators. In still another scandal, Grant's Secretary of War, W.W. Belknap, accepted bribes from a post-trader in the Native American territory; Belknap would have been impeached had he not resigned.

FOREIGN RELATIONS UNDER GRANT

President Grant by fortunate choice made Hamilton Fish Secretary of State. Fish proved to be an unusually able diplomat who peacefully settled serious conflicts with Great Britain. In foreign relations the record of the Grant administration is considered quite constructive.

The Attempt to Annex Santo Domingo—Grant in 1869 fell in with a scheme of speculators to take over Santo Domingo. He submitted a treaty to the Senate, but there it was opposed by Charles Sumner, who recognized the dishonesty involved. Grant persistently tried to secure Senate approval. Later Sumner was deposed from the chairmanship of the Senate Committee on Foreign Relations when Grant had his revenge.

The Fenians—A secret Irish American brotherhood known as the Fenians organized in the 1850s to help achieve freedom for Ireland. After the Civil War they planned to use Union veterans of the Civil War to conquer Canada and exchange it to Britain for freedom for Ireland. In 1866 the Fenians invaded Canada from the United States at the Niagara River and fought a battle with the Canadian militia. After a second invasion in 1870 the United States arrested the Fenian leaders and took other steps to prevent other invasions of British Canada. The incidents may have made the British more willing to recognize their error in aiding the Confederacy.

✪✪✪ **The Treaty of Washington (1871)**—On behalf of the United States, Secretary of State Sumner made large claims against Great Britain for damage payments for the depredations of the Alabama and other British-built cruisers that had destroyed American shipping during the Civil War. Settlement was prevented for several years by the preposterous claims of Sumner and British reluctance to make any reasonable settlement. When Hamilton Fish became Secretary of State he quietly worked out a settlement in the Treaty of Washington in 1871. 1) In this treaty the British admitted their unneutral behavior and agreed to submit the claims to arbitration under conditions that assured the United States an award. As a consequence the Alabama Tribunal met at Geneva and awarded the United States $15,500,000 indemnity.

2) Another provision of the Treaty of Washington resulted in an award of $2,000,000 to Britain for property lost by her subjects in the Civil War. 3) Still another British claim against the United States over American

fishing privileges resulted in an arbitration award of $5,500,000 to Britain. 4) A final provision led to settlement by arbitration of the exact boundary between the United States and British Columbia in the maze of islands in the Puget Sound. These awards constituted another landmark in the long record of peaceable settlement of serious disputes between the two countries and of victory for the principle of arbitration in international law.

○ **The Cuban Revolt**—A ten-year-long revolt of Cuba against Spain began in 1868; the United States, although sympathetic with the Cubans, adopted a policy of neutrality. In 1873 the Spaniards captured the *Virginius,* a ship illegally flying the American flag, and proceeded with the execution of those aboard, including some Americans. Hostilities were avoided and Spain agreed to make damage payments to families of those executed.

○ **The Burlingame Treaty**—Anson Burlingame, the American minister to China during the 1860s, drew up this agreement (1868), which permitted unrestricted Chinese immigration to the United States. Large numbers of Chinese were entering California at the time; strenuous but unsuccessful efforts were soon made in California to limit drastically the incoming surplus of labor.

○○ THE ELECTION OF 1872

The most notable feature of this presidential election year was the revolt of the liberal Republicans; the liberals were tired of the vengeful Reconstruction policy, wished to promote honesty in government, and stood for various reforms. The regular Republicans renominated Grant; the liberals, foreseeing this, formed the Liberal Republican Party and chose Horace Greeley as their candidate. Greeley, the liberal and famous editor of the *New York Tribune,* had already been chosen by the Democratic Party as their presidential nominee. In the hard-fought campaign the Republicans waved the "Bloody Shirt" in an emotional appeal for their war hero; both sides engaged in false charges. The eccentric Greeley lost; the Republicans controlled enough African American votes in three states still unreconstructed to gain victory for Grant. The revolt of the liberals forced the Republicans to take steps for more honest government.

POSTWAR ECONOMIC PROBLEMS

Postwar adjustments in the economy to peacetime conditions brought sudden panic, and steps to resume the prewar convertibility of currency to gold brought sustained deflation and its consequent hardship to debtors and farmers.

⊙⊙ The Panic of 1873—The Postwar depression struck in 1873 in America; it began as a panic precipitated by the failure of Jay Cooke and Company. The failure of this firm that had led in financing the Civil War shocked American businessmen. Causes of the panic and depression were the overexpansion in railroad building and in industry during the business boom following the Civil War. A panic in Vienna in 1873 initiated the financial troubles in America.

⊙⊙ Money Controversy After the Civil War—Farmers and other debtor groups suffered from falling prices due to the shrinkage in the nation's money supply following the Civil War. During the war large quantities of irredeemable paper money known as greenbacks were put into circulation by the federal treasury; this was necessary because of insufficient specie to meet the monetary needs of the country. The plentiful supply of cheap money caused prices to rise and made it easy for debtors to repay their obligations in the depreciated greenback currency.

At the end of the war the treasury ceased to issue greenbacks; in fact, withdrew them from circulation. The conservative business interests in the dominant Republican Party were beginning to take steps leading to eventual return to a specie basis; a reduction in the floating supply of greenbacks was necessary to accomplish this. Prices of agricultural commodities fell sharply and other prices less steeply, but enough to create hardship for debtor groups. In 1868 the Democratic Party in its platform adopted the "Ohio Idea," which called for redemption of federal bonds in greenbacks instead of gold. This idea was favored by the debtor classes but was not adopted.

In 1870 in the Legal Tender Cases the Supreme Court ruled that the greenbacks were not legal tender for debts created prior to issuance of the greenbacks in 1862. But Grant appointed two new justices who reversed this decision in 1871 by declaring the greenbacks constitutional—but this only recognized the validity of those already in circulation and did not relieve the money shortage.

⊙⊙ The "Crime of '73"—In 1873 another step was taken that prevented any increase in the money supply. Congress approved a bill recommended by the treasury that discontinued the purchase and coinage of silver, which had become relatively scarce. By coincidence the silver supply increased and the price fell just as silver coinage was stopped. To the debtors this seemed a deliberate step by the creditor interests to prevent the supply of cheap silver from flowing into the nation's money supply. Thus they protested violently against the demonetization of silver and referred to the act as the "Crime of '73." They began to agitate for the remonetization of silver as another way to increase the amount of money in circulation.

⊙⊙ Resumption Act—In 1875 Congress yielded to financial interests to provide for a resumption of redeemability of the nation's paper money in gold. The act went into effect in 1879. It created creditor confidence in the soundness of the American dollar but further increased the burden of the debtors.

○○ Greenback Party—In 1875 the Greenback Party was organized to give expression to the debtors who demanded an increased money supply. In 1878 the disgruntled labor groups joined to form the Greenback Labor Party. Their platforms demanded the increased use of greenbacks and the free coinage of silver on a parity with gold. In 1878, at its peak, the party elected 15 representatives to Congress and many state officials.

○○ Farm Distress After the Civil War—The usual wartime prosperity of farmers came to an end soon after Appomattox. The worldwide depression beginning in 1873 brought a further drop in prices. In fact, the long-term trend of farm prices tended downward until 1896. The shrinkage in the money supply only aggravated the more fundamental difficulty of overproduction. New agricultural lands were being opened not only in western America but in Canada, Argentina, Australia, and Russia. The farmers believed the difficulty was one of underconsumption caused by high prices due to the additional charges of middlemen.

○○ The Grangers—In 1867 Oliver H. Kelley, an employee in the Department of Agriculture, organized the Patrons of Husbandry, popularly known as the Grangers. This national organization began as a secret order, like the various lodges, to provide social life and educational meetings for farm families. After farm prices fell further in 1873 the Grangers became predominantly a political movement. The Grangers complained of various business interests, whom they blamed for the poor economic status of the farmer. They opposed monopolistic sellers of the things farmers had to buy, especially machinery; they blamed the middleman for increasing the price of farm goods by the time they reached the consumer; they particularly blamed the railroads for multiple economic abuses.

By 1874 the Grangers had gained much political strength over the nation, and in most states had sufficient influence to secure the passage of laws regulating the railroads and grain elevators. It was at this time that the railroad commissions were created as public utility regulatory bodies in the states.

In addition to social and political activity the Grangers established consumer and manufacturing cooperatives; these failed from lack of experience of their managers, but much valuable experience brought later success to such ventures. The Grange movement reached its peak about 1879 but still operates as one of the leading farmers' organizations.

○○ THE ELECTION OF 1876

A third-term movement for Grant was squelched and the way left open for the magnetic, moderate James G. Blaine. His candidacy for the nomination apparently would have succeeded except for the news of the favors he had accepted from a railroad for helping it secure a federal land grant in 1869. The liberal but colorless Civil War general and governor of Ohio, Rutherford B. Hayes, won the nomination. The Democrats appealed to the conservatism of the times and the desire for reform by choosing Samuel J. Tilden, governor of New York and the dragon-slayer who had made himself nationally famous by bringing an end to the Tweed Ring in New York City.

The election returns produced the most disputed election in American history. Tilden won 264,000 more popular votes than Hayes but of the undisputed electoral votes Hayes had 165 to 184 for Tilden. Twenty electoral votes were disputed; 19 of these were in the three Southern states of Louisiana, South Carolina, and Florida. The Republicans would have to win every disputed elector to win the presidency. These states submitted two sets of election returns, one favoring each party, to Congress.

Congress had no law or precedent for settling such a dispute, but finally agreed to appoint an Electoral Commission of 15 with five members from each—the House, the Senate, and the Supreme Court. The membership was made up of seven Republicans, seven Democrats, and one nonpartisan. When the nonpartisan member resigned from the Supreme Court, he was necessarily replaced by a Republican, since all remaining members of the Supreme Court were Republican. The strictly partisan vote gave every point in dispute to the Republicans. The dispute was decided just a few days before the new President was inaugurated. A political bargain between the two parties secured the assent of the Democrats to the decision of the Electoral Commission in return for the withdrawal of the remaining federal troops in Louisiana and South Carolina. Thus was military Reconstruction terminated.

CHAPTER BOOK LIST

Carpenter, John A., *Ulysses Grant: A Biography* (1974). Excellent one-volume biography.

Grant, Ulysses S., *Personal Memoirs* (Premier). A modern abridgment.

Grob, Gerald N., *Workers and Utopia: A Study of Ideological Conflict in the American Labor Movement, 1865–1900* (1961). The transition of American labor.

Hale, W.H., *Horace Greeley: Voice of the People* (Collier). Biography of a leader who reflected his time.

Kirkland, Edward C., *Industry Comes of Age: Business, Labor, and Public Policy, 1860–1897* (1967). Detailed survey.

Liddell-Hart, B.H., *Sherman—Soldier, Realist, American* (Praeger).

Nevins, Allan, *Hamilton Fish: The Inner History of the Grant Administration* (1936).

Randall, J.G. and Donald, David, *The Civil War and Reconstruction* (1961).

Rodman W. Paul, *The Far West and the Great Plains in Transition, 1859–1900* (1988). The last frontier for the farmer and miner.

Taylor, G.R. and Neu, I.D., *The American Railroad Network, 1861–1890* (1956).

Trelease, A.W., *White Terror: The Ku Klux Klan Conspiracy* (1971).

Van Deusen, Glyndon G., *Horace Greeley: Ninteenth-Century Crusader* (1953).

Weinstein, Allen, *Prelude to Populism: Origins of the Silver Issue, 1867–1878* (1970). The first phase of the silver controversy.

Wilson, Woodrow, *Division and Reunion: 1829–1889* (Collier). The scholar-President's history of the period before and after the Civil War.

REVIEW QUESTIONS

MULTIPLE CHOICE

1. Before becoming President, Grant (1) spent much of his early life in Kentucky (2) became a successful businessman (3) promoted policies of harsh Reconstruction (4) served creditably in the Mexican War but resigned the army several years later.

2. Grant's weaknesses as President included all *except* (1) the appointment of poorly qualified persons (2) lack of critical appraisal of his subordinates (3) permitting reckless currency inflation (4) taking advice from dishonest and self-seeking persons.

3. The two speculators who plotted the gold conspiracy were (1) Jay Gould and Jim Brady (2) Jim Fisk and Jay Gould (3) Tom Nast and Jim Fisk (4) Boss Tweed and Sam Tilden.

4. The wrongdoing in the Credit Mobilier scandal was (1) the wholesale bribery of members of Congress (2) the bribery of members of Grant's cabinet (3) the misappropriation of construction funds lent the railroads (4) the creation of a railroad monopoly.

5. Which of Grant's cabinet members resigned to avoid impeachment for accepting bribes? (1) Hamilton Fish (2) W. W. Belknap (3) Zachary Chandler (4) Schuyler Colfax.

6. The Fenians (1) wanted to annex Canada to the United States (2) were encouraged by Grant's administration (3) goal was to take Canada and exchange it for freedom for Ireland (4) sought to force Britain to settle the Alabama claims.

7. The Treaty of Washington did all of these except (1) settle the fisheries dispute once again (2) give the British a favorable settlement in the Alabama claims (3) set an early example of successful arbitration (4) finally provide for settlement of the boundary between the United States and Canada.

8. The Burlingame Treaty (1) provided for the importation of Chinese contract labor to the United States (2) created a loose alliance of America and China (3) permitted unrestricted Chinese immigration to the United States (4) stopped Chinese immigration to the United States.

9. The most significant development in the election of 1872 was the (1) split in the Democratic Party (2) reelection of Grant (3) creation of a special commission to determine the victor (4) split in the Republican Party.

10. The "Crime of '73" is a term given to the (1) resumption of the gold standard (2) Supreme Court decision declaring greenbacks legal tender (3) demonetization of silver (4) dishonesty in treasury bond refunding operations.

11. The Grangers' main achievement was the (1) founding of farmers' marketing cooperatives (2) passage of state laws against trade monopolies (3) founding of farmers' consumer cooperatives (4) establishment of railroad commissions in the states.

12. The election of 1866 was unique at its time because of all *except* which one? (1) Republican interference in the election in some Southern states (2) the means adopted to settle the disputed election (3) an agreement to withdraw federal troops from the South (4) the election of a liberal Republican.

TRUE-FALSE

13. The moral climate of the post-Civil War period accounts for much of the corruption of Grant's administration.

14. The Grant administration expected business to uphold high ethical standards such as Grant himself lived by.

15. The postwar period experienced continued inflation, which hurt the debtor classes.

16. Oakes Ames acted as an agent for the Credit Mobilier in its bribery of Congressmen.

17. In 1873 Congress voted itself a 100 percent salary increase.

18. Overexpansion in railroad building was an important cause of the Panic of 1873.

19. Silver was demonetized in 1873 because it had become relatively scarce, but immediately, thereafter it became more plentiful.

20. Debtor farmers for decades after the Civil War suffered from a long-term decline in prices.

21. The Farmers' Grange was organized originally as a political agency but by 1875 concentrated upon social and educational activities.

22. In the 1880s the Grange died out completely.

23. The election of 1876 was actually settled by a political compromise rather than by a fair election.

COMPLETION

24. The corner on gold that caused great losses to many businessmen in 1869 was called the _____ gold conspiracy.

25. The _____ was a notoriously corrupt group of politicians operating in New York City before 1871. They were exposed through the efforts of the cartoonist _____ and prosecuted by a lawyer named _____ who later was the Democratic presidential nominee.

26. The _____ was a railroad construction company guilty of wholesale bribery of members of Congress.

27. The _____ during Grant's term was guilty of defrauding the government of excise taxes on liquor.

28. It was _____ who prevented an attempt to dishonestly annex Santo Domingo. Grant's able Secretary of State was _____ .

29. The Democratic nominee in the election of 1872 was _____ who was also nominated by the _____ but was defeated by _____ .

30. The Panic of 1873 began with the failure of _____ a great investment banking firm.

31. In the Legal Tender Cases the Supreme Court finally ruled that _____ were legal tender.

32. The redemption of all money in gold was provided for by the _____ of 1785. Opposing the gold standard, there arose a new political party called the _____ Party.

33. The Patrons of Husbandry was founded by _____ .

34. The Democratic presidential candidate in 1876 was _____ and the _____ Republican _____ received the most popular votes but _____ was elected when the dispute was settled by _____ .

CHRONOLOGY / CHAPTER 4

1856   Bessemer-Kelly steel-refining process developed.

1859   "Drake's Folly" started first oil boom. Pike's Peak and
            Comstock Lode mining booms.

1860   Chicago became leading meat-packing center.

1861   Morrill Tariff brought American manufacturers protection
            against imports.
            Pacific Telegraph completed.

1862   Union Pacific and Central Pacific railroads chartered.

1863   National Banking Act passed to provide better currency and
            banking facilities.

1866   Atlantic Cable operates successfully.

1867   Farmers' Grange organized.

1868   Fourteenth Amendment gave business corporations same
            constitutional protection as "persons."

1869   Union Pacific and Central Pacific railroads completed across
            the continent.

1872   Westinghouse automatic airbrake for railroads improved and
            patented.

1873   Andrew Carnegie concentrated business interests in the
            manufacture of steel.
            Panic of 1873.

1876   Bell invented telephone.

1882   Rockefeller had gained control over 90 percent of oil
            refineries.

1883   Three more transcontinental railroads completed: Southern
            Pacific, Santa Fe, and Northern Pacific.

1893   Great Northern Railroad completed to the Pacific by
            James J. Hill.

1901   United States Steel became first billion dollar corporation.

Chapter

4

ECONOMIC GROWTH AFTER THE CIVIL WAR, 1865–1900

The presidential victory of the Republican Party in 1860 and the secession of the powerful agrarian states of the South placed the federal government in the hands of the business interests of the North and East. In the years that followed occurred the fundamental change from an agricultural to an industrial nation. The political changes of the Civil War and Reconstruction were the violent manifestations of this profound change. Statistics of the nation's economy provide ample evidence of the rapid growth of business and urban life in America.

CAUSES OF INDUSTRIAL GROWTH

Numerous political and economic factors combined to favor the rapid advance of the nation's industry.

●●● **Political Factors Promoting the Postwar Industrial Growth—** The Republican Party, the political instrument by which the machinery of the federal government was managed by business interests, enacted a number of laws highly favorable to business.

1) The Morrill Tariff (1861) reestablished high protective rates. These higher rates assured manufacturing industries higher profits, freedom from foreign competition, and at the same time provided an indirect subsidy at the expense of other groups. Industry expanded with confidence as high tariffs were maintained as a permanent national policy.

2) The National Banking Act (1863) provided a satisfactory banking system and uniform national bank notes, and swept away the inefficiency and confusion of state bank notes. Subsequent financial measures assuring a "sound money" and adoption of the gold standard provided a boon to banking and creditor interests.

3) The various enactments chartering railroad companies and providing subsidies in the form of land grants and loans to the 42 transcontinental railroads created a great new industry, which was essential to the industrial complex of the nation.

4) Special protection of business corporations against action by the state governments was deliberately written into the Fourteenth Amendment. This provision provides that no state may enforce any law that would "deprive any person of life, liberty, or property, without due process of law." Afterwards the Supreme Court defined corporations as "persons" and extended to them the special protection that individuals received by the Fifth Amendment against the federal government.

5) The momentum given business by the enormous profits during and after the Civil War greatly accelerated industrial growth.

6) The friendly attitude of government after 1861 provided a climate of freedom, and executive and judicial decisions encouraged business in innumerable ways. Although business interests claimed adherence to laissez-faire theory, they sought government interference in economic affairs when it was favorable to them.

✪✪✪ **Economic Factors Promoting Industrial Growth**—In the mid-nineteenth century many economic factors operated to make industrial growth possible. 1) Nature endowed America with abundant resources. Fertile soil yielded abundant crops; forests provided a surplus of lumber for export; coal, iron, and oil deposits yielded great wealth; gold, silver, copper, and lead deposits were abundant.

2) Investment capital came from war profits and other income; European capital flowed into the favorable business climate created by protective government; and American mines in the West produced great fortunes in gold and silver and put money in circulation. Much investment capital flowed from shipping into industry.

3) The large supply of cheap labor necessary for industrial growth was provided by the millions of veterans released at the end of the war and by the movement of farm population to the cities. In addition to this were the increasing numbers of immigrants coming in year after year. Many new immigrant nationalities, such as the Chinese and southern and eastern Europeans, provided cheap, unskilled labor for building the railroads and operating mines, mills, and factories.

4) New technologies, such as mass production, made possible by the application of the principle of interchangeable parts, and almost innumerable inventions, created new industries or increased production and made it more efficient.

5) Improved transportation and rapid communications made possible the growth of nationwide business firms. Raw materials could be brought together by the railroads from all parts of the country and the finished products marketed over vast domestic and foreign markets. Telegraphy provided managers better control over widespread business operations.

6) The new postwar industries may be considered as still another special factor in the growth of industry.

THE TRANSCONTINENTAL RAILROADS

By providing efficient transportation the railroads were fundamental to the growth of other industries. The extension of rails across the continent to the Pacific coast tied the resources of the West to the industry of the East. At the same time branch lines over the territories opened the new frontiers of the range cattle industry and of agriculture on the Pacific coast, in the intermountain region, and over the Great Plains. The railroads made an economic unit of the nation, and they made possible the rapid settlement of half the nation's territory within a single generation. The railroads themselves produced a great market for the new steel industry. The construction of transcontinental lines marked the greatest period of railroad expansion.

✪✪ The Union Pacific and Central Pacific Railroads—In 1862 the absence of Southern opposition permitted Congress to proceed with the long-discussed transcontinental railroads by chartering two lines that together would connect Chicago and San Francisco. The two lines met near Ogden, Utah, to complete in 1869 the first transcontinental railroad. The Union Pacific built westwards from Omaha and the Central Pacific built eastwards from San Francisco. The initial subsidies provided in 1862 proved insufficient to attract the necessary capital, and in 1864 more liberal terms provided federal land grants of 20 square miles of land along the right-of-way for each mile of track laid. Loans were provided liberally; they took the form of second mortgage railroad bonds purchased by the federal government. The amount of the loans was $16,000 per mile for track laid through level lands, $32,000 per mile through rolling country, and $48,000 through mountainous terrain.

The construction was done by companies created by the larger, controlling stockholders. The generous terms of these contracts enabled these insiders, really grafters, to accumulate immense fortunes at the expense of the smaller stockholders and the government. The Credit Mobilier was the construction company for the Union Pacific, and the Crocker Corporation built the Central Pacific. The Crocker Corporation created the great fortunes of California's Big Four: Leland Stanford, Charles Crocker, Collis P. Huntington, and Mark Hopkins. Problems of securing labor and materials had to be overcome. Large numbers of Chinese were imported to construct the Central Pacific; both railroads used many Irish immigrants and war veterans. Boisterous terminal towns cared for the needs and catered to the vices of the laborers as the lines were pushed forward. The tracks were hastily laid to collect the government subsidies, and rebuilding had to begin as soon as the roads were "completed."

✪ The Southern Pacific—The next railroad company to complete a transcontinental line was the Southern Pacific, a corporation begun in California and controlled by the owners of the Central Pacific. The

Southern Pacific followed the thirty-second parallel or southernmost route along the Gila River just north of the Mexican border; at first it built in California to the Arizona boundary and later took over the bankrupt Texas Pacific. In January 1882, connections were completed with St. Louis, and in 1883 connections were completed with New Orleans.

✪ **The Atchison, Topeka, and Santa Fe**—The next railroad completed was the Santa Fe, across the Southwest. This corporation, by absorbing other lines and through the aid of federal land grants, completed connections in 1883 between California and St. Louis, connections that generally followed the old Santa Fe Trail and the thirty-fifth parallel route.

✪ **The Northern Pacific Railroad**—The Northern Pacific built along a northern route from Lake Superior to Portland, Oregon. The construction of this road was halted, like other Western railroads, by the Panic of 1873. But in 1881 it was reorganized by Henry Villard and completed in 1883. It, too, received liberal land grants from the federal public domain.

✪ **The Great Northern and Other Transcontinental Railroads**— After the construction of the first four transcontinentals, still other roads were completed. Among these the Great Northern has received by far the greatest praise of historians. James J. Hill, the hero among the railroad builders, got control in 1889 of a northern route owned by a company that had gone into bankruptcy. This reorganized railroad, the Great Northern, built to the Pacific at Tacoma, Washington, in 1893. Hill is praised for having built his road without federal subsidies and for having promoted settlement and agricultural prosperity along the railroad.

Numerous other railroads built into the Far West, and some completed lines to the Pacific. In the East, railroad financiers consolidated railroads into great systems. Commodore Vanderbilt extended the New York Central to Chicago. Other large systems consolidated were the Erie, the Pennsylvania, and the Chesapeake and Ohio.

Technical Improvements in the Railroads—Technical improvements in roadbeds and rolling stock were made steadily as the network spread over the nation. Steel rails replaced iron rails and heavier rails replaced light rails. After the war, roadbeds were better prepared and great steel bridges built to span the rivers. In 1864 George Pullman built the first sleeping car and was soon building dining and other special purpose cars. In 1872 the Westinghouse automatic airbrake was in use, and uniform gauge tracks came to be adopted about 1870. Better and heavier steam locomotives were put into service.

POSTWAR INDUSTRIES

The leading new industries after the Civil War were steel, petroleum, meat packing, and flour milling.

○○ **The Steel Industry**—The phenomenal growth of steel production in the central states after the Civil War resulted from the adoption of the Bessemer process. Bessemer, an English inventor, developed the method and applied it successfully during the ten years preceding 1866. At this same time an American named Kelly also developed the new process. In 1868 the "open-hearth" process was introduced from Europe. The Bessemer process produced lower-cost steel and predominated until around 1900; it reduced the price so that steel replaced iron for many uses. Abundant deposits of coal in Pennsylvania and the East and iron ore from Michigan and the Mesabi Range in Minnesota provided most of the raw material. Andrew Carnegie, a Scottish immigrant of much intelligence and personal charm, after success in steel and other business ventures, concentrated upon the manufacture of steel, beginning in 1873. By achieving the efficiencies of large-scale production and through clever salesmanship, Carnegie became by far the nation's greatest steelmaker. He amassed an immense fortune by his activities centered at Pittsburgh. In 1901 he sold his steel works to a financial group guided by the genius of J.P. Morgan. This merger became the United States Steel Corporation, the first billion-dollar corporation in America. Carnegie devoted the rest of his life to philanthropy by building libraries, creating benevolent trusts, promoting international cooperation, and creating research institutions.

○○ **The Petroleum Industry**—The beginnings of the oil industry occurred in the five years immediately before the Civil War; George H. Bissell, a businessman, was responsible. He sent a sample of oil from western Pennsylvania to the noted Yale chemistry professor Benjamin Silliman, who reported that it could be refined into various products such as paraffin and, most important, a fuel for illumination. Bissell hired Edwin Drake to drill a well with the same equipment that had been developed for drilling deep wells for producing salt. In 1859 "Drake's Folly" started gushing oil and set off the first oil boom in America in western Pennsylvania.

A new industry grew rapidly, since there was a large national market for kerosene for lamp fuel. Kerosene replaced whale oil and other illuminants and became the chief refined product from petroleum until the combustion engine created a larger market for gasoline. Enterprising businessmen started other oil well drilling ventures in other parts of the nation. By 1870 oil production and refining had become a leading industry.

John D. Rockefeller was the business genius who came to dominate the oil industry; he created the monopoly of the Standard Oil Company and by 1882 had gained control of over 90 percent of the nation's oil refineries.

○○ **Meat Packing**—In 1860 Cincinnati, or "Porkopolis," yielded to Chicago its leadership as the nation's meat-packing center. Philip Armour, the first prominent tycoon in the livestock slaughtering and meat industry, in 1865 concentrated his plants in Chicago where the Union Stockyards had been incorporated. Another leader, Nelson Morris, in Chicago experimented with shipping dressed beef to the Atlantic cities. Gustavus F. Swift perfected the refrigerator car and thereby opened a vast market for fresh meat as contrasted with earlier "packing" of pickled, salted, and smoked meat products.

Flour Milling—Flour milling was revolutionized into a large-scale industry by the introduction from France and Hungary of the "New Process" for milling. Millers in Minneapolis, in particular Washburn and Pillsbury, applied the New Process and made numerous improvements; they made large fortunes and established the leadership of Minneapolis in this industry. This new method of milling consisted of the use of a succession of chilled-iron rollers, which crushed the hard wheat, and of screens that separated the parts of the grain. This process opened the northern Great Plains to agriculture by creating a market for the hard-kerneled varieties of wheat that would grow in the harsh climate of that region.

CHAPTER BOOK LIST

Adams, C.F., and Adams, Henry, *Chapters of the Erie* (Cornell). Unscrupulous tycoons struggle to control the railroad.

Atherton, Lewis, *The Cattle Kings* (1961).

Cochran, T.C., and Miller, William, *The Age of Enterprise* (Torchbooks). Interpretive, stimulating social history of American industry.

Cochran, T.C., *Railroad Leaders, 1845–1890* (1966). Analytical study of railroad executives.

Cochran, Thomas C., *Basic History of American Business* (Anvil).

Fogel, Robert, *Railroads in American Economic Growth* (1964).

Hacker, L.M., *The Course of American Economic Growth and Development* (1970).

Josephson, Matthew, *The Robber Barons* (Harvest). Biographical study of capitalists after the Civil War.

Kirkland, Edward, *Business in the Gilded Age* (1952). Stresses fierce competition.

Miller, William, ed., *Men in Business: Essays in the History of Entrepreneurship* (Harvard) (1952). Attacks rags to riches thesis.

Nevins, Allan, *Study in Power: John D. Rockefeller* (1953). Influence of Rockefeller on American business development.

North, Douglas C., *Growth and Welfare in the American Past* (1966).

Riegel, R.R., *The Story of Western Railroads* (1926). Best survey of the transcontinentals.

Taylor, G.R., and Neu, Irene D., *The American Railroad Network, 1861–1890* (1956).

Warner, W.L., and Abegglen, James, *Big Business Leaders in America* (Atheneum).
Wiebe, Robert H., *The Search for Order, 1877–1920* (1968).

REVIEW QUESTIONS

MULTIPLE CHOICE

1. The National Banking Act of 1863 proved helpful to business interests because it (1) required higher interest rates (2) placed the nation on a firm gold standard (3) provided a uniform currency (4) favored the debtor classes.

2. The Fourteenth Amendment included a clause designed to protect business corporations by (1) making citizens of all persons born in the United States (2) requiring payment of the national debt in gold (3) defining states' rights (4) extending the special protection of individuals to corporations.

3. Which statement regarding industrial growth after the Civil War is not true? (1) Abundant raw materials formed the basis of great industries (2) growth was uninterrupted by depressions or panics (3) immigration provided an adequate supply of labor (4) new inventions greatly aided the growth of new industries.

4. The construction of the transcontinental railroad to California was delayed in the 1850s chiefly because of (1) the Native American danger (2) disagreement between the North and South (3) opposition of private enterprise to what would necessitate a government subsidy (4) technological problems awaiting solution.

5. Which proved to be the largest source of financing in the construction of the Central Pacific Railroad? (1) Local aid (2) state aid (3) federal aid (4) private financing.

6. Which of these railroads was first to receive an extensive federal land grant? (1) Illinois Central (2) Central Pacific (3) Northern Pacific (4) Union Pacific.

7. Of these transcontinental railroads, which did not receive a federal land grant? (1) Northern Pacific (2) Great Northern (3) Central Pacific (4) Southern Pacific.

8. The key to the growth of the steel industry after 1865 was the (1) use of the Bessemer process (2) return of peace (3) export market for American steel (4) construction of the railroads.

9. The first oil boom in the United States occurred in the year (1) 1851 (2) 1859 (3) 1870 (4) 1880.

10. The petroleum industry by 1900 (1) had experienced long continued competition   (2) had come to be dominated by monopoly
(3) suffered from wasteful overproduction (4) had not yet become
a major industry.

11. The revolution in flour milling about 1870 (1) made use of soft
wheats feasible (2) was purely an American discovery (3) gave
Minneapolis leadership in the industry (4) opened California to
wheat growing.

TRUE-FALSE

12. The Civil War represented a transition from agricultural leadership
to business leadership in the United States.

13. A great scarcity of labor after 1865 hindered the growth of industry
in America.

14. The construction of the transcontinental railroads marked the greatest period of railroad expansion.

15. As soon as the first transcontinental railroad was built, rebuilding
had to begin because of hasty construction to collect the government subsidies.

16. The last of the great railroads to be built was the Southern Pacific.

17. Immediately south of the Canadian border was built the Northern
Pacific Railroad.

18. Commodore Vanderbilt constructed the Great Northern Railroad.

19. Carnegie's steel interests were concentrated in the Chicago area.

20. The revolution in flour milling made it possible to find a market for
the hard wheats grown on the Northern Great Plains.

COMPLETION

21. The author of the tariff act under Lincoln was _____ .

22. What is the number of the civil rights amendment to the
Constitution? _____ .

23. The first transcontinental railroad was linked when the two lines
met near _____ , Utah.

24. The eastern part of the first transcontinental railroad was named the
_____ .

25. The southernmost transcontinental railroad was the _____ ;
next, to the north of it, was the _____ Railroad.

26. The inventor of the sleeping car was _____ .

27. An American named _____ discovered a new steelmaking
process at the same time that _____ did so in England.

28. The leading steel manufacturer up to 1900 was _____ ; his steel interests were bought by a Wall Street financial wizard named _____ and became a part of a new giant firm named the _____ .

29. The first businessman to discover oil was _____ ; _____ drilled the well that brought an oil boom in western _____ . The great chemist who analyzed the properties of petroleum was _____ , and the business genius who came to dominate its refining was _____ .

30. The last names of three early leaders in the meat-packing industry are: _____ , _____ , _____ .

CHRONOLOGY / CHAPTER 5

1848   Gold discovery resulted in California population boom in 1849.

1857   James Birch operated first stage line across the West.

1858   Butterfield stage line put in operation under federal contract.

1859   Pike's Peak and Virginia City mining booms. Oregon admitted.

1860s   Many Native Americans wars over the Far West.

1860   Pony Express began operation but ceased in 1861.

1861   Russell, Majors, and Waddell operated first stage line through the central route.

1863   Homestead Act passed.

1864   Nevada admitted.

1867   Abilene, Kansas, first "cow town" sprang up. Nebraska admitted.

1869   First transcontinental railroad completed.

1870s   Last of the great Native American wars fought.
Cattle Kingdom spreads over the West.

1874   Black Hills gold rush began.
Barbed wire patented by Glidden.

1875   Custer's defeat by Sioux at Little Big Horn River.

1876   Colorado admitted.

1880s   Range cattle industry declines.

1883   Disappearance of last large buffalo herd. Downturn of cattle boom began.

1885   Geronimo captured.

1887   Dawes Severalty Act provided for individual ownership of land by Native Americans.

1889   Four omnibus states admitted, two others in 1890.
First land rush in Oklahoma.

1890   Battle of Wounded Knee, last Native American outbreak.
American frontier substantially closed.

1924   Native Americans gain full citizenship.

1934   Wheeler-Howard Act reversed Native American policy so as to conserve native culture.

Chapter

5

THE FAR WEST AND THE
NEW SOUTH, 1865–1890

Great changes already under way in the Far West followed immediately upon the close of the Civil War. The settlement of the Far
West took the form of successive frontiers that introduced population and rapidly developed the region. Before the Civil War the
mining frontier brought in tens of thousands of settlers to California
and thence into the intermountain regions. In the absence of mineral deposits other regions were opened first by the cattlemen. The
final frontier was that of the farmer; actually, the cattlemen's frontier and that of the farmer were the result of the extension of the
railroads—which should be more emphatically recognized as the
railroad frontier.

The South necessarily experienced important changes in its institutions as a result of the war and Reconstruction. The changes
taken together are referred to as the "New South."

THE MINERAL FRONTIERS OF THE WEST

When the gold in California easily recoverable by individual miners
with simple equipment and methods was exhausted, prospectors
looked for new fields. They were rewarded with rich discoveries in various parts of the Rockies and intermountain regions.

The Pike's Peak Rush—The next great rush occurred in 1859 in
Colorado after small deposits of gold were found near present-day
Denver. The newspapers in Missouri, by exaggerated accounts, stirred
up a mad rush from the East. Over 100,000 prospectors took part in the
Pike's Peak Gold Rush, many in wagons bearing their motto of "Pike's
Peak or Bust." About half of these prospectors returned East disappointed, but profitable strikes were made subsequently. Since many
stayed to engage in farming, business, and in mining, Colorado, like
other mining regions, gradually acquired a permanent population, territorial status, and, finally, statehood in 1876.

✪ **The "Fifty-Niners" in Nevada**—The fabulous Comstock Lode in Mt. Davidson in the Washoe Mountains in western Nevada caused a great mining boom there that lasted for decades. The great inrush of population, though insufficient for statehood, was seized upon under the political necessities of the Civil War to create the state of Nevada in 1864 and provide additional Republican strength in the national capital. Gold and silver both were taken in immense quantities from the Comstock Lode, and Virginia City became the principal mining city in Nevada.

✪✪ **Mining Booms in Other Western States**—As the miners spread eastward from the gold fields of California, many new lucky strikes were made. Mining towns sprang up in Idaho and Montana in the early 1860s; Arizona, too, received its share of miners. The last great mining rush occurred in the Black Hills of South Dakota after 1874. Deadwood became the wildest of any of the mining communities. It was here that "Wild Bill" Hickock, Calamity Jane, and others of their kind held forth and many remained permanently in the Boot Hill cemetery. Eventually most of the claims were bought out by the Homestake Mining Company.

✪ **The Mining Frontier**—The successive mining rushes brought a sudden mass of population into communities where no established machinery of law enforcement existed. Bad men of all kinds came in to prey on the mining population. The mining camps all passed through certain successive phases. In the first phase, a lonely prospector made the discovery of easily recoverable gold or silver. The second phase came with the sudden inrush of miners, disorderly elements, and the outbreak of a wave of crimes. The response of the honest elements came when the crimes could no longer be tolerated. In this third phase miners organized themselves as vigilantes to execute a rough and speedy justice to clean out the wrongdoers. Now, legally constituted agencies of law enforcement were established, and the camps settled down into relatively law-abiding communities.

The larger areas, as distinguished from mining camps, passed through the successive stages from unorganized to organized territories and then to statehood.

As the mining frontier passed away, the methods of mining changed from the use of simple tools and devices used by a few individuals in surface mining to the use of heavy machinery and equipment, deep tunneling, and heavy powered equipment for processing gold- and silver-bearing ores. Highly capitalized, speculative corporations bought out the mining claims and came to dominate the mineral deposits.

✪ COMMUNICATIONS BEFORE THE RAILROADS

The gold rush in California created the need for transcontinental transportation. Before the railroads penetrated the West, stage and freight lines were established. Even before this, the first public carriers between the East and California were ships operating around Cape Horn or to Panama, where passengers took the isthmian railroad to catch another ship for California. The first contract for an overland stage line was made in 1857 by the Post Office Department with James Birch of California; he operated mail stages monthly from San Antonio to San Diego. In 1858 John Butterfield put stages into operation also along the southern route but connecting St. Louis and San Francisco. Concord coaches carried passengers and mail, and wagons hauled freight.

In 1861 the famous firm of Russell, Majors, and Waddell became the leading stage line; on account of Confederates in the Southwest, the line was shifted to the central route across the plains and mountains. When this latter firm went bankrupt in 1862, the coarse, domineering tycoon Ben Holladay took over, but he shrewdly sold out to the Wells Fargo Company in 1866 before the completion of the transcontinental railroad. The much-publicized Pony Express was only a short-term demonstration of the feasibility of a central transportation route and was operated by the firm of Russell, Majors, and Waddell. It began in 1860 but was discontinued in 1861 when the Pacific Telegraph completed its line across the West. Many other firms not so well known operated a network of stagecoach and wagon freighting lines all over the West, mainly to serve mining towns before the railroads were extended into these remote areas.

NATIVE AMERICAN PACIFICATION IN THE FAR WEST

A lull in the almost continuous history of Native American fighting in America occurred after the War of 1812. The lull was interrupted mainly by the Seminole and the Black Hawk wars around 1840. But widespread, bloody Native American wars were renewed, beginning with the gold rush in California, and continued until the late 1870s when the Native American tribes were all finally beaten beyond any possibility of further practical resistance.

✪ **Outbreak of Native American Wars in the West**—The first mining boom in the Far West, the California gold rush, brought a horde of aggressive Americans across the Native American-occupied plains into California. At first conflicts between Native Americans and the miners who overran their lands brought on a succession of campaigns in California lasting from 1849 until the early 1870s. These "wars" killed off the relatively large number of peaceful Native Americans of California. The need to protect emigrants along the trails leading to California, Santa Fe, and Oregon and to open the way for the transcontinental railroad, brought treaty negotiations with the various tribes for the purpose of concentrating them in smaller reservations. The tribes were separated and each limited to its own well-defined hunting grounds. But it proved impossible to keep whites out of Native American hunting grounds when mineral discoveries were made.

The Cheyenne-Arapaho War broke out in 1861 when the "fifty-niners" overran Native American lands in eastern Colorado. The war lasted until 1864, by which time this region had become devastated by the Native Americans. The bloodshed was ended with the Chivington massacre when an encampment of sleeping Cheyennes, who had already surrendered, were attacked by the Colorado militiamen. Over 450 Native American men, women, and children were killed.

The Sioux War, 1865–1867, broke out next in Wyoming and Montana. The Sioux War was caused by the defeat of the Minnesota Sioux in a minor war in 1862, by anger over the Chivington massacre, and by mining activities in Montana. The Sioux greatly hampered the building of forts and their maintenance in Montana. The massacre of all the men of the army's Fetterman party was the bloodiest episode of this war.

During the 1860s Native American depredations and wars were, in fact, widespread over the Far West. In the southern Great Plains the Comanche and Kiowa raided into Texas and Oklahoma into the middle 1870s. The Civilized Tribes in Oklahoma joined the Confederacy during the Civil War. In the Southwest the Navajos fought until 1867, but the Apaches continued their plundering for two more decades.

Later Native American Wars—During the 1870s numerous wars were fought against Native Americans who grew discontented with confinement on the reservations and the shabby treatment they received there. Another Sioux War broke out in 1875 when miners trespassed the Black Hills in the Sioux reservation. It was during this campaign that General George A. Custer and his force of over 200 cavalrymen lost their lives when they fell into a Sioux ambush in the Battle of the Little Big Horn (River) in Montana. Soon their leader, Crazy Horse, and his men were captured, but Sitting Bull fled to Canada and stayed there for several years.

In the Pacific Northwest the Nez Percé under Chief Joseph rose in rebellion but were soon defeated and removed to a reservation in Oklahoma. When Geronimo, the Apache leader, was captured in 1885, the recurrent Native American raids finally ceased in New Mexico and Arizona.

A final Native American outbreak, the Ghost Dance War, resulted from a religious frenzy among the mistreated Sioux in their Black Hills Reservation. The Native Americans, numbering about 200, who left the reservation were massacred in the Battle of Wounded Knee in 1890.

⊘ New Federal Native American Policy—The Chivington massacre of 1864 caused heavy protests in Congress against treatment accorded the Native Americans and led to the adoption of new policies. The Peace Commission, sent out in 1867 to stop the Sioux War, introduced a policy of "Small Reservations" to remove and isolate Native Americans in remote places. At the same time there began a policy of treating the Native Americans as individuals and as wards of the government instead of recognizing the tribes as separate nations. The new policy was endorsed by Congress in 1871. The Indian Office helped the tribes organize councils to undermine the power of the chiefs. One step followed another in the direction of educating the Native Americans and trying to change them into the pattern of the white man's culture. In 1883 a system of federal courts relieved the chiefs of their judicial powers.

∞ **The Dawes Act, 1887**—Among the humanitarians who worked to win public support for a more just treatment of the Native Americans, the best known was Helen Hunt Jackson. As the author of *A Century of Dishonor and Ramona,* she aroused public opinion. The leading consequence of this agitation was the Dawes Severalty Act, which provided for individual ownership of land, to become effective after a trust period of 25 years. In 1906 the Burke Act permitted a shortening of the trust period.

In 1924 the Native Americans were given full citizenship. In 1934 the New Deal reversed the policy of forcing the Native American to conform to the white man's ways when Congress passed the Wheeler-Howard Act. This last revision of policy sought to conserve the Native American tribal culture.

THE RANGE CATTLE INDUSTRY

Several developments concurred during the two decades after 1865 to make possible the spectacular spread of the open-range cattle grazing industry over the Great Plains. The growth of a population of consumers in the industrial cities of the East created the market for beef; the extension of the railroads into the Plains provided transportation; and the killing of the buffalo and pacification of the Native Americans removed these obstacles from the grazing lands.

The Disappearance of the Buffalo—Millions of buffalo roamed the Great Plains and Rocky Mountain areas; they constituted the chief livelihood of the Native Americans of those regions. The large-scale killing of the buffalo began with the construction of the Union Pacific Railroad; the buffalo were used to feed the railroad laborers. Next, professional hunters, organized in parties and employing repeating rifles, slaughtered them for the hides, which were converted into "buffalo robes." Hunters killed them for sport, and railroad passengers shot them for the same reason. The southern buffalo disappeared by 1875, and in 1883 the northern herd was killed except for a small number. Later the bones were gathered up in wagons and shipped East by the trainload to be ground into fertilizer or to make carbon for refining sugar. The destruction of the buffalo deprived the Native Americans of their food supply and forced them to depend on a government beef supply at the reservations.

✪✪ **Origins of the Range Cattle Industry**—The Great Plains range cattle industry originated in south Texas, where it was developed by the Mexicans. Cattle grew wild in Texas long before the Civil War; during the war they multiplied in large numbers. When the Kansas Pacific Railroad was extended to Abilene, Kansas, in 1867 the first "cow town" sprang up. Enterprising Texans began driving herds here to sell to buyers who shipped them East by rail to the packing houses. The price differential between Texas and the railheads was great enough to make the long drives quite profitable. As settlers moved into Kansas, the railroads were extended farther west and new cow towns sprang up at places like Newton, Ellsworth, and Dodge City. The Chisholm Trail through west Texas was the best known of the cattle trails.

✪ **Spread of the Cattle Kingdom**—As word spread of the lush profits to be made in cattle grazing on the free public lands, more Texans extended the grazing into west Texas, the Texas Plains, the Indian Territory, and Kansas. In the 1870s grazing spread rapidly into the Northern Plains in Colorado, Wyoming, Montana, and the Dakotas. It was found that in ordinary winters cattle would thrive by grazing on dry grass in the northern Plains. The Texas longhorns were bred to Hereford bulls and to eastern cattle to produce a much better type of beef animal. The killing of the buffalo and the confinement of the Native Americans opened more rangeland. As packers turned to canning the beef and using refrigerated railway cars, the market increased and extended to Europe. Cattle came to be sold for fattening on Northern corn. The profits attracted more and more enterprisers. The demand for breeding stock created a further rise in price as the boom began to feed on itself.

Management of the Cattle Ranges—Since the cattlemen grazed their herds on free public lands and in areas where no local government had been established, it became necessary for them to develop their own codes to regulate the use of the range and identify and protect their cattle. "Range rights" of those who first used the land were recognized. An individual's range usually extended from a stream to the divide separating it from the next sizable stream. There was no fencing, but cowboys riding the range worked to keep the cattle on their proper range. Voluntary extra-legal organizations, the livestock associations, were organized to register each cattleman's brand and conduct "round-ups" for returning strays to their rightful owners, for protection against thieves, and to otherwise enforce the codes that were devised.

✪ **The Break-up of the Range Cattle Industry**—Overexpansion of the cattle industry and boom conditions marked by high cattle prices and heavy profits—of as much as 30 percent a year—led to over-crowding of the ranges and overproduction of cattle. Everybody seemed to rush in to enjoy the high profits; they often borrowed money at extremely high interest rates. Cattle companies organized in England and Scotland invested large sums. Prices kept rising until 1883, when drought forced increased marketing of stock.

The crash came in 1884 when $35 cattle sold for $10. Prolonged drought kept prices sliding until 1887. Heavy losses were suffered from unusually cold winters and heavy snow and ice that covered the dry grass. A combination of low prices and heavy losses precipitated wide-spread bankruptcy. Other factors bringing an end to the industry were the coming of the "nesters," homesteaders who had a legal right to claim and fence the land. Sheepherders also crowded the ranges in the 1880s. Cattlemen learned that they would have to acquire their own land, breed better cattle, and grow winter feed. Cattle raising became a stable business confined to fenced ranches.

THE FARMERS' FRONTIER IN THE FAR WEST

The agriculture of the small farmer of the East had to undergo radical changes under the semiarid climate of the intermountain regions and of the Great Plains. New methods, new equipment, and new crops had to be devised or introduced. These changes are particularly characteristic of, and are usually associated with, Great Plains farming. This last frontier of the farmer developed rapidly after the Civil War when the railroads, more than anything else, opened these wide spaces to settlement. By 1890 agricultural communities had fairly well completed the settlement of the last farmers' frontier, that of the Great Plains. The main adjustments that the farmer had to make were due to a climate less favorable to agriculture than that of the East. The chief problem was the lack of water in any form.

⊙ **The Role of the Railroads in the Farmers' Frontier**—If the railroads had not been developed earlier, they would have had to be invented to open the Far West to agriculture. There were no suitable streams, as in the East, to provide water transportation. The railroads provided transportation first for marketing cattle, and then transportation for heavy, bulky farm crops at low rates, as compared with other possible transportation. In large areas the railroads first introduced potential settlers to the land during railroad construction. As the railroads were built they made great efforts to settle the land with farmers; they accomplished this by advertising their own land and by systematic encouragement of immigration from both the East and from Europe.

Settlement generally followed the railroads after they were built. The rails brought in heavy materials needed by the settlers, such as lumber, fuel, and fencing materials, which were not present on the Plains.

Lack of Timber—On the Great Plains the first problem faced by the settler was the lack of timber. In the subhumid East, where trees grew readily, he had come to depend upon wood for housing, fencing, fuel, and other purposes. In the absence of timber he had to get along with dugouts or sod houses for shelter until he could afford to have lumber shipped in for frame houses. For fencing, barbed wire had to be invented, since rail or wood fences were too expensive. Joseph F. Glidden in Illinois in 1874 first began the manufacture of suitable barbed wire. Sales of the new wire multiplied many times as the farmers fenced the West. For fuel the pioneer settlers had to manage with twisted grass and other plant materials until coal or wood could be purchased.

The Lack of Moisture for Crops—Insufficiency of rainfall beyond the ninety-eighth meridian made it necessary for farmers to devise a system of agriculture known as dry farming. Extensive irrigation was not practiced in the West until large-scale projects were built after the frontier days by the federal government. Dry farming employs special methods of cultivation to retain moisture in the soil and depends on drought-resistant crops. The United States Department of Agriculture made worldwide searches to introduce drought-resistant crops, grasses, and trees. The most successful of these were the hard or durum wheats now grown over the Great Plains.

Farmers and ranchers had to plant thinner and utilize larger acreages in the semiarid West. This brought about the use of large power machines needed to cover the ground quickly. Large fields and level land invited the use of sulky gang plows and large seeding and harvesting machines. In 1878 the twine binder was invented; and in the 1880s, the header for harvesting grain. Steam power developed rapidly on the large farms. Settlement of the Plains greatly speeded the use of power and large machines on farms everywhere.

✪ **Land Laws and the West**—Liberal laws by which individuals could secure title to federal lands and land grants to the states for various purposes disposed of much of the public domain in the West and aided rapid settlement.

The Homestead Act (1863) offered free land to encourage settlement by family farmers. Although the act was much talked of as one to aid the small farmer, in actual results its role in aiding the small farmer and promoting Western settlement has been greatly exaggerated. Much of the best land in quality and location was granted to the railroads or bought in large blocks by land speculators. Other land was acquired fraudulently under the Homestead Act by ranchers and timber companies. The Homestead Act applied to semiarid lands mostly, and therefore offered too small a unit to support a family. Land could not be taken up under the Homestead Act until surveyed; speculators and others acquired much of the best land before it was surveyed.

Land grants were made to the states, as under the Morrill Act, to subsidize agricultural and mechanical colleges, but this land was sold to speculators, who in turn sold it to individuals at increased prices.

The railroad land grants took a large chunk out of the public domain and included much good land with the all-important advantage of proximity to rail transportation. This land was sold at a price averaging $5 an acre.

Lands originally reserved for the Native Americans but later taken over by the government were sold to speculators until 1887.

The Timber Culture Act (1873) permitted homesteaders to increase their original 160 acres by acquiring an additional 160 acres by planting trees. About 10,000,000 acres were taken under this act.

The Desert Land Act (1877) sold 640 acre blocks at $1.25 an acre on proof the land had been irrigated. Much land was taken fraudulently by large ranchers and irrigation companies under this act.

The Timber and Stone Act (1878) permitted individuals to buy 160 acres "unfit for cultivation" for its timber and stone. Under this act land was taken fraudulently at a fraction of its value by timber companies.

CHANGES IN THE SOUTH AFTER THE CIVIL WAR

After the war the South attracted much more industry than ever before. A new pattern appeared in Southern politics, and agriculture underwent certain changes after the abolition of slavery.

○○ The New South—The term "New South" refers to the growth of industry that had become so apparent in the South during the 1880s. A prominent editor in Atlanta, Henry W. Grady, advocated the promotion of industry as the principal goal of the South. How is the growth of industry in the New South to be explained? 1) Most of the new industry developed in the upper South, where water power and labor were available. 2) The Bourbon Democrats (the successors to the pre-war Southern Whigs) favored industry. 3) The presence of raw materials determined the kinds of industries: textile mills and other factories that manufactured cotton, tobacco, lumber, and processed cottonseed. Deposits of iron and coal near Birmingham, Alabama, made this city a center of iron and steel manufacture. The industrial growth of the South has continued to the present; the same favorable factors of abundant labor and raw materials, a friendly political climate, and supplies of fuel and power still encourage its growth.

⊙⊙ Politics in the South—The Reconstruction experience of the South identified the Republican Party with outside rule and caused Southern whites to look to the Democratic Party as one properly identified with the states' rights thinking of the South. Once the South was left free, the whites dominated politics through the single-party system of the Democrats. The "Solid South" became a stronghold of the national Democratic Party, and until 1928 all Southern states appeared as a single block in the Democratic column. Within the Democratic Party itself the Bourbon, or well-to-do Democrats, usually managed to keep control. The one-party system prevented a healthy rivalry between parties.

By numerous devices the whites kept the African Americans away from the polls. In addition to intimidation and threats, legal devices were employed. Poll taxes came into use. In the 1890s some states passed laws against anyone voting whose ancestor had not voted before 1867—these were the "grandfather clauses." Property qualifications, literacy tests, and examinations over the Constitution were also used. In 1915 the Supreme Court declared the "grandfather clauses" unconstitutional, but other laws to restrict voting remained in effect.

⊙ The Agricultural System in the South—It was 1870 before agricultural production was fully restored in the South. Much of the difficulty was in devising a new labor system. The freedmen resented working in gangs and would not abide by written labor contracts. Hence there developed a system of individual cultivators working as tenants for a share of the crop. Large numbers of landless white farmers, as well as the African Americans, worked as sharecroppers. Combined with tenancy was the crop-lien system, under which a tenant was furnished supplies on credit but had to give a lien on his harvest. He usually found himself unable to pay his debt, and state laws prevented his changing landlords until he cleared his debts. This created a system closely resembling peonage. Landlords in the cotton areas required their tenants to produce a single cash crop, usually cotton; this perpetuated the one-crop system.

CHAPTER BOOK LIST

Branch, E.D., *Hunting of the Buffalo* (Bison).

Bronson, Edgar, *Reminiscences of a Ranchman* (Bison).

Cash, W.J., *The Mind of the South* (Vintage). Interpretive.

Conway, John, *Apache Wars* (Monarch). Brief story of cruel Native American raids.

Fite, Gilbert C., *The Farmer's Frontier, 1865–1900* (1966).

Garland, Hamlin, *Boy Life on the Prairie (Bison)*. Pioneer farm life on the Northern plains.

Graham, W.A., *Story of the Little Big Horn* (Collier). Custer's last fight.

Greener, William S., *The Bonanza West: The Story of the Western Mining Rushes, 1848–1900* (1963).

Hagan, William T., *American Indians* (University of Chicago).

Mitchell, Broadus, and Mitchell, G.S., *Industrial Revolution in the South* (1968).

Nixon, Raymond B., *Horace W. Greeley* (1969).

Sandoz, Marie, *The Cattlemen From the Rio Grande Across the Far Marias* (1958).

Winther, Oscar, *Transportation on the Trans-Mississippi West Frontier, 1865–1890* (1964). Authoritative survey.

Woodward, C. Vann, *Origins of the New South, 1877–1913* (1951). The standard work.

Woodward, C. Vann, *The Burden of Southern History* (Vintage). Essays on the character of the South.

REVIEW QUESTIONS

MULTIPLE CHOICE

1. The last of the great mining booms in the Western states occurred in (1) South Dakota (2) Nevada (3) Colorado (4) Arizona.

2. The mining frontier was significant in all the following *except* (1) most of the Western states received their initial population boom from metal discoveries (2) American gold caused a worldwide increase in the money supply and stimulated prosperity in the fifties (3) California gold helped win the Civil War (4) in the long run gold proved a blighting influence on the culture and economic well-being of California.

3. The conduct of the vigilantes in bringing criminals to justice may best be described as (1) uniformly fair but hasty (2) nearly always deliberate, accurate, and fair (3) ranging from fairness to the grossest forms of mob violence (4) so unfair as to have never been preferable to existing conditions.

4. The initial impetus to extensive transportation development in the Far West came from the (1) settlement by farmers (2) mining frontier (3) military needs (4) fur traders.

5. Which item below does *not* match correctly the location and name of a Native American tribe? (1) Cheyenne and Arapahoes, Colorado (2) Sioux, Northern Great Plains (3) Nez Percé, the Southwest (4) Apaches, New Mexico and Arizona.

6. Which event caused the introduction of the "Small Reservation" policy in managing the Native American tribes? (1) Fetterman massacre (2) Custer's massacre (3) Nez Percé War (4) Chivington massacre.

7. Which was *not* a factor in introducing the range cattle industry to the West? (1) The invention of barbed wire (2) slaughtering of the buffalo (3) pacification of the Native Americans (4) extension of the railroads.

8. The range cattle industry of Texas (1) was primarily Spanish in origin (2) drove no cattle to the East until after the Civil War began (3) was influenced most by American cattle and ranching practices from east of the Sabine (4) would have been permanent except for the invention of barbed wire.

9. Which factor was probably least effective in the decline of the range cattle industry? (1) Drought (2) overexpansion (3) sheepgrazing (4) barbed wire fencing.

10. The range cattle kingdom (1) never spread to the cold climate of the Northern Great Plains (2) expanded rapidly with such technological advances as railroads, refrigeration, and large packing plants, as well as through foreign investment (3) expanded on lands to which title was acquired by fraudulent means (4) ended chiefly because it was more efficient to feed blooded stock, which could not be bred under open range conditions.

11. The last agricultural area to be opened in the West was in (1) the intermountain region (2) California (3) Oregon (4) the Great Plains.

12. Which factor probably did the most to open the last agricultural areas of the Far West? (1) Mining booms (2) railroad transportation (3) dry farming (4) liberal immigration policies.

13. The Homestead Act was less helpful than commonly thought mainly because (1) compliance provisions were too onerous (2) it applied only to semiarid lands (3) much of the best land was taken up (4) ranchers successfully intimidated "nesters" who tried fencing their land.

14. The growth of industry in the South after 1865 was encouraged least by which of these factors? (1) Availability of labor and raw materials (2) favorable federal policies in the South (3) friendliness of the Bourbon Democrats (4) presence of coal and water power.

15. Which device used to keep African Americans from voting in the South was discontinued first? (1) Poll taxes (2) special examinations (3) grandfather clauses (4) literacy tests.

16. Which feature was least characteristic of the agriculture of the New South? (1) Use of labor contracts (2) crop-lien system (3) one-crop system (4) sharecropping.

TRUE-FALSE

17. "Wild Bill" Hickock and Calamity Jane were associated with the mining boom at the Comstock Lode.

18. The first contract for an overland stage line to California was made with Ben Holladay.

19. The highly profitable Pony Express provided swift mail service for a decade before it was supplanted by the railroads.

20. The lull in the Native American wars on the frontier was ended by the coming of whites, mainly because of the mining booms.

21. The Comanche tribe was especially destructive in Utah.

22. The last notable Native American outbreak was the Ghost Dance War.

23. There was no economic motive for killing the buffalo.

24. The cattlemen on the open range made use of public lands for livestock, and thus had the boon of free grazing.

25. The greatest problem of farming in the Great Plains was the lack of credit.

26. The last frontier of the farmer in the West followed the extension of railroads into new lands.

27. Dry farming practice came to make much use of machinery.

28. Most of the best land in the West was claimed by small farmers under the Homestead Act.

29. The Desert Land Act gave 640 acres of land to settlers on proof it was unfit for irrigation.

30. After the abolition of slavery, the labor of the African American was utilized through a system of tenancy known as sharecropping.

31. The crop-lien system in the "New South" helped establish the one-crop system there.

COMPLETION

32. The next great mining rush after the California gold rush was in 1859 in the vicinity of _____ in Colorado and another in Nevada at _____ City.

33. Before legally constituted law enforcement came to the mining towns, evildoers were punished by the _____ .

34. The last great mining boom in the West was in the _____ of South Dakota; the main town there was _____ .

35. Before the railroads came to the West passengers were carried by _____ .

36. Identify these Native American chiefs with their tribes: Sitting Bull _____ , Chief Joseph Geronimo _____ .

37. General Custer was killed at the _____ River.

38. The Native Americans were given land ownership in severalty by the _____ Act in the year _____ . The writer who defended the Native Americans was _____ who wrote two famous books about the Native Americans which were entitled _____ and _____ . The Native American was given citizenship in the year _____ .

39. The New Deal reversed Native American policy in the _____ Act in 1934.

40. The first great cow town was built at _____ , Kansas.

41. The best known of the cattle trails was the _____ Trail.

42. The cattlemen governed themselves through extralegal organizations called _____ . The peak of cattle prices in the boom came in the year _____ .

43. Homesteaders who fenced in farms in the rangelands were called _____ .

44. The farmers' last frontier in America occurred in the _____ region.

45. The inventor of barbed wire was named _____ .

46. Conservative Democrats who favored business and industry in the South were called _____ Democrats.

47. The steel industry in the South centered in _____ , Alabama.

THE CONSERVATIVE PERIOD, 1877–1900

CHRONOLOGY / CHAPTER 6

1866   National Labor Union organized.

1869   Knights of Labor organized.

1877   Hayes inaugurated as President. Reconstruction ended in
          South.

          National railroad strike.

1878   Greenback-Labor Party organized.

          Bland-Allison Act passed.

1879   Treasury resumes redemption of greenbacks in gold.

1882   Chinese Exclusion Act.

1881   Garfield (Rep.) inaugurated; assassinated after four months.
          Arthur became President.

          AF of L organized.

1883   Pendleton Act created Civil Service Commission.

          "Mongrel Tariff" failed to reduce rates.

1884   Blaine (Rep.), most prominent political figure of his time, lost
          presidential election to Cleveland (Dem.).

1885   Cleveland began his first term as President.

1886   Wabash case nullified state regulation of interstate railroads.

1887   Interstate Commerce Commission created to regulate
          interstate railroads.

          Dependent Pension Bill vetoed by Cleveland.

1888   Tariff main issue in presidential campaign of Harrison and
          Cleveland. Harrison (Rep.) elected.

1889   Harrison inaugurated.

1893   Cleveland began his second term.

Chapter

6
POLITICAL DEVELOPMENTS, 1877–1889

National politics during this period were chiefly characterized by a failure to come to grips with the economic problems of the times. Protests against business domination of politics remained ineffective for the most part. The leading problems were the need for tariff reform, the conflict of labor and capital, and the regulation of the railroads and of business combinations. Too much attention was given to personalities of contenders in the political contests.

HAYES AS PRESIDENT

Rutherford B. Hayes came to the Presidency with a record of honesty and high purpose as governor of Ohio. As Governor he had supported the merit system; he advocated it vigorously in the campaign in 1876. His support of the merit system in the federal government weakened his influence with his party. He was a religious man and his wife refused to serve alcohol in the White House. Able persons were chosen for his cabinet but not regular party men. He restored faith in the Republican party after the corruption of the Grant administration.

✪✪✪ **Hayes and the South**—Hayes' first important act was the withdrawal of federal troops from South Carolina and Louisiana, the last two of the occupied states. Democratic administrations in these states immediately replaced the Republican carpetbag officials when military reconstruction ended. Federal steps taken to enforce civil rights for African Americans were halted, and white supremacy became a dominant condition over the whole South.

✪ **Fight Against the Spoils System**—Frustration marked Hayes' attempts to introduce the merit system. He made commendable appointments, including the civil service reformer Carl Schurz, but incurred the angry hostility of his own party leaders. He gained a partial victory in a fight over "senatorial courtesy"—a custom that gave senators the right to approve or disapprove appointments of federal officials within the senator's state. The battle against such patronage was so hard-won that presidents no longer ignore the rule of "senatorial courtesy." Opposed to Hayes in this fight were two prominent, conservative, regular Republicans and spoilsmen, Chester A. Arthur and the imperious Roscoe Conkling, both of New York.

○○ The Monetary Problem—Hayes endorsed the "sound money" policies of his party. He backed the successful efforts of his Secretary of the Treasury, John Sherman, to accumulate a gold reserve of $100,000,000 so that the purpose of the Resumption Act could be realized. In 1879 the Treasury resumed the redemption of the greenbacks in gold, i.e., adopted the gold standard. This hard money policy caused a continual appreciation in the value of the dollar to the benefit of the creditor class and to the detriment of the debtors. Farm prices continued their long-term decline.

The Greenbackers voiced their objections by organizing the Greenback-Labor Party in 1878, a successor to the National Greenback Party that had organized in 1875. Western farmers gave the party much support in the party's demand for an increased money supply. The party lasted until 1884 when it merged with the Anti-Monopoly Party.

The "Silverites" paralleled the Greenbackers' agitation by demanding the resumption of silver coinage. Silver-mining interests joined these reflationists and demanded free and unlimited coinage of silver at a price ratio of "sixteen to one"; this would have raised the price of silver in terms of gold and insured an unlimited market for the output of Western mines. It appealed to those who favored inflation and higher prices.

The Bland-Allison Act was passed in 1878 by a Democratic Congress over Hayes' veto; it provided for limited purchases of silver for coinage, but the law was so administered as to bring no visible relief to hard-pressed debtors.

○○ Labor Strife—Labor disorders on a national scale occurred for the first time in America in a paralyzing railroad strike in 1877. The strike had been called in response to a cut in wages. Federal troops were called out in Maryland and twice sent into Pennsylvania; over the nation scores of workers were killed or injured in riots. Millions of dollars in property were destroyed but the workers returned to their jobs at lower wages. The Molly Maguires, a murderous terrorist labor organization, operated in the coal district of eastern Pennsylvania at this time. A Pinkerton detective gathered evidence that resulted in the conviction and hanging of ten of them in 1877.

○ Denis Kearney and Chinese Exclusion—Denis Kearney, an Irish agitator, led a movement of unemployed workingmen in San Francisco in the late 1870s. The Workingmen protested against the employment of low-wage Chinese labor and condemned the railroads that employed them. The agitation caused Congress to enact a law to restrict Chinese immigration, but Hayes vetoed it as a violation of the Burlingame Treaty with China. In 1880 a new treaty negotiated with China permitted Congress to legally pass an exclusion act; this was done in 1882.

✪✪ GARFIELD'S ELECTION AND ASSASSINATION

The long depression of the seventies was followed by several years of buoyant prosperity and expansion in the 1880s. A political move was made to nominate ex-President Grant for a third term, but the "Stalwarts," under the spoilsman Roscoe Conkling, had too much opposition from another faction, the "Half-Breeds," under James G. Blaine. The deadlock was broken at the nominating convention by the choice of the "dark horse" James A. Garfield of Ohio who had the approval of the reformers. The Stalwarts had to be conciliated with the selection of Chester A. Arthur of New York as Vice President.

The Democrats chose General Winfield S. Hancock, a Union officer who had fought at Gettysburg. Their party, too, was divided—between the Northern and Southern Democrats.

The campaign lacked any real emphasis upon issues of the day, as the Democrats seemed not to be conscious yet of the problems of money, tariff, and monopoly. The campaign revolved around personalities. The Democratic platform did favor low tariffs, but Hancock declared the issue unimportant. The Greenback candidate was James B. Weaver of Iowa. The Republicans barely managed to win but did regain control of Congress, as well as of the Presidency. Garfield was assassinated, only four months after his inauguration, by a disappointed office-seeker. The shock of his death brought national resentment against the system of rewarding men for party work by giving them political office.

ARTHUR AS PRESIDENT

When Vice President Chester A. Arthur succeeded to the Presidency upon Garfield's death, he turned over a new leaf and rose to the demands of high office. He fought and exposed corruption within his own party.

✪✪ **Civil Service Reform**—The Pendleton Act in 1883 authorized the President to create a three-member Civil Service Commission. The lowest offices in the federal government were classified and open competitive examinations required for applicants. The law was passed when the Democrats won control of the House in 1882, but Arthur sincerely supported the law and subsequent presidents placed more and more jobs under the classified lists.

✪ **Arthur's Constructive Measures**—1) On Arthur's recommendation Congress in 1882 created a tariff commission. This body recommended 20 percent reductions, but the attempt in Congress only produced the "Mongrel Tariff." Lobbying by special interests and log-rolling (vote-trading) by members of Congress killed tariff reform. 2) The President aided the prosecution of party members guilty of the Star-route frauds in Western mail contracts. 3) He vetoed extravagant pork barrel rivers and harbors appropriations. 4) He supported the construction of the first "iron" ships for the navy.

✪✪✪ **Election of 1884**—Arthur's good record lost him the support of the Stalwarts in 1884, but the liberals did not forget his past as a spoilsman. The presidential nomination went instead to James G. Blaine. Blaine, from Maine, had served in the House and Senate since 1863. His personal charm, like that of Henry Clay, won him a large following of supporters. The "Mulligan letters," which earlier had revealed his acceptance of financial favors in return for his political influence in securing a land grant for an Arkansas railroad, were now brought up against Blaine again and possibly cost him the victory in the election.

The Democrats nominated the bluntly honest reformer and conservative governor of New York, Grover Cleveland. He had risen rapidly in New York from county sheriff to mayor of Buffalo to the governor's office. Cleveland had the support of the Mugwumps, or liberal Republicans, but lost other votes because of the revelation of his bachelorhood involvement in an instance of personal immorality.

During the campaign a Protestant minister in New York referred to the Democratic party as the party of "rum, Romanism, and rebellion." This appeal to religious prejudice cost the Republicans many votes and in itself undoubtedly lost the pivotal state of New York for Blaine. Because Blaine failed to denounce the statement, it came to be assumed that he had endorsed it.

Cleveland won by a popular lead of only 23,000 votes, and his party won control of both houses of Congress. In the race Prohibitionist and Greenback candidates each won over 150,000 votes.

CLEVELAND AS PRESIDENT

President Cleveland was plagued by hungry Democrats who had been out of federal office since 1861. Considering the pressure he had to withstand, he resisted well the spoilsmen in his own party; he extended the civil service by almost doubling the number of classified positions. He appointed two ex-Confederates to his cabinet.

✪ **Pension Bill Vetoes**—A law enacted in 1862 provided pensions for Union veterans of the Civil War who had suffered war-connected disabilities and the dependents of those who had died in military service. Many veterans delayed filing their claims until long after the war. Dishonest veterans took advantage of this situation to file claims for disabilities suffered since the war or to make false claims. These claims, if denied by the Pensions Bureau, were presented as private bills by congressmen.

Cleveland studied these claims carefully and vetoed hundreds of them. The veterans organization, the Grand Army of the Republic, and the Republican party advocated careless liberality. In 1887 Congress passed, without regard to the nature of the disability, a Dependent Pension Bill providing lavish pensions to veterans no longer able to earn a living. Cleveland vetoed this bill. Cleveland's attempt to return captured Confederate flags to the South also aroused bitter Northerners.

THE TARIFF PROBLEM

The greatest problem in Cleveland's first term was the tariff.

○ **Origin of the Issue**—The Republican administration had maintained protective tariffs on imports from foreign countries since the Morrill Tariff (1861). The "Mongrel Tariff" (1883) failed to reduce rates. The large annual surplus of revenue now drained the nation's monetary supply and caused a depressing influence on the economy. The Civil War debt was being paid as the bonds matured. Since the national banknotes were supported by federal bonds, the retirement of these bonds would have further reduced money in circulation. The treasury surplus, resulting from high tariffs, encouraged extravagance, yet business interests wished to maintain protective tariff rates.

In 1887 Cleveland and the Democrats identified themselves more strongly with the cause of low tariffs by the introduction of the Mills Bill to reduce substantially the existing rates. The Republicans countered with a measure of their own to maintain high rates. Neither bill passed but the debates in Congress made the tariff the main issue in the campaign of 1888. The tariff continued as a lively issue in subsequent political campaigns.

○ **High Tariff Arguments**—In the demands for protective tariffs certain arguments have been used to win support for high rates. 1) It has long been argued in America that new, or "infant," industries need protection against well-established foreign competition that might deliberately seek to destroy American competition by price cutting. Industries, however, cling to protection long after they have become well-established. 2) Labor unions within protected industries argue that American labor needs continued protection against the competition of goods produced by low-paid workers abroad. Such competition can cause unemployment here in certain industries by depriving American-made goods of the domestic market. 3) The argument of self-sufficiency says that America must be able to produce essential goods within its own boundaries because of the possibility of foreign sources being cut off by war or a lack of shipping in wartime. The argument is that critical industries must be preserved and workers' skills maintained for the ever-possible needs of national defense or survival. 4) The need to maintain a favor able balance of trade by producing goods in America instead of paying gold for imports is argued when there is a strong outflow of gold.

⦾ **Free Trade Arguments**—Those who favor either low tariffs or free trade maintain that 1) free competition in international markets promotes national specialization in industries in which a country possesses natural advantages. Each nation produces what it can produce best and at the lowest cost. By exchanging goods, the whole free market enjoys a greater abundance, since all goods are produced more efficiently or where they can be produced at the lowest cost. America has a high standard of living within the large free trade area of the 50 states; the whole world could raise its standards of consumption similarly by removing trade barriers. 2) High tariffs in America raise the cost of goods to farmers and other consumers to the selfish advantage of protected industries. 3) It is argued that efficient producers can meet foreign competition without the benefit of tariffs. 4) American export industries such as agriculture are injured by tariffs, for if foreign nations cannot sell to the United States they cannot earn the dollars to pay for the goods we would like to sell them. 5) Trade barriers are an important cause of international friction and war. In a free market a country may buy what it needs instead of resorting to force to obtain such things as raw materials for its industry and consumer goods for its people.

⦾⦾⦾ **The Tariff Issue in Politics**—In American politics the protectionists have traditionally been the Republican Party and its predecessors. They have favored the tariff not only for protection of leading industries, but as a favored means of producing revenue for the federal government. The Democratic Party has traditionally supported free trade or low tariffs, and has looked upon low tariff duties as primarily a means of producing revenue. It is recognized that tariffs promote monopolies and that they give an indirect subsidy to protected industries at the expense of consumers and the unprotected industries. Industry has enjoyed a great advantage over other groups in being better-organized and more able to raise funds to lobby for its interests in Congress. Industrialists after the Civil War fought effectively to maintain the advantages of protective tariffs.

THE RAILROAD INDUSTRY

The railroads were at first hailed as the lifeblood of communities, and everything was done to subsidize and encourage their construction. Although they were public utilities, they fell under the control of men who managed them strictly as private property, without regard to the public interest.

⦾⦾⦾ **The Abuses of the Railroads**—The railroad builders and managers used their power in many ways to increase private fortunes and dominate politics. 1) In building the roads the insider-stockholders organized construction companies to enrich themselves by paying extravagant sums for construction contracts with companies owned by themselves. These high construction costs increased the bonded indebtedness of the railroads and their total capitalization. They used the overcapitalization to justify charging the public unreasonable rates for carrying freight and passengers. 2) The railroads were guilty of issuing watered stock. Watered stock results from the issuance of securities with a nominal value in excess of money actually invested in a business enterprise. Watered securities arose from the sale of securities at large discounts or from the practice of insiders voting themselves stocks as bonuses or as excessive compensation for their services in organizing the corporation. With too much stock outstanding, the railroads often found it impossible to maintain dividends on stock and interest on bonds, or they justified exorbitant rates to maintain dividends and interest payments. 3) Speculator-managers of railroad companies like Jay Gould, Jim Fisk, and Daniel Drew manipulated their securities or speculated in them solely for private enrichment.

4) Rebates of freight charges paid to large shippers gave these larger companies an additional advantage over their small competitors, who lacked the bargaining power to demand rebates from the railroads. Farmers and small-businessmen were outraged by various other unfair practices in railroad rates. 5) Another unfair type of discrimination occurred when railroads reduced rates in a locality where competition from another railroad forced them to do so but made up losses by overcharging customers where there was no competition. 6) Similarly, railroads made a practice of charging less for carrying freight over a long haul where competition existed and making up the loss of profits by charging more over a short haul where there was no competition.

7) The earliest method used to eliminate competition between different railroads, so they could charge all the traffic would bear, was the pooling device. The two main types of pools were territorial and profit-pooling. Competing lines would agree to divide territory or to prorate profits among themselves to halt competition.

8) The railroad managers also used their enormous financial power to corrupt government officials at all levels. Through political pressure of lobbyists or by outright bribery, they secured special favors from legislators or local officials. Bribery might take the form of free passes to politicians and officeholders. Contributions to campaign funds prevented unfavorable legislation and helped secure lower taxation.

✪ **Railroad Consolidations**—Since the early history of the railroads, the stronger companies created larger and larger systems by absorbing other lines. More and more railroads came to be interstate in character; they were either outside the jurisdiction of state regulatory bodies or more powerful than the state governments themselves. This situation made federal regulation necessary. The integration of railroads into fewer and larger systems came about because 1) better-managed railroads bought up the weaker lines or bought other lines to achieve a more efficient system or to assure monopoly advantages. 2) After depressions, bankrupt railroads were bought by financially stronger lines. 3) Railroad magnates created great systems through such devices as holding companies and leaseholds.

✪✪ **Railroad Regulation by the States**—The states first undertook to regulate the railroads by creating specialized bodies, the railroad commissions. This was the leading achievement of the Grangers in the agricultural states in the 1870s. Under the commissions regulation took the form of setting maximum rates. In some cases rates were fixed by the railroad commissions.

✪✪ **The Granger Cases**—The railroads and grain elevator companies invoked the newly ratified Fourteenth Amendment to protect themselves against what they charged amounted to a confiscation of private property without due process of law (considered confiscation because regulation denied them adequate returns on their investments). But in the case of *Munn v. Illinois* (1876) the United States Supreme Court held that these properties were "public utilities" and therefore subject to public regulation.

In a second important case, *Peik v. the Chicago and Northwestern Railroad,* the Supreme Court ruled that the Granger laws were not in violation of the interstate commerce powers of the Federal Constitution, even though the laws incidentally regulated railroads operating in other states. In the absence of federal legislation the states were free to regulate interstate railroads.

✪✪✪ **The Wabash Case (1886)**—In the case of *Illinois v. the Wabash Railway,* state regulation as upheld in the Granger cases received a severe setback. The regulatory statute of Illinois was held unconstitutional in its regulation of an interstate railroad that passed through Illinois. Here the Court reversed its decision in the Peik case and nullified most state laws regulating railroads, since most railroads were interstate in their operations. It followed that interstate railroads were therefore subject to regulation only by Congress, and the Court suggested action to this end.

Cullom Committee—Since 1870 minor parties and progressives had been asking for federal regulation or ownership of the railroads as a means of eliminating the various abuses. The Wabash Case and public opinion made it clear that Congress must act. The Senate appointed the Cullom Committee in 1886 with a large range of powers to investigate the problem and make recommendations. This committee traveled and studied the problem thoroughly and made its report in favor of federal regulation.

✪✪✪ **The Interstate Commerce Act**—In 1887 Congress passed this act, whereby 1) it created the Interstate Commerce Commission of five members to enforce provisions of the law. 2) The act made rebates, pools, and unjustifiable discriminations illegal, and 3) required railroads to charge "reasonable and just" rates and to publish such rates. 4) It gave the Commission the power to investigate complaints and make decisions subject to review by the courts.

The creation of this independent agency to exercise special powers of regulation in a difficult economic area brought into action the first such body. Since then Congress has created many similar independent regulatory agencies staffed by specialists. These agencies combine legislative, executive, and judicial functions. It was significant that Congress accepted the principle of federal regulation. But the courts did not support the Interstate Commerce Commission and effectively reduced its powers. It did not become really effective until the Presidency of Theodore Roosevelt.

THE ORGANIZATION OF LABOR

During the 1880s the nationally organized labor unions became more active and effective. The rise of nationwide business organizations and of monopolies made it necessary for workers, like the farmers, to organize large-scale bargaining units and pressure organizations to match the power by which industry had come to exploit so effectively both farmers and laborers. Before the Civil War labor had never organized more than local unions nor organized national unions of more than a limited number of workers within a particular skill.

⊙ **The National Labor Union**—In 1866 this organization was founded; it combined into a federation a wide variety of skills and crafts; it lasted only until 1873. It had weakened itself by going into politics under the name Labor Reform Party (1872) and by promoting general reforms rather than working for such specific labor goals as higher wages and fewer hours.

⊙⊙⊙ **The Knights of Labor**—This union was organized as a lodge in 1869 by Uriah S. Stephens. The aim of the Knights was to create "one big union," all-inclusive and built upon individual members (instead of being a federation of existing unions) and with few restrictions as to occupation of its members. After 1878 the Knights fell under the domination of Terence V. Powderly and expanded by 1886 to a membership of 700,000. The Knights advocated general reforms such as the income tax and government ownership of railroads and telegraph lines. They organized consumers cooperatives, but they failed for lack of sound management. The Knights advocated arbitration of disputes but had to resort to boycotts and strikes. The Knights proved successful in winning a major victory in a strike against the Missouri Pacific Railroad in 1885 and won many minor victories the same way. These victories accounted for its rapid growth.

OO The Decline of the Knights—In 1886 railroad shopmen under the Knights went on strike against the Texas and Pacific Railroad when one of their foremen was fired. By strike and sabotage they stopped all freight traffic in the Southwest on over 5,000 miles of track. Public opinion at first sympathized with the strikers, but later turned against them, and the strike was lost. In the same year the May Day strikes occurred in support of the eight-hour day. On May 4 occurred the Haymarket Riot as a consequence of these May Day strikes.

At Haymarket Square in Chicago, foreign-born anarchists were addressing an orderly crowd when police tried to break up the meeting. When a bomb was thrown into the column of policemen, fighting broke out between the crowd and the police. Seven police were killed in the whole affair and 60 seriously wounded; the civilians suffered slightly smaller losses.

Public opinion reacted violently against the Knights of Labor, who had participated in these events. The public demanded that someone be punished, although no one could be found who was responsible for the bombing. Nevertheless, seven anarchist leaders were brought to trial and convicted on the assumption that their encouragement had caused someone to throw the bomb; four were hanged. The Knights had welcomed almost everyone into membership and now were blamed by public opinion for anarchist violence. Skilled workers became dissatisfied with the unwise promotion of conflicts by the unskilled workers and withdrew in great numbers after 1886. Membership declined rapidly, and soon after 1890 the organization disappeared entirely.

OOO Rise of the American Federation of Labor—This federation of existing unions, organized in 1881, thrived and expanded upon the dissatisfaction of skilled workers with the Knights of Labor; it differed sharply from the Knights in several of its characteristics. 1) Its unit of membership was the labor union instead of the individual; 2) the AF of L was an exclusive organization representing the interests of the "aristocracy of labor," the skilled workers; 3) it was conservative in its acceptance of the capitalist system, and only wished to share in its benefits; 4) it worked to achieve specific goals, such as the eight-hour day, higher wages, job tenure, and abolition of child labor; 5) it avoided "going into politics" but supported whichever party was most favorable to its goals; 6) it avoided such violent weapons as sabotage but freely used the strike, boycott, and sympathetic strike.

OOO Samuel Gompers and the AF of L—Labor unions, like business corporations, tend to remain under the dominating leadership of some self-perpetuating strongman. In the AF of L this leader was Samuel Gompers; he served every year except one as president of the Federation from 1885 until he died in 1924. Gompers established a reputation of cooperating with government.

The conservatism of the AF of L under Gompers enabled it to survive and win great gains for the small minority of workers that it represented. However, these gains were often extended to labor outside the AF of L It helped win higher wages, better working conditions, the eight-hour day, the closed shop (which permitted employers to hire only union members), and secured legislation outlawing yellow-dog contracts (contracts by which employers hired workers only on condition they would never join a union). Innumerable federal and state laws favorable to labor were passed. The member unions set up funds to provide sickness and unemployment benefits for their members.

The great railway brotherhoods of skilled workers resembled the AF of L and remained outside the Federation, but usually cooperated with it.

○ **Gains Made by Labor**—While many employers resisted the demands of the unions, the workers did gain many concessions. In 1868 the eight-hour day was established in federal public works and in 1892 for all federal employees. Oriental exclusion (1882) and the prohibition of the importation of contract labor (1885) were realized in answer to labor demands. The principle of arbitration of disputes involving interstate carriers was realized by law in 1898. State laws limited women and children to a ten-hour day, and laws were passed to provide better working conditions.

○○ THE ELECTION OF 1888

The Democrats renominated President Cleveland in 1888. After Blaine refused to be a candidate, the Republicans chose Benjamin Harrison, the grandson of William Henry Harrison. Cleveland had made the tariff question the main issue of the campaign. Cleveland was accused of favoring free trade when he only wanted tariff reductions; the tariff issue enabled the GOP to raise generous campaign funds, and Cleveland's anti-pension vetoes cost him the support of the GAR (Grand Army of the Republic, the pressure organization of Civil War Union veterans). Funds were used scandalously in crucial states to get out the vote. Cleveland received a plurality of 100,000 votes, but in losing the electoral vote of the pivotal state of New York, he lost the election to Harrison. The Republicans won control of both houses of Congress. The publication of a private letter written by the British minister, Sackville-West, in favor of Cleveland probably switched enough British-hating Irish voters in New York State to account for the defeat of Cleveland there. Cleveland forced the minister's departure for his indiscretion.

CHAPTER BOOK LIST

Broehl, W.G., *The Molly Maguires* (1964). Thorough.
Brown, T.N., *Irish-American Nationalism* (1966).
Buck, Solon, *Granger Movement* (Bison). Standard.
Burr, Susan S., *Money Grows Up in American History* (1964).
Callow, A.B., *The Tweed Ring* (1966). Fascinating.
Dinnerstein, Leonard, and Geier, F.C., *The Aliens* (1970).
Goldman, Eric F., *Rendezvous With Destiny* (Vintage). Outstanding, stimulating; reform movements since 1860.
Josephson, Matthew, *The Politicos* (Harcourt).
Morgan, H. Wayne, *The Gilded Age* (1970).
Nugent, Walter T.K., *Money in American Society 1865–1880* (1968). Basic.
Pelling, Henry, *American Labor* (University of Chicago). Authoritative, narrative history.
Shannon, F.A., *American Farmers's Movements* (Anvil). Brief survey.
Taft, Philip, *The American Federation of Labor in the Time of Gompers* (1970). Scholarly.
Unger, Irwin, *The Greenback Era* (1964).

REVIEW QUESTIONS

MULTIPLE CHOICE

1. As President, Hayes may be best characterized as (1) reactionary and honest (2) liberal but cynical (3) religious and honest (4) a weak spoilsman.

2. Which problem was least important in government in the 1880s? (1) The tariff (2) government revenues (3) conflict of labor and capital (4) regulation of business combinations.

3. Which of these classes did *not* favor free silver? (1) Debtors (2) farmers (3) those with money on loan (4) silver miners.

4. The Greenback movement (1) was a consequence of the debtor status of the West after the Civil War (2) called for the redemption of greenbacks in gold (3) demanded the withdrawal of paper money and the substitution of silver (4) was supported by Eastern Republicans.

5. The most significant effect of Garfield's assassination was the (1) introduction of civil service (2) succession of Arthur to the Presidency (3) resignation of Blaine as Secretary of State (4) passage of the "Mongrel Tariff."

6. Blaine lost the election of 1884 possibly for all these reasons *except* (1) "rum, Romanism, and rebellion" (2) the "Mulligan Letters" (3) his personality (4) the unblemished reputation of Cleveland.

7. Which was *not* a policy pursued by Cleveland? (1) Tariff reform (2) extension of the Civil Service (3) critical examination of claims for Civil War pensions (4) support of monetary inflation.

8. Those who favored high tariffs in the 1880s desired them mainly because (1) they increased the foreign market for agricultural exports (2) they increased profits of manufacturers (3) the government sorely needed the revenue (4) of the danger of war.

9. High tariffs are detrimental to all *except* (1) consumers of goods protected by tariffs (2) farmers producing for the export market (3) manufacturers in protected industries (4) importing and shipping interests.

10. The railroads practiced several kinds of rate discrimination *except* (1) favoring farmers and small-businessmen (2) giving rebates to large shippers (3) charging more where there was no competing railroad (4) charging more on a short haul where there was no competition.

11. The railroads did all *except* (1) form pools to eliminate competition (2) bribe public officials (3) consolidate companies to eliminate competition (4) discourage freight traffic in areas they served.

12. The Wabash case (1) granted rate-making powers to the federal government (2) denied the states the power to regulate interstate railroad traffic (3) declared railroad mergers to be monopolistic (4) reduced railroad rates.

13. The creation of the Interstate Commerce Commission is especially significant because (1) it was passed under a Republican administration (2) it caused a split in the Democratic Party (3) it was the first federal business regulatory agency created (4) it won the immediate good will of the railroads.

14. The first nationwide labor organization to accept individual members regardless of union affiliation was the (1) Knights of Labor (2) American Federation of Labor (3) National Labor Union (4) Molly Maguires.

15. For the first time labor unions began organizing on a national scale after the Civil War because (1) communications developments made it possible (2) farmers had begun nationwide organizations (3) corporation and business operations had become national in scope (4) politicians encouraged it.

16. The Knights of Labor declined for all reasons except (1) the Haymarket riot (2) the rise of the American Federation of Labor (3) dissatisfaction of skilled workers (4) its membership was too exclusive.

17. The American Federation of Labor (1) organized militant political parties (2) was relatively conservative and accepted the capitalistic system (3) welcomed all true manual workers (4) favored radical reforms.

18. The AF of L did not work for (1) government ownership of industry (2) the eight-hour day (3) prohibiting yellow-dog contracts (4) the closed shop.

19. Which was not a typical goal of organized labor in the 1880s? (1) Abolition of the blacklist (2) better hours and wages (3) liberal immigration laws (4) anti-injunction laws.

20. In the election of 1888 (1) Cleveland was elected (2) Cleveland won the most popular votes (3) Blaine won the most popular votes (4) Harrison won the most popular votes.

TRUE-FALSE

21. Hayes supported the merit system while President; he also supported the gold standard.

22. The long-continued deflation after the Civil War injured the creditor classes.

23. The Greenbackers and "Silverites" aimed at basically opposing goals.

24. Nationwide labor disorders occurred for the first time in the railroad strike of 1877.

25. Garfield is often spoken of as a martyr for the cause of civil service.

26. As President, Arthur made a reputation for honesty; he was not renominated by his party.

27. Cleveland found it difficult to resist the spoilsmen in his party, but did manage to double the number of positions under the Civil Service.

28. Cleveland vetoed many pension bills because of his Confederate sympathies.

29. The large treasury surplus and the retirement of Civil War bonds increased money in circulation and promoted prosperity.

30. Both labor unions and industrialists in protected industries favor high tariffs.

31. Free trade promotes economic specialization; tariffs give an indirect subsidy to protected industries.

32. Railroad regulation was first undertaken by the federal government.

33. The Cullom Committee opposed federal regulation of the railroads.

34. Anarchists were active in America in the 1880s.

35. The unit upon which the American Federation of Labor is built is the individual workman.

36. The AF of L, being too conservative, gained little for the cause of labor.

37. Sackville-West may very well have caused Cleveland's defeat in 1888.

COMPLETION

38. Hayes came from the state of _____ and became President in the year _____ .

39. The custom that a president respects the wishes of senators in appointing high federal officials in the state is known as _____ .

40. The United States returned to the gold standard by the _____ Act, which went into effect in _____ .

41. The Silverites won a small victory in the _____ Act of 1878.

42. Opposed to the Republican _____ in the early 1880s were the Republican faction called the _____ .

43. When Garfield died he was succeeded in the Presidency by _____ . Civil Service was enacted into law by the _____ Act.

44. Cleveland came from the state of _____ ; his opponent Blaine came from the state of _____ .

45. Cleveland made an issue of the tariff question in 1887 by attempting to pass the _____ to reduce rates.

46. As for tariff policy, the Democrats traditionally have favored free trade or low tariffs for producing _____ , while the Republicans have favored high rates, otherwise known as _____ tariffs.

47. The practice of returning a part of freight charges to favored shippers is known as giving _____ ; excessive issues of securities in corporation finance are known as _____ .

48. Railroads were first regulated by an agency named the _____ .

49. The greatest leader of the Knights of Labor was _____ .

50. Which President served two terms but not successively? _____ .

51. GAR stands for _____ ; GOP stands for _____ .

MATCHING

52. Roscoe Conkling	a. Radical agitator in San Francisco
53. John Sherman	b. Organizer of the AF of L
54. Denis Kearney	c. Secretary of the Treasury under Hayes
55. James A. Garfield	d. His career blighted by the "Mulligan Letters"
56. James B. Weaver	e. "Stalwart" Senator from New York
57. James G. Blaine	f. Elected President in 1888
59. Uriah S. Stephens	g. Founder of the Knights of Labor
60. Samuel Gompers	h. "Dark horse" winner in 1880
61. Benjamin Harrison	i. Leading Greenback candidate
	j. Railroad financier and speculator
	k. Western railroad builder

CHRONOLOGY / CHAPTER 7

1882   Standard Oil Trust Agreement, followed by trusts in other
      industries.

1889   Harrison (Rep.) inaugurated as President.
      Four Western states admitted: North Dakota, South Dakota,
      Montana, and Washington.

1890   Wyoming and Idaho admitted.
      Sherman Silver Purchase Act increased silver and paper
      money.
      McKinley Tariff raised protective rates still further.
      Sherman Antitrust Act.

1891   Farmers' Alliance became the Populist Party.

1892   Election shows growing strength of Populists.

1893   Cleveland began second term.
      Panic of 1893, followed by severe depression.
      Cleveland takes steps to restore gold reserve.
      Homestead Strike.

1894   Wilson-Gorman Tariff failed to reduce rates and included
      provision for income tax.
      Pullman strike.
      "Coxey's Army" marched on Washington.

1895   Income tax declared unconstitutional.

1896   Utah admitted.

1907   Oklahoma admitted.

1912   Arizona and New Mexico admitted.

Chapter

7
POLITICAL DEVELOPMENTS, 1889–1896

A greater awareness of national problems began to manifest itself in the political parties about 1890. Protests of the Populists did the most to force attention to the problems arising from big business influence in the nation's politics.

THE PRESIDENCY OF BENJAMIN HARRISON, 1889–1893

Benjamin Harrison, dignified and honest but cold in personality, never was able to win personal friends or strongly influence people. Three other Republicans provided leadership for the party in power during his single term: James G. Blaine was made Secretary of State, Thomas B. Reed became Speaker of the House, and William McKinley provided leadership as chairman of the House Committee on Ways and Means. Presidential support of the new civil service was only nominal, but Theodore Roosevelt was appointed to the Civil Service Commission.

✪✪ **Czar Reed**—The Republicans had such a weak majority in the House that they found it difficult to maintain a quorum so that legislation might proceed. When the Democrats wished to stall action on a measure, they refused to answer roll call, as they were permitted to do under existing rules, even when physically present on the floor. Reed, therefore, changed the rules and declared a quorum if he could *see* members present. By these single-handed changes Reed won the title of "Czar" and overcame the obstructive tactics of the Democratic opposition. His rules helped to expedite the business of the House so effectively that they became permanent.

✪ **Republican Legislation**—A large volume of legislation was passed under Harrison; liberal appropriations of this Congress caused it to be dubbed the "billion-dollar Congress." Money was appropriated under the Dependent's Pension Act, which provided 92 pensions for all disabled Civil War veterans and dependent widows and minor children of veterans. River and harbor improvements were lavishly voted and more funds provided for the new steel naval vessels. A Federal Elections Bill, or "Force Bill," designed to give the federal government enough control over voting to assure the vote for the African American in the South, failed to pass.

✪ **Statehood in the Far West**—The admission of four states in the West that had been held up by Democratic majorities in the House now passed the all-Republican Congress. In 1889 North and South Dakota, Montana, and Washington became states. In 1890 Wyoming and Idaho were admitted. The Republican majority in the Senate was strengthened by the admission of these new states. Nebraska had been admitted in 1867, Colorado in 1876. In 1896 Utah was finally admitted after the Mormons at last gave up polygamy. Oklahoma, long delayed by the Native American problem, entered the Union in 1907. When Arizona and New Mexico were admitted early in 1912, the mainland of the United States had all become organized as states.

✪✪ **The Sherman Silver Purchase Act**—This law was passed in 1890 in order to win the support of Western-state members of Congress for the McKinley Tariff Bill. This silver purchase act required the treasury to buy 4,500,000 ounces of silver each month at the market price. The silver was to be paid for with legal tender treasury certificates redeemable in gold. The act brought a substantial increase in money in circulation.

✪✪ **The McKinley Tariff (1890)**—This act revised tariff rates on manufactured goods to a new peacetime high level and rewarded industrialists for their contributions to the Republican Party's election victory. To prevent an embarrassing surplus in the treasury, raw sugar was placed on the free list and a bounty of two cents per pound provided for American sugar producers. The prohibitive rates on imports had the intended effects of excluding some imports altogether and of reducing tariff revenues. Public resentment of the higher rates was reflected in the congressional elections of 1890 when the Democrats won a startling total of three fourths of the membership of the House; nine of the Populist candidates won election.

THE PROBLEM OF THE MONOPOLIES

Among the consequences of the growth of big business in America after the Civil War was the rise of the problem of monopoly control and price-fixing in vital industries. Monopoly violated the American economic system ideally governed by free competition and enabled monopolists to fix prices for maximum profits to the detriment of competitors and consumers.

✪✪ **Early Devices for Achieving Monopoly**—Pools were first used to achieve concentration of control in a given industry. Pools were arranged during the 1860s and 1870s but especially after 1873. By "pooling," companies in the same industry avoided competing with each other by agreeing to divide the market or to place all profits in a common fund to be prorated according to agreement. Members of pools frequently broke their agreement.

The trust proved to be a more effective device for achieving monopoly. Under trusts former competitors combined by entrusting the stock of competing companies to the hands of a board of trustees in return for trust certificates. The trustees voted the stock of all the companies and managed them as a unit.

The best known of the trusts was Rockefeller's Standard Oil Company agreements beginning in 1879. Rockefeller ruthlessly drove out competition and soon controlled over 90 percent of refinery capacity in the nation. In 1882 the Standard Oil Trust Agreement gave Rockefeller control over 40 subsidiary and associate firms and created the most powerful industrial organization in the country. Its main purpose was to control the marketing of oil and fix prices for maximum profits. It set the example for other trusts that soon followed, as in whiskey (1887), sugar (1887), and tobacco (1901). While the trusts were guilty of price-fixing, crushing smaller competitors by all kinds of foul means, and political corruption, they possessed certain inherent economic advantages such as efficient, low-cost, large-scale production, distribution of a superior product, and full utilization of byproducts.

The *holding company* became the next widely used device for eliminating competition among business firms after the antitrust laws began to take effect. A holding company is a corporation created for the specific purpose of buying and holding shares of operating corporations in order to manage them for whatever advantages may be desired. Holding companies acquire control of other companies by buying physical properties or stock and by leasing agreements. While business professed to believe in a system of freedom of enterprise and competition, many sought to abolish such freedom by establishing monopoly control. Government intervention was demanded to preserve freedom of enterprise.

✪✪✪ **The Sherman Antitrust Act (1890)**—Attempts by the state legislatures to regulate great business combines proved as ineffective as early regulation of the railroads. The Supreme Court stood in the way of effective regulation by the states when it ruled that corporations were "persons" under the Fourteenth Amendment and could not be deprived of "life, liberty or property without due process of law." The Grangers, the anti-Monopoly Party (1884), labor organizations, and popular writers demanded regulation that would give the public protection against monopolies. In response to these demands, the Republican Congress under Harrison in 1890 passed the Sherman Antitrust Act. This act 1) made conspiracies in restraint of trade illegal in interstate commerce;

2) provided fines and imprisonment for violations; and 3) prescribed three-fold damages in court to any person proving he had been injured by the competition of a business monopoly.

❍❍ **Failure to Enforce the Sherman Act**—In the wording of the anti-monopoly law the courts and the corporation lawyers found loopholes that made the act ineffective. The courts rendered unfriendly decisions in the few cases brought by the government, but the greatest failure of the act came from the failure of Harrison, Cleveland, and McKinley to enforce the law vigorously. Monopolies abandoned the trust for the holding company device. The Sherman Act came to be applied against labor unions instead of being applied to break corporate monopolies.

THE ELECTION OF 1892

For the first time since the Civil War a third party succeeded in winning votes in the Electoral College, in 1892. This was the Populist Party, which originated as a protest movement among the farmers of the South and West.

❍❍❍ **Causes of the Farmers' Discontent**—The greatest cause of discontent among farmers over the country was their conviction that the business interests in the nation were exploiting them. 1) They attributed falling farm prices to the deflationary monetary system maintained for the benefit of the creditor classes; the debtor farmers continued to ask for an increase in the money supply. They felt this could be achieved by the free coinage of silver. 2) Farmers suffered from the burden of heavy debts and of high interest rates. In the boom years of the early eighties farmers were sought out and pressed to accept loans from agents of Eastern capitalists who were seeking safe high-yielding mortgage investments in Western farms. When drought or low prices returned, the debts were resented by the farmers. In the South, farmers stayed in debt under the crop-lien system. 3) The Interstate Commerce Act and state laws did little to lower freight rates of the railroad monopolists. 4) Manufacturers enjoyed tariff protection and monopoly pricing while the farmer had to sell in an unprotected market depressed by overproduction. 5) Awareness of the seemingly carefree life in the growing cities contrasted with the hardships and monotony of homesteading in the West. 6) The risks of crop failure from drought, hail, windstorms, grasshoppers, and other hazards of nature brought frustration and desperation.

❍❍ **The Farmers' Alliances**—When the Grangers declined in the late 1870s, another farmers' organization, the Alliance, began to take its place in leading the farmers' protest. In 1891 the alliance had organized itself into the Peoples' or Populist Party. Actually two separate Alliances were organized, one in the South, the other in the North. Both were similar to the Patrons of Husbandry in their efforts to help the farmers. At first the Alliances tried to gain control of the machinery of the dominant party of each section; the new party came to be known as the Populists even before they formally organized in 1891. In 1890 under various names these third parties sent, in all, 53 Congressmen to Washington. Rousing speakers appealed to the farmers in the election of 1890; among these colorful personalities were "Sockless" Jerry Simpson and Mary Lease of Kansas, Ignatius Donnelly of Minnesota, James B. Weaver of Iowa, and "Pitchfork" Ben Tillman of South Carolina.

✪✪✪ **Demands of the Populists**—The Populists completed their organization in 1891. In 1892 a second convention adopted the Omaha Platform, which included these planks: 1) Most prominent of all was the demand for currency inflation in the form of silver or paper. 2) They favored government ownership and operation of the railroads, telephone, and telegraph systems. They also favored such innovations as 3) the graduated income tax, 4) the Australian (secret) ballot, 5) a postal savings system, 6) the initiative and referendum, 7) direct election of United States senators, and 8) shorter hours for labor. All have been realized since, although the demands seemed extreme and frightful to conservative classes.

✪✪ **Outcome of the Election of 1892**—The Democrats renominated Cleveland for the presidency and the Republicans renominated Harrison; money and tariff reform were the main issues. Cleveland won because of his reputation for honesty and his stand on the tariff question. The Populists, or People's Party, nominated James B. Weaver, who won over a million popular votes and 22 electors in the silver and agricultural states of the West. The Populists elected many members of both houses of Congress and came to believe they would win the national election in 1896. The Alliances passed off the scene—they had been absorbed by the Populist Party.

PROBLEMS OF CLEVELAND'S SECOND ADMINISTRATION

Tumultuous events after 1893 formed the background of the hardest fought presidential election in American political history.

✪ **The Panic of 1893**—Within a few weeks after Cleveland's inauguration, the nation found itself in a money panic that turned into a severe four-year depression. The panic and depression had these causes: 1) The loss of purchasing power by the farmer eventually dragged down the rest of the economy, 2) bankruptcy of the overexpanded railroads, 3) stock manipulation and speculation, and 4) depression in Europe were prominent contributing factors. 5) Almost certainly, fear of creditors that free silver might cause the devaluation of the dollar contributed also.

The depression that ensued proved to be one of the worst America has experienced. Within six months thousands of businesses failed; 400 banks closed; 56 railroads, including some of the largest, went bankrupt; and the treasury's gold reserve fell steadily.

✪ **The Gold Reserve**—When Cleveland became President the gold reserve had already fallen to only $100,000,000, which had come to be accepted by financiers as the minimum reserve necessary to assure continuance of gold redeemability of the dollar. When the panic struck, the reserve fell steadily as silver certificates were redeemed and gold hoarded by frightened people. President Cleveland had to meet the emergency; he called Congress in special session and secured the repeal of the Sherman Silver Purchase Act. But the drain on the reserve continued and the reserves needed to be restored.

Cleveland sought to restore the gold reserve by selling three issues of bonds for gold. He succeeded only after the third issue was sold at a discount in a deal with the Morgan and other Wall Street firms, who agreed to obtain gold from abroad and to use their influence to prevent any further withdrawals of gold. The inflationists were not interested in maintaining the gold standard; Western and Southern Democrats condemned Cleveland and bolted the Democratic party to join the Populists.

The Wilson-Gorman Tariff—An alliance of Eastern Democrats and Eastern Republicans wrecked Cleveland's campaign pledge to reduce tariffs. Log-rolling in the Senate eliminated most of the reductions in the original bill. The sugar tariff was restored and the principle of low tariffs forgotten. In general, rates remained about as high as ever. An income tax provision of the act was declared unconstitutional by the Supreme Court in a 5-4 decision in 1895.

✪ **The Homestead Strike**—This strike occurred just before the Panic of 1893 and introduced the country to a series of violent labor disturbances during the years of depression that followed. The Homestead strike broke out against the Carnegie Steel Company when Carnegie's partner Henry C. Frick, an ardent enemy of organized labor, proposed a reduction in piecework rates. The steel workers union refused to accept the reduction, and Frick closed the Homestead plants. When 300 Pinkerton guards were brought in to protect the plant, they were attacked by the strikers and run out of town; many were killed and injured on both sides. Militia were called in. Public opinion turned against the workers when an anarchist tried to assassinate Frick. After five months of strife the workers resumed their jobs at reduced pay.

✪✪ **The Pullman Strike (1894)**—Employees of the Pullman Palace Car Company went on strike when their wages were cut by about one third. In a model example of corporation paternalism, Pullman had built a company town where employees rented housing and bought from company stores. Pullman made no reduction in rents and prices in the company town when he reduced wages. Workers on strike cut Pullman cars out of trains and left them on side tracks. The strike spread over the West to San Francisco, and traffic came to a standstill when the American Railway Union aided the strikers with a sympathetic boycott. The Railroad Managers Association took up the fight for the railroads. Mobs joined both sides and millions of dollars worth of property was destroyed.

A court order, or injunction, was obtained to prevent the strikers from doing anything to interfere with the United States mail. When the injunction was disobeyed, President Cleveland sent troops to Chicago to keep the trains moving; he did so even though Governor John P. Altgeld insisted they were not needed. The able and vigorous leader of the American Railway Union, Eugene V. Debs, was sentenced to six months in jail for contempt of court. While in jail Debs studied socialism; after his release he became the leader of the Socialist Party.

Coxey's Army—Many unemployed workers, suffering from the hard times of the early nineties, joined numerous marching demonstrations to call attention to their plight. By far the best known of these was the army of marchers led by General Jacob S. Coxey of Ohio. He led 500 demonstrators to Washington to impress Congress. Coxey advocated public works programs to provide jobs and the issuance of greenbacks to pay for them and to increase money in circulation. The economic philosophy of the times did not permit Coxey's petition to be taken seriously; his men were arrested in Washington for walking on the grass.

CHAPTER BOOK LIST

Faulkner, H.O., *Politics, Reform, and Expansion* (1959).

Ginger, Ray, Altgeld's *America: The Lincoln Ideal Versus Changing Realities* (1958).

Hicks, J.D., *The Populist Revolt* (Bison). Thorough, scholarly.

Hoogenboom, Ari, *Outlawing the Spoils* (1961).

Morgan, H. Wayne, *The Gilden Age: A Reappraisal* (1963).

Nevins, Allan, *Grover Cleveland* (1954). Also good for general history.

Rosenboom, Eugene H., *History of Presidential Elections* (1964).

Sievers, H.J., *Benjamin Harrison* (1959).

Wiebe, Robert H., *The Search for Order, 1877–1920* (1967).

Woodward, C. Vann, *Origins of the New South 1877–1913.*

REVIEW QUESTIONS

MULTIPLE CHOICE

1. Czar Reed's changes in the parliamentary rules of the House (1) became permanent because they helped curb an obstructive minority (2) were unnecessary and gave unfair advantage to the Republican majority (3) had to be discarded as too controversial (4) never did become effective.

2. Utah was admitted to the Union (1) soon after the Utah War (2) immediately after the Edmunds Act outlawed polygamy (3) not until after the Mormon Church formally abandoned polygamy (4) as one of the Omnibus states with the blessings of the Republican majority in 1890.

3. Which pair of states were *not* admitted in either 1889 or 1890? (1) Wyoming and Idaho (2) Montana and Washington (3) Oregon and Nebraska (4) North and South Dakota.

4. Which two states were last to be admitted? (1) Utah and Arizona (2) Oklahoma and Washington (3) Idaho and Montana (4) Arizona and New Mexico.

5. Which was the Republican Party least interested in during the 1880s? (1) Protective tariffs (2) economy in government (3) pensions for veterans (4) the gold standard.

6. The Sherman Silver Purchase Act (1) was passed to get Western states to support the McKinley Tariff (2) did little to increase the use of silver (3) was passed by a Democratic Congress (4) was intended to ease the nation off the gold standard.

7. The McKinley Tariff (1) generally reduced rates substantially (2) repealed the tariff on raw sugar (3) increased tariff revenues substantially (4) helped the Republicans elect more members in the next election.

8. The trust was first prominently used in which industry? (1) Oil production (2) railroads (3) oil refining (4) meat packing.

9. Which statement gives in correct time order the introduction of the various monopoly devices? (1) Trusts, pools, holding companies (2) pools, holding companies, trusts (3) holding companies, trusts, pools (4) pools, trusts, holding companies.

10. The Sherman Antitrust Act (1) immediately became an effective weapon against monopoly (2) was not enforced in the 1890s (3) was repealed under McKinley (4) was early declared unconstitutional.

11. In the midterm election of 1892 which party made the greatest gains? (1) Republican (2) Populist (3) Democratic (4) Socialist.

12. For which hardship could the farmer most expect or hope for political relief? (1) Overproduction (2) high interest rates (3) high prices for manufactured goods he had to buy (4) high risks of loss from natural hazards.

13. The Panic of 1893 struck during the administration of (1) Cleveland (2) McKinley (3) Harrison (4) Blaine.

14. To meet effectively the fall in the gold reserve Cleveland (1) increased subsidies to gold miners (2) imposed import controls (3) amended the Sherman Silver Purchase Act (4) sold gold bonds to J.P. Morgan and Company.

15. Which tactic was *not* used to stop the Pullman strikers in 1894? (1) Federal troops (2) the injunction (3) jailing (4) arbitration.

16. Not involved in the Pullman strike in 1894 was (1) Eugene V. Debs (2) Governor Altgeld (3) President Cleveland (4) Jacob S. Coxey.

TRUE-FALSE

17. Benjamin Harrison was both a strong leader and a strong personality.

18. The Republican Congress under Harrison produced very little legislation.

19. The Sherman Silver Purchase Act represented a substantial victory for paper money and silver advocates but was repealed in a few years.

20. The Populists made strong gains in the election of 1890.

21. Business combinations and large-scale operation provide no real economic advantages to the nation as a whole.

22. Business monopoly is consistent with the free enterprise economic system.

23. In its first decade the Sherman Antitrust Act was largely nullified by judicial decisions.

24. The Populist movement met little success in the South in any form.

25. Most of the Populists' demands have since been enacted into law.

26. Fear that the gold standard might not be maintained was one cause of the Panic of 1893.

27. Cleveland's remedy for the fall in the gold reserve pleased the Populists.

28. In keeping with the tradition of the Democratic Party, Cleveland took the side of labor in the Pullman Strike.

29. Coxey's Army caused Congress to pass a law to provide jobs through a public works program.

COMPLETION

30. Harrison appointed _____ Secretary of State.

31. Two important measures passed in 1890 in a package were the _____ Tariff and the _____ Act. Passed in the same year was the first federal antimonopoly law, the _____ Act.

32. Successor to the Grangers as the spokesman for the farmer was an organization called the _____ .

33. The Populists favored the secret ballot, also known as the _____ ballot.

34. Cleveland's tariff law named the _____ Tariff failed to bring reductions in rates.

35. Two great strikes occurred in Cleveland's second term; they were the steel or _____ strike and the railroad or _____ strike.

CHRONOLOGY / CHAPTER 8

1891   Organization of Populist Party.

1892   Election shows growing strength of Populists.

1893   Panic and depression, the background of discontent and political revolt.

1894   *Coin's Financial School* published.

1895   Income tax declared unconstitutional.

1896   Hardest fought election in American politics; Bryan candidate of both Democrats and Populists but defeated by McKinley, Republican.

Signs of recovery from depression.

1897   McKinley inaugurated as President.

Dingley Tariff raised protective rates still further.

1898   Spanish-American War.

1900   McKinley reelected. Main campaign issue was annexation of Philippines.

Gold Standard Act passed.

Chapter

8

THE ELECTION OF 1896 AND THE MCKINLEY ADMINISTRATION, 1896–1901

> The presidential campaign and election of 1896 thoroughly threshed out the political issues arising from the distress of the preceding years. Although not as significant as the election of 1860, the election of 1896 was the hardest fought and the most interesting in American politics. The Republican victory, the gradual return of better times, the Spanish-American War, and other developments quieted the demands for monetary reform and inflation.

✪ **Popular Discontent with the Major Parties**—Cleveland's policies, as conservative as most Republican policies, lost him the support of his party. By his repeal of the Sherman Silver Purchase Act and the restoration of the gold reserve under terms that favored Wall Street, the failure of the Wilson-Gorman Tariff, and the use of federal troops to break the Pullman strike, Cleveland made too many enemies in his own party. The Democrats were blamed for the depression. Low prices for wheat and cotton hurt the party in power. The popular mind associated both the Democrats and Republicans with excessive conservatism.

✪ **The Populist Enthusiasm**—In the election of 1894 the Populists increased their vote by over 40 percent over that of 1892. Six Populists were elected to the United States Senate. In the West and the South, Populist speakers attracted large crowds. The Republicans, in the election of 1894, won a two-to-one lead over Democrats in the House and won control of the Senate also. Both Populists and Republicans expected to win in 1896.

The issue of silver was the most prominent one in the background of the campaign, not only because of Populist agitation but also the popularity of a small book by William H. Harvey called *Coin's Financial School* (1894). The book sold by the hundreds of thousands of copies. Illustrated and in simple language, it advocated the free coinage of silver at the ratio of sixteen to one. Mine owners in the Western states were also asking for an increase in silver coinage.

✪✪✪ **The Nominations**—The Republican leader, Marcus A. Hanna, an Ohio steelman and capitalist, dominated the Republican convention. Governor William McKinley of Ohio, Hanna's close friend, won the nomination. McKinley had authorized the tariff act named for him and generally took a conservative position.

The Democrats had become thoroughly divided by the time their convention met. Cleveland's monetary policies had alienated Southern and Western Democrats, but Eastern Democrats kept a conservative stand. The convention appeared leaderless until William Jennings Bryan of Nebraska, in his famous Cross of Gold speech, spoke out against the gold standard: "You shall not crucify mankind upon a cross of gold." Bryan's vigorous oratory won him the nomination as he took the convention by storm. Here he began his long career as the Democratic leader in national politics. Bryan's running mate for the vice presidency represented a concession to the conservative Northeast: they chose Arthur Sewall, a banker from Maine.

The Populist convention faced an embarrassing problem since the Democrats had adopted their free-silver plank and had nominated a free-silver advocate whom they could not beat. The free-silver goal was too important to sacrifice; they, too, nominated Bryan, but instead of endorsing Sewall, the Populists chose for the vice presidency Tom Watson, a Populist orator from Georgia. In order to avoid splitting the free-silver vote, the Populists were forced, by Democratic strategy, to practically merge with the Democrats.

✪✪✪ **The Party Platforms**—The Republican platform pledged maintenance of the gold standard, upheld the principle of protective tariffs, and condemned the Cleveland administration. The silverites gained control of the Democratic convention and adopted the plank for unlimited coinage of silver at the ratio of sixteen to one and adopted other Populist demands including tariff reduction, the income tax, and antitrust measures. The Populists supported virtually the same platform they had adopted in 1894.

✪✪✪ **The Campaign and Its Results**—Three main factors influenced the vote during the campaign: the untiring oratory of Bryan, the millions in campaign funds easily collected by the Republicans from industrialists, and the confusion of the Populists. The Populists supported Bryan, but the "educational" campaign of the Republicans frightened the cautious into supporting McKinley. Bryan seemed too radical to many voters. The heavily populated states of the North and East won the election for the Republicans.

The outcome of the election strengthened the conservative Republicans and kept them in power until McKinley's assassination placed Roosevelt in the Presidency. The election broke the Populist Party as a separate political entity, but its program remained very much alive in the Progressive movement and in the Democratic Party.

○ **William Jennings Bryan**—The Nebraska Democrat remained as a perennial candidate for his party's nomination until he died in 1925. He received the Democratic nomination in 1900 and in 1908, and joined Henry Clay as a thrice-defeated candidate of a major party. Bryan's power, aside from his superb oratorical magic, was derived from his role as a spokesman for the debtor, the farmer, and the small businessman. His enemies dismissed him as a golden-voiced, shallow-brained demagogue; his friends saw him as a sincere defender of little men everywhere against selfish, aggressive business plutocrats.

○ **McKinley Legislation**—With decisive control of Congress, the Republicans proceeded to enact their program in a special session. The Dingley Tariff (1897) raised rates to a new all-time high level.

The money controversy was settled by the Gold Standard Act of 1900, which, in effect confirmed and reinforced the gold standard as the basis of the American monetary system.

The returning farm prosperity that had helped McKinley win the election continued until after World War I. An important cause of returning national prosperity was the substantial addition to the world's money supply from increased output of gold. New gold came from the outpourings of the Australian, South African, and the Klondike rushes, as well as from the application of the new cyanide process for recovery of more gold from ore in the refining process. The Spanish-American and Boer wars also added a stimulus to business activity in America.

CHAPTER BOOK LIST

Coletta, Paolo E., *William Jennings Bryan, Political Evangelist, 1860–1908* (1969).

Cunningham, Raymond J., *Populists in Historical Perspective* (1968).

Darden, Robert F., *The Climate of Populism* (1965).

Faulkner, H.O., *Politics, Reform, and Expansion* (1959).

Goldman, Eric, *Rendezvous With Destiny* (Vintage). American reform movements, includes populism.

Hesseltine, William B., *Third-Party Movements in the United States* (Anvil). Excellent brief survey.

Hofstadter, Richard, *The Age of Reform From Bryan to F.D.R.* (Vintage). Pulitzer prize book. Populism, Progressivism, and the New Deal.

Jones, Stanley L., *The Presidential Election of 1896* (1964).

Leech, Margaret, *In the Days of McKinley* (1959).

Morgan, H. Wayne, ed., *The Gilded Age* (Syracuse University).

Pollock, Norman, *A Populist Response to Industrial America* (1963).

Woodward, C.V., *Origins of the New South* (1951).

REVIEW QUESTIONS

MULTIPLE CHOICE

1. Popular discontent with the major parties arose from the similarity of their policies on all *except* which of the following (1) Tariff (2) gold standard (3) labor problem (4) monopoly problem.

2. Which factor does *not* help account for the Democratic defeat in 1896? (1) The depression in the years preceding the election (2) the charge of radicalism against Bryan (3) Bryan's public speaking qualities (4) campaign contributions by industrialists.

3. In its outcome the election of 1896 (1) killed all hopes of realizing the Populist reforms (2) marked the end of the Populist hopes as a political party (3) showed the North opposed the gold standard (4) closed the political career of Bryan.

4. During McKinley's administration (1) deflation continued (2) prosperity returned (3) tariff rates were lowered (4) peace reigned.

TRUE-FALSE

5. The McKinley victory marked the downfall of the Populist Party and the free silver issue.

6. The Populists were strongest in the Far West and in the Northeast.

7. The Democratic platform in 1896 abandoned policies Cleveland had stood for.

8. McKinley waged a vigorous speaking campaign in 1896.

9. Returning prosperity helped the Republicans win in 1896.

COMPLETION

10. A popular book favoring free silver written by William H. Harvey was entitled _____ .

11. The businessman leader of the Republican Party in 1896 was

    _____ .

12. William Jennings Bryan won the Democratic nomination in 1896 by his famous _____ speech. He was also nominated by the _____ Party.

13. The Populists nominated _____ of the state of _____ for Vice President in 1896.

14. Bryan came from the state of _____ . In his political career he was nominated and defeated _____ times for the Presidency.

15. After the election McKinley's administration passed the _____ Tariff.

CHRONOLOGY / CHAPTER 9

1875 Hawaiian reciprocity treaty opened American market for more Hawaiian sugar.

1889 First Pan-American Conference held in Washington.
Naval war threatened over Samoa.
Fur seal controversy caused by American seizure of Canadian vessels.

1890 Admiral Mahan published *Influence of Sea-Power Upon History*.

1891 Controversy with Chile over street riot against sailors off *USS Baltimore*.

1893 Republic of Hawaii offers annexation to United States but rtreaty ejected by Cleveland.

1895 British and Venezuela boundary controversy brought threat of war between United States and Britain.
Jameson raiders captured by Boers in South Africa leads to Boer War.
Cuban revolt began against Spain.

1898 Spanish-American War fought in Philippines and Cuba.
Hawaii annexed.
Treaty of Paris with Spain gave Cuba independence, ceded Philippines, Guam, and Puerto Rico to the United States and Germany.

1899 Open Door policy began.
Philippine Insurrection began.

1900 Foraker Act established civil government in Puerto Rico.

1901 Platt Amendment made Cuba an American protectorate.

1916 Jones Act extended power of local self-government in Philippines.

9

FOREIGN AFFAIRS IN THE 1890s

The United States on numerous occasions after the Civil War manifested a growing interest in overseas possessions and participation in hemispheric and world affairs. There were several developments to account for both the drift away from isolationism and towards imperialism. 1) The growth of industry after the Civil War awakened Americans to the need for markets for exports of manufactured goods. 2) The rapid occupation of vacant land and development of the nation in the decades preceding 1900 exhausted the opportunities at home for lush profits for business investment. 3) The profits of American business generated funds seeking an opportunity for higher rates of return than were available at home. 4) The rise of the new imperialism in Europe set an example for the United States. American imperialism found an outlet for expression in Latin America and in the Pacific. The British assumption of "the white man's burden," and their boast that "the sun never sets on the British flag," appealed to many American leaders as a model for the United States to follow.

AGGRESSIVE FOREIGN POLICY UNDER CLEVELAND AND HARRISON

Several unrelated disputes in the late 1880s and early 1890s under both Republicans and Democrats showed America's willingness to assert her growing power.

Foreign Affairs in the Eighties—In 1881 Blaine as Secretary of State demanded in vain that the British give up their rights in Panama under the Clayton-Bulwer Treaty (1850) which gave Britain and the United States joint control over any canal dug across the isthmus by either of the two. When Garfield died, Blaine resigned his post. When reappointed in 1889 by Harrison, Blaine resumed his vigorous policies.

Blaine realized Clay's old dream of promoting cooperation among the nations of America; in 1889 he arranged the meeting in Washington of the First Pan-American Congress.

○ **Hawaii and the United States**—First American contacts with the Hawaiian Islands were made by vessels calling for provisions or trade and by missionaries in the early nineteenth century. In 1875 American sugar planters, who earlier had established themselves on the islands, secured a treaty of reciprocity with the United States. This treaty opened a larger market for Hawaiian sugar in America. In 1882 an amendment to the treaty gave the United States a naval base at Pearl Harbor.

In 1893 American sugar growers, with the aid of a force of American Marines, overthrew the Hawaiian monarchy under Queen Liluokalani, substituted a republic, and offered annexation to the United States. Blaine signed the treaty of annexation, but President Cleveland, recognizing the interference in Hawaiian affairs, withdrew the treaty. He did, however, recognize the new Republic of Hawaii.

In 1898, after the United States had established a strong interest in the Far East by annexing the Philippines, it became necessary to annex Hawaii for the construction of naval bases. By joint resolution the Republican Congress in 1898 overwhelmingly voted for annexation.

Samoa—In the Samoan Islands in the South Pacific the United States acquired by the agreement of 1872 the harbor of Pago Pago. England and Germany also wished to acquire these islands. In 1889 a German attempt to annex the islands brought naval vessels of two other powers—the United States and England—to the harbor at Pago Pago. A hurricane put the three fleets out of action and the three powers then agreed to a tripartite protectorate. In 1899 England withdrew for compensation elsewhere and the islands were divided between the United States and Germany.

○ **The Controversy with Chile (1891)**—Blaine's appointee as minister to Chile, Patrick Egan, made the mistake of taking sides in a Chilean revolution. The ill-feeling created in Chile exploded in a brawl between Chileans and American sailors on shore leave from the Baltimore in Valparaiso. Two American sailors were killed and others seriously wounded. The United States, by threatening war, forced Chile to pay an indemnity. The uncompromising stand of the American government created much ill-will in Latin America, undoing the friendliness created at the Pan-American Conference.

The Fur Seal Controversy—This dispute with Great Britain, also known as the Bering Sea Controversy, arose over the taking of fur seals in the Bering Sea. In 1889 Canadian sealing vessels were seized by American revenue vessels; the United States contended that the Bering Sea was a closed sea solely within the jurisdiction of the United States and that the Canadian vessels were poaching in American waters. The American government also contended that the seals belong to the United States since these valuable fur-bearing animals used the American owned Pribilof Islands as their breeding grounds. Blaine, as Secretary of State, inherited the dispute and aggressively upheld the American contentions against Britain. War was threatened over the issue. Finally, Blaine agreed to arbitration; the international tribunal decided against all the far-reaching American claims but recommended joint action to regulate the slaughter of the seals. In 1911 the United States, Britain, Japan, and Russia finally reached a satisfactory agreement regulating the harvesting of the pelts.

❍❍ **Venezuelan Boundary Controversy (1895)**—Danger of war between the United States and Britain arose in 1895 in a move by President Cleveland to uphold the Monroe Doctrine against Britain. The dispute arose over the boundary between Venezuela and British Guiana when gold was discovered in the disputed area. Great Britain refused the American request to submit the dispute to arbitration. Defiantly, Cleveland requested that Congress give him authority to appoint a commission to determine the proper boundary which the United States would defend on behalf of Venezuela. The dispute reached a crisis in 1895, but the British suddenly agreed to submit the dispute to arbitration. The award favored Britain with the larger part of the disputed territory.

This controversy was especially significant. 1) It upheld the Monroe Doctrine against a European power trying to enlarge its territory at the expense of an American state. 2) It was another victory for the principle of arbitration in international disputes. 3) Britain's unexpected reversal of position came from her alarm in 1895 when the Boer War broke out in South Africa. Britain discovered she had no international friends but instead had a powerful rival in Europe in the rising power of Germany. England's conciliatory attitude at this time marked an historic turning point in British-American relations to feelings of cordiality that eventually made them allies in World War I.

THE SPANISH-AMERICAN WAR, 1898

The Spanish-American War was not a big war, yet it marks a significant turning point in that it brought world recognition of the United States as a great power.

❍❍ **Cuba and the United States**—The proximity and strategic location of Cuba have always made this island of special concern to the United States. Before the Civil War some Southerners had desired the annexation of Cuba; after the war Cuban insurrectionists tried to get American aid in their struggle for independence. Spain held on to the "Pearl of the

Antilles" tenaciously; it was the last best remnant of her great empire in America. Partly due to a depression in the sugar industry, caused by the increased rates against sugar in the Wilson-Gorman Tariff Act, the Cubans again revolted in 1895.

✪✪✪ Causes of the Spanish-American War—Several factors and events brought on the war against Spain. 1) In the larger background were the advocates of the new imperialism and of a big navy. Of minor importance were the fairly substantial investments in Cuba and trade relations with the island. Probably of much more consequence was the desire for naval bases in Cuba and in the Spanish possessions in the Pacific. The American public enjoyed the thought of assuming the burdens and glory of empire; the popularity of the war indicated this.

2) Many historians have judged yellow journalism in America as the most important single cause of American involvement in the war. The rival Hearst and Pulitzer papers, in order to increase circulation, wrote lurid headlines of the Spanish atrocities against the Cubans. General Weyler's policy of forcing Cuban guerrillas and civilians into miserable concentration camps where they died by the tens of thousands became the basis of accounts which stirred the sympathy of the American public.

3) The de Lome letter aroused the anger of Americans and helped bring war nearer. This was a private letter written by the Spanish minister in Washington to a friend. The letter was stolen and published; it stated that McKinley was a "spineless politician" (almost exactly what Theodore Roosevelt said of McKinley). De Lome resigned his post.

4) The explosion of the battleship *Maine* in Havana harbor served as the immediate cause of war. Americans assumed that Spain was responsible, and "Remember the Maine" became the war cry of the nation.

✪✪ Attitude of the Governments of Spain and the United States—The Spanish government and President McKinley both wished to avoid war. The fighting could have been avoided and its avowed purposes achieved without war. The Spanish government realized it could not win a war against the United States and certainly not one immediately off the American coast. On April 9, 1898, McKinley received telegraphed concessions from Spain on every point demanded regarding Cuba. Nevertheless McKinley sent his war message to Congress, April 11. He did so because of popular demand for war. McKinley feared that if the demand was not met, his administration and his party would be ruined. Business and financial interests sought to avoid the war since it would increase taxes and disturb trade.

✪✪ Preparation of the Navy—The American navy fortunately was in an excellent state of readiness; it ranked third among world fleets. The construction of an iron navy had been started in the administration of Chester A. Arthur as a way of expending some of the surplus revenue from the high tariffs.

Of no small significance in the development of a strong navy were the writings of Alfred Thayer Mahan, a retired navy captain and author of numerous books on naval strategy and history. His most influential book, *The Influence of Sea Power Upon History, 1660–1783*, published in 1890, showed that naval superiority had decided the outcome of great struggles of the past. His arguments were exploited by propagandists for a big navy and modern battleships.

Another big navy advocate who personally, as Assistant Secretary of the Navy, helped prepared the navy for war was Theodore Roosevelt. He glorified the exploits of the American navy in his book *The Naval War of 1812* (1882). Roosevelt ordered Commodore George Dewey of the American Far Eastern Fleet to station at Hong Kong to pounce upon the Spanish Philippines in case of war.

○ **Role of the Navy in the Pacific**—The nature of the conflict gave the navy the leading role in winning the war. Recently built steel battleships and preparations in the immediate months before the outbreak of the war placed the navy in a state of readiness. Dewey at Hong Kong carried out his orders, steamed into the large Manila Bay, and easily sank the decrepit Spanish fleet there but had to wait for three months for troop reinforcements to capture the city of Manila. Manila was taken on August 13, with the help of Filipino insurgents under Emilio Aguinaldo.

An interesting event in Manila harbor helped strengthen the new British policy of friendliness with the United States. The Germans with five warships at Manila had a stronger force than Dewey and on several occasions had aroused Dewey's anger. The friendly cooperation of the commander of a British force, also present, smoothed over the friction with the German commander. America became grateful for what it considered a strong manifestation of British friendship.

○○ **The Navy in the Atlantic**—In the Atlantic the navy's strategy was to blockade Cuban ports and prevent Spanish reinforcements from being landed. In this the navy failed, and Admiral Cervera slipped his wretched fleet into Santiago harbor. There Lieutenant Hobson failed in an attempt to sink an old ship in the narrow mouth of the harbor to bottle up the Spanish fleet; nevertheless, the nation, craving a hero, hailed Hobson for his daring attempt.

After the army had landed and occupied the heights overlooking Santiago, Cervera made a dash to escape. In a running sea battle south of Cuba his entire fleet was sunk at a cost of one American killed and sixteen wounded.

○○ **Preparation of the Army for War**—The army had been neglected since the Civil War and the country had to pay in confusion and unnecessary loss of life in the Spanish-American War. Political appointments and old age characterized the officers; the commander of the invasion of Cuba, the 300-pound General William R. Shafter who had to be lifted into his saddle, symbolized the army's inefficiency. The sudden increase in the size of the army led to unbelievable confusion in camp in Florida where the troops boarded ship for Cuba.

Congress voted an increase in the regular army and authorized the enlistment of 125,000 volunteers. A special provision for the benefit of Theodore Roosevelt permitted three regiments of volunteer cavalry. Roosevelt resigned as Assistant Secretary of the Navy and recruited his "Rough Riders."

The army bound for Cuba embarked at Tampa, Florida, in great confusion. The "Rough Riders" seized one of the troop transports to make sure they would not miss out on the adventure—but in the confusion they were unable to take their horses with them. In Cuba the men suffered from the heat in their improper heavy uniforms, they used black powder instead of the new smokeless powder, and had to eat spoiled food and "embalmed" beef. The lack of proper sanitary precautions caused most of the 5,000 deaths; bullets killed less than 400. The blunders of the army resulted in a thorough overhauling that put it in an efficient condition when it was needed the next time, in World War I.

✪✪ **The Army in Action in Cuba**—The army landed near Santiago and found itself facing an even less efficient foe. Two engagements were won on the approach to Santiago, the battles of El Caney and San Juan Hill. When the heights overlooking the harbor were taken, the Spanish fleet was forced out of Santiago harbor and destroyed. General Nelson A. Miles rushed his expedition to Puerto Rico to take it before the armistice was signed on August 12. The "glorious" and easy little war ended in less than four months after it had been declared.

✪✪✪ **The Treaty of Paris, 1898**—The commissioners from the two nations met in October 1898, to draw up the terms of the Treaty of Paris. McKinley wisely appointed three members of the Senate to the peace commission in order to give that body representation in drafting the terms of a treaty it would be asked to ratify.

The terms provided 1) that Cuba would be granted independence but Spain would retain the heavy Cuban debt. 2) Puerto Rico, Guam, and the Philippines were ceded to the United States. 3) The United States agreed to pay $20,000,000 for the Philippines. The United States had now acquired an overseas empire for itself and the burden of governing alien peoples.

✪✪✪ **The Decision to Keep the Philippines**—McKinley's decision to keep the Philippines mirrored the sentiment of the American people who had suddenly become imperialist-minded. We had fought to free Cuba; why not free the Philippines? McKinley consulted his conscience and decided 1) we should assume the responsibilities of Christianizing and civilizing the native population. 2) Americans were carried away with the idea of enlarging the national prestige by ruling an empire.

3) Businessmen expected to find opportunities for profit in investments and loans, in developing a source of raw materials for industry, and in selling in the Philippine market. 4) The islands would give America a base for conducting a large trade in the Far East. 5) Finally, there was the real possibility that the islands would fall into the hands of Germany, Japan, or some other power with ambitions in East Asia.

○ **Ratification of the Treaty**—Some Republicans as well as many Democrats in the Senate opposed the subjugation of an alien people. Democratic votes under the influence of William Jennings Bryan ratified the treaty by only two votes over the necessary two-thirds majority. Bryan opposed imperialism but, it is charged, he convinced a few Democrats that if they would approve the annexation of the Philippines they would provide a useful issue for the presidential campaign of 1900.

○○○ **Consequences of the Spanish-American War**—The "splendid little war" required little national effort but it had far-reaching significance. 1) The results of the war marked the complete end of the great Spanish empire in America that had begun with Columbus. 2) The acquisition of possessions in the Pacific immediately made the United States active in the affairs of the Orient. American involvement with other powers marked a sharp turn away from the isolationism of the past. 3) The United States became recognized as a world power. 4) The war, in bringing the North and the South together in a common effort, helped erase much of the heritage of hate of the Civil War.

○ **Cuba After the War**—Cuba realized its independence soon after the war when peace had been restored and American troops withdrawn. Under American occupation a program of sanitation was carried out; Doctor Walter Reed identified the mosquito that carried the yellow fever and the disease was brought under control. However, Cuba became an American dependency under the status of a protectorate. The Platt Amendment (1901), a rider to an army appropriation bill passed by the American Congress, stipulated 1) that without American consent Cuba could make no international agreements likely to impair her sovereignty; 2) that Cuba could not assume any indebtedness that might give foreign powers an excuse for intervention; 3) that the United States itself could intervene if necessary to preserve the independence and political stability of Cuba; and 4) two naval bases were to be granted to the United States.

Under the Platt Amendment the United States subsequently intervened in Cuba either by sending in troops (1906, 1912, 1917) or more often by diplomatic persuasion. Greatly increased American investments and economic power in Cuba served further to subordinate Cuba to the United States. Of the two naval bases established there, only Guantanamo Bay has been retained to the present.

Puerto Rico—The bloodless occupation of Puerto Rico was followed by rapid progress under the American military supervision in sanitation, road building, and in public finance. By the Foraker Act (1900) Congress established civil government in Puerto Rico, including the first elective legislature in any of the newly acquired lands. The Foraker Act set a pattern for the government of the other possessions.

❍ The "Insular Cases"—In general, the pattern of government established in the new island possessions resembled governments previously established by Congress in the mainland territories. After 1900 when the Supreme Court was called upon to decide certain cases involving the status of the new territories, it agreed in general that they were under almost complete control of Congress rather than having the same rights under the Constitution as citizens of the states. Thus it was decided that the Constitution does not necessarily follow the flag. For example, the Puerto Ricans were not made American citizens until 1917. The Filipinos were never made citizens but remained *nationals* of the United States.

❍ The Philippine Insurrection (1899–1902)—The Filipinos were upset by the decision of Congress not to grant independence as had been granted to Cuba. They had been fighting the Spanish for independence and did not see the logic of changing masters. The Filipinos fought under their leader Emilio Aguinaldo, who had been returned to the islands by Admiral Dewey. The cruel war lasted until Aguinaldo was captured in a daring invasion of his camp by the disguised General Funston and his men.

By objective standards the insurrection was a war of considerably larger proportions than the Spanish-American War. The war cost more in lives, money, and time. Aguinaldo had 70,000 men under his command and the war lasted from 1899–1902. Of course, its international consequences were not so far-reaching as the results of the Spanish-American War.

The Republicans and Democrats both declared themselves in favor of Philippine independence. They differed mainly in how soon the Filipinos should be introduced to self-government and eventual independence realized. The Democrats were more sympathetic with Philippine aspirations for self-government and independence.

In 1900 William Howard Taft headed a Philippine Commission to establish civil government. In 1901 Taft was appointed governor. With the assistance of Filipino members, the Taft Commission exercised executive and legislative functions and prepared a framework of government. In 1907 a Philippine assembly met for the first time. Schools were organized and many American teachers sent to the islands. The Jones Act of 1916 extended native participation in legislation by adding an elective senate to the existing elective lower house. Leonard Wood was appointed governor-general in 1921; he engaged in controversy with the Filipino legislature. After 1926 new governors restored a friendly spirit of cooperation.

CHAPTER BOOK LIST

Beale, Howard K., *Theodore Roosevelt and the Rise of America to World Power* (Johns Hopkins).

Dulles, Foster R., *Prelude to World Power* (1965).

Freidel, Frank, *Splendid Little War* (Dell). Excellent account of the brief Spanish-American War.

Mahan, A.T., *Influence of Sea Power Upon History* (American Century). Reprint of the big navy advocate's influential history on the significance of navies in winning wars.

May, E.R., *Imperial Democracy* (1961).

McCormack, T.J., *China Market* (1967).

Perkins, Dexter, *Hands Off: A History of the Monroe Doctrine* (1941). Popular.

Pratt, Julius W., *Expansionists of 1898* (Quadrangle).

Roosevelt, Theodore, *The Rough Riders* (Signet).

Varg, Paul A., *Open Door Diplomat* (1952).

REVIEW QUESTIONS

MULTIPLE CHOICE

1. After 1890 the United States began to take a greater interest in foreign affairs for all reasons *except* for (1) our foreign commitments (2) the need for export markets (3) the influence of the new imperialism (4) the end of the frontier had exhausted the lush opportunities for profits at home.

2. The chief American economic interest in Hawaii by 1893 was in (1) sugarcane plantations (2) military bases (3) ranching (4) whaling.

3. Blaine's greatest achievement as Secretary of State was (1) defense of the Alaskan fur seals (2) getting permission to dig the Panama canal (3) calling the first Pan-American Conference (4) the correction of Chile.

4. The Fur Seal Controversy was settled at first (1) by an arbitration award favorable to the United States (2) by treaty agreement to limit the harvest of seal pelts (3) Canadian and British agreement to American contentions (4) by an arbitration award favorable to Canada.

5. The settlement of the Venezuelan Boundary Controversy was significant for all of these reasons *except:* (1) it demonstrated the strong foreign policy of McKinley (2) it reinforced the Monroe Doctrine (3) it marked a turning point in British-American relations (4) it was a victory for the principle of arbitration.

6. Many historians consider which to have been the most influential cause of the Spanish-American War? (1) Sinking of the Maine (2) American investments in Cuba (3) the de Lome letter (4) yellow journalism.

7. As for the attitude of the governments of Spain and the United States before the Spanish-American War (1) both wanted war but American citizens did not (2) the McKinley administration wanted war but Spain did not (3) neither wanted war but their people did (4) Spain wanted war but the United States did not.

8. In the Spanish-American War Spain was ready to concede to American demands (1) after her navy was defeated in Manila Bay (2) after the army victory at San Juan Hill (3) even before the war began (4) only after the Philippines were completely occupied.

9. America's best preparation for the Spanish-American War was revealed by the experiences (1) with army weapons (2) with sanitation and food (3) of the navy (4) in army transportation.

10. Which was not a provision of the Treaty of Paris of 1898? (1) The annexation of Hawaii (2) the annexation of Guam (3) acquisition of the Philippines (4) independence of Cuba.

11. Who was chiefly responsible for the American decision to keep the Philippines? (1) The Filipinos (2) the McKinley administration (3) William Jennings Bryan (4) Spain.

12. Which was *not* a consequence of the Spanish-American War? (1) Recognition of the United States as a world power (2) Spain lost her last possession in America (3) the United States became involved in Asiatic affairs (4) Cuba became an American colony.

13. The Platt Amendment was designed to (1) insure American economic supremacy in Cuba (2) assure the preservation of democracy in Panama (3) keep Cuba from falling under the control of a power other than the United States (4) enforce sanitary measures in Panama.

14. In general the decisions made in the "Insular Cases" (1) extended the same constitutional rights to the colonies as enjoyed by citizens of the states (2) recognized the colonies as the same as the former mainland territories (3) placed the colonies under the Department of the Interior (4) recognized only such constitutional provisions as extended by Congress.

15. The Philippine Insurrection (1) ended with a grant of self-government to the islands (2) lasted longer than the Spanish-American War (3) was quickly suppressed (4) was caused by Spanish intrigue.

TRUE-FALSE
16. In 1881 Blaine secured changes in the Clayton-Bulwer Treaty by agreement with the British.
17. The United States won Hawaii from Spain in 1898.
18. The controversy with Chile improved American relations with Latin America.
19. The American claims in the Fur Seal Controversy were generally upheld by the arbitration tribunal.

COMPLETION
20. Americans in 1893 overthrew the Hawaiian monarchy under Queen _____ . However, President _____ blocked the annexation of Hawaii. Annexation came in _____ not by treaty but by _____ .

21. The United States acquired an interest in Samoa by a treaty in 1872 that gave us the harbor of _____ . For a time the United States shared control of the islands with _____ and _____ .

22. In 1891 a controversy in Chile arose when sailors from the naval vessel _____ were granted leave in _____ . Chile was forced to pay _____ for the American casualties suffered there.

23. The Fur Seal Controversy was related to the _____ Islands in the _____ Sea.

24. The Spanish-American War began after the sinking of the battleship _____ in _____ harbor.

25. Two influential books had emphasized the importance of naval power before 1898. State author and title of each _____ , _____ ; _____ , _____ .

CHRONOLOGY / CHAPTER 10

1859 Darwin published *Origin of Species.*

1862 Morrill Act began establishment of land grant colleges.

1869 Wyoming territory granted woman suffrage.

Resurgence of temperance movement.

1873 Kindergarten introduced into United States at St. Louis.

1874 Women's Christian Temperance Union organized.

1879 Christian Science Church established in America.

Salvation Army organized in America.

Progress and Poverty published by Henry George.

1880 "New Immigration" brought several changes in kinds of immigrants to United States about 1880.

1881 Carnegie began to give money for city libraries.

1882 Chinese Exclusion Act prohibits Chinese immigration.

1887 Hatch Act began establishment of agricultural experiment stations.

Dawes Act alloted land in severalty to Native Americans.

1888 *Looking Backward* published by Edward Bellamy.

1890s Southern states pass "grandfather clauses" to restrict African American suffrage.

1890 Census report indicates that the American frontier ended about 1890.

1893 Anti-Saloon League organized.

1896 *Plessy v. Ferguson* recognized separate but equal schools for African Americans as constitutional.

Chapter

10
SOCIAL DEVELOPMENTS, 1865–1900

> Social problems and changes arose out of the background of labor-capital conflict, the rapid industrial growth, the large inflow of immigration, and the influence of science.

MORAL LAXITY AND REFORM

An abominable letdown in public and private morals manifested itself after the Civil War and became so widespread as to arouse determined reformers to their best efforts.

● **The Newly Rich and the Poor**—A crop of newly rich, made up of war profiteers, Western miners, and speculators and manipulators of stocks and bonds, loudly displayed their wealth in vulgar forms of "conspicuous consumption." Outstanding among these was Jim Fisk, who plundered the Erie Railroad of millions, led the "Black Friday" gold conspiracy, maintained a harem of actresses, and died in a gunfight with a business and amatory rival.

Many had grown rich from the new industries and other businesses; much of this accumulation and concentration of wealth in the hands of a small minority of "robber barons" came from unethical practices, heartless aggressiveness, political influence, and the exploitation of labor. At the bottom of the economic ladder, poverty, unemployment, disease, and insecurity prevailed among slum dwellers of the cities of the East and among rural and pioneering families in the South and West.

● **Corporate Dishonesty**—The absence of adequate protection of the small investor made it easy for crooks to sell fraudulent stocks and bonds to the gullible public. So many fortunes in oil and mining had been made that it was easy to find "investors" who would buy worthless "blue-sky" stocks and bonds in nonexistent enterprises. Banks and insurance companies went broke with heavy losses to depositors and policy holders while their managers continued to live in luxury.

● **Early Advocates of Reform**—There were educated and cultured men who took the lead in publicizing the evils of the day and arousing demands for reform. An outstanding leader among the liberals in politics was Carl Schurz, one of the liberals who fled Germany after the failure of the revolutionary movements there in 1848. He enjoyed a highly successful career in America as a lecturer and statesman; he was an advocate of civil service reform and one of the liberal Republicans who opposed the Grant administration.

Two journalists who used the press to influence public opinion were E.L. Godkin and George William Curtis. Godkin founded the *Nation,* a weekly newspaper; it was widely read by educated leaders for its interpretation of current events and critical understanding of the weaknesses in American society. G.W. Curtis, the noted editor of *Harper's Weekly,* reached a more popular audience through his publication and as a lecturer.

THE RISE OF THE CITIES

The rapid growth of industry with its large concentrations of factory workers brought a corresponding growth in the size of American cities. Improvements in agricultural technology permitted fewer farmers to produce foodstuffs and released others who accelerated the migration from country to town. The "new immigration" added to city population. Railroad transportation promoted growth of the cities in obvious ways. New York had long since become the nation's largest city. City growth was aided by the coming of trolley cars (1887), elevated railroads and subways, steel bridges, electric arc lights, the incandescent lamp, skyscrapers, and knowledge of sanitation.

✪✪ THE OLD AND NEW IMMIGRATION

About 1880 a noticeable change occurred in the characteristics of immigrants. These changes, referred to as the "new immigration," came about because of a marked increase in the number of immigrants from southern and eastern Europe. They contrasted with the old immigration that came from northern Europe. The new immigrants came from the Latin or Slavic countries; in religion they were Roman Catholic, Orthodox, or Jewish; they found it more difficult to learn English, were not so easily assimilated, and often formed solid cores of unassimilated population in large cities; they became laborers at low wages in the cities, lived in slums, and easily came under the control of political machines.

American labor unions took a strong lead in demanding restrictions upon immigration. First came the Chinese Exclusion Act of 1882; in the same year another law restricted undesirable persons such as paupers, the insane, and criminals. In 1891 the list of prohibited persons was enlarged and the office of the federal superintendent of immigration was created.

The immigrants came to America to escape poverty and seek economic opportunities, to escape the dominance of the upper classes and for freedom of religion, freedom from compulsory military service and educational opportunity. They were generally welcomed as workers, farmers, and consumers. They contributed their special abilities, skills, and cultural assets; and among them were many men of genius.

DEVELOPMENTS IN RELIGION AND EDUCATION

Several developments in religion may be observed. Great progress was made in education along several lines during the last half of the nineteenth century.

✪ Science and the Churches—When Charles Darwin, the English naturalist, published the Origin of the Species, he contradicted the literal Biblical explanation of man's creation. In America as elsewhere organized religion had to reconcile its teachings with the mass of pertinent scientific evidence. Leading ministers like Henry Ward Beecher and Lyman Abbot worked to reconcile religion and science. These modernists in religion were attacked by others who clung to the literal interpretations of the Bible and sought to discredit the theory of evolution. Dwight L. Moody was one of many fundamentalists whose strength resided in rural areas and especially in the South.

The historical study of religion by trained scholars, especially study of the origin of the Bible, discovered and pointed out discrepancies of one kind or another. Orthodoxy had to face the additional challenge of the comparative study of religions. Bigotry was disturbed by similarities in religious allegories, in beliefs, and in moral teachings.

Changes in Church Denominations—The new immigration greatly increased the number of non-Protestants in the population. The Roman Catholics and Jews increased enough to obtain considerable political significance. Roman Catholics stood out more strongly than ever as the largest single denomination, but no country could offer such variety of choice among the different denominations. Still another new and important denomination, Christian Science, of purely American origin, was founded by Mary Baker Eddy in 1879. The Salvation Army came from England to America in 1879.

✪ Advances in Education—Much progress was made in the extension of educational opportunities in the public school systems after 1865. Probably the outstanding development was the growth of the high schools. The South made relative progress in establishing free public schools. The *kindergarten,* introduced at St. Louis in 1873, was widely adopted. Catholic parochial schools became common. Teacher training, or normal schools, increased to about 300 by 1900 and helped teaching win recognition as a profession.

Higher education for African Americans in normal and industrial schools got underway. Here Booker T. Washington arose as a great educational leader in his position as head of Tuskegee Institute. The Chautauqua movement helped to fill the vacuum in adult education; it featured entertaining lectures and enrolled tens of thousands annually in home study courses. In 1881 Andrew Carnegie began giving money to establish libraries; tax-supported town libraries were established in most towns of any size by 1900.

In college and university education 1) the Morrill Act (1862) gave subsidies of federal lands for founding colleges to offer education in the agricultural and mechanical arts. 2) Under the Hatch Act (1887) agricultural experiment stations were founded with federal funds and in connection with the land grant colleges. 3) Private philanthropy founded several great universities. Johns Hopkins was outstanding among these since it established the first high quality graduate school in America. As other graduate schools were founded, American scholars no longer needed to go to Germany. 4) Charles W. Eliot of Harvard introduced the "elective system" to American colleges.

✿✿ ECONOMIC REFORMERS

First among the authors of books advocating economic reform was Henry George. In 1879 he published *Progress and Poverty,* which dealt with the problem of unequal distribution of wealth in America. He believed that land was the source of wealth and advocated a "single tax" on land to deprive its owners of the unearned increment in values due to population growth. Although a Jeffersonian agrarian, his egalitarian ideas influenced socialist thought in America and England.

Another widely read and influential book advocating economic reform was *Looking Backward* (1888), a novel published by Edward Bellamy. "Nationalist" clubs were formed over the country to promote his utopian socialist ideas.

More radical reformers introduced the ideas of anarchism from Europe. Anarchists advocated the violent overthrow of government since they believed governments existed mainly to preserve property rights and the resultant inequalities. Radical socialists introduced Marxian ideas from Europe after 1865 and later organized the Socialist Labor Party (1877). Eugene V. Debs, the American labor leader, organized the more moderate Socialist Party in the 1890s; it soon became the most popular of the American socialist parties.

❖ THE FIGHT FOR WOMEN'S RIGHTS

The struggle for greater equality for women, especially the right to vote, began well before the Civil War. Susan B. Anthony and Elizabeth Cady Stanton after the Civil War continued the movement for woman suffrage. This movement was supported by temperance reformers. Women were first allowed to vote in school elections. Wyoming first granted woman suffrage in 1869 as a territory and in 1890 as a state; other western states soon followed Wyoming's lead.

Many women's colleges were established after 1865. Coeducation paralleled this reform as state institutions of higher education opened their doors to women. Educational opportunity permitted women to qualify for better jobs. More and more women went to work in the business world. The states also passed laws to give women greater equality with men in holding property and money.

❖ THE PROHIBITION MOVEMENT

In 1869 a resurgent temperance movement, aroused by the growth of alcoholic consumption during the Civil War, the opposition to recent immigrants, and the demonstrated unity of the brewing industry, organized the Prohibition Party. The evangelical Protestant churches joined the movement to urge various restrictions on liquor traffic and in 1874 the Women's Christian Temperance Union organized; Frances E. Willard became its leader. Later (1893) the Anti-Saloon League organized. Notorious among prohibitionists but of doubtful help to the cause was the hatchet-swinging barroom assailant, Carry Nation. The prohibitionists won local option laws, and by 1890 statewide prohibition laws had been enacted by seven states.

❖ CIVIL RIGHTS

With the failure of social reconstruction and the withdrawal of federal troops from the South, the whites were left to deal with the race problem as they chose. When "Jim Crow" laws provided for segregation of African Americans in the schools and other public places they were upheld by the Supreme Court. After 1890 the South reacted strongly against the Federal Elections Bill by passing the "grandfather clauses" to deny the franchise to African Americans. In 1896 the Supreme Court in *Plessy v. Ferguson* interpreted the Fourteenth Amendment as permitting separate but equal school facilities for African Americans. Lynching and other violence were employed to maintain white supremacy in the South while the North also fell short of the goals of equality.

PHILOSOPHICAL DEVELOPMENTS

American philosophers, like ministers, had to find a place for Darwinism in their thinking. Before Darwinism and the Civil War, American thought generally followed the lines of Emerson's transcendentalism. This romantic and optimistic philosophy held that God intervened directly in the lives of men and that men had a spark of the divine which, with freedom of choice, gave them the ability to achieve a perfect society. But the industrial revolution in America after 1865 brought aggression and conflict between the social classes. Darwin's theory of biological evolution indicated that man was a biological organism subject to the same laws of competition and struggle as other forms of life; it suggested that God did not create man according to the literal interpretation of *Genesis* and did not guide him always.

Two philosophers, pioneer sociologists, dealt with the philosophical implications of Darwinism. The first, William Graham Sumner at Yale, argued that man was a product of his environment, controlled by mechanistic forces but had limited freedom to work out his destiny. Within these limits men should be left free from government controls to compete with each other and without government favoritism to any group. Thus he used Darwinism to support the laissez faire, free enterprise philosophy of the earlier decades. He became known as the leading spokesman of social Darwinism.

Lester Ward, also a Darwinian, argued differently in his books in sociology. Ward thought that man with his intelligence differed from brute animals. Through government man should devise institutions to control his evolution. Some leading theologians took up this line of thought to justify the amelioration of the evils of industrial society.

From this thinking developed a distinctive American philosophy, pragmatism. Pragmatism began with Charles Peirce, William James helped formulate it, and later John Dewey further developed and expounded this concept. Basically, pragmatists were practical philosophers who judged human institutions by their consequences. Whatever worked satisfactorily was the answer to man's social problems. Truth, like institutions, was relative; the answers might change with changing times; there were no absolute answers. Thus the reaction to Darwinism varied. In the business community it was used, by men like John D. Rockefeller, to justify the gospel of wealth; this thinking Horatio Alger reflected in his success novels written to inspire boys to struggle for success through effort and sacrifice.

⊙⊙ HISTORIOGRAPHY

The most discussed of all American historians, Frederick Jackson Turner, started on the road to fame in 1890 when he read his challenging paper *The Significance of the Frontier in American History*. The young historian startled American historians into thinking along new lines and pointed to the effect of America's 400-year experience of expanding along new frontiers into vacant land. The existence of the frontier, he said, explained why Americans became democratic, individualistic, and otherwise developed distinct characteristics from their European ancestors. Since his time, American historians have given undue attention to confirming or contradicting Turner's loosely formulated ideas.

CHAPTER BOOK LIST

Addams, Jane, *Twenty Years at Hull House* (Signet). Abridged; on reform movements.

Barker, C.A., *Henry George* (1956).

Bremmer, Robert H., *American Philanthropy* (University of Chicago). A survey of American givers.

Cochran, T.C., and Miller, William, *The Age of Enterprise: A Social History of Industrial America* (Torchbooks).

Fine, Sidney, *Laissez Faire and the General Welfare State* (1956).

Handlin, Oscar, *Immigration as a Factor in American History* (Spectrum).

Handlin, Oscar, *The Uprooted* (1951). From immigrants' viewpoint.

Higham, John, *Strangers in the Land: Patterns of American Nativism, 1860–1925* (1955). Best on the subject.

Jones, Maldwyn A., *American Immigration* (Chicago). Why they came and their influence.

Josephson, Matthew, *Robber Barons* (Harvest).

Miller, Perry, ed., *American Thought, Civil War to World War I* (1954).

Mumford, Lewis, *The City in History* (1961).

Steffens, Lincoln, *Shame of the Cities* (American Century).

Wittke, Carl, *We Who Built America* (Western Reserve). Survey of immigrant groups.

REVIEW QUESTIONS

MULTIPLE CHOICE

1. The following are true of the "new immigration" *except* they (1) were predominantly Catholic or Jewish in religion (2) tended to learn English quickly (3) were poor and uneducated (4) tended to form solid cores in the cities.

2. Immigration laws before 1900 did not (1) exclude the Chinese (2) establish the quota system (3) restrict undesirable persons (4) select immigrants by national origin.

3. The term "new immigration" refers to what population trend in the United States? (1) The large increase in immigration from southern and eastern Europe (2) a westward shift in the geographical center of the American population (3) the immigration trendtoward more poverty-stricken peoples (4) the increase in immigration of Orientals.

4. Which was *not* a prominent development in religion after 1865? (1) Decrease in Roman Catholics (2) modernists reconciled religion with the findings of science (3) fundamentalists stubbornly clung to literal interpretations of the Bible (4) Christian Science was founded.

5. Which was *not* an educational development after the Civil War? (1) The lyceum movement (2) establishment of agricultural experiment stations (3) higher education for African Americans (4) the Chautauqua movement.

6. Henry George's greatest influence in American economic thought was to (1) call attention to the increase in tenant farming (2) stimulate interest in radical socialism (3) promote Utopian socialist colonies (4) stimulate thought about the unequal distribution of wealth.

7. Women were first given the right to vote in (1) the South (2) in the Northeast (3) in a Western territory (4) in the Midwestern states.

8. John Dewey as a philosopher advocated (1) social Darwinism (2) progressivism (3) pragmatism (4) Hegelianism.

9. The American historian who developed the frontier thesis to explain the peculiarities of American politics, culture, and character was (1) Henry Adams (2) Brooks Adams (3) F. J. Turner (4) William D. Howells.

TRUE-FALSE

10. An outstanding social development after 1865 was the rapid growth of American cities.

11. Labor unions have nearly always opposed liberal immigration policies.

12. The Morrill Act of 1862 provided for the establishment of land-grant colleges.

13. Soon after the Civil War the prohibition movement was revitalized.

14. In 1890 the Federal Elections Bill considerably increased voting by African Americans in the South.

15. The ideas of Darwin were used mostly to provide an intellectual defense against government regulation of business.

16. The philosophy of pragmatism is essentially European in origin.

COMPLETION

17. Worthless stocks sold in fraudulent schemes are known as _____ stocks.

18. A leading liberal Republican who fled Germany after 1848 was _____ .

19. The year _____ is usually taken as the turning point from the "old" to the "new" immigration.

20. The clash between the _____ and the modernists in religion was started by Charles Darwin's book entitled _____ .

21. The founder of Christian Science was _____ .

22. Noted for donating money for libraries was _____ .

23. The first high quality graduate school in America was _____ .

24. The greatest early leader of the moderate socialists was _____ .

25. The historian who called attention to the frontier in American history was _____ .

MATCHING

26. E.L. Godkin

27. Henry Ward Beecher

28. Booker T. Washington

29. Charles W. Eliot

30. Henry George

31. Edward Bellamy

32. Frances E. Willard

33. Susan B. Anthony

34. Carry Nation

35. "Jim Crow"

36. John Dewey

a. Introduced elective system in colleges

b. Direct action prohibitionist

c. WCTU

d. Racial segregation

e. Woman suffrage leader

f. Leading Congregationalist minister

g. *Looking Backward*

h. Tuskegee Institute

i. Pragmatist

j. *Progress and Poverty*

k. Founder of the Nation

l. Wrote books to inspire boys

THE PROGRESSIVE ERA
1901–1914

CHRONOLOGY / CHAPTER 11

1900 McKinley defeated Bryan (Dem.) for Presidency on issue of Philippines.

1901 McKinley assassinated in September following inauguration for his second term; Theodore Roosevelt became President.

1902 Roosevelt forced mine owners to arbitrate dispute with United Mine Workers.

Employees liability laws (workmen's compensation) passed in states after 1902.

Newlands Reclamation Act passed to irrigate desert lands in West.

Elkins Act provided punishment for acceptance of rebates.

1903 Department of Labor and Commerce created.

1904 Supreme Court ordered dissolution of Northern Securities Company.

Roosevelt elected President.

1906 Hepburn Act finally made ICC an effective regulatory agency.

Pure Food and Drug Act passed.

1907 Brief Panic of 1907.

1908 Taft (Rep.) elected President.

National Conservation Commission appointed by Roosevelt.

Aldrich-Vreeland Act created National Monetary Commission.

1909 Taft inaugurated President. Progressives enacted most of their reforms during his administration.

11

THE DOMESTIC REFORMS OF THEODORE ROOSEVELT, 1901–1909

Theodore Roosevelt brought to the Presidency vigorous, able, and practical political ability. Although he has been criticized for not doing more to achieve the goals of the Progressive Movement and promote social justice, he is recognized for his contributions as a realistic liberal. He led the nation in steps to preserve democracy against plutocracy; he set an example and roused Progressives in the states to correct the abuses of power and halt political corruption by entrenched wealth. His political judgment told him where he could succeed; to have moved too quickly would have jeopardized his success. The need for reform existed because predatory business monopolists, by corrupting politicians, threatened to destroy democratic government.

THE ACHIEVEMENTS OF THEODORE ROOSEVELT

Upon assuming office, "that damned cowboy," as Hanna had called him, reassured his conservative party with tact and restraint but still spelled out the changes he favored. He soon made it clear that he would crusade for reform in many of the domestic issues of the day. He made it clear he believed in vigorous presidential leadership. He did not trouble himself excessively about the role of the legislative and judicial branches. Where his predecessors had failed, he used the power of the federal government to curb monopolies and regulate business. He demonstrated greater political leadership than economic understanding.

✪ **Roosevelt's Rise in Politics**—Theodore Roosevelt, born to a wealthy and aristocratic family in New York, enjoyed the advantages of education and travel. After graduating from Harvard he chose to go into politics. When his political career was temporarily stalled, he went into ranching in South Dakota and produced several works in American history. He established a reputation for honesty, energy, courage, and humanitarianism in his early political offices. Before becoming President he served successively as Assistant Secretary of the Navy, Rough Rider, and governor of New York.

⊙⊙ The Election of 1900—The Republican convention in 1900 ran smoothly under the guidance of the industrialist Senator Marcus A. Hanna. McKinley was renominated. Roosevelt's fame in Cuba won him the nomination for the Vice Presidency; he had the support of his friends who thought he deserved it and of his enemies who wished to place him in a do-nothing position. The Republican Party maintained its earlier position on the gold standard and the tariff issues. On the important issue of the Philippines, they favored prosecution of the war against Aguinaldo and his Filipino rebels and the retention of the islands.

The Democrats renominated Bryan for the Presidency and chose Adlai E. Stevenson as his running mate. Free silver was advocated but imperialism and retention of the Philippines became the main issues. The Democrats also opposed the blacklist and the injunction in labor relations and monopolies in business. Several smaller parties nominated candidates, including the Populists. Prosperity had returned to the country and the Republicans won a substantial victory.

In the September following his second inauguration (1901) President McKinley was killed by an anarchist. Roosevelt became President.

⊙⊙ Demands for Reform—Roosevelt had the backing of various groups in his fight for correction of the evils of big business. Among them were the intellectuals. Thorstein Veblen, author of *The Theory of the Leisure Class* and other writings in economics, influenced intellectuals against "predatory wealth." John Dewey, the philosopher and educator, advocated the use of man's intelligence to plan and shape his environment for progress. These leaders provided the philosophical basis of Progressivism.

Another group, more numerous, more vociferous and more popular, were the "muckrakers." They were journalists who wrote for the general reader and exposed the evils in the business world. Popular magazines carried their articles for a decade. Among the leaders of the muckrakers were Ida M. Tarbell who exposed the methods of John D. Rockefeller in building up the Standard Oil Company, and Lincoln Steffens, the most able of the muckrakers, who exposed business interests as the source of political corruption and the wirepullers behind the bosses in the political machines. Upton Sinclair, the crusading novelist, exposed in his work *The Jungle* the filthy conditions and the sale of diseased animal products in the meat-packing industry.

Labor unions and socialist leaders took an aggressive role in politics and in arousing workers to protest against their exploitation. The Socialist

Party under Eugene V. Debs gained considerable strength as it gave warning of what might happen if the existing economic evils were not remedied. Unskilled workers, ignored by the American Federation of Labor, joined the Industrial Workers of the World under the leadership of "Big Bill" Haywood. They were a noisy, militant, undisciplined lot who agitated among miners, lumberjacks, and agricultural workers, especially in the West. They advocated violent and radical measures to secure better conditions for the working classes.

○ **The Anthracite Coal Strike (1902)**—Roosevelt first exhibited his vigorous leadership in the anthracite coal strike in Pennsylvania in 1902. In this incident his administration became branded as the "Square Deal" as he called his program for fair treatment for labor and the public as well as for capital.

The causes of the strike were typical of the time. The United Mine Workers sought to provide organized leadership to protect miners against existing exploitation. The miners wanted fewer hours, higher wages, and recognition of their union. They complained of having to live in company housing and buy at company stores. The miners went on strike when the owners refused to negotiate.

Roosevelt intervened on behalf of the public and the workers and tried to mediate the quarrel at a White House conference. The mine owners refused to permit arbitration. Roosevelt's threat to use federal troops to reopen the mines persuaded the owners to submit the case to a board of arbitration appointed by the President. The board granted a pay increase and a nine-hour day but not union recognition.

Roosevelt many times recommended to Congress legislation to give federal protection to women and children in industry and to limit the use of the injunction, but no legislation passed. He did secure an employers' liability law to protect injured workers on interstate railroads.

○○○ **Anti-Monopoly Enforcement by Roosevelt**—Roosevelt first heeded the public outcry against monopoly abuses by having his Attorney General bring suit against the Northern Securities Company. This corporation was purely a holding company, created to merge the Great Northern, Northern Pacific, and Burlington railroads into a single system. In the Northern Securities case in 1904 the Supreme Court reversed an earlier decision and declared this merger to be a violation of the Sherman Antitrust Act and ordered dissolution of the holding company. In all, Roosevelt brought 25 indictments of trusts but lost more cases than he won. Roosevelt did not seek to eliminate big business but only to end its abuses. Bigness was not necessarily bad. The Supreme Court later, in the "rule of reason," agreed with Roosevelt's approach.

○ **Regulation of the Railroads**—Roosevelt's chief aim with respect to the railroads was to extend the powers of the Interstate Commerce Commission. In 1903 the Elkins Act made the acceptance of rebates punishable, as well as the granting of them. In 1906 the Hepburn Act greatly increased the regulatory power of the Interstate Commerce Commission and finally made it an effective body. Its most important new authority gave it the power to fix maximum rates.

✪✪ Conservation Under Roosevelt—Conservation of natural resources was one of Roosevelt's strongest interests. With the last public lands being taken over for private purposes and public awareness of the rapid depletion of natural resources, the need for action had come to be accepted. The first major measure came in 1891 under President Harrison; Congress provided that the president could set aside reserves of public forest lands; Harrison, Cleveland, and McKinley all set aside such reserves. Roosevelt set aside 125,000,000 acres or three times the acreage reserved by his predecessors.

In the Carey Act of 1894 Congress first tried to encourage the states to build irrigation projects to reclaim desert lands; this act was unsuccessful. In 1902 Roosevelt had Congress pass the Newlands Reclamation Act. It provided that proceeds from the sale of federal lands in the West be put into a revolving fund for the construction of projects to irrigate the arid lands.

✪ Election of 1904—Roosevelt desired election as President in his own right. Mark Hanna, his greatest threat and rival, died early in 1904. Roosevelt's popularity forced his party to nominate him. The Democrats took a conservative turn and chose Alton B. Parker, a New York lawyer of impeccable character. The campaign was mild in comparison with others and Roosevelt won a more resounding victory than any president since 1872.

Pure Food and Drug Act (1906)—This act of Congress and the Meat Inspection Act resulted from the muckrakers' exposures of the food and drug industries. The Pure Food Act forbade the use of harmful drugs, chemicals, and preservatives in foods and drugs sold in interstate commerce. In 1911 the act was amended to forbid misleading labels on such goods.

✪ The Panic of 1907—The renewed prosperity coming in the late 1890s was briefly interrupted by a severe money panic in 1907. Conservatives claimed Roosevelt had caused the jolt by destroying confidence in business. The panic was partly caused by the issuance of watered stock by recently merged corporations. The money panic itself revealed that weaknesses in the nation's currency and banking system had aggravated the crisis. Consequently, Congress passed the Aldrich-Vreeland Act in 1908 which created the National Monetary Commission to study and recommend reform of the currency and banking system.

✪ Election of 1908—Roosevelt's popularity in 1908 remained great enough to have won him the nomination again; instead he chose

William Howard Taft of Ohio as his successor, and he wrote the party platform besides. The conservatives and liberals both approved of Taft. The Democrats nominated Bryan only to have him suffer defeat again— for the third and last time. The Republican platform included much that pleased the Democrats.

THE PROGRESSIVE MOVEMENT

The Progressives gained momentum during Roosevelt's two terms. He encouraged the reform movement in the states and in local government as a means of rooting special interests out of control of government and returning it to the control of the people.

✪✪ **La Follette and Other Progressives**—A more thoroughgoing Progressive than Roosevelt was Robert M. La Follette, the reform governor of Wisconsin for three terms beginning in 1900. He forced through the Wisconsin legislature a program of legislation to regulate corporations, and to provide conservation and good government free of business domination. From 1906 to 1925 La Follette fought for Progressive measures as United States Senator from Wisconsin.

The Progressive movement brought other leaders into prominence; in New York Charles Evans Hughes exposed evils in the life insurance companies; in California Hiram Johnson, elected as a Progressive governor in 1910, ended the domination of California politics by the Southern Pacific Railroad and passed an extensive program of Progressive reforms.

✪✪✪ **Political Reforms in the States and Cities**—The Progressives accomplished the most in the states and cities. The laws passed there are indicative of what they stood for. Much of their program they borrowed from the Populists and other protest movements going back to about 1870. 1) Direct primary election laws in the states took control of the choice of party nominees from the political bosses. This reform was the real key to the success of the Progressives in winning control of state governments. 2) The initiative and referendum laws created a procedure for direct legislation by the people. Laws are initiated by petition where the legislature fails to act and may be passed by ballot of a majority of the voters. 3) The recall was introduced to give voters an opportunity to vote to remove an unpopular official and elect another in his place. 4) The direct election of United States senators was strongly favored by the Progressives. This they realized by final approval of the Seventeenth Amendment by the states in 1913. Before 1913 members of the Senate were chosen by the state legislatures; often these legislatures had been bribed to elect a corporation nominee. 5) In city government some of the same reforms were introduced as were adopted by the states. The "com mission form" of government, made up of an elected commission which in turn chose a city manager, was introduced. 6) Employer's liability (or workers' compensation) laws were passed by the states beginning with Maryland in 1902; these laws put the burden of proof upon the employer to show that he was not responsible for loss of life or for injury to his employees. The old common law assumed the party injured to be responsible unless proven otherwise. Employers protected themselves against such claims by taking out insurance on employees. 7) Most states passed laws to regulate the employment of women and children.

CHAPTER BOOK LIST

Chalmers, David M., *The Social and Political Ideas of the Muckrakers* (Citadel).

Ekirch, Arthur A., *Progressivism in America* (Watts).

Goldman, Eric, *Rendezvous With Destiny* (Vintage). Includes reform of the Progressive era.

Harbaugh, W.H., *Power and Responsibility: The Life and Times of Theodore Roosevelt* (1961).

Hofstadter, Richard, *The Age of Reform* (1955).

Kolko, Gabriel, *The Triumph of Conservatism, 1900–1916* (1963).

Mowry, G.E., *The California Progressives* (1951).

Mowry, G.E., *The Era of Theodore Roosevelt, 1900–1912* (1958). A leading work.

Mowry, G.E., *Theodore Roosevelt and the Reform Movement* (1946).

Mowry, George, *Theodore Roosevelt and the Progressive Movement* (American Century).

Swades, Harvey, *Years of Conscience: The Muckrakers* (Meridian). A very excellent anthology from the muckrakers; shocking.

Wiebe, Robert H., *Businessmen and Reform: A Study of the Progressive Movement* (1962).

Woods, J.A., *Roosevelt and Modern America* (Collier). Brilliant account of the presidency of Theodore Roosevelt.

REVIEW QUESTIONS

MULTIPLE CHOICE

1. Theodore Roosevelt as President (1) showed great concern for legal and judicial aspects of his acts (2) thought Congress best represented the needs of the people (3) thought the President should assume a vigorous role in defense of national and popular needs (4) was unassuming and modest.

2. Roosevelt was nominated in 1900 for the Vice Presidency because (1) his party was looking for a liberal candidate to succeed McKinley (2) he threatened to bolt the party and join the Democrats (3) he would represent industrialist interests (4) his friends thought he deserved it and his enemies wanted to render him harmless.

3. The author of *The Theory of the Leisure Class* was (1) Thorstein Veblen (2) William Jarnes (3) Herbert Spencer (4) Edward Bellamy.

4. Roosevelt settled the anthracite coal strike in 1902 by (1) forcing the mine owners to arbitrate the dispute (2) dictating a settlement (3) urging Congress to intervene (4) use of the army and the injunction.

5. Roosevelt in fighting the trusts did all of the following *except* (1) direct his Attorney General to prosecute antitrust suits (2) win the case against the Northern Securities Company (3) create the Department of Labor and Commerce 4) condemn bigness as evil *per se*.

6. The Newlands Reclamation Act of 1902 (1) created a revolving fund to finance the construction of irrigation projects (2) provided for the preservation of wildlife (3) matched federal with state funds to encourage conservation projects of many kinds (4) provided for the restoration of deforested lands.

7. The most important outcome of the Panic of 1907 was (1) the creation of an emergency currency (2) abandonment of the gold standard (3) the creation of the National Monetary Commission (4) the charges made against Roosevelt.

8. The central purpose of Progressivism was to (1) promote economic equality (2) encourage moral reform (3) promote political and economic democracy (4) give farmers a greater voice in politics.

TRUE-FALSE

9. Theodore Roosevelt was an insincere opportunist who rode the coattails of the Progressive movement to high political office.

10. Roosevelt's success may be explained by his care to avoid overstepping the limits of the President's authority.

11. Roosevelt was a spoilsman in his early political career.

12. In 1900 the Democratic Party favored free silver, the prevention of monopoly, and legislation to benefit labor.

13. Roosevelt's program took the name "Square Deal" when he took up the cause of labor in the anthracite coal strike.

14. In his antitrust suits Roosevelt lost more cases than he won.

15. The promotion of conservation by the presidents began with Roosevelt.

16. The election of 1904 was fought bitterly by the radical Democratic nominee Alton B. Parker.

17. The nation recovered quickly from the money panic of 1907.

18. The initiative, referendum, and recall were enacted into law in many states during the Progressive movement.

COMPLETION

19. Theodore Roosevelt came from the state of _____ ; before becoming President he served as _____ in the Navy Department.

20. The author of The Theory of the Leisure Class was _____ .

21. Journalists after 1900 who exposed the evils of big business were called _____ . One of them who publicized Rockefeller's methods of creating the Standard Oil monopoly was named _____ . A novelist who exposed filthy conditions in the meat-packing industry was _____ in his book _____ .

22. The greatest leader of the IWW was _____ .

23. Laws to protect employees and their families against economic insecurity in case of death or injury of a wage earner are known as _____ laws.

24. Under Roosevelt two laws were passed to regulate the railroads; they were the _____ and the _____ .

25. In 1904 Roosevelt's chances of winning his party's nomination were uncertain until the death of his rival _____.

26. In the election of 1908 the Republican _____ ran against the Democrat _____ .

27. A noted leader of the Progressives in California was _____ .

28. Direct election of United States senators was required by the _____ .

CHRONOLOGY / CHAPTER 12

1879	De Lesseps began effort to build Panama Canal.
1894	Sino-Japanese War began.
1899	Open Door notes sent.
	First Hague Conference met.
1900	Boxer Uprising, Chinese anti-foreign rebellion.
1901	Hay-Pauncefote Treaty opened way for United States construction of Panama Canal.
	Platt Amendment imposed on Cuba.
1902	British-Japanese military alliance.
	Venezuelan debt controversy; Drago doctrine enunciated.
1903	Hay-Herran Treaty with Colombia rejected by Colombia's senate.
	Hay-Bunau-Varilla Treaty with Panama gave United States lease on Canal Zone.
	Alaska Boundary Dispute settled.
1904	Russo-Japanese War began.
	Roosevelt Corollary to Monroe Doctrine announced.
1905	Treaty of Portsmouth ended Russo-Japanese War.
1906	Actual construction of Panama Canal began.
	Algeciras Conference called by Roosevelt to settle French-German dispute over Morocco.
1907	1907–1908 Gentlemen's Agreement reached between United States and Japan settled disputes over segregation and immigration of Japanese.
	Second Hague Conference met.
1908	Root-Takahira Agreement to soothe relations with Japan.
1914	Panama Canal completed.

12
FOREIGN RELATIONS UNDER THEODORE ROOSEVELT, 1901–1909

> Theodore Roosevelt's advocacy of a big navy foretold the vigorous role he would exercise in foreign affairs. The expansionists that dominated the nation's thinking during the Progressive Era gave the President all the support he needed in his aggressive foreign policies.

AMERICAN RELATIONS IN THE PACIFIC

The acquisition of the Philippines immediately involved the United States in the problem of China. Since the defeat of China in the Sino-Japanese War (1894–1895), the imperialistic powers of Europe threatened to dismember and dominate the parts of China in the same way that Africa had been taken over by these same powers. Our newly acquired position in the Philippines would be valueless if these powers should come to monopolize China.

✪✪✪ **The Open Door Policy**—John Hay, McKinley's able Secretary of State, undertook to halt the absorption of China as threatened by the "spheres of influence," "concessions," bases, and ports held by foreign powers. Great Britain also had an interest in keeping all of China open to trade and had made proposals of an alliance to this end. Hay in 1899 sent notes to Great Britain, Germany, France, Italy, Japan, and Russia asking them to agree to the Open Door Policy in China. When they substantially agreed, Hay declared the policy to be in effect. This policy meant that all nations having special areas in China would leave them open on free and equal terms to the trade of other nations.

✪✪ **The Boxer Uprising**—A nationalist society of Chinese known as the Boxers reacted against the humiliation of foreign occupation in 1900 by staging a rebellion against the foreign settlement at Peiping. About 300 foreign missionaries, businessmen, and diplomats were killed. The powers immediately sent in troops to restore order. The United States took the lead in organizing these troops as an international police force and secured the agreement to withdraw and preserve Chinese independence. The intervening powers forced China to pay large indemnities. When the United States found it had been awarded more than its losses, it returned in all $17,000,000 of the original award of almost $25,000,000. Grateful China set aside the larger part of the Boxer indemnity to send Chinese students to American colleges.

OO The Russo-Japanese War—Russia and Japan both expected to obtain further advantages in China after the settlement of the Boxer Uprising. Russia maintained her troops in Manchuria after the other powers had withdrawn. Japan felt that she could not permit Russian occupation to endanger her access to China as a market and source of necessary raw materials for her growing industry. In 1902 Japan entered into a military alliance with Britain which in effect permitted Japan to realize her plans to drive Russia out of Manchuria without fear of attack from any ally of Russia.

The Russo-Japanese War began in 1904 with a surprise attack on Russia. The Japanese soon defeated Russian forces, but both nations were weakened enough to desire peace. Roosevelt offered his services in peace-making and helped negotiate the Treaty of Portsmouth (New Hampshire) in 1905. Japan won territories from Russia, but Roosevelt persuaded her not to force Russia to pay a large cash indemnity the Japanese felt they badly needed. Japan blamed Roosevelt for the loss of the indemnity. Roosevelt wanted neither power to become so strong as to gravely threaten the Open Door in China.

O The Gentlemen's Agreement—The Japanese, proud of their recent victory over Russia, deeply resented the American discrimination in California against the large number of recent Japanese immigrants there. Roosevelt eventually forced the San Francisco school board to stop its policy of segregation of Japanese children in its schools and worked to satisfy California by halting the wave of Japanese immigration there. He worked out, in an exchange of notes in 1907 and 1908, the Gentlemen's Agreement by which Japan agreed to stop the immigration of laborers to the United States.

The Root-Takahira Agreement (1908)—Friendly relations between the United States and Japan ceased after 1905; it became apparent that Japan did not intend to respect the Open Door in either Manchuria, where she had superseded the Russians, or in Korea. Roosevelt's attempt to soothe relations with Japan led to the Root-Takahira Agreement. The two nations agreed to maintain the Open Door in China, support Chinese independence, and respect each other's possessions in the Pacific.

THE PANAMA CANAL

The lengthy voyage of the battleship *Oregon* from the Pacific coast around South America to Cuba during the Spanish-American War dramatized for the whole American people the military need of an isthmian canal. The newly acquired possessions in the Atlantic and Pacific made it more important than ever to shift naval units as speedily as possible. Its commercial uses were obvious.

✪✪✪ **Early Developments in Panama**—The isthmian canal project was the subject of the Clayton-Bulwer Treaty that denied either Britain or the United States exclusive control over any canal either might construct in Panama. In 1901 the new diplomacy of Britain, arising from the German threat in Europe, brought a willingness to abrogate the Clayton-Bulwer Treaty.

In 1879 the French Canal Company under Ferdinand de Lesseps, engineer of the Suez Canal, began digging a canal in Panama. The company failed because of mosquito diseases and unexpected engineering problems.

The Hay-Pauncefote Treaty with Britain in 1901 released the United States from the restrictions of the Clayton-Bulwer Treaty. The treaty of 1901 gave the United States a free hand in building, controlling, and policing a canal that would be open to all nations on equal terms.

The agent of the New Panama Canal Company, Philippe Bunau-Varilla, made a bid to sell out to the United States in an effort to salvage something from their unsuccessful efforts at canal building. Before Bunau-Varilla's efforts, Congress had tended to favor a route through Nicaragua. The clever French lobbyist took advantage of the volcanic explosion of Mount Pelee in the West Indies to convince Congress that any canal dug along the proposed route through Nicaragua would be endangered by an active volcano there. Although an engineer's report favored the Nicaraguan route, Congress voted in favor of the Panama route in 1902.

✪ **The Hay-Herran Treaty (1903)**—Since Congress was willing to pay the offering price of $40,000,000 of the New Panama Canal Company for its rights in Panama, the next step was to secure canal rights from Colombia. The Hay-Herran Treaty as negotiated gave the United States such a lease for $10,000,000 cash and an annual rental of $250,000. To the great disgust of Roosevelt, the Colombian Senate held out for better terms and refused to ratify the treaty. Roosevelt was impatient to get the canal started before the election of 1904.

✪✪ **Panamanian Independence**—Bunau-Varilla, too, was in a hurry since his company's franchise would expire in 1904; he, therefore, took advantage of the almost annual attempts of Panama to break away from Colombia. He financed and planned another revolt. President Roosevelt, who had knowledge of the plans cooperated by dispatching an American naval vessel to prevent Colombia from landing troops to crush the rebellion. He broke all precedents by recognizing Panama's independence an hour after the movement began and later boasted: "I took Panama."

✪✪✪ **Hay-Bunau-Varilla Treaty (1903)**—Fifteen days after Panamanian independence this treaty between the United States and Panama gave the United States a perpetual lease of a zone ten miles wide across Panama. Colombia's rightful complaints were finally quieted in 1921 by a payment of $25,000,000. Roosevelt's haste proved expensive in terms of both money and good-will.

Construction of the Canal—Actual construction did not begin until 1906. The problem of sanitation, chiefly responsible for the French defeat, had to be overcome first; Colonel W.C. Gorgas practically eliminated the tropical diseases there. Major George W. Goethals, an army engineer, directed the construction of the canal. In August 1914 the first ocean vessel steamed through the new waterway.

CARIBBEAN RELATIONS UNDER ROOSEVELT

The Panama Canal project, as well as the Monroe Doctrine, made it doubly important to the United States to keep any enemy power from obtaining a foothold in the Caribbean. Roosevelt's aggressive attitude was branded the "Big Stick" policy.

✪✪ **The Venezuelan Incident of 1902**—Great Britain, Germany, and Italy blockaded the ports of Venezuela in order to force the dictator of the country to pay debts owed by Venezuela to their citizens. Roosevelt, acting behind the scenes, exerted pressure against Germany to withdraw and agree to arbitration. The Hague Tribunal reviewed the case and Venezuela agreed to apply a third of her customs receipts to repayment of the debt.

✪ **The Drago Doctrine**—Luis Drago, the Argentine minister of foreign affairs, took the Venezuelan incident as the occasion for announcing that no nation should have the right to use unpaid debts as an excuse for military intervention. The American State Department and the Second Hague Conference (1907) agreed to a slightly modified version.

The Roosevelt Corollary—This assertion by Roosevelt, an enlargement of American powers claimed under the Monroe Doctrine, stated that the United States would intervene in the domestic affairs of any weak or negligent state in the Caribbean or Central American area to keep it from giving excuse for intervention by any outside power. This policy was vigorously applied in Santo Domingo in 1905.

✪ RELATIONS WITH THE BRITISH

The new British policy of friendship toward the United States manifested itself not only in the canal diplomacy but in the Alaskan boundary dispute. A dispute over the boundary between Alaska and Canada arose following the Klondike gold rush (1897–1899). The Canadians based their claims upon the reinterpretation of a boundary treaty of 1825. Their object was to secure a land passage across the Alaskan panhandle to the Pacific. The commission appointed to settle the dispute included an Englishman who voted consistently with the American members to give the United States a highly favorable decision in the settlement of the disputed points.

The restoration of friendly relations between the United States and Britain, as realized in the Hay-Pauncefote Treaty, permitted Britain to leave to the United States Navy the protection of the interests of both nations in the Caribbean area. Treaties of alliance with Japan and France likewise permitted Britain to withdraw her naval units from the Far East and the Mediterranean respectively. Britain needed her navy at home to offset the growing threat of Germany.

AMERICAN DIPLOMATIC RELATIONS WITH EUROPE

Roosevelt's participation in diplomatic events in Europe marked a further step away from America's old policy of isolationism.

✪ **The Hague Conferences**—In 1899 the First Hague Conference met in response to a worldwide feeling that steps should be taken to promote world peace. The Conference recommended three means for settling disputes and avoiding war: 1) mediation, 2) international commissions of inquiry, and 3) the establishment of a Permanent Court of Arbitration. The United States submitted the first case for settlement to the newly established Court.

President Roosevelt took the lead in calling the Second Hague Conference in 1907; he failed in an effort to establish an international court of justice to settle disputes. Nevertheless, minor progress was made toward promoting arbitration.

Arbitration Treaties—Early in his administration Roosevelt began negotiating treaties with foreign powers by which they agreed to submit certain disputes to the Hague Tribunal. The negotiation of these arbitration treaties was continued by subsequent administrations. The Central Powers in World War I, however, refused to sign such agreements.

The Algeciras Conference—Roosevelt called this conference to settle the Moroccan Crisis of 1905–1906. Germany feared that France was about to exclude her from Morocco. At Algeciras, Spain, Roosevelt helped work out a settlement more favorable to France than to the Germans.

CHAPTER BOOK LIST

Beale, H.K., *Theodore Roosevelt and the Rise of America to World Power* (Collier). Impact of Roosevelt upon American foreign policy.

Campbell, Charles, *Special Business Interests and the Open Door Policy* (1968).

Du Val, Jr., M.P., *And the Mountains Will Move* (1947). Construction of the Panama Canal.

Healy, David, *United States Expansion* (1970).

LeFeber, Walter, *The New Empire: An Interpretation of American Expansion* (1963).

Lena, Sidney, *The Forging of the American Empire from the Revolution to Vietnam* (1971).

McCormick, Thomas J., *China Market: American Quest for Informal Empire* (Quadrangle).

Munro, Dana G., *Intervention and Dollar Diplomacy for the Caribbean* (1960).

Pratt, Julius W., *Expansionists of 1898* (Quadrangle).

Pringle, H.F., *Theodore Roosevelt, A Biography* (Harvest). A famous Pulitzer Prize biography of Theodore Roosevelt: Slights Roosevelt's achievements.

Roosevelt, Theodore, *Rough Riders* (Signet).

Williams, William A., *The Tragedy of American Diplomacy* (1963).

REVIEW QUESTIONS

MULTIPLE CHOICE

1. The main purpose of the Open Door policy in China was to (1) keep Japan out of China (2) preserve Chinese independence against Russia (3) keep China open to all countries on equal terms (4) open all coastal ports to foreign trade.

2. All are true of the Russo-Japanese War *except* which one? (1) It strengthened friendship between the United States and Japan (2) it made Japan the leader of the Asian nations (3) it won Russian territories for Japan (4) it increased Japanese pride.

3. Which treaty released the United States from the terms of the Clayton-Bulwer Treaty? (1) Hay-Herran (2) Hay-Bunau-Varilla (3) Hay-Pauncefote.

4. The determining factor in the choice of the Panamanian route for the canal was the (1) refusal of Nicaragua to lease a route (2) the lower grades to be crossed over Panama (3) lobbying efforts of Bunauvarilla (4) friendship with Colombia.

5. The Panama Canal was completed in (1) 1904 (2) 1914 (3) 1907 (4) 1910.

6. Roosevelt helped Panama win independence by (1) warning Colombia not to interfere (2) sending a naval vessel to prevent Colombia from landing troops (3) landing troops in Panama (4) making a large payment to Colombia.

7. The Drago Doctrine announced that (1) no nation had the right to use military force to collect an unpaid debt (2) only the United States could use force to make Latin-America pay her debts (3) no nation had the right to interfere in the internal affairs of another (4) the Monroe Doctrine was to be made multilateral.

8. The Alaskan Boundary Dispute (1) was settled by arbitration (2) arose over claims to Klondike gold fields (3) left Canada highly pleased (4) was settled in favor of the United States.

9. The Hague Conference in 1907 (1) was given only grudging American support (2) was given the full support of President Roosevelt (3) established an international court of justice (4) made no progress in its objectives.

TRUE-FALSE

10. The aim of the Open Door Policy was to help the United States gain a territorial foothold in China.

11. After the Boxer Uprising the United States expressed its policy of friendship for China by returning over half of the Boxer indemnity.

12. In many ways the Russo-Japanese War represented important developments in Asia and had far-reaching consequences.

13. In the Root-Takahira Agreement Japan acceded to the Open Door Policy.

14. Britain did not manifest her new policy of friendship to America in the negotiations to abrogate the Clayton-Bulwer Treaty.

15. Roosevelt won the Nobel Peace Prize for his cautious deliberations in securing rights from Colombia to dig the Canal.

16. Panama had never sought independence until encouraged to do so by Roosevelt and Bunau-Varilla.

17. In the Alaskan Boundary Dispute the British deliberately sought to further friendship with the United States.

COMPLETION

18. The active Secretary of State under McKinley and Roosevelt was named _____ .

19. The _____ in 1900 was the Chinese reaction to foreign interference; the rebellion centered at _____ .

20. The Russo-Japanese War was concluded by the Treaty of _____ in the year _____ . Japan resented the fact that she received no _____ from Russia.

21. The American-Japanese Agreement in 1907–1909 regarding immigration is known as the _____ . Trouble had arisen when Japanese children were segregated by the _____ school board.

22. In Asiatic matters the United States and Japan tried to come to an understanding in the _____ Agreement.

23. A French engineer who failed to dig the canal in Panama was named _____ .

24. A rejected alternative canal route to that in Panama was that along the _____ River in _____ .

25. Sanitation was introduced to the Panama Canal Zone by Colonel _____ and the construction of the canal was directed by Major _____ .

26. Roosevelt's aggressive foreign policy was given the name _____ policy.

27. The chief aggressor in the Venezuelan Incident of 1902 was the government of _____ ; the reason was a valid _____ claim.

28. Roosevelt eulogized the Monroe Doctrine to assert American right to intervene to require Latin-American nations to meet their obligations in the _____ .

29. In the _____ Roosevelt departed from American isolationist policy to help settle a quarrel over Morocco.

CHRONOLOGY / CHAPTER 13

1909   Taft inaugurated as President.
        Taft discredited by Payne-Aldrich Tariff, which failed to
            reduce protective tariff rates.
1910   Progressives revolted against "Cannonism" in Congress.
        Mann-Elkins Act placed interstate communications utilities
            under ICC.
        Roosevelt and Taft split.
        Ballinger-Pinchot controversy led to Pinchot's removal.
        Democrats win midterm congressional elections.
1911   Supreme Court dissolved Standard Oil Company in an
            antitrust suit.
        "Rule of Reason" decisions of Supreme Court permit large
            corporations where competition exists.
1912   "Bull Moose" presidential election campaign leads to victory
            of Wilson (Dem.).
1913   Sixteenth (income tax) and Seventeenth (popular election of
            United States senators) amendments ratified.
        Wilson inaugurated as President.

13
TAFT AND THE ELECTION OF 1912, 1909–1913

> Taft's single term represents an extension of the Progressivism of Roosevelt. Although his political mistakes would cost him the reelection, Taft's record in office is one of modest but numerous achievements.

✪✪ TAFT'S CAREER AND CHARACTER

Before he became President, William Howard Taft, had demonstrated his ability as a judge in Ohio and in the federal courts, and as an attorney. Under Roosevelt he served as the first civil governor of the Philippines and then served as Secretary of War, until Roosevelt chose him for the presidential succession.

Taft was trained as a lawyer and his experience had been in legal and judicial capacities; he had not engaged in politics in the sense of campaigning for office until nominated for the Presidency; he detested politics as such. He was conservative in that he did not assert the power of his office to personally fight for reforms and dramatize issues as Roosevelt had done. He was concerned about the legal limits of his power where Roosevelt was not. These characteristics made Taft seem timid and conservative. Lacking Roosevelt's political shrewdness, he made political blunders. These qualities alienated the Progressives, lost him the friendship of Roosevelt, and gave him a reputation for ineffectiveness. Actually he was a mild Progressive and his administration succeeded in accomplishing numerous Progressive reforms.

TAFT'S POLITICAL INEPTNESS

A series of events and laws cost Taft his initial popularity.

✪✪ **The Payne-Aldrich Tariff**—Taft called a special session of Congress to legislate tariff reductions. The House passed a bill with moderate reductions but in the Senate tariff rates were revised upward to suit the views of the wealthy industrialist senators. Progressive Republican insurgents led by Senator La Follette strongly opposed the bill, but the House and the President accepted it. Taft lost much of his support in the West when he defended the Payne-Aldrich Tariff Act in an address at Winona, Minnesota.

○ **The Dismissal of Pinchot**—In another incident Taft lost the support of Progressives when he gave the impression he had joined the anti-conservationists. Gifford Pinchot criticized his superior in office and, in published articles, protested the return to private interests of certain waterpower sites and coal lands. In publicly criticizing the action of the Secretary of the Interior, R.A. Ballinger, Pinchot was guilty of insubordination. Taft reviewed the case carefully and dismissed Pinchot for insubordination. The people could not see the administrative logic of Taft's action; they only saw that a friend of conservation had been fired.

○ **The Fight Against "Cannonism"**—Under Taft the Speaker of the House, Joseph G. Cannon, an ultra-conservative, used the powers of his office to block progressive legislation. The Progressive Republicans led by George W. Norris of Nebraska joined the Democrats in a revolt to reduce the powers of the office of the Speaker. They succeeded in making fundamental changes that reduced the Speaker's powers of appointing committee members. They freed members of the House from a large degree of party discipline. Taft again refused to take the side of the Progressives. Taft's loss of popularity brought Republican defeat in the congressional elections of 1910, and the Democrats won overwhelming control of the House.

Canadian Reciprocity—After the election, Taft drafted a reciprocity treaty with Canada providing mutual reductions in tariff duties. Western farmers opposed the provisions for tariff reductions on imports of Canadian foodstuffs. When the Canadians suspected that the treaty would lead to eventual union with the United States, their Parliament refused to ratify it. Taft was further discredited.

○○ **"Dollar Diplomacy"**—The Taft administration followed a foreign policy in the Caribbean area of encouraging and protecting American investments there. The Secretary of State, Philander C. Knox, followed a similar policy in China and induced American bankers to join a consortium of powers in financing railroads. "Dollar Diplomacy" in the Caribbean led to military intervention in Nicaragua that lasted into the 1920s. Cuba and Honduras were occupied by American troops during Taft's administration.

ACHIEVEMENTS OF TAFT

Solid but seemingly minor achievements of Taft in the Progressive program were overlooked because of his political ineptitude.

✪ **The Mann-Elkins Act (1910)**—This law sponsored by Taft greatly increased the powers of the Interstate Commerce Commission. Most important, it extended its jurisdiction to include telephone, telegraph, and cable lines.

✪ **Conservation**—Taft withdrew oil lands from public entry and bought back forest lands from private companies. Public land laws were improved.

✪ **Prosecution of Trusts**—Taft brought more than twice as many antitrust suits against monopolies than did Roosevelt. The Supreme Court dissolved both the Standard Oil Company and the American Tobacco Company at this time. The "rule of reason" was also handed down by the Court; it said that only those combinations guilty of "unreasonable" restraint of trade should be punished. Many of the antitrust proceedings had been begun under Roosevelt.

✪ **Other Progressive Measures**—1) The establishment of the postal savings system provided a safe haven for and returned interest on small savings of individuals. This measure provided tangible benefits to the common man, especially in areas where banks did not exist. American banks were not then adequately regulated to provide for the safety of deposits.

2) The parcel post was liberalized to permit the delivery of large packages on rural routes; this act enabled farmers to escape the monopoly of small town merchants in the day before automobiles became common; the liberalized parcel post stimulated the growth of the great mail order houses.

3) The Department of Labor was made independent of the Department of Commerce. 4) The eight-hour day was provided for workers on government contracts. 5) The income tax was legalized by ratification of the Sixteenth Amendment to the Constitution, and 6) popular election of United States senators was introduced by the Seventeenth Amendment.

THE ELECTION OF 1912

This contest is of unusual significance and interest because of the personalities and parties involved and the outcomes.

✪✪ **Schism Among the Republicans**—Well before the nominating conventions, Robert M. La Follette organized the Republican insurgents as the National Progressive Republican League. The Progressives advocated reforms to enable the people to end the rule of political bosses and regain control of government; the organization represented farmers, workers, and small businessmen.

Roosevelt had supported the anti-Taft insurgents since his return from Africa, but he refused to support La Follette, who had organized the Progressives. Instead he announced his own candidacy for the Republican nomination.

⊙ **The Republican Party**—Taft delegates were chosen for the Republican nominating convention. In the states that had already adopted the preferential primaries, the voters chose delegates to support Roosevelt. But Roosevelt had entered the race for the delegations too late, and Taft won the nomination on the first ballot.

⊙⊙ **The Bull Moose Party**—The defeated Progressives withdrew and later met as the Progressive Party to nominate Roosevelt. The new party became known as the "Bull Moose" Party because of the expression used by Roosevelt at the convention. La Follette was bitterly disappointed at having been pushed aside after his strenuous efforts in organizing and demonstrating the strength of the Progressives.

⊙⊙ **The Democratic Party**—The split among the Republicans assured the Presidency to the Democratic nominee and led to a strenuous fight at the Democratic convention. The contest was not resolved until 46 ballots had been held. Senator Champ Clark from Missouri had the backing of Eastern Democrats and conservatives. After Bryan shifted his support to Wilson, the New Jersey liberal won the nomination. The Democratic platform promised a definite program of reform legislation.

⊙⊙⊙ **Results of the Election**—The split among the Republicans helped give the victory to Wilson, but the Democrats also won control of both houses of Congress. Roosevelt ran second and Taft third. The Socialist Party won nearly a million votes for their perennial candidate, Eugene V. Debs. The strength of the three reform candidates indicated the social unrest that prevailed. The second Democratic candidate since 1860 had won the Presidency. Millions of voters had shown their willingness to violate the anti-third term tradition by voting for Roosevelt.

CHAPTER BOOK LIST

Hays, S.P., *Conservation and the Gospel of Efficiency* (Atheneum).

Hays, S.P., *Response to Industrialism: 1885–1914* (University of Chicago). Effects of the business growth on society and politics.

La Follette, Robert M., *Autobiography: A Personal Narrative of Political Experiences* (first published in 1912; University of Wisconsin).

Link, Arthur S., *Woodrow Wilson and the Progressive Era 1910–1917* (Harper & Row).

Madison, Charles A., *Critics and Crusaders, A Century of American Protest* (Ungar). Perceptive geographical essays. A wide-ranging book that could be listed here under several different chapters.

Manners, William, *A Friendship that Split the Republican Party* (1969).

Maxwell, R.S., *La Follette and the Rise of the Progressives in Wisconsin* (1956).

Mowry, George C., *The Era of Theodore Roosevelt 1900–1912* (Harper & Row).

Wilonsky, Norman W., *Conservatives in the Progressive Era: The Taft Republicans of 1912* (1965).

Wilson, Woodrow, *New Freedom* (Spectrum).

REVIEW QUESTIONS

MULTIPLE CHOICE

1. Taft had a reputation as (1) an Old Guard Republican (2) a Progressive Republican (3) a superb politician (4) being militant in foreign relations.

2. Taft dismissed the popular conservationist Gifford Pinchot because (1) Pinchot criticized his boss in published articles (2) Pinchot was an overly eager conservationist (3) Taft was opposed to conservation (4) Pinchot was a Progressive.

3. "Boss" Cannon, Speaker of the House, was (1) defeated and stripped of his special powers (2) upheld in the exercise of his powers in the House (3) opposed actively by Taft (4) defeated by Old Guard Republicans.

4. On which of these did Taft *not* make gains for the cause of Progressivism (1) conservation (2) regulation of public utilities (3) prosecution of trusts (4) tariff reduction.

5. The person most responsible for leading the revolt of the Progressives before the campaign of 1912 was (1) Gifford Pinchot (2) Robert M. La Follette (3) Hiram Johnson (4) Theodore Roosevelt.

6. Which was *not* a candidate in the election of 1912? (1) Theodore Roosevelt (2) Eugene V. Debs (3) Woodrow Wilson (4) Robert M. La Follette (5) William Howard Taft.

7. The greatest rival of Wilson's for the Democratic nomination in 1912 was (1) Champ Clark (2) William Jennings Bryan (3) William G. McAdoo (4) Oscar Underwood.

8. In the election of 1912 the correct ranking of the candidates according to votes received was (1) Taft, Wilson, Roosevelt, Debs (2) Wilson, Roosevelt, Taft, Debs (3) Wilson, Taft, Debs, Roosevelt (4) Wilson, Roosevelt, Debs, Taft.

TRUE-FALSE

9. Before his nomination for the Presidency Taft had demonstrated his political shrewdness by winning several elective offices.

10. Taft's weakness was his seeming timidity and lack of flair for marshaling public opinion for his policies.

11. Taft's legislation almost entirely was of a conservative character.

12. Taft prosecuted business monopolies more vigorously than did Roosevelt.

13. Liberalization of the parcel post aided the large mail order houses.

14. Wilson won the nomination in 1912 with the support of Champ Clark.

COMPLETION

15. Roosevelt chose _____ as his successor to the Presidency.

16. Early in his administration Taft lost popularity by defending the attempt at reform in the _____ Tariff.

17. The Secretary of the Interior criticized by Pinchot was named _____ .

18. The fight against "Cannonism" was led by _____ of Nebraska.

19. Taft's foreign policy in the Caribbean was called _____ by his critics.

20. The powers of the Interstate Commerce Commission were increased under Taft by the _____ Act.

21. In the post offices over the country Taft established the _____ .

22. Taft established a new position in the cabinet, that of the Secretary of _____ .

23. The Progressive Party in 1912 was nicknamed the _____ Party.

THE WILSON ADMINISTRATION AND WORLD WAR I, 1913–1921

CHRONOLOGY / CHAPTER 14

1910   Revolution began in Mexico by Madero.
1912   Panama Canal Tolls Act modified at British insistence.
1913   Wilson inaugurated.
        Underwood Tariff substantially reduced rates.
        Department of Labor organized separately.
        Federal Reserve Act revised nation's banking system.
        Huerta-led counter-revolution caused murder of Madero.
            Wilson refused to recognize Huerta and began "Watchful
            Waiting" policy.
1914   World War I broke out in Europe.
        Clayton Antitrust Act improved upon the Sherman Antitrust
            Act.
        Federal Trade Commission created to enforce fair trade
            practices.
        Smith-Lever Act provided funds for farm extension education.
        American forces landed at Vera Cruz, Mexico.
1915   La Follette Seamen's Act improved lot of sailors in merchant
            marine.
        American intervention in Haiti.
1916   Wilson reelected by narrow margin.
        Federal Farm Loan Act passed to provide long-term farm
            credits.
        Marines intervene in Santo Domingo.
        General Pershing sent to Mexico to take Villa.
1917   Smith-Hughes Act provided federal aid for vocational
            education.
        Virgin Islands purchased from Denmark.
1919   Eighteenth Amendment (prohibition) ratified by states and
            implemented by Volstead Act.
1920   Nineteenth Amendment (woman suffrage) ratified.

Chapter

14
WILSON'S FIRST TERM, 1913–1917

> The strong support for progressivism in the election of 1912 and Democratic control of Congress enabled Wilson to secure passage of his large program of important domestic reforms. After 1915 the country became distracted by the war in Europe and by international problems.

THE WILSON ADMINISTRATION

Wilson labeled his program of reform the "New Freedom." His first term saw the fulfillment of most of the reforms desired by the Progressives.

❂❂ **Wilson's Career and Character**—Woodrow Wilson was born in a Presbyterian minister's family in Virginia; he was the first Southerner to be elected President since pre-Civil War days. Before entering politics he had enjoyed a successful teaching career as a professor of government and history. From the presidency of Princeton University he moved to the governor's office in New Jersey. As governor he aroused enough public pressure against the indifferent state legislature to pass a program of popular reform legislation. Hence he was promoted for the Presidency and elected in 1912, the first and only earned Ph.D. to hold that office.

Wilson's upbringing in a minister's family made him probably the most religious person in the presidency. His language and his policies reflected religious upbringing and much concern with the morality of his actions. As a very superior person intellectually, he unfortunately made others conscious of his contempt for their intellectual inferiority. His cold, self-righteous personality further handicapped him in interpersonal political relationships. He loved people in the abstract rather than as individuals. He exercised remarkable political skill with groups but ultimately alienated all his personal friends. The domestic reforms he won corrected some existing evils and deficiencies, improved government, and helped preserve equality of opportunity for individuals.

⊘ **Wilson and His Cabinet**—Wilson repaid his political debt to Bryan by making him Secretary of State but had no liking for him. Bryan proved more able than expected; his leading work was the negotiation of about thirty treaties by which the signatory nations agreed to postpone hostilities in cases of dispute—"cooling-off" treaties, they were called. Later Bryan resigned in protest against Wilson's policies leading to war with Germany. William G. McAdoo became Secretary of the Treasury.

Wilson chose five Southern-born Democrats for his cabinet, relatively unknown men since the Democrats had been out of federal office since Cleveland. Wilson's most influential adviser and political assistant, Edward M. House of Texas, never held a cabinet post.

WILSON'S PROGRAM OF REFORM

Wilson exerted strong presidential leadership, in the tradition of Jackson and Theodore Roosevelt, to secure passage of a large program of legislation.

⊘⊘⊘ **The Underwood Tariff (1913)**—The new President called a special session of Congress to deal immediately with the need to lower tariff duties. In order to dramatize the tariff issue, he addressed Congress in person, the first President to do so since John Adams. Lobbyists representing special interests threatened to promote the log-rolling that had wrecked so many earlier attempts to reform tariffs. Wilson and his allies in Congress exposed their unsavory methods by publicity and squelched them by threatening punitive action. Substantial reductions were made; the resulting losses in revenue were made up by passage of the graduated income tax as permitted by the recently ratified Sixteenth Amendment.

⊘⊘ **The Federal Reserve Act (1913)**—The next fulfillment of Wilson's program brought a much-needed revision of the nation's money and banking system.

In the background of the Federal Reserve Act, the panic of 1907 had emphasized the need to create a more elastic monetary system by which credit and the money supply could be expanded and contracted according to the needs of trade and of different regions of the country. To the investigation of the National Monetary Commission controlled by the Republicans was added the investigation by the Democratic-controlled Pujo Committee. The Pujo Committee revealed the operations of the Wall Street "money trust" and its tie with the dominant business corporations of the country. The investigations disclosed weaknesses to be remedied and studied features of more advanced central banking systems in several foreign countries.

The Federal Reserve System was devised mainly by Senator Carter Glass of Virginia, a longtime Senate specialist in banking legislation. The chief provisions of the Act follow. 1) It created 12 regional Federal Reserve banks in as many districts drawn along economic and geographic lines. These districts avoided the danger of a highly centralized system and thus achieved some Democratic consistency with the Jacksonian tradition. 2) The Federal Reserve banks were to be "banker's banks." Private bankers subscribed the stock to found them and the system served banks, not individuals. 3) Control of the system was placed under a Board of Governors, some chosen by member banks and others appointed by the president of the United States. 4) The banks were to accept deposits and make loans to member banks. All national banks were required to join the system. 5) The Federal Reserve banks issued a new uniform currency, the Federal Reserve notes. The notes in time constituted about 90 percent of the nation's currency in circulation and superseded the national bank notes. The Federal Reserve notes passed into circulation when loans were obtained from member banks. The needed elasticity was provided by this feature since money could be expanded with borrowings and contracted by their repayment. 6) Numerous services were provided to the nation's banks and the United States government.

The Federal Farm Loan Act (1916)—This law created 12 Federal Land Banks in a system resembling the Federal Reserve banks. The act made long-term land mortgage credit available at reasonable rates of interest and on suitable terms to farmers through cooperative farm loan associations. This act marked the first entry of the federal government into agricultural credits; the failure of private lenders to provide satisfactory terms of credit necessitated government action.

✪✪✪ **The Clayton Antitrust Act (1914)**—Experience had revealed the need for further improvement in antimonopoly laws. This law 1) defined in detail unfair practices in business competition. 2) Certain types of interlocking directorates and holding companies were forbidden. 3) Labor unions were exempted from the antitrust laws and the use of the injunction limited in labor disputes. The provisions of this act are difficult to generalize since they were numerous, technical, and highly qualified, but the act had the effect of remedying the weaknesses of the Sherman Antitrust Act.

✪ **The Federal Trade Commission (1914)**—Created by Congress in the pattern of the Interstate Commerce Commission, this agency received extensive powers to enforce fair trade practices. It operates by issuing "cease and desist" orders to stop violations of fair competition. Injunctions can be issued against business firms by the federal courts if the Commission's orders are not obeyed. Such companies may appeal decisions of the Commission to the circuit court of appeals.

✪✪ **Legislation for Labor and Agriculture**—1) The La Follette Seamen's Act (1915) required better wages, food, accommodations, and treatment for sailors in the merchant marine. 2) The Adamson Act (1916) made great concessions to strike-threatening railroad workers, the greatest being the eight-hour day. Wilson did not wish the threatened strike to interfere with the flow of war supplies to the Allies. 3) The Smith-Lever Act (1914) provided dollar-matching federal funds to the states for farm extension (educational home demonstration) work. 4) The Smith-Hughes Act (1917) similarly provided funds for agricultural, industrial, and home economics education in the public schools.

✪✪ **Prohibition and Woman Suffrage**—In Wilson's second term wartime idealism helped secure two more reforms by constitutional amendment. The Eighteenth Amendment was passed by Congress in 1917 and ratified by the states early in 1919; it prohibited "the manufacture, sale, or transportation of intoxicating liquors." The Volstead Act (1919) spelled out the details of prohibition. The desire to conserve grain during the war helped bring ratification in 1917 and 1918.

The Nineteenth Amendment passed by Congress in 1919 and 1920 gave the vote to women; more exactly, it prohibited the denial of suffrage on account of sex.

WILSON'S FOREIGN POLICY

Wilson, like his Progressive predecessors, continued a policy of intervention to protect American interests in Latin America.

✪ **The Panama Canal Tolls Act (1912)**—Looking forward to the completion of the canal, Congress passed a schedule of tolls for the ships that would use it. American vessels in coastwise trade were exempted from payment of tolls. Great Britain insisted strongly that the exemption violated the equality of treatment provided in the Hay-Pauncefote Treaty. Wilson made an urgent plea before Congress for repeal of the exemption. Congress complied. It was understood that the British in return agreed to support Wilson's policy in dealing with the revolutionary troubles in Mexico. Wilson undoubtedly wished to preserve friendship with Britain in troubled Europe.

✪ **Caribbean Relations**—In 1916 the marines went to Santo Domingo to prevent a revolution and maintain financial responsibility there. Troops remained until 1924 but American control of the customs remained.

In Nicaragua Wilson maintained control initiated under Taft. In 1914 a treaty negotiated with the republic granted the United States the right to dig a canal there as well as maintain naval bases. In effect Nicaragua was continued as an American protectorate.

The United States intervened in Haiti in 1915 to prevent European intervention and maintain financial solvency.

Not only in the three countries involved but in all of Latin America, American occupation was resented and American motives suspected.

○ **Purchase of the Virgin Islands (1917)**—The need to establish naval defenses for the approaches to the Panama Canal explains the purchase of the Virgin Islands. Denmark received $25,000,000 in payment.

THE REVOLUTION IN MEXICO

Mexico's history since independence in 1821 was marked by chronic revolutionary unrest and instability. In 1876 the despot Porfirio Diaz placed himself at the head of a dictatorship that lasted until 1910. Diaz, who preserved safety of property and life, retained the support of foreign investors and wealthy proprietors in Mexico.

○○ **The Overthrow of Diaz**—In 1910 an idealistic young liberal, Francisco Madero, led the successful revolt against Diaz and, among other reforms, worked to distribute great estates to the landless peons. In 1913 General Victoriano Huerta led a conservative counter-revolution of the landholders and murdered Madero.

The "Watchful Waiting" Policy of Wilson—While 25 other countries recognized the *de facto* regime of Huerta, who was friendly to foreign interests, Wilson branded him a murderer and refused to recognize him. Huerta represented the investors and conservative Mexicans and did not genuinely represent the cause of the people of Mexico.

Huerta made reprisals against Americans and in 1914 arrested a small force of American sailors at Tampico. Wilson demanded an apology and later captured the city of Veracruz to prevent German arms shipments from reaching Huerta. To prevent a war that seemed certain, the ABC Powers (Argentina, Brazil, and Chile) offered mediation. Wilson accepted but Huerta refused. Huerta now rapidly lost support and fled Mexico. The United States withdrew its troops.

Wilson and Carranza—Meanwhile Carranza, who had revolted against Huerta, won recognition from Wilson. Carranza, however, was unable to maintain order in Mexico; his former ally, Francisco Villa, defied Carranza in northern Mexico and carried on attacks against foreigners, including Americans. In March 1916, in retaliation for American support of Carranza, Villa killed 17 persons in Columbus, New Mexico, in a border raid. Wilson secured Carranza's assent to send an invading force under General John J. Pershing to capture Villa. Resentment in Mexico and the approach of war with Germany caused the futile American expedition to be withdrawn.

The Mexican Constitution of 1917—This document marked a great turning point in Mexican history; in a few years it brought peace to Mexico and it represented a final victory for the masses of plain people of Mexico. The Constitution of 1917, 1) favored workers and peasants, 2) provided for gradual appropriation of mineral resources, and 3) the redistribution of large landed estates. These features caused further friction between the United States and Mexico, but provisions for compensating foreigners for expropriated oil, mining, and land properties brought good will and eventual improvement in relations.

CHAPTER BOOK LIST

Clendenen, C.C., *The United States and Pancho Villa* (1961).

Cline, H.F., *The United States and Mexico* (1953). A survey.

Filler, Louis, *Crusaders for American Liberalism: The Story of the Muckrakers* (Collier).

Link, A.S., Wilson, *The New Freedom* (1956). Both history and biography.

Link, Arthur, *Woodrow Wilson and the Progressive Era, 1910–1917* (1954). An analysis of the sources of progressivism.

Meier, Matt S., and Rivera, Feliciano, *The Chicanos: A History of Mexican-Americans* (1972).

Quirk, R.E., *An Affair of Honor: Woodrow Wilson and the Occupation of Vera Cruz* (1962).

REVIEW QUESTIONS

MULTIPLE CHOICE

1. Wilson's Presidency was unique in all these respects except which? (1) First President with an earned Ph.D. (2) first to address Congress in person since Jefferson (3) first Democrat reelected since Jefferson (4) first President elected from the South since before the Civil War.

2. Which of the following facts about the Underwood Tariff is incorrect? (1) Substantial tariff reductions were made (2) it included an income tax (3) it was one of Wilson's last reform measures (4) it was passed by a special session of Congress.

3. The Federal Reserve Act of 1913 included all the following provisions except (1) it provided for 12 district banks (2) it was to be founded entirely with federal funds (3) all national banks had to join it 4) it issued a new type of currency.

4. The Clayton Antitrust Act (1) forbade most holding companies (2) did very little to prevent monopolies (3) outlawed the "blacklist" as used against labor leaders (4) exempted labor unions from antitrust laws.

5. Of these fundamentals of popular government which was the last to be realized? (1) freedom of speech and press (2) separation of church and state (3) popular representative government (4) universal adult suffrage.

6. President Wilson did which in relations with the Caribbean nations? (1) Reversed the policies of his Republican predecessors (2) halted British inroads in the Caribbean (3) encouraged revolution against dictators (4) continued substantially the policies of his predecessors in the Caribbean.

7. The United States purchased the Virgin Islands to (1) give indirect aid to Denmark (2) gain important national resources (3) initiate a Caribbean expansionist policy (4) establish naval defenses at the approaches to the Panama Canal.

8. Wilson's policy toward Mexico during her revolutionary turmoil was one of (1) supporting whoever happened to be in power (2) friendship for Huerta (3) strict nonintervention (4) opposition to Huerta.

TRUE-FALSE

9. Wilson appointed many Southern-born Democrats to his cabinet.

10. Wilson's most effective action against the enemies of tariff reform was his defeat of the lobbyists of special interests.

11. Most of the nation's currency in circulation is made up of Federal Reserve notes.

12. Wilson's administration achieved relatively few gains for organized labor.

13. Prohibition and woman suffrage both became law in Wilson's second term.

14. The Mexican constitution of 1917 brought friendlier relations between the United States and Mexico.

COMPLETION

15. President Wilson's program of reform legislation was known by the phrase _____ .

16. Wilson came from Virginia and served as president of _____ University before becoming _____ of _____ .

17. Wilson appointed _____ as Secretary of State; he negotiated numerous so-called _____ treaties.

18. The _____ is the name of Wilson's tariff reform law. He succeeded in passing the tariff in spite of attempts at trading votes by congressmen, which practice is known as _____ . The tariff law included provisions for an income tax as permitted by the recently ratified _____ Amendment.

19. To lend money to farmers the Wilson administration passed the _____ in 1916. To enforce fair trade practices the _____ was created; this agency issues _____ orders to stop unfair practices.

20. Railroad trainmen were given the eight-hour day by the _____ .

21. The _____ Act provided for educational home demonstration for farmers and the _____ Act provided for vocational education in the public schools.

22. Leader of the revolution in Mexico in 1910 was _____ who was murdered by _____ whom Wilson refused to recognize during his Mexican policy of _____ . During the Mexican troubles Wilson sent General _____ into Mexico to capture _____ .

CHRONOLOGY / CHAPTER 15

1909   Declaration of London drew up rules of international law in time of war.

1914   August, World War I began in Europe.

1915   February, *Lusitania,* British passenger ship, sunk.

        March, *Arabic,* British vessel, sunk.

1916   *Sussex,* French ship, sunk.

        United States takes "preparedness" measures; defense legislation enacted.

        Colonel House sent to Europe to propose terms for peace.

        Presidential election returned Wilson to office as the peace candidate.

1917   Virgin Islands purchased from Denmark.

        Lansing-Ishii Agreement to preserve Open Door policy in China.

        January, Germany announced resumption of unrestricted sinkings in war zone around British Isles.

        March, Zimmermann note released, influenced public opinion against Germany.

        March, Russian Revolution broke out.

        April 6, Congress declared war on Central Powers.

1918   Wilson offered Germany peace on basis of Fourteen Points.

        Summer, American "doughboys" engage in full offensive against German lines.

        November 11, Armistice ended World War I.

1919   January, Wilson went to Versailles Peace Conference. Peace treaty defeated in Senate.

1920   Treaty of Versailles defeated again in Senate. Harding (Rep.) elected President.

1921   Congress under Harding made separate peace agreement with Germany by joint resolution.

Chapter

15
THE FIRST WORLD WAR, 1914–1918

A century of relative peace in the Western world ended in 1914 with the outbreak of World War I. America had been involved in the previous general wars of Europe and again found it impossible to remain neutral.

●● EUROPEAN BACKGROUND

Ever since the defeat of Napoleon, Great Britain had dominated the world without serious challenge. The unification of most of Germany under Prince Bismarck's guidance created a new imperial power strong enough to challenge Britain's position in international politics and commerce. Soon after 1900 most European nations, and a few others, began to polarize, according to the interpretation of their particular national interests, around these two powers. Leading the Central Powers in the Triple Alliance were Germany and Austria-Hungary; the Triple Entente represented the more solid alliance and included Britain, France, and Russia. Each camp engaged in an armaments race; incident after incident threatened to throw off a spark that would ignite the war.

Ultimately the match that lit the powder barrel came with the assassination of Archduke Ferdinand of Austria-Hungary in June 1914. The numerous alliances caused most of Europe to be drawn into the war that began when Austria-Hungary threatened to attack Serbia. As in the War of 1812, the *direct* ostensible cause of American entry in the war arose from efforts to uphold its rights at sea as a neutral nation.

AMERICA BEFORE ENTRY IN WORLD WAR I

With the outbreak of war in Europe Wilson proclaimed American neutrality and soon afterwards asked the nation to be neutral "in fact as well as in name." The government soon became involved in efforts to uphold America's rights at sea against the two sea powers, Britain and Germany, each of whom was seeking to destroy the other's foreign trade.

●● **Relations with Great Britain**—Britain immediately sought to enforce a blockade against Germany according to her own interpretation of international law. Wilson asked all nations to respect the rules drawn up with the Declaration of London (1909), which Britain had refused to sign. Britain instead enlarged the rights of a belligerent in certain practices offensive to the United States. 1) Britain enlarged the list of contraband of war to include foodstuffs and other goods not previously accepted as contraband. 2) Britain invoked the doctrine of continuous voyage to stop American goods being shipped to neutral countries bordering Germany. 3) Britain enforced her blockade against neutral shipping to Germany, not along the German coastline, but by inspecting ships all over the world. 4) Britain limited American commerce with Germany's neutral neighbors to what had existed before the war broke out—to prevent goods being transshipped to Germany. 5) Britain set up a blacklist of American firms trading with Germany.

Wilson sent notes of protest to the British for these violations of international law but did nothing to apply sanctions. Americans soon learned to live with the British regulations and government officials privately agreed that a British victory was in America's interest. Besides, America found a profitable market with the Allies for all it could produce.

●● **German War Operations and America**—Germany, lacking equality of surface naval craft with Britain, employed a new weapon, the submarine; it did so to enforce strangulation of the British Isles and to break the British blockade. In February 1915, Germany declared that all enemy ships in waters around the British Isles would be sunk on sight and warned neutral vessels to avoid these waters. Germany also warned citizens of neutral countries not to travel on Allied ships. The United States asserted that Germany must observe the rule of visit-and-search before sinking vessels; this rule made Germany's new weapon too vulnerable to destruction from armed merchantmen. Germany protested that it would abandon unrestricted submarine warfare if the United States would, among other demands, force the British to observe the Declaration of London.

●● **The Sinking of the *Lusitania***—The British ship *Lusitania* was sunk by a torpedo near Ireland in February 1915, with the loss of over 100 American lives. Wilson sent successive notes to Germany to persuade her to abandon unrestricted submarine warfare. Secretary of State Bryan resigned because he believed Wilson's policies would lead to war, and Robert Lansing replaced him. After the sinking of still another British ship, the *Arabic,* in August 1915, Wilson protested more strongly and Germany agreed to abandon such sinkings unless provisions were made to protect the lives of noncombatants.

●● **The Sussex Pledge**—When the French ship *Sussex* was sunk in March 1916, with the loss of two American lives, Wilson sent an ultimatum to

Germany demanding safety for the lives of passengers. In May, to avoid war, Germany made the Sussex Pledge not to sink merchant ships without saving lives of those aboard.

○ **Public Reaction to the War**—Public opinion was divided in sympathy for the belligerents. Since there was no likelihood of America restraining the British, German Americans hoped for neutrality and peace. Antimilitarists and peace societies organized to oppose American involvement.

Other organizations and individuals, like Theodore Roosevelt and General Leonard Wood, campaigned for military preparedness. Wilson after a time abandoned his opposition to strong preparedness and in 1916 asked Congress to pass several defense measures.

Defense Legislation (1916)—Congress now 1) passed the National Defense Act to increase the size of the army and bring the state militia under the federal government. 2) In August Congress appropriated money for the construction of battleships and other naval fighting vessels. 3) In September the United States Shipping Board was created and received money to buy and build merchant vessels to be operated under its own management. 4) A Council of National Defense was created by Wilson to make plans to mobilize the material resources of the nation in case of war.

In 1916 Wilson sent Colonel House to Europe as his personal agent to propose terms for peace. England, France, and Germany showed no willingness to negotiate a peace.

○○ **The Election of 1916**—The possibility of America's entry in the war in Europe made this the leading issue in the election. The Democrats renominated Wilson and endorsed his domestic reform legislation. The Democratic slogan "He kept us out of war" gave an implied promise that neutrality would be maintained.

The Republicans nominated the Supreme Court Justice Charles Evans Hughes and the Progressives renominated Theodore Roosevelt. Roosevelt refused the nomination and asked his supporters to rejoin the Republican Party, but they supported Wilson as the more progressive. Hughes avoided the war issue, since the Republicans were divided between pacifists and interventionists.

Wilson won by a narrow margin in both the popular vote and electoral college. The outcome hinged on the vote in California which, to everyone's surprise, swung over to Wilson the day after the election. Hughes lost in California because he failed to seek the support of the Progressive Hiram Johnson while campaigning there. Wilson won the states of the South and West.

○ **Wilson's Peace Proposals**—After the election Wilson asked the belligerents to state the terms by which they would conclude the war. Again the terms of both sides were irreconcilable. Wilson stated his own conditions for a just "peace without victory"; these terms foreshadowed the first provisions of the Fourteen Points but nothing came of this effort.

✪✪✪ Immediate Causes of American Entry in the War—1) Germany's unrestricted submarine warfare was the most important immediate cause and, superficially, was the main cause of American entry in the war. In January 1917, Germany announced resumption of a sink-on-sight submarine campaign against all ships around the British Isles. Wilson immediately broke diplomatic relations with Germany upon this abandonment of the Sussex Pledge. When he asked Congress for authority to arm merchant vessels, a long filibuster in the Senate under Robert M. La Follette defeated his request. Wilson used instead a statute dating to the War of 1812 to arm merchant ships. After eight American ships had been sunk, Wilson, on April 2, called a special session of Congress and asked for a declaration of war. The war resolution was passed on April 6.

2) The Zimmermann note, intercepted by the British and released by the State Department on March 1, influenced public opinion against Germany. This message from Germany to Mexico promised Mexico the return of Texas, New Mexico, and Arizona if Mexico would enter the war against the United States and invite Japan to do the same.

3) The Russian Revolution, which resulted in the overthrow of the Tsarist autocracy in March 1917, made it easier for the United States to join the Allies in the cause of democracy. Now the administration would not have to apologize for its alignment with the Russian autocracy.

✪✪✪ Background Causes of American Entry—The events immediately preceding the declaration of war do not fully explain America's taking up the Allied cause. 1) Basically the English background of the influential majority of the American people caused them to identify themselves with the British cause. This background included language, literature, law, and other aspects of a common culture.

2) American credits with Britain from the sale of munitions and other supplies were stressed at one time as a cause of pro-British sentiment. It was said that the repayment of the obligations gave influential financial interests a heavy stake in a British victory. This factor is probably greatly exaggerated since these same interests stood to lose profits and pay heavier taxes in case of war.

3) The British flood of sensational propaganda made a great psychological appeal as contrasted with the German's logical and legalistic presentation of their case. Furthermore, the British controlled the cables and other communications by which war news reached America; news had to be favorably slanted before newsmen could transmit it to America. British propaganda created stories of atrocities, especially in connection with the German invasion of Belgium in disregard of Belgium's neutrality.

4) Germany's manifest militarism in creating and boasting of her powerful armaments, as well as her entry in the world race for colonial

possessions, alarmed Americans. It was felt that German victory represented a threat to American interests and institutions.

THE UNITED STATES IN WORLD WAR I

Soon after declaring war the United States government learned of the
desperate situation of the Allies and of their large requirements for men,
ships, munitions, and foodstuffs. Speedy mobilization of material
resources was needed.

✪ **Mobilization for War**—1) The greatest and most pressing need was
manpower for the military services. In May 1917, Congress passed a
Selective Service Act that required all men of stipulated ages to register
for military service. The total armed forces of the United States, including both volunteers and draftees, reached about 4,000,000. Half of these
were shipped overseas and about a third saw active service there. 2)
The War Industries Board, headed by Bernard M. Baruch, was created
to control the manufacture of war matériel. 3) The War Shipping Board
was created to build the bridge of ships needed to transport men and
supplies and replace losses from submarine sinkings. A vast program of
ship construction got underway.

4) A Railroad Administration assumed government control of the railroads after they proved incapable of avoiding confusion in moving the
vast shipments of goods needed. 5) A Fuel Administration exerted its
efforts to conserve coal and oil and increase their production. Daylight
saving time was instituted to conserve electricity. 6) A Food Administration was created and placed under Herbert Hoover. Meat and wheat
were conserved for shipment overseas, and farmers were paid higher
prices to encourage production, which rose by a fourth.

✪ **Control of Public Opinion**—The administration showed much interest in winning public support for the war effort and suppressing dissension. Congress established immediately the Committee on Public Information under an able journalist, George Creel. This agency printed books,
wrote editorials, made motion pictures, published a daily *Official Bulletin,*
and spread striking posters. The war was "sold" as a holy crusade; it was
a "war to end war" and "a war to make the world safe for democracy."

Most Americans were loyal, but some Socialists regarded it as a "capitalistic" war. The tone of wartime propaganda aroused a hysteria
against all things German; Wilson accepted this unnecessary persecution
as a matter of course. Congress passed the Espionage Act (1917) and the
Sedition Act (1918) to prevent any possible obstruction of the war effort.

✪ **Financing the War**—One of the most important contributions to victory was made in the form of loans and supplies to the Allies. 1) More
money was raised by bond sales than by taxes. Liberty and Victory bonds

were sold in high-pressure campaigns; many poor were compelled to borrow money at prevailing high interest rates to buy bonds to prove their loyalty. 2) Tax money was raised by increasing rates in the individual and corporation income levies. A corporation excess profits tax was passed. Excise taxes increased in kind and in amount. The cost of the war amounted to about 35 billion dollars; almost 10 billion dollars went to the Allies as loans.

The Navy in the War—The navy under Admiral William S. Sims went to war first; for a time it was thought naval service would be our main contribution to the Allies, until the pressing need for men was revealed after war had been declared. The American navy performed four main services by 1) fighting submarines, 2) convoying troop ships, 3) laying a barrage of mines across the North Sea to bottle up German submarines, and 4) enforcing the blockade against Germany. The navy lost no ships in action; two were lost after the war was over in sweeping up the mine barrage in the North Sea.

✪✪ **The Army in the War**—General John J. Pershing was placed at the head of the American Expeditionary Force (AEF) sent to France. It was seven months after the declaration of war before the army saw action in battle. The Germans had hoped to win the war before the American "Doughboys" could go into action. The defeat of the Italians and the surrender of the Russians permitted Germany to rush more troops to the Western Front in France.

In May 1918, the Germans approached within 40 miles of Paris. At Pershing's determined insistence the American army assumed responsibility for the defense of a definite sector of the battle front instead of being absorbed into British and French units. At the Battle of Chateau-Thierry the Americans helped halt the advance. In June the Germans were driven out of Belleau Wood. The Second Battle of the Marne saw the beginning of German retreat. The St.-Mihiel and Meuse-Argonne offensives involved over 1,000,000 American troops. The Germans kept falling back from these attacks.

✪✪✪ **The Wilson Peace Offensive**—In January 1918, Wilson announced his Fourteen Points to Congress as a basis for a just peace in Europe. The first provisions called for 1) the abolition of secret diplomacy, 2) freedom of the seas for all, 3) freedom of trade among nations, 4) armament reduction, 5) the disposal of colonies of the defeated powers in the interest of the colonials, and 6) the League of Nations. Other provisions related to the national aspirations of particular nations and boundary adjustments.

The Germans were showered with printed circulars announcing the Fourteen Points as a basis of peace. The terms seemed so reasonable that the people, tired of war, rebelled, forced the German Kaiser to flee to Holland, and set up a parliamentary government. The Fourteen Points, in conjunction with Allied offensives, hastened German surrender. Marshal Ferdinand Foch, supreme commander of the Allied forces, negotiated the Armistice, and the war ended on November 11, 1918, before the Allied forces had been able to invade German territory. A total of 130,000 Americans died in the war, well over half being from disease. A wartime epidemic of influenza in 1918 took the lives of many civilians as well as causing a heavy death toll among military personnel.

THE DIFFICULTIES OF MAKING PEACE

Resentment against the losses and sacrifices of the war in both America and Europe made it difficult for President Wilson to realize the just and idealistic peace he desired.

✪✪✪ **Wilson's Frustrations in Peacemaking—1)** By electing Republican majorities in both houses of Congress, the American people repudiated the Wilson administration in the congressional elections in November 1918, even before the war was over. This was the first repudiation of a wartime administration in American history. The people were tired of the war and the sacrifices it required. In spite of this defeat at the polls, Wilson presumed to speak for the nation by going to the Peace Conference—at Versailles, France, in January 1919—without taking with him effective Republican advisers in close touch with their party, nor did he take with him any members of the Senate.

2) Wilson's promises in the Fourteen Points had been made in opposition to secret treaties committed to a division of the spoils of war among the Allies. Wilson hoped to overcome these commitments at the negotiations.

3) The British and French had chosen leaders pledged to vengeance upon the Germans who were held responsible for having caused the war. The Allies expected to dictate unusually harsh terms against the defeated powers. 4) The danger of the spread of Communism over Europe forced Wilson to accept compromises to restore peace quickly.

✪✪✪ **The Treaty of Versailles—**The Peace Conference was dominated by the Big Four: Wilson, David Lloyd George of England, Georges Clemenceau of France, and Vittorio Orlando of Italy. Wilson hoped to modify the harsh terms demanded by the Allies and secure acceptance of the Fourteen Points. Facing these diplomats, Wilson had to compromise many of the points he had hoped to write into the peace treaty.

The terms of the Treaty of Versailles 1) stripped Germany of all her colonies, and 2) forced Germany to surrender Alsace-Lorraine and other border areas to Poland, Belgium, and Denmark. 3) Germany was forced to accept the war-guilt clause. This clause required Germany to make full reparations for the cost and damage of the war. 4) Germany's assessment was to be determined later by the Reparations Commission. 5) Germany was to be completely disarmed and the Allies were committed to work toward disarmament among themselves. 6) Finally, Wilson induced the Allies to accept the League of Nations. The League, Wilson thought, would peacefully settle friction resulting from injustices in the treaty.

✪✪✪ **The League of Nations**—The terms of the Covenant provided for: 1) a Council of nine, made up of the five leading powers (the United States, France, Britain, Italy, and Japan) and four others elected by the Assembly. 2) An Assembly made up of delegates from all member nations; 3) a permanent Secretariat at Geneva to handle the routine business of the League.

The purposes of the League were: 1) to respect and preserve the territory and independence of its members; 2) to consider disputes likely to lead to war; 3) to apply military and economic sanctions against nations guilty of aggression; 4) to plan armament reduction; and 5) to establish a Permanent Court of International Justice.

✪✪✪ **American Opposition to the Treaty**—Members of the Republican majority in the Senate were determined to defeat the treaty. Their leader, Henry Cabot Lodge, intensely disliked Wilson personally; other members of the Senate objected to Wilson's failure to consult that body in drafting the terms of the treaty; some opposed the concessions made to the selfishness of the Allies, and many opposed American membership in the League of Nations. American minorities of various national origins opposed the treatment accorded their fatherlands. Many Americans suffered disillusionment from the initial idealism of the war and now felt that the United States ought to withdraw from the futile attempt to remake Europe. Others objected that the country would become involved in another European war. Republicans wished to capitalize the dissatisfaction for political advantage.

Two groups sought to defeat the treaty: the "Irreconcilables"—including Hiram Johnson, William E. Borah, and La Follette—wished to reject it completely; the reservationists under Lodge followed the strategy of modifying the treaty so much that Wilson himself would oppose it. This last group succeeded. Wilson was so dissatisfied with the reservations introduced into the treaty in the Senate that he advised his own followers to vote against it. He tried to take his battle to the nation but broke down from exhaustion and never fully recovered.

Peace was made with Germany by joint resolution passed under Harding in 1921. Later the United States negotiated separate peace treaties with Austria and Hungary which the Republican Senate ratified promptly in 1921.

CHAPTER BOOK LIST

Beuhrig, Edward, *Woodrow Wilson and the Balance of Power* (1955).

Blum, John M., *Woodrow Wilson and the Politics of Morality* (1956).

Cohen, Warren I., *The American Revisionists: The Lessons of Invention in World War I* (1967).

Garraty, J.A., *Henry Cabot Lodge: A Biography* (1953). Best biography of Lodge.

Hoover, Herbert, *Ordeal of Woodrow Wilson* (McGraw-Hill). Sympathetic account of Wilson's fight for the League of Nations.

Levin, N. Gordon, *Woodrow Wilson and World Politics: America's Response to War and Revolution* (Oxford).

Link, Arthur, *Wilson the Diplomatist* (1957).

Link, Arthur, Wilson, *The Struggle for Neutrality* (1960).

Luebke, Frederick C., *Bonds of Loyalty: German-Americans in World War I* (1974).

May, Ernest R., *The World War and American Isolationism* (1959).

Nye, Russel G., *Midwestern Progressive Politics, 1870–1958* (Michigan State University Press).

Peterson, H.C., and Fite, Gilbert, *Opponents of War 1917–1918* (University of Washington Press).

Snyder, L.J., *Historic Documents of World War I* (Anvil). Selections with brief introductions.

REVIEW QUESTIONS

MULTIPLE CHOICE

1. In World War I (1) the United States fought on the side of the Triple Entente (2) Italy fought on the side of Germany (3) the United States fought on the side of the Triple Alliance (4) Russia and Germany fought on the same side.

2. In World War I Britain did all *except* (1) enlarge the contraband list (2) enforce the doctrine of continuous voyage (3) abide by the Declaration of London (4) blacklist American firms trading with Germany.

3. In World War I Germany did all *except* (1) establish a war zone in waters surrounding the British Isles (2) permit citizens of neutral countries to travel on Allied ships (3) ask that the United States require Britain to observe the Declaration of London (4) practice sabotage in the United States.

4. Bryan resigned as Wilson's Secretary of State because (1) Wilson threatened to remove him (2) of popular criticism against him (3) he believed Wilson's policies would lead to war (4) he hoped to win the Democratic nomination in 1916.

5. In World War I public opinion (1) remained strictly neutral until Wilson asked for war (2) remained disinterested in the war until the sinking of the *Lusitania* (3) preponderantly favored the Allied nations (4) was evenly divided between the two opposing sides.

6. In the election of 1916 (1) the Republican candidate pledged war against Germany (2) Wilson won by a strong majority (3) the Democrats gave an implied promise to stay out of the war (4) Roosevelt ran on the Progressive ticket.

7. All were immediate causes of American entry in World War I *except* (1) the trouble with Mexico (2) the Zimmermann note (3) the Russian Revolution (4) Germany's sinking of American merchant vessels.

8. Which was probably the least influential in causing the United States to enter World War I? (1) The British background of a majority of Americans (2) British propaganda (3) popular fear of a German victory (4) British debts to the United States.

9. In the mobilization for World War I the United States government did all *except* (1) take the railroads under complete government control (2) preserve reasonable tolerance and freedom of speech (3) conserve fuel for the war effort (4) vigorously seek to propagandize the war effort.

10. During World War I the United States financed the war effort by every means *except* (1) issues of "printing press" money (2) sell bonds by high pressure campaigns (3) levy excess profits taxes on corporations (4) increase excise taxes.

11. During World War I the navy (1) lost no ships in battle (2) was required to make little effort (3) used aircraft carriers (4) was under the supreme command of Admiral Halsey.

12. The army in World War I (1) included a ranger unit under Theodore Roosevelt (2) saw little severe fighting (3) was under the command of General Leonard Wood (4) was under the command of General John J. Pershing.

13. Wilson's Fourteen Points included all *except* (1) the abolition of secret diplomacy (2) a League of Nations (3) freedom of the seas for all (4) freedom of religion and freedom from want.

14. In the elections of 1918 Wilson's party (1) won a strong victory (2) lost votes to the Socialists (3) suffered defeat (4) won a weak victory.

15. The Treaty of Versailles has been judged by many to have been an unjust peace for all *except* (1) it failed to carry out the Fourteen Points as promised (2) the amount of reparations assessed against Germany (3) the compromises made to satisfy the secret agreements of the European Allies (4) the independence of Poland.

16. American opposition to the Treaty of Versailles included all *except* (1) the "Irreconcilables" (2) Congressmen willing to compromise (3) Wilson and those loyal to him (4) the reservationists under Lodge.

17. Opposition to Wilson and the Treaty of Versailles developed because of all *but* which of the following? (1) Wilson was too friendly with Clemenceau and Lloyd George (2) the upsurge of isolationism (3) Wilson refused to make certain changes (4) Wilson failed to consult Republican congressional leaders.

TRUE-FALSE

18. Up to 1917 Britain showed a scrupulous regard for American shipping rights.

19. The Wilson administration did not defend American neutral rights in such a way as to interfere seriously with the British war effort.

20. To explain American entry in World War I in terms of German submarine warfare is probably superficial.

21. Preceding entry in World War I the greatest pacifist opposition to Wilson's policies came from Progressive senators in the West and Midwest.

22. The Wilson administration did its utmost to preserve freedom of speech and oppose intolerance in World War I.

23. World War I was financed partly by the issuance of paper money.

24. The defeat of Russia's Tsarist government in 1917 made it easier for the United States government to represent the war as a crusade for democracy.

25. In World War I German propaganda proved more influential in America than British propaganda.

26. General Pershing was successful in his insistence that Americans be given responsibility for a definite sector of the battle front.

27. The Fourteen Points helped to hasten German surrender.

28. Minorities in America sympathetic with the lands of their origin supported the Treaty of Versailles.

COMPLETION

29. World War I began in Europe after the assassination of _____ of _____ .

30. Germany's violations of international law involved the use of a new weapon, the _____ . The outstanding ship sinking was that of the _____ , a ship belonging to _____ .

31. Germany promised not to sink any more ships without saving passengers in the _____ Pledge.

32. The notable advocate of strong action against Germany was _____ .

33. The United States _____ was created to buy and build ships for the government.

34. The presidential election in 1916 pivoted on the vote in the state of _____ and _____ was defeated, undoubtedly because he failed to seek the support of the Progressive _____ .

35. In appealing to America's sense of fair play, British propaganda made the most of Germany's invasion of "little" _____ .

36. The wartime Food Administration was headed by _____ and the War Industries Board by _____ .

37. The American army sent to Europe in 1917 was called the _____ ; the soldiers were nicknamed _____ .

38. Wilson's basis for a just peace in Europe was stated in the _____ .

39. During World War I a great many civilians as well as soldiers died from _____ .

40. By the Treaty of Versailles, Germany was stripped of its _____ , forced to accept the _____ clause and required to pay full _____ for the cost of the war.

41. In the Senate the leader of Wilson's opponents fighting the Treaty of Versailles was _____ .

MATCHING

42. David Lloyd George   a. Bryan's successor as Secretary of State

43. Charles Evans Hughes   b. Head of the American Expeditionary Force

44. John J. Pershing   c. Wilson's closest personal adviser

45. Robert Lansing   d. Strong isolationist in World War I

46. Colonel House   e. British wartime leader

47. William S. Sims   f. Supreme commander of Allied forces

48. George Creel   g. Committee on Public Information

49. Ferdinand Foch   h. Admiral of the navy

50. Robert M. La Follette   i. Opposed Wilson for Presidency in 1916

51. Vittorio Orlando   j. Italian leader at Versailles

     k. Secretary of Treasury under Wilson

THE ERA OF CONSERVATIVE REPUBLICANS, 1921–1933

CHRONOLOGY / CHAPTER 16

1920   Election termed a "solemn referendum" on the League of Nations.

Overwhelming victory for Harding.

Esch-Cummins Act returned railroads to private owners.

Merchant Marine Act returned shipping to private enterprise.

1921   Harding inaugurated.

Washington Conference met to deal with naval disarmament and relations of Pacific powers.

1922   Fordney-McCumber Tariff revised rates upward.

1923   President Harding died. Coolidge (Rep.) succeeds to Presidency.

1924   Teapot Dome and other scandals revealed in years following Harding's death.

Adjusted Compensation Act gave "bonuses" to World War I veterans.

Coolidge elected to succeed himself. La Follette, nominee of Progressive Party, won over five million votes.

Dawes Plan provided economic relief for Germany.

1925   Scopes Trial in Tennessee.

1927   Better relations between U.S. and Mexico begin.

Kellog-Briand Pacts drawn up.

1928   Hoover (Rep.) elected President.

Geneva Naval Disarmament Conference failed.

McNary-Haugen Farm Bill vetoed by Coolidge.

Sacco and Vanzetti executed in Massachusetts.

1929   Hoover inaugurated as President.

Stock market crash.

1931   Hoover moratorium postponed payment of intergovernmental war debts.

1933   Payments on intergovernmental war debts ceased.

Chapter

16
HARDING AND COOLIDGE, 1921–1929

In the 1920s the United States, disillusioned by the war, reacted against the ideals of internationalism of the Wilson administration. In domestic affairs most of the Progressive reforms had already been achieved and the people lacked enthusiasm for further reforms in a period of considerable prosperity. The nation almost overwhelmingly endorsed the return to "normalcy" of the prewar days. Yet the Republicans in the decade of the twenties accepted a large degree of international cooperation rather than returning completely to isolationism.

THE HARDING ADMINISTRATION

Harding's administration suffered several parallels with the Grant administration: it followed a great war with the accompanying cynicism and moral relaxation, it suffered from several notorious cases of corruption, and it was characterized by a strong favoritism to the business community.

❂❂❂ **The Election of 1920**—This election showed the extent of the rejection of the idealism of Wilson. The leading Republican candidates General Leonard Wood and Governor Frank Lowden of Illinois blocked each other in the nominating convention. The deadlock was broken by the selection of Warren G. Harding, a dark horse candidate and United States Senator from Ohio. The New Englander, Calvin Coolidge, who had made a national reputation by overcoming the Boston police strike in 1920, was chosen as Harding's running mate.

The Democrats chose James M. Cox, Governor of Ohio, as the presidential nominee and Franklin D. Roosevelt, Assistant Secretary of the Navy under Wilson, as his running mate. Wilson spoke of the campaign as a "solemn referendum" on the Treaty of Versailles and the League of Nations.

The Republicans hedged on the issue of the League, and their confused campaign speakers appealed to the wishful thinking of both those who favored and those who opposed the League of Nations. The Democrats fully endorsed Wilson's record and clearly supported the League. The election returns gave Harding a resounding popular majority of nearly 7,000,000 popular votes and 404 electoral college votes to Cox's 127.

✪✪ Harding and His Cabinet—In his early career Warren G. Harding had been the editor of a small-town newspaper in Ohio. In 1914 he won election to the United States Senate and remained there until nominated for the Presidency. In many ways Harding was the direct opposite of Wilson. Harding was genial, friendly, nonintellectual, and satisfied with things as they were. He chose three cabinet members of great ability— Herbert Hoover, Secretary of Commerce; Charles Evans Hughes, Secretary of State; and Andrew W. Mellon, Secretary of the Treasury— but he chose two others who disgraced his administration—Albert B. Fall, Secretary of the Interior, and Harry M. Daugherty, Attorney-General. Lacking in critical judgment, Harding chose "friends" who betrayed the trust he placed in them.

✪ Demobilization of the Railroads—Even before Harding took office the Republican Congress in 1920 passed the Esch-Cummins Act to demobilize the railroads. This act 1) provided for the return of the railroads to their owners; 2) it gave the Interstate Commerce Commission authority to determine the fair value of railroad investment and fix rates to permit a fair return. 3) Combinations of railroad systems were encouraged in order to promote efficiency. 4) A Railway Labor Board was created to settle labor disputes.

The attitude of government to the railroads had necessarily changed. New forms of competition were taking customers away; they received competition from trucks, buses, and private automobiles. Henceforth, government policy would seek to assist the railroads by encouraging mergers and by recognition of their financial problems.

✪ The Merchant Marine—The Merchant Marine Act of 1920 brought a halt to wartime shipbuilding and authorized the Shipping Board to sell ships to private companies and to operate ships itself. The shipping problem was difficult to solve. The nation needed an adequate fleet of ships in case of war, but private enterprise could not compete successfully with foreign shipping that enjoyed lower wage scales. Yet, in principle, the Republicans abhorred government-run enterprises and direct subsidy.

In 1928 the Jones-White Act took a step toward answering the problem by providing an indirect subsidy of loans for shipbuilding and main contracts to ship operators. This act stimulated the modernization and enlargement of the American merchant marine.

Adjusted Compensation for Veterans—After World War I the American Legion arose to make itself the spokesman for war veterans. Congress responded to their plea for additional compensation for wartime sacrifices veterans had made when others stayed home to earn high wages and profits. The Adjusted Compensation Act of 1924 gave a "bonus" to each veteran in the form of a 20-year endowment policy; the value of the policy was determined by the length and nature of service. Veterans could borrow against these policies at a moderate interest rate. The next main goal of the veterans' lobby was the redemption of these policies in cash.

✪✪✪ **The Washington Conference, 1921–1922**—The Harding administration soon showed its opposition to the League of Nations. In an effort to make a response to the demand for world peace, Harding endorsed the happy decision of Secretary of State Hughes to do something positive in international relations. Also in the background of the Washington Conference was the threat of Japanese aggression in the Pacific and of a naval armaments race.

In 1915 Japan had attempted to place China under complete domination; Japan took advantage of the European powers' preoccupation with war to present oppressive Twenty-one Demands. The Lansing-Ishii Agreement (1917) resulted from the effort of the United States to commit Japan to an affirmation of the Open Door and of Chinese territorial integrity; in the treaty Japan reaffirmed both. The United States, however, did recognize that Japan had special interests in China.

✪✪✪ **The Washington Conference Treaties**—Three treaties were negotiated at the conference.

The Treaty of Naval Limitations, or Five-Power Treaty (1921),   1) agreed to fix a ratio of naval strength among the five naval powers. The ratio of 5-5-3-1.7-1.7 was adopted to fix the relative tonnage of capital warships. For each five tons of capital warships maintained by the United States and Britain, Japan could keep three tons and France and Italy 1.7 tons each.   2) The powers agreed to a ten-year holiday in the construction of new ships. In the United States some tonnage had to be scrapped to conform to the ratio. The agreement was one of noteworthy success toward naval disarmament. The treaty was renewed in 1930 but abrogated by Japan in 1936 when the naval armaments race was resumed.

In the Four-Power Pact (1921) between the United States, Britain, France, and Japan the signatory nations agreed to respect each other's possessions in the Pacific area and to confer in case of threats from other powers.

In the Nine-Power Pact (1922) interested nations agreed to maintain the Open Door in China and in general to respect the interests of China. This was a rebuff to Japan and it soon violated the agreement.

✪✪ **The Harding Scandals**—The most notorious case of corruption under Harding was the Teapot Dome scandal. The case originated with oil reserves on public lands at Teapot Dome in Wyoming and Elk Hills in California. Secretary of the Navy Denby was induced to transfer these naval oil reserves to the Department of the Interior under Albert B. Fall. Fall in turn leased them to private oil companies. Fall received at least two "loans" from oilmen Doheny and Sinclair totaling $125,000. Fall resigned from the cabinet and was convicted of bribery later; the leases were canceled.

In the Veterans' Bureau, the forerunner of the Veterans Administration, the Director, Charles R. Forbes, was sentenced to Leavenworth federal prison for graft in connection with the purchase and sale of hospital supplies. His graft cost the government $200,000,000. The Alien Property Custodian was convicted of criminal conspiracy to defraud the government; he had sold German chemical patents, confiscated during the war, at giveaway prices. In still another high level case, Attorney-General Daugherty was dismissed from office for selling liquor permits and pardons and for other dishonest practices.

Harding's Death—Harding's death came suddenly in 1923 after he returned from a trip to Alaska. His death was possibly due indirectly, whatever the immediate cause, to the shock of the revelations of large-scale corruption by those he had carelessly trusted. Vice President Coolidge succeeded to the Presidency.

THE COOLIDGE ADMINISTRATION

Calvin Coolidge had risen in politics as a conservative and honest office holder. He was nicknamed "Silent Cal" for his quiet personality; businessmen liked the do-nothing policies of this mediocre President and the people saw no need for dynamic leadership. He praised the business world and preached and practiced economy in domestic life and in government. He did not obstruct revelation of the Harding scandals or the prosecution of the wrongdoers.

○○ **The Election of 1924**—The appeal of Coolidge's negative policies in a time when most of the country enjoyed prosperity won the Vermonter the nomination of his party. The Democratic Party suffered badly from a deadlock at their convention. On one side were the rural, Southern, farmer, pro-Ku Klux Klan elements; on the other were the urban, Northern, labor, anti-Klan elements. The deadlock was finally broken with the nomination of a conservative New York lawyer from Wall Street named John W. Davis.

With both major parties having conservative candidates, the Progressive Party gained much support from the disgruntled farmers and liberals. They were combined with the Socialists in this campaign. The Progressives adopted a platform calling for government ownership of waterpower and the railroads, for farm relief, pro-labor laws, and other progressive measures; Robert M. La Follette became their Presidential candidate.

Coolidge won in a landslide with almost twice the popular vote of Davis. But La Follette won almost 5,000,000 votes.

✪✪✪ **Republican Business and Labor Policies**—The pro-business attitude of the Harding-Coolidge years manifested itself in a number of legislative measures, in administrative policy, and in the courts.

In general these administrations sought to return to a laissez-faire policy by getting the government out of businesses where it had operated during the war. The controls of regulatory agencies were relaxed. Appointments to regulatory agencies, such as the Interstate Commerce Commission, represented the business interests that were supposed to be under regulation. The government got rid of its ships under giveaway terms and established subsidies for their private operators. The Secretary of the Treasury, Andrew Mellon, repeatedly secured tax reductions from Congress—reductions that benefited the largest taxpayers, both individuals and corporations. The large sums left in their hands helped release money that went into the stock market boom of this decade.

The Fordney-McCumber Tariff Act (1922) increased duties in line with traditional Republican protectionism. Mergers were permitted among corporations in spite of the antitrust statutes. The courts rendered decisions unfavorable to organized labor; the labor movement declined. The government refused to complete and operate the Muscle Shoals Project on the Tennessee River. It did not favor government production of cheap electricity or fertilizer for farmers as Senator George W. Norris desired. Nothing was done to relieve the distress of farmers, and low farm prices gave industry cheap raw materials and food for their workers.

✪✪ **International Debts**—Two kinds of intergovernmental obligations inherited from the war remained to plague relations between the former Allies. These were the reparations assessed against Germany under the war-guilt clause of the dictated peace of Versailles and the debts owed the United States by its wartime Allies. While Americans thought the Allies should gratefully repay these debts without hesitation, the Allies hoped the United States would reduce or cancel them in consideration of the heavy losses Europe had suffered as compared with those of the United States in the war. Furthermore, they insisted on making their payments contingent upon Germany's payments of reparations to them.

In 1924 the Dawes Plan and in 1929 the Young Plan scaled down the principal amounts owed and also arranged for the United States to lend money to Germany to promote its economic recovery. The United States during the twenties negotiated treaties with our debtors to reduce interest charges and extend the time for repayment.

When the Great Depression struck, the nations were unable to meet their obligations. President Hoover, to prevent a financial crisis, declared a one-year moratorium on the debt payments in 1931. The payments were not continued after 1933 except by Finland. The Finns owed a much smaller debt and enjoyed a better market for exports to America.

Competent economists, including Lord Keynes, recommended soon after the war that the debts could not be repaid and should be canceled to permit European economic recovery, which was dependent upon Germany, and to prevent irritation among the nations involved. The debts had been incurred by the purchase of goods and could only be repaid in the same way, but American tariffs prevented the sale of European goods in American markets.

○ **Foreign Relations in the Caribbean and Mexico**—In the Caribbean area American troops were gradually withdrawn—from Santo Domingo in 1922 and Nicaragua in 1925.

In Mexico the nationalization of foreign-owned, including American, oil and mineral properties threatened the loss of large investments and war with Mexico. In 1927 a turn in relations came when Dwight L. Morrow was appointed as Ambassador to Mexico. Charles A. Lindbergh, a national hero after his solo flight from New York to Paris, visited Mexico City in the same year. These were the beginning of a renewal of friendly relations.

○ **Peace and Disarmament**—An attempt by France and the United States to outlaw war resulted in the Kellogg-Briand Pact (Pact of Paris) in 1927. The French Premier Aristide Briand suggested the pact to Secretary of State Frank B. Kellogg under Coolidge. Sixty-two nations eventually signed this agreement that renounced war in favor of peaceful means for the settlement of disputes. It proved to be ineffective since there was no machinery for its enforcement.

The United States took part in the World Court when three famous American jurists served upon the tribunal, but never became a member due to Senate reservations. In 1945 the United States joined the International Court of Justice as a part of the United Nations.

Naval disarmament begun by the Treaty of Naval Limitations (1921) was taken up again in the Geneva Conference in 1927 in an effort to prevent competitive construction of cruisers, destroyers, and submarines. France and Italy refused to participate and nothing was accomplished.

The London Conference met in 1930 under President Hoover's invitation. It sought to apply the ratio of the Five-Power Treaty to smaller ships. It, too, failed since France and Italy refused to ratify it.

CHAPTER BOOK LIST

Allen, Frederick L., *Only Yesterday* (Bantam). Exceptionally readable and popular social history of the 1920s.

Bailey, Thomas A., *Wilson and the Peacemakers* (Macmillan).

Hicks, John D., *Republican Ascendancy, 1921–1933* (1960).

Kennan, George, *American Diplomacy 1900–1950* (Mentor).

La Follette, R.M., *La Follette's Autobiography: A Personal Narrative of Political Experiences* (Wisconsin).

Link, Arthur S., *Wilson the Diplomatist* (Johns Hopkins).

Murray, Robert K., *Red Scare* (McGraw-Hill).

Russell, Francis, *The Shadow of Blooming Grove: Warren G. Harding* (1968).

Schriftgiesser, Karl, *This Was Normalcy* (1948). On politics; very critical of the times.

Smith, Gene, *The Shattered Dream: Herbert Hoover and the Great Depression* (1970).

Wilson, Jean Hoff, *Herbert Hoover: Forgotten Progressive* (1975).

Wilson, Jean Hoff, *The Twenties: The Critical Issues* (1972).

REVIEW QUESTIONS

MULTIPLE CHOICE

1. In the presidential campaign of 1920 what was the position of Harding and Cox in regard to the League of Nations? (1) Both favored it (2) Both opposed it (3) Harding's position was ambiguous but Cox favored it (4) Cox's position was ambiguous but Harding favored it.

2. The presidential election of 1920 showed that (1) the Democratic Party had abandoned Wilson's idealism (2) almost any Republican could have won (3) the United States was ready for a strong-minded president (4) the American people favored the League of Nations.

3. The election of 1920 resulted in (1) a Democratic Congress with a Republican president (2) a Democratic House with a Republican Senate (3) control of Congress and the presidency by the Republican Party (4) control of Congress and the presidency by the Democrats.

4. Legislation affecting the merchant marine in 1920 (1) fixed the pay of American seamen at the level maintained by foreign operators (2) kept the federal government from owning and operating merchant ships (3) provided subsidies for American shipping interests (4) avoided hidden subsidies by the use of mail contracts.

5. The Esch-Cummins Act of 1920 provided that (1) labor unions in the railroad industry should determine leading policies of operation (2) railroads might merge, contrary to previous laws (3) efficient and inefficient railroads could not be merged (4) decreased government control over railroad rates.

6. The Treaty of Naval Limitations of 1921 gave Japan a ratio of ships that was (1) equal to that of the United States (2) three fifths that of the United States (3) 1.7 to 5 of American tonnage (4) equal to that of France.

7. The most publicized of the Harding scandals was the (1) Teapot Dome (2) corruption in Veterans Bureau (3) fraud by the Alien Property Custodian (4) sale of liquor permits by Daugherty.

8. Coolidge won the Presidency in 1924 (1) because the nation was satisfied with a rather passive federal administration (2) because La Follette split the Democratic Party   (3) in the House of Representatives (4) but was defeated for reelection.

9. During the 1920s the labor movement (1) met unusual success (2) declined in effectiveness   (3) was dominated by the IWW (4) was promoted by favorable state legislation.

10. Economic experts believe that international war debts of World War I (1) should have been collected in full (2) should have been largely canceled by the United States (3) could have been paid (4) would cement closer ties between the Allies.

11. The Kellogg-Briand Pact was signed during the Presidency of (1) Hoover (2) Harding (3) Coolidge (4) Roosevelt.

TRUE-FALSE

12. In many ways Harding represented a strong contrast to the things Wilson stood for.

13. By 1920 the railroads had reached a point where they needed the sympathetic concern of government.

14. Under Harding the veterans of the recent war were voted cash bonuses by Congress.

15. The Washington Conference dealt mainly with problems in the Pacific and in Asia.

16. The United States supported the Open Door in China by both the Lansing-Ishii Agreement and by the Nine-Power Treaty.

17. During the 1920s the American people were more eager than ever to assert American leadership in foreign affairs and to continue reform in domestic affairs.

18. The Democratic Party suffered much internal dissension, mainly over the civil rights issue in its convention in 1924.

19. In many ways the pro-business sympathies of the Republican Party manifested itself during the 1920s.

COMPLETION

20. Harding died in the year _____ after a trip to _____ .

21. The Secretary of the Navy _____ played a role in the scandals over the oil reserves at Teapot Dome and _____ .

22. The great powers interested in Pacific territories agreed in the _____ Pact to respect each other's possessions.

23. Wilson spoke of the campaign of 1920 as a _____ on the Treaty of Versailles and the League.

24. The _____ project advanced by Senator Norris for the production of cheap fertilizer for farmers was never supported by the Republican presidents in the 1920s.

25. The United States sought to solve the war debts problem in 1924 by the _____ Plan and in 1929 by the _____ Plan.

26. A turn in relations with Mexico came in 1927 when _____ was appointed Ambassador.

MATCHING

27. Clarence Darrow
28. James M. Cox
29. Leonard Wood
30. John T. Scopes
31. Calvin Coolidge
32. Charles Evans Hughes
33. Albert B. Fall
34. Robert M. La Follette
35. Andrew W. Mellon
36. Frank B. Kellogg

a. Convicted Secretary of the Interior

b. Violated Tennessee anti-evolution law

c. Called the Washington Conference in 1921

d. Progressive nominee in 1924

e. Defense attorney in anti-evolution trial

f. Defeated by Harding for Republican nomination

g. Conservative Secretary of the Treasury

h. Defeated Davis in 1924

i. Democratic presidential nominee in 1920

j. Came from New England

k. Coolidge's Secretary of State

l. Secretary of Agriculture

CHRONOLOGY / CHAPTER 17

1900   Automobile manufacture increases rapidly after 1900.

1903   Wright brothers flew their heavier-than-air machine at Kitty Hawk.

1919   Alien radicals deported to Russia.

1920s Decade of revolt in manners and morals.
           Decade of general prosperity.

1921   Brief postwar depression.

1923   Intermediate Credit Act extended further credits to farmers.

1924   Immigration Act of 1924 permanently limited immigration by application of quota system.

1925   Ku Klux Klan began to subside rapidly.
           Scopes Trial for violation of Tennessee anti-evolution law.

1926   Radio came into popular use.

1927   Lindbergh made solo flight across Atlantic.

1928   Sound films introduced.

1929   Stock market crash.

1933   Prohibition Amendment repealed by Twenty-first Amendment.

Chapter

17
ECONOMIC AND SOCIAL
DEVELOPMENTS OF
THE 1920s, 1921–1933

In economic and political matters the twenties were years of reaction and conservatism. But in manners, customs, morals, and literature it was a time of revolt.

ECONOMIC DEVELOPMENTS

During the twenties the United States enjoyed unusual prosperity, except for the farmer. New industries added to the prosperity and almost everybody enjoyed an increase in the standard of living.

● **The Depression of 1921**—A short primary postwar depression began in 1921 as a part of the readjustment to a peacetime economy. It occurred, more specifically, due to the cessation of wartime loans to Europe and Europe's inability to buy from the United States. Europe's agricultural recovery lessened the demand for America's war-stimulated agricultural abundance. American consumers went on a buyers' strike against prices driven too high by speculative hoarding. High American tariffs discouraged foreign trade. Agricultural prices and consumer goods fell sharply in price. A slow, steady recovery set in during 1922, and by 1924 the prosperous twenties began for most groups in the economy.

●● **Urban Prosperity and New Industries**—During the decade of the twenties the American standard of living improved more rapidly than ever before. A small core of unemployment remained, and some industries, such as textiles and coal mining, suffered chronic depression, but most urban dwellers and many farmers lived much better than ever before. People had more leisure time to enjoy popular spectator sports and engage in outdoor recreation.

The automobile, radio, and motion pictures became available to nearly everyone. "Talking pictures" had become common in 1928. Mass production made the new gadgets and entertainment available, and the mass entertainment, with the national advertising that supported the radio, brought a greater uniformity in manners and customs. Installment buying increased the market for consumer goods by enabling families to buy certain items on credit. Mass merchandising in groceries at "chain stores" and in miscellaneous goods at variety store chains brought lower prices to consumers.

○○ **The Automobile**—After the combustion engine had been harnessed to the horseless carriage about 1900, this new rubber-tired "automobile" caught on rapidly. It was Henry Ford who visualized the low-cost production of an automobile that almost everyone could afford. In 1908 he developed the "Model T" and in a few years had already developed a market for several hundred cars per day. Soon after the war it seemed that almost every family had managed to buy a car. Most early automobile makers were forced out by the few large and efficient firms that came to dominate the market.

The automotive revolution in transportation, like the coming of the railroad, had vast repercussions on the total economic life of the nation. Allied industries sprang up. Highway construction and improved roads became necessary. The petroleum industry multiplied its output as gasoline became its leading product. The pattern of town growth began to stretch towns out along the roads. Filling stations and garages became an all too familiar part of the American scene. The rubber and steel industries benefited enormously. About one in every seven persons came to depend directly upon the automobile for his livelihood. Touring became a popular sport; the farmer became less isolated from life in the towns.

Aviation—This new industry of the twenties had its beginning about 1903 when Orville and Wilbur Wright flew their heavier-than-air machine briefly at Kitty Hawk, North Carolina. World War I stimulated the industry when several thousand planes were produced for the military service.

In 1926 the Air Commerce Act and in 1927 the solo flight of Lindbergh gave an impetus to commercial aviation, and in a few years commercial aviation became established.

○○ **The Farm Problem**—Millions of acres of land were plowed up during World War I to produce food and fiber to win the war. Government subsidies and exhortation encouraged this expansion.

After the war European agriculture recovered and needed fewer imports of goods. Increased production for export by foreign agriculturists helped produce a surplus in world markets. In the United States consumers changed their diet and ate less wheat and meat. The use of machines and the substitution of gasoline-powered tractors for draft animals both increased the production and released tens of millions of acres from the production of feedstuffs for draft animals. This increased the production of crops for the market. The surplus crops kept average prices low. Many farmers had bought land in the prosperous war years at high prices and later found interest payments extremely burdensome. Many were foreclosed and tenancy increased.

⚭ **The Farm Bloc**—Members of Congress in both parties from the farm states combined to seek government relief for the farmer. The Intermediate Credit Act (1923) extended intermediate term credit to farmers. The McNary-Haugen Bill passed Congress in 1927 but President Coolidge vetoed it; 1928 he vetoed it again. These bills called for devices to subsidize the export of surpluses of farm produce.

SOCIAL DEVELOPMENTS

Rapid social changes in the 1920s brought greater freedom in morals and sharp changes from the earlier Victorian customs. The Nineteenth Amendment, ratified in 1920, gave women the right to vote. The broad-mindedness of the twenties in social customs was offset by a narrow provincialism with respect to foreign influences. The wartime spirit of sacrifice and idealism had resulted in the ratification of the Prohibition Amendment to the Constitution. The problems of enforcing it and strong minority opposition kept the issue alive in politics.

⚭ **Prohibition**—The century-old movement for the prohibition of the sale and consumption of alcoholic, intoxicating beverages realized its goal of nationwide prohibition in 1919 in the Eighteenth Amendment and the Volstead Act.

The long campaign of opposition to alcoholic beverages was based upon various claims that intoxicants 1) caused crime and lawlessness, 2) were injurious to health, 3) caused poverty and increased the tax burden, 4) were a waste of national resources and reduced the efficiency of workers, and 5) created great hazards to life and property in a mechanized society.

The rural and Protestant communities, especially in the South, supported prohibition while the cities and the more recent immigrants opposed it. In the political contests in the 1920s prohibition remained one of the main issues and one that the average voter felt most strongly about. Candidates were classified as either "wet" or "dry." The Democratic Party, except in the rural South, included more "wets" than the Republican Party.

During the twenties, people became progressively more dissatisfied with the operation of prohibition. 1) Many objected to and defied the law as an unjustified interference in personal morals. 2) Speakeasies and other hidden establishments catered to the drinking public. 3) Gangsterism, bootlegging, political corruption, and other evils flourished on the illegal liquor traffic. 4) Prohibition seemed to be creating a disrespect for the law. 5) Absence of regulation caused the sale of poisonous liquor with consequent blindness, permanent injury, and death. 6) When the depression struck, it was argued that repeal would help bring an end to the hard times and produce tax revenues on liquor sales.

In the 1932 campaign the Democrats promised repeal. Following their victory, Congress submitted a repeal amendment to the states. They rushed to ratify the Twenty-first Amendment by special state conventions. This was the first amendment to be so ratified. Repeal returned the control of the liquor traffic to the states where various solutions were worked out for its regulation.

○ **Intolerance of the 1920s**—The Communist Revolution in Russia in 1917 and agitation elsewhere convinced Americans that the Reds were a serious threat to the United States. Two explosions contributed to the "Big Red Scare" of 1919–1920: a bomb exploded at the home of Attorney-General Palmer in 1919 and in 1920 a blast in Wall Street killed 38 persons. In December 1919, 249 alien radicals were deported to Russia on a special ship. Reactionaries seized upon the red scare to condemn Socialists and labor leaders. The wave of anti-foreignism probably prejudiced a judge and jury who gave the death penalty to Sacco and Vanzetti, alien Italian anarchists, on very weak evidence.

The Ku Klux Klan—The revived Klan grew rapidly and became active over the whole country in the early 1920s. It attacked minorities and non-conformists who deviated from the pattern of 100 percent Americanism as determined by the prejudices of the Klansmen. The movement subsided, about 1925, after people became aware of its abuses and its national leaders were found guilty of misappropriating funds or using the organization to make money for themselves.

○○ **The Immigration Act of 1924**—In 1917, Congress over President Wilson's veto, passed a literacy test requirement to restrict immigration. A flood of immigrants started coming in after the war. Congress passed the Emergency Immigration Act in 1921 as a stopgap until a permanent well-considered law could be written. The Immigration Act of 1924 1) limited immigration to an annual quota for each country of two percent of Americans of that national origin residing in the United States in 1890. 2) An overall limit of 150,000 immigrants per year was fixed.

The law gave further offense to the Japanese by excluding them and other nationalities from the Far East. The "national origins" system was later modified by adoption of the census of 1920, but it still favored immigrants of northern Europe. There were no quota restrictions on immigration from other nations of the Americas, but the wide latitude of administrative discretion permitted restriction by property requirements and by other means of selection.

○○○ **Life in the Twenties**—The war experience, for whatever the reason, brought an end to Victorianism in American manners and morals during the "Roaring Twenties." A time of disillusionment, materialism, and prosperity, everyone seemed bent upon having a good time in this "Jazz Age." Women defied the older conventions; they started wearing dresses that grew progressively shorter during the decade; they bobbed their hair, wore lipstick and rouge, smoked in public, and adopted some of the manners of men. The automobile worked a profound effect upon the living habits of people and upon the manners and morals of youth. The popularization of Freud brought on a frank interest in and exploitation of sex. A new generation of writers, employing a realistic style, addressed themselves to the issue of sex as well as to the social problems of the day. Educational enrollments in high schools and colleges vastly increased; John Dewey introduced his revolutionary ideas into the public schools.

✪ The Scopes Trial—The struggle between religious fundamentalists and modern science came to a climax in the famous "Monkey Trial" at Dayton, Tennessee. In the summer of 1925 a young high school teacher of science, John T. Scopes, was brought to trial for violation of the Tennessee anti-evolution law. The noted skeptic, Clarence Darrow, as defender of Scopes, found himself opposing the famous fundamentalist, William Jennings Bryan, who strove to defend the literal interpretation of the Bible. Technically, Scopes was found guilty in the sensational case and was fined, but the cause of the fundamentalists suffered such embarrassment and ridicule at the hands of the defense and by national commentators that no such effort has since been made to defy the teachings of modern science.

CHAPTER BOOK LIST

Asbury, Herbert, *The Great Illusion: An Informal History of Prohibition* (1950).

Burlingame, Roger, *Henry Ford* (New American Library). Brief biography by a historian of American business.

Cargill, Oscar, *Intellectual America* (1941). Literature and thought of the 1920s.

Commager, H.S., ed., *America in Perspective* (New American Library).

Grebstein, S.N., *Monkey Trial* (Houghton Mifflin).

Handlin, Oscar, *American People in the Twentieth Century* (Beacon).

Hicks, John D., and Saloutos, Theodore, *Twentieth Century Populism* (1964).

Kirschner, Don S., *City and Country: Rural Responses* (1970).

Leuchtenberg, W.E., *Perils of Prosperity: 1914–1932* (University of Chicago). Survey history of the period.

Murray, R.K., *Red Scare: A Study in National Hysteria, 1919–1920* (1955).

Stone, Irving, *Carence Darrow for the Defense* (Bantam). Abridged; life of the great criminal lawyer who defended Scopes at Dayton, Tennessee.

Weeks, R.P., *Commonwealth vs. Sacco and Vanzetti* (Prentice Hall). A book of primary source materials.

REVIEW QUESTIONS

MULTIPLE CHOICE

1. The main cause of the depression of 1921 was (1) monetary policies (2) a decline in American exports to Europe (3) war scares (4) greater use of machinery in industry.

2. The prosperity of the twenties was due to all of the following *except* (1) installment buying (2) mass merchandising (3) mass production (4) higher prices for agricultural staples.

3. The automobile in the twenties had the same far-reaching effects upon the nation that might best be compared with the influence the (1) railroads exerted during the seventies and eighties (2) canals had in the 1830s (3) airplanes had in the 1930s (4) steamboats had in the 1820s.

4. Prohibition of alcoholic beverages was most strongly supported by (1) the South (2) the foreign element in the cities (3) the Democrats (4) the working class in the cities.

5. Immediately after World War I all of the following occurred *except* (1) a renewed interest in international cooperation (2) speculation in land (3) impatience with alien radicals (4) a large number of strikes.

6. The main opposition to the Ku Klux Klan arose because (1) its membership resorted to violence to enforce extralegally its own moral and political concepts (2) it was fundamentally an anti-Jewish society (3) politicians abhorred it as an intolerant movement (4) it enforced strict morals during the wild twenties.

7. Which is *untrue* of the Immigration Act of 1924? (1) It established a quota system (2) it excluded legally all Japanese immigration (3) it favored immigration from Northern Europe (4) it did not greatly curtail European immigration.

8. Which was *not* a new mass industry of the twenties? (1) Civilian air transportation (2) radio (3) movies (4) chain stores.

COMPLETION

9. The manufacturer of the low-cost automobile that almost everyone could afford was _____ .

10. Famous for his solo flight in 1924 was _____ .

11. The term _____ designates a combination in support of agricultural legislation of both Republicans and Democrats beginning in the 1920s.

12. The leading farm relief measure vetoed by Coolidge was known as the _____ Bill.

13. The major party having the most opponents of Prohibition was the _____ Party; Prohibition was repealed by the _____ Amendment in the year _____ .

14. The most notorious case of intolerance in the 1920s was the case of two Italian anarchists named _____ and _____ .

15. The prosecution in the Scopes Trial was headed by _____ .

16. The first successful airplane flight was made by the _____ brothers.

CHRONOLOGY / CHAPTER 18

1928   Hoover (Rep.) elected President. Alfred E. Smith (Dem.) lost states in the Solid South.

1929   Hoover inaugurated President at time of apparent permanent prosperity.

Agricultural Marketing Act created Federal Farm Board.

September–October, stock market panic, immediately followed by severe depression in winter of 1929–1930.

1930   Hawley-Smoot Tariff raised rates to highest level ever reached in United States.

1931   Moratorium declared by Hoover on payment of intergovernmental war debts.

1932   Franklin D. Roosevelt (Dem.) elected President, main issue was the depression.

Home Loan Bank Act passed to save homes from foreclosure.

Reconstruction Finance Corporation created.

Bonus Army routed from Washington.

Norris-LaGuardia Act forbade use of injunctions in labor disputes.

1933   February–March, Great Depression hit bottom, partly caused by uncertainty in transition of the presidency.

Roosevelt inaugurated as President.

Twentieth ("Lame Duck") Amendment and Twenty-first (Prohibition repeal) Amendment ratified.

Chapter

18

HOOVER AND THE GREAT DEPRESSION, 1928–1933

> Hoover suffered the misfortune of falling heir to the Great Depression that resulted from accumulated maladjustments and evils in the American economy during the terms of his predecessors. During most of his term in office Hoover dealt in a limited and tardy way with the resulting economic anguish.

❂❂ **The Election of 1928**—Coolidge could have had the Republican nomination for a third term but he refused, in answer to questions of newsmen, with this simple statement, "I do not choose to run." The brilliant engineer Herbert Hoover, who served as Coolidge's businessmen's Secretary of Commerce, was quickly chosen by the nominating convention. The Democrats chose the honest and sincere Alfred E. Smith, the forceful and popular governor of New York.

Smith conducted an energetic campaign and denounced both prohibition and the favoritism of the Republicans to industrialists. Hoover straddled the prohibition issue by referring to prohibition as "the noble experiment."

Again the Republicans won an overwhelming victory. The country, still prosperous except for the farmers, was in no mood to abandon the party that claimed credit for the prosperous state of the economy. Hoover's reputation for an engineer's skill and efficiency, his successful career, and his middle western background helped him win. Smith, because of his Catholicism, his anti-prohibition stand, and his Eastern big city background, could not even win the discontented farmers of the Midwest. For the first time since Reconstruction, the states of Texas, Florida, Virginia, and North Carolina voted Republican. The radio, widely used in an election campaign for the first time, hurt Al Smith with his accent from the "Sidewalks of New York."

❂❂ **The Coming of the Depression**—The prosperity of the twenties was limited in scope, unsoundly based, and more apparent than real.

Agriculture and some industries such as textiles and coal mining remained chronically depressed. The prosperity of business corporations, as reflected by their growth and the rising prices of their securities, was enjoyed by only a small segment of the population. The failure of the small recessions of 1924 and 1927 to develop into serious depressions caused prognosticators of the business world to acclaim that the wisdom of the business leaders had introduced a "New Era" of freedom from drastic fluctuations in the business cycle. This optimistic belief in permanent prosperity caused mad speculation in city real estate, particularly in Florida, and extreme speculative overvaluations of corporation securities and brisk trading in the stock exchanges. When Hoover took office in the spring of 1929 he declared the soundness of the nation's economy. Very few expected the panic and collapse in the economy that struck in the fall of 1929.

❂ **The Federal Farm Board**—To appease the unhappy farmers and head off more radical legislation, President Hoover called Congress in special session to pass the Agricultural Marketing Act of 1929. This act established a Federal Farm Board to encourage farmers' marketing cooperatives to organize. The Farm Board 1) loaned money to the cooperatives to promote the storage and orderly marketing of farm produce; 2) at the same time it sought to discourage production where surpluses had depressed prices; 3) the Board itself purchased surpluses of cotton and wheat to prevent price declines. After two years and accumulated surpluses which it could not market, the Board ceased its purchases, and wheat and cotton fell to new low prices far below the costs of production.

❂ **The Hawley-Smoot Tariff**—Hoover undertook tariff revision also. By this act the traditional log-rolling by congressmen carried tariff rates to an all-time high, even exceeding the rates of the Fordney-McCumber Act of 1922. Leading economists urged Hoover to veto the measure. They pointed out that 1) it would raise consumer prices; 2) it would protect inefficient businesses; 3) it would injure farmers by limiting the ability of foreign countries to buy American exports; and 4) it would bring reprisals from other countries who stood to lose their market in the United States. Hoover signed the bill. The predictions were borne out; the tariff helped to create further barriers to international trade and good will and thereby contributed to the depression.

❂❂❂ **The Panic and the Depression**—Only a few observers cast doubts on the soundness of the economy in the summer of 1929, but certain weaknesses were noted. Too much money was being diverted to stock market speculation, the building boom was declining, surpluses existed in industry as well as in agriculture.

To discourage speculation on borrowed money, the Federal Reserve Board raised its discount rate in the summer of 1929. In October, the English did the same in order to attract funds back home. This touched off selling in the New York Stock Exchange. Within a month stock prices declined about 37 percent. In successive market breaks for the next three years prices reached new lows after temporary recoveries. Soon all markets in commodities and real estate reflected the onset of depression. The depression became worldwide. Unemployment in the winter of 1929–30 mounted into the millions by the fall of 1930. The extended depression, the worst in American history, reached a bottom in 1933. Recovery was not complete when severe depression recurred in 1937. Only the coming of World War II ended the depression.

✪✪✪ **Causes of the Depression**—Economists came to agree upon the basic causes of the Great Depression. 1) The overexpansion of agriculture and the consequent chronic depression in the twenties eventually helped pull the rest of the economy down with it. 2) Overexpansion had occurred in industrial capacity, particularly in the important automobile industry. 3) Labor-saving machines caused technological unemployment. Unemployed and underpaid workers could not sustain the demand for industrial goods. 4) Concentration of money among wealthy individuals and surpluses in business corporations deprived farmers and workers of purchasing power. 5) As in the prosperity phase of most business cycles, the overexpansion of credit encouraged speculation and overinvestment. Installment buying of consumer goods introduced a new factor creating wide swings and instability in purchasing power. 6) The international trade decline due to tariff barriers was another factor. 7) Overspeculation in securities, land, and commodities touched off the panic and made the depression worse than it might have been.

✪✪✪ **Hoover's Steps to Fight the Depression**—Hoover accepted the need, more than any president before him, for government attack upon depression. His failure to act more vigorously may be explained 1) by his philosophy that expected measures of a voluntary nature by business and labor and action by local government to carry the burden of recovery and relief; 2) the belief that the depression would be short-lived, that prosperity was "just around the corner," justified inaction. 3) Hoover believed the causes of depression were fundamentally international and that the burden of intergovernmental debts was primarily responsible. He emphasized the need for international solutions for the crisis.

Hoover at first held a series of conferences in Washington to secure the voluntary cooperation of business in maintaining wages and continuing plant expansion. He asked labor to spread the work by accepting part-time employment so that more persons could stay on payrolls. In 1930 Hoover asked Congress to appropriate funds for public works projects. He caused Congress to establish the Reconstruction Finance Corporation to lend money to state and local governments to create jobs and to banks, railroads, and other large corporations to prevent bankruptcy and to help create jobs.

The Home Loan Bank Act of 1932 established Home Loan Banks to refinance home mortgages for individuals in danger of losing their homes by foreclosure. Hoover declared a one-year moratorium in 1931 in the payment of international debts. Hoover opposed the payment of the veterans' bonus which would have both discharged this obligation and created purchasing power among many families. The Bonus Army of unemployed veterans and others that marched to Washington and camped in the city were routed by the army upon Hoover's orders. In the Norris-La Guardia Act (1932) the Democrats joined Republican insurgents to forbid the use of injunctions in labor disputes.

✪✪✪ **The Election of 1932**—The midterm election of 1930 gave the Democrats control of Congress; as the depression grew worse it became clear that the Republicans could not avoid blame for the depression and that the Democratic presidential nominee would win. This made a lively convention for the Democrats. Al Smith expected Franklin D. Roosevelt to nominate him again, but Roosevelt worked for the nomination himself and won it. John Nance Garner of Texas ran for Vice President with Roosevelt. The Republicans renominated Hoover. The victory of the Democrats reached landslide proportions.

✪ **The Interregnum**—The transition of the Presidency from Hoover to Roosevelt left the country without a vigorous hand to deal with depression. During this "interregnum" the uncertainty as to the policies of the new administration created uncertainty and fear. Withdrawal of deposits from banks brought on a financial crisis and the depression touched bottom when Roosevelt came in office. The outgoing Hoover and the incoming Roosevelt could not cooperate and each distrusted the other; Hoover tried to commit Roosevelt to certain financial policies but Roosevelt necessarily refused to reveal his intentions until he had the powers of office.

✪ **The Twentieth Amendment**—This so-called "lame duck" amendment was ratified in 1933 to keep members of Congress defeated in the November elections from having to legislate. It abolished the short session of Congress that met in December in even numbered years. "Lame duck" congressmen were those whose wings had been clipped by defeat in the election. The amendment specified that Congress should convene on January 3rd and moved the date of the president's inauguration up to January 20th.

CHAPTER BOOK LIST

Alexander, David, *Panic: The Life and Times of the Stock Market Crash* (Regency).

Allen, F.L., *Only Yesterday: An Informal History of the Nineteen Twenties* (Harper & Row).

Bernstein, Irving, *The Lean Years: A History of the American Worker, 1920–1933* (Houghton Mifflin).
Current, R.N., *Secretary Stimson: A Study in Statecraft* (1954). Diplomacy under Hoover.
DeConde, Alexander, *Herbert Hoover's Latin-American Policy* (1951).
Ferrell, R.H., *American Diplomacy in the Great Depression* (1957).
Galbraith, John, *The Great Crash* (Sentry). Causes and effects of the stock market panic in 1929.
Hicks, John D., *Republican Ascendancy, 1921–1933* (1960). Clearly written.
Romasco, A.U., *The Poverty of Abundance* (1965).
Schwarz, Jordan A., *The Interregnum of Despair: Hoover Congress and the Depression* (1959).
Shannon, D.A., *Great Depression* (Spectrum).
Sobel, Robert, *The Great Bull Market: Wall Street in the 1920s* (1968).
Warren, H.G., *Herbert Hoover and the Great Depression* (Norton).
Wilson, Joan Hoff, *Herbert Hoover, Forgotten Progressive* (1975).

REVIEW QUESTIONS

MULTIPLE CHOICE
1. The election of 1928 (1) revealed general economic discontent (2) gave the Republicans a narrow victory (3) gave victories to the Republicans in several states of the South (4) was a mandate for prohibition repeal.

2. From 1923 to early 1929 behavior of business cycles (1) registered sharp fluctuations (2) was indiscernible (3) created the belief that a serious depression would never return (4) created unrest and alarm.

3. Which pair designates Republican tariff acts after 1921? (1) Fordney-McCumber and Smoot-Hawley (2) Esch-Cummins and Aldrich-Vreeland (3) Underwood-Simmons and Aldrich-Vreeland (4) Mellon-Borah and Smoot-Hawley.

4. Hoover's policies in dealing with the depression have been criticized for all reasons below *except* that he (1) postponed action in the belief prosperity was just around the corner (2) deprecated the domestic causes of the depression (3) depended too much on voluntary action (4) did less than earlier presidents had done in similar crises.

5. Which statement is *incorrect?* Hoover (1) opposed all government interference in economic matters (2) was educated as an engineer (3) opposed any government activity he considered socialistic (4) held high office under a Democratic president.

6. The payment of the veterans' bonus after 1930 was opposed by (1) Hoover (2) Roosevelt (3) by neither Hoover nor Roosevelt (4) by both Hoover and Roosevelt.

7. In its consequences the election of 1932 is most comparable with the election of (1) 1892 (2) 1828 (3) 1908 (4) 1920.

8. All are true of the Twentieth Amendment to the Constitution *except* (1) it eliminated unproductive "lame duck" Congresses (2) it changed the date of the president's inauguration (3) it limited presidents to two terms (4) it specified that Congress would meet early in January of each year.

TRUE-FALSE

9. In the election of 1928 the Republicans won a quite narrow victory.

10. The Democratic candidate took his position on the Prohibition issue by declaring it to be a "noble experiment."

11. In 1928 the radio for the first time was used in a presidential campaign.

12. When it struck, the depression was very severe because it was so widely anticipated.

13. The Federal Farm Board failed because it could do nothing to reduce the production of agricultural surpluses.

14. One cause of the Depression was that too much money had been diverted to speculation of one kind or another.

15. After 1930 Hoover faced a further difficulty of having to work with a Congress dominated by Democrats.

COMPLETION

16. In the election of 1928 the Republican presidential candidate who was _____ ran against the Democrat _____ .

17. The most depressed sector of the economy in the 1920s was _____ ; to bring relief President Hoover created the _____ .

18. Hoover's high tariff measure was the _____ Tariff.

19. The Great Depression began with panic in the _____ in the fall of _____ . During the early months of the Depression government officials promised that prosperity was _____ .

20. Hoover had Congress create a great lending agency known as the _____ and created the _____ to refinance homes in danger of foreclosure. The use of the injunction in labor disputes was forbidden by the _____ Act.

21. In 1932 Franklin D. Roosevelt, instead of helping _____ win the Democratic nomination, worked for it himself.

22. During the transition of the presidency referred to as the _____ , Hoover and Roosevelt failed to reach agreement.

THE NEW DEAL, 1933–1939

CHRONOLOGY / CHAPTER 19

1933 Roosevelt inaugurated as President.
Depth of depression reached in bank closings; "banking holiday" proclaimed in March by Roosevelt.
New Deal relief agencies created: CCC, FERA, PWA, CWA.
NRA and AAA created to promote recovery of industry and agriculture.
Other important legislation: TVA, banking reform, U.S. Employment Service, FDIC, and FCA.

1934 Beginning of two-year drought that created "Dust Bowl" in Great Plains.
Reciprocal Trade Agreements Act.
SEC created. National Housing (FHA) Act and other New Deal recovery and reform measures passed.

1935 Works Progress Administration (WPA), Resettlement Administration, REA created.
NRA declared unconstitutional.
National Labor Relations Act passed.
Social Security Act passed.
Public Utility Holding Company Act passed.
CIO organized within the AF of L

1936 Roosevelt reelected by landslide over Landon (Rep.).
AAA declared unconstitutional; replaced by Soil Conservation and Domestic Allotment Act.
Merchant Marine Act provided subsidies for shipping.
Veterans' "bonus" passed over President's veto.

1937 Roosevelt's campaign to reform the Supreme Court failed.
Recession of 1937–1938 began.
Farm Security Administration created.

1938 Fair Labor Standards Act and AAA of 1938 passed.
CIO organized independently of AF of L

1939 Hatch Act passed to regulate political activities of federal employees.

Chapter

19
THE DOMESTIC REFORMS OF THE NEW DEAL, 1933–1939

> The New Deal introduced such sharp changes in the relationship between individuals and the federal government that the term "revolution" may be applied here as appropriately as to any other turning point in the national history. Basically, however, it represented necessary modifications to ensure the preservation of the American political and economic system; in several measures the demands of earlier protest groups, such as the Populists, found fulfillment. The accumulated evils and maladjustments of the years of national complacency and neglect, as well as the particular problems caused by the Great Depression, caused the New Deal to enact a flood of new legislation.

THE NEW DEAL

During the interregnum Roosevelt laid his own plans for dealing with the nation's problems after his inauguration and chose advisers to help him achieve his goals.

◆◆◆ **Career and Character of Roosevelt**—Franklin Delano Roosevelt, like his distant relative Theodore Roosevelt, enjoyed the advantages of upbringing in a wealthy and cultured family. He served as Assistant Secretary of the Navy under Woodrow Wilson; in 1920 he ran for Vice President. In 1921 both his legs were crippled by an attack of infantile paralysis. His handicap did not keep him from his reading and from corresponding with Democratic Party leaders. In 1928 he was elected governor of New York and enacted a modest program of liberal legislation; his understanding of human nature and his personality won him support and popularity.

Roosevelt very early demonstrated his forceful and dramatic leadership. He gained favorable publicity by winning the good will of the press. His well-timed fireside radio chats to the nation built up popular support. He exerted strong leadership with members of Congress. He induced Congress to give him much discretionary power in legislation. He gave his program the popular label, the "New Deal."

✪✪ **Roosevelt and His Cabinet**—The more important early members included Cordell Hull from Tennessee who became Secretary of State; Henry Morgenthau, Jr., Secretary of the Treasury; Harold L. Ickes, Secretary of the Interior; James A. Farley, Postmaster-General; Henry A. Wallace, Secretary of Agriculture; and Frances Perkins, the first woman cabinet member, headed the Labor Department. Like many other presidents, Roosevelt gathered men outside his cabinet as close personal advisers; he made use of the talent of the nation's universities instead of limiting his advisers to businessmen. The business leadership characteristic of the Hoover administration had been pretty well discredited by the depression and revelations of betrayal of public trust among some of their more prominent figures. Roosevelt's specialists, experts, and men of ideas were referred to as the "brain trust."

✪✪✪ **Philosophy of the New Deal**—Instead of choosing either the rightist policies of the fascists or the leftist policies of extreme socialists as some world leaders were doing at the time, Roosevelt chose a middle course of preserving both private enterprise and democratic institutions. His innovations consisted of a large number of measures to plan and regulate the economy of the nation by government controls. He sought to restore prosperity to the nation. Instead of pursuing early plans for international solution of economic problems in the London Economic Conference, which met in June 1933, Roosevelt suddenly decided to concentrate upon a domestic program of economic rehabilitation. The program had three goals: relief, recovery, and reform. In addition to planning, Roosevelt expected to take an approach of experimentation in the effort to find workable solutions for economic problems. New Deal philosophy operated to put money into the hands of the "forgotten man" at the bottom of the economic system. The Democrats charged that, by contrast, the Republicans had poured money in at the top of the economic heap and that so little of it filtered down that it failed to create mass purchasing power.

NEW DEAL MEASURES AND EVENTS

Roosevelt first had to deal with the emergencies of financial collapse and unemployment. During the "hundred days" after Roosevelt's inauguration Congress quickly enacted the early New Deal measures.

✪✪ **The Banking Crisis**—With depositors making runs on banks and forcing them to close, Roosevelt faced an immediate and serious crisis upon his inauguration. The new President's first act was to declare, on

March 5, a bank holiday to close all banks until they could be opened again after public confidence had been restored in them. He called Congress in special session on March 9. Within a few hours Congress passed an Emergency Banking Act that 1) provided for the examination of all banks and reopening of those found to be sound. 2) The Act called into the treasury all gold and gold certificates and thereby took the nation off the full-fledged, or gold coin, standard. 3) Emergency currency was authorized by the Act.

❂ **New Deal Relief Measures**—Roosevelt preferred work relief to the dole system as a means of enabling the unemployed to secure basic food and shelter for survival. The following agencies were organized to provide jobs and relief.

1) The Civilian Conservation Corps (CCC) was created in April. It employed young men from destitute families. They were put to work in various outdoor conservation projects in forests and parks. The 1,600,000 youths lived in camps under semi-military discipline; most of their small wages were sent home to sustain their families.

2) The Federal Emergency Relief Administration (FERA) provided relief funds for food, clothing, and shelter to the unemployed until they could find jobs or work relief.

3) The Civil Works Administration (CWA) later gave work relief to 4,000,000 persons.

4) The Public Works Administration (PWA) provided large projects of permanent construction, such as buildings and waterworks, to be built under contracts with private firms.

5) In 1935 the Works Progress Administration (WPA) created jobs in government projects of all kinds. It provided jobs for a wide variety of talents—in writing, acting, painting, teaching, and other white collar jobs. The National Youth Administration (NYA) under the WPA provided small jobs on campus for high school and college youths to enable them to earn enough to stay in school. Some of these temporary agencies mentioned above lasted several years but none survived the depression.

❂❂❂ **Monetary Reform**—The New Deal did not hesitate to adopt monetary reforms to promote inflation—more correctly, reflation—to bring relief to debtors and provide the stimulus of an enlarged currency supply. In several acts Congress granted the President discretionary powers to inflate the currency. He was authorized 1) to issue treasury notes; 2) to reduce the gold content of the dollar up to 50 percent; 3) to introduce unlimited amounts of American silver into the national currency by purchasing it at prices above world free market quotations. Under these laws the government later raised and stabilized the price of gold at $35 per ounce. In effect this devalued the dollar in terms of gold. The Gold Clause Act (1935) canceled gold clauses in all financial contracts and made such obligations payable in any legal tender. Thus the New Deal did not hesitate to embrace the seemingly radical monetary policy of Bryan in 1896.

✪✪✪ Agriculture Under the New Deal—The pressing need of farm owners was for relief from the threat of foreclosure. In May 1933, the Farm Credit Administration was created to refinance farm mortgages at low interest rates. The Frazier-Lemke Act (1934) postponed farm mortgage foreclosure. When the Supreme Court found the latter act unconstitutional, a second Frazier-Lemke Act (1935) replaced it with certain changes. The Resettlement Administration (1935) bought submarginal farms to help owners resettle on lands that would provide an adequate living income. After 1937 the Farm Security Administration (FSA) took over the job of aiding and lending money to submarginal farmers.

The experience of the Hoover Farm Board proved that farm prices could be raised only by reducing acreage and production. New Deal measures followed this approach. The Agricultural Adjustment Administration (AAA, May, 1933) 1) made rental payments to farmers for retiring acreage from cultivation in the basic crops and paid subsidies for reducing the numbers of hogs and cattle. 2) This act levied a processing tax against processors of farm crops in order to raise money to finance the subsidies to farmers. Millions of acres were retired and farm prices improved, but in 1936 the Supreme Court found the law unconstitutional. The law was held to be in violation of states rights and the tax was considered in violation of the taxing power accorded Congress; it was considered a tax for the benefit of a special group rather than for the general welfare.

The Soil Conservation and Domestic Allotment Act was passed in 1936 and the second Agricultural Adjustment Act in 1938 to renew the program and still meet the objections of the Supreme Court. Under these laws 1) farmers were paid to follow soil conservation practices for the benefit of the nation. Payments were made to farmers to plant soil building crops in the place of market staples. 2) A program of acreage allotments and 3) one of marketing quotas was prepared in order to keep surpluses down. 4) Farmers were given commodity loans to support prices and to withhold surpluses from the market. Desirable prices for different staples were determined by the principle of "parity," one of restoring the farmers' equality of purchasing power to that of other groups.

The Bankhead-Jones Act (1937) authorized the Farm Security Administration to establish a program to assist selected tenant farmers in buying larger farms under long-term, low-interest loans.

In 1934–1935 severe drought created dust-bowl conditions in the Great Plains, and many farmers abandoned their farms to seek jobs in California. In parts of the South the New Deal farm program had the effect of driving tenant farmers off the land. The farm measures did not bring prosperity but did provide much relief to distressed farmers.

✪ **The National Recovery Administration (NRA)**—This measure was passed to maintain higher wages and prices in businesses of all kinds. It was placed under the World War I administrator Hugh S. Johnson, who made patriotic appeals for the support of its goals. The law opposed ruinous competition by encouraging trade associations, such as barbers and dry cleaners, to adopt codes of fair competition which prescribed wages, hours, and prices. It provided for minimum wage rates. Its important Section 7a required that workers be granted genuine rights of collective bargaining.

The NRA resulted in the drafting of hundreds of codes. "Chiselers" resorted to all kinds of subterfuges to gain advantage over competitors instead of abiding by the codes. The public complained of rising prices; liberals charged that the act encouraged monopoly. In any case, it proved unworkable. The Supreme Court in the Schechter case declared it unconstitutional, because 1) the act delegated law-making power to the president; 2) it violated the rights of the states; and 3) illegally gave the federal government control over commerce in the states. Certain provisions of the act were revived in subsequent labor legislation. The most significant outcome of the act was the stimulus it gave to unionization of labor.

✪✪✪ **Labor Under the New Deal**—After some experimenting and the downfall of the NRA, the New Deal passed the National Labor Relations Act sponsored by Senator Wagner of New York. This "Wagner Act" created, in 1935, a National Labor Relations Board (NLRB) to determine bona fide bargaining agents for workers and otherwise protect the recognized rights of collective bargaining. The NLRB became the umpire for enforcing fair practices on the part of labor and management in conducting collective bargaining. Employers not accustomed to dealing with unionized labor resented the act as one giving unfair advantages to the unions.

The United States Employment Service (1933) was created to provide offices where workers could locate jobs and thereby avoid "frictional unemployment," that is, unemployment due to the time lost in shifting from one job to another.

✪✪ **The TVA and Utility Regulation**—Since World War I Senator George Norris of Nebraska had worked to make public use of the water power of the Tennessee River. The Democratic Platform in 1932 had promised the development of publicly-owned electric power. The Tennessee Valley Authority was created, as a public corporation with multiple goals and powers to develop an area including parts of seven states. All parts were tributary to the Tennessee River.

The purposes of the TVA were 1) to create a yardstick for determining the cost of producing electricity that could be used to help regulate electric power rates over the whole country; 2) to build dams to produce low cost electricity for the Tennessee Valley residents; 3) to help prevent the disastrous annual floods below the Tennessee River; 4) to manufacture low-cost nitrate fertilizer to rebuild worn-out farms; 5) to rehabilitate in other ways the whole Tennessee Valley area; 6) to provide cheap water transportation; and 7) to promote conservation and develop recreational facilities.

The project set a model for similar programs in the Columbia River Basin where the Grand Coulee and Bonneville Dams were built and in the Missouri River Valley. Arid land reclamation was an important achievement in the Northwest due to these river projects.

The Rural Electrification Administration (REA, 1935) created a national program to bring electricity to rural areas which had been by-passed by privately owned utilities. Private utilities followed a practice of extending power lines to "skim off" profitable markets but by-passed areas not yielding sufficient profits.

The Wheeler-Rayburn Act (1935) with its "death-sentence" clause provided for the elimination of the multiplicity of layers of utility holding companies created during the twenties. Electric utility holding companies had created complex corporations to satisfy the speculative mania for stock issues and as a way of justifying higher utility rates.

○○ Housing—1) The Home Owners Loan Corporation (1933) modified and continued the Hoover measure to provide refinancing for existing homes in danger of foreclosure. 2) The Federal Housing Administration (FHA, 1934) was created to insure home mortgages created by private financing on new construction and was later extended to existing houses. One of its purposes was to revive the construction industry. 3) The United States Housing Authority subsidized projects by local governments in slum clearance and construction of low-rental housing in the cities.

○○ Banking Reforms—The Glass-Steagall Banking Act (1933) created the Federal Deposit Insurance Corporation (FDIC) under federal control to provide insurance of individual bank deposits. This measure practically ended the chronic evil of bank failure under the old laissez-faire system. The Glass-Steagall Act also forbade commercial banks from engaging in investment banking (selling securities), curtailed the use of depositors funds for making speculative investments, and made many technical reforms to strengthen the banking system.

○ The Regulation of Securities—The financial collapse revealed shocking abuses of public trust by corporations in creating new issues of stocks and bonds. Abuses in the security markets, too, called for reforms to protect the public and preserve one of the benefits of the American capitalistic system, individual investment in privately owned corporations.

The Securities Act of 1933 provided for the registration and disclosure of full information about new issues of securities. In 1934 the act was revised. The Securities and Exchange Commission (SEC) was also created. The SEC was given the power to regulate new issues of securities and regulate the security markets. These measures did much to protect the investing public but did not apply to smaller corporations or to certain security transactions outside the major exchanges.

✪✪✪ **The Social Security Act (1935)**—Europe since the 1880s had begun to adopt social security to protect the masses from various forms of insecurity such as unemployment and old age. There was insufficient demand for such protection in the United States until depression-born want struck large numbers of retirement age persons. Radical rabble-rousers then took advantage of the situation and threatened to force the passage of unworkable schemes. This agitation, however, served to arouse action by the federal government. The Townsend Plan, originated by Dr. Charles Townsend and supported by thousands of clubs, demanded pensions of $200 a month for the aged. At this same time Huey Long of Louisiana and Father Coughlin were criticizing Roosevelt's New Deal and promising radical solutions for the depression.

The Social Security Act provided 1) a federal program of old age insurance beginning at the age of 65 for retired persons and benefits for dependent survivors of workers who died; these benefits were financed by a tax on both employers and employees. 2) The same law established a system of federal aid to the states for forms of assistance to several types of indigent persons: pensions for the aged, maternal and child health services, and aid for crippled children and the blind. 3) This same law established a system of unemployment benefits administered by the states but financed by payroll taxes. The Federal Social Security Board administered all these benefits.

The Social Security Administration in time issued social security numbers to almost all persons; probably no measure of the New Deal affected so many individuals. Amendments have repeatedly extended the coverages to more persons, have increased the taxes to support it, and the benefits and amounts paid. The system created a workable means by which individuals made compulsory contributions to provide security for themselves and their dependents.

The Merchant Marine Act (1936)—The New Deal accepted the necessity of direct subsidies to maintain a strong merchant marine to meet the needs for ocean transportation in the emergencies of war. This act created a new agency, the Maritime Commission, to take cognizance, in cooperation with the navy, of the shipping needs of the nation in wartime. The Commission subsidized both shipbuilding and ship operation to insure that ships, shipbuilding facilities, and experienced seamen—all under American control—would be ready for an emergency. Without these subsidies America's shipping needs would be supplied by lower cost foreign shipbuilders and shipping lines.

✪✪ Election of 1936—The great changes introduced by the New Deal aroused angry opposition among a minority. In the campaign the opposition stated its objections. 1) The New Deal's spending was greatly increasing the national debt; 2) the New Deal was too socialistic, and it had encouraged labor to make extravagant demands; 3) Roosevelt was accused of using federal funds to build a political machine to perpetuate his party in office; 4) the New Deal in many ways had violated the Constitution.

The Republicans chose Alfred M. Landon, a midwestern Calvin Coolidge, to contest Roosevelt for the Presidency. The Democrats won by a landslide; in the electoral college Roosevelt won 523 votes. Landon won only 8 electoral votes, in the two states of Maine and Vermont, to make this the most one-sided election since 1820. The Democrats won overwhelming control of both houses. The voters had repudiated the "rugged individualism" of the "economic royalists," as Roosevelt referred to Republican opponents. *The Literary Digest,* the leading news weekly, predicted a Landon victory; the magazine went out of business as a consequence of its error. The Gallup Poll successfully predicted the outcome and established itself in this field by the use of scientific sampling of various segments of voters.

✪✪✪ Roosevelt and the Supreme Court—Roosevelt took his victory as a complete endorsement of the New Deal. He now sought to remove the greatest obstacle to its further success, the Supreme Court. Roosevelt criticized the conservatism of the "nine old men" who, he said, followed precedents of the "horse-and-buggy days." Six of them were over 70 years of age. The Court had invalidated many of the most vital New Deal laws; Roosevelt had had no opportunity to appoint any member to the Court.

The President now had his friends in Congress sponsor a law to permit a president to appoint as many as six additional justices to the Court where incumbent justices over 70 did not choose to retire. For the first time Roosevelt found many former political leaders and supporters combined against him. A storm of opposition in the country and among conservative Democrats arose over the "Court Packing Bill." Roosevelt had to abandon his measure, but the attack did bring results. Even as the debate was going on in Congress, the Court handed down several decisions favorable to New Deal measures, some of which it had invalidated previously. Beginning in 1937 resignations and death opened vacancies which Roosevelt filled with staunch New Dealers. The controversy showed 1) how difficult it is for one branch of government to override another; 2) the support for the independence of the Court; and 3) the Court's willingness to give heed to political as well as legal considerations in interpreting the nation's laws.

✪ The Fair Labor Standards Act (1938)—This "Wages and Hours Law" provided the normal work week of 40 hours and minimum wages of 40 cents an hour in firms producing for interstate commerce. It also revived the anti-child-labor provisions of the NRA. The success of this and other legislation has killed the demand for a child labor amendment. As time passed, the minimum wage was revised upward.

The Recession of 1937–1938—After substantial recovery from the 1933 lows in the economy, the administration took several steps in 1936 and 1937 to reduce the burden of expense in fighting the economic depression. The result was a sudden and severe recession beginning in 1937. Heavy federal spending was resumed and the economy made considerable recovery by the fall of 1938. Full employment did not return until World War II. In the congressional elections of 1938 the Republicans gained enough strength to effectively oppose the administration.

Roosevelt successfully urged reorganization of the executive departments of the federal government in the interest of efficiency and economy; Congress authorized the reorganization plans. Also in 1939, the Hatch Act was passed to forbid federal employees in the lower ranks from engaging in political activities.

✪✪✪ **Changes in Organized Labor**—New Deal laws that encouraged labor unionization helped strengthen the militant leader of the unskilled workers, John L. Lewis. Lewis, the head of the United Mine Workers, organized the Committee for Industrial Organization within the AF of L Lewis advocated the organization of a single, large union within each industry— unions that would combine all crafts and also unskilled workers. The AF of L under William L. Green opposed this principle. When the CIO unions organized by Lewis were expelled, the new organization became permanent in 1938 as the Congress for Industrial Organization (CIO).

The CIO employed a new weapon known as the "sitdown" strike. Instead of maintaining pickets to prevent "scabs," non-union men, from taking their jobs, they remained within the company plants. The union won strikes in the automobile industry and recognition from steel companies as well in 1937. Much violence accompanied the CIO strikes. The Supreme Court in 1939 outlawed the sit-down strike since it in effect confiscated private property.

CHAPTER BOOK LIST

Allen, Frederick L., *Since Yesterday* (Bantam). Another popular, accurate history of a decade, the 1930s and the Great Depression.

Conkin, Paul, *The New Deal* (Rev. ed., 1975).

Friedel, Frank, *Franklin D. Roosevelt* (3 vol. biography, 1952, 1954, 1956). Thorough study.

Hofstadter, Richard, *Age of Reform* (Vintage). Begins with W. J. Bryan.

Ickes, Harold L., *The Secret Diary of Harold L. Ickes* (1954). By Roosevelt's Secretary of the Interior.

Johnson, George, *Eleanor Roosevelt* (Monarch). Brief biography.

Kindelberger, Charles P., *The World in Depression, 1929–1939* (1973).

Lash, Joseph P., *Eleanor and Franklin* (1971).

Leuchtenberg, William, *Franklin D. Roosevelt and the New Deal: 1932–1940* (1963).

McCoy, D.R., Angry Voices, *Left-of-Center Politics in the New Deal Era* (1959).

Romasco, Albert U., *The Poverty of Abundance: Hoover, the Nation, the Depression* (Oxford).

Schlesinger, A.M., Jr., *The Coming of the New Deal* (Houghton-Mifflin).

Schlesinger, Jr., A.M., *The Age of Roosevelt* (3-vol., 1958, 1959, 1960). Excellent general history.

Shannon, D.A., *Great Depression* (Spectrum).

Tugwell, R.G., *In Search of Roosevelt* (1972). By an early liberal member of FDR's brain trust.

Wester, Dixon, *Age of the Great Depression, 1929–1941* (1948). A general history, vivid and readable.

Williams, T.H., *Huey Long* (1967).

REVIEW QUESTIONS

MULTIPLE CHOICE

1. In the early years of the New Deal Roosevelt (1) sought advice from very few others (2) relied heavily upon a "Brain Trust" for advice (3) consulted business leaders mainly (4) sought advice only from politicians in his cabinet.

2. Before coming to the Presidency, Roosevelt had been in every position *except* (1) the governorship of New York (2) Assistant Secretary of the Navy (3) candidacy for previous national office (4) a seat in Congress.

3. The policies of FDR revealed (1) a rejection of the capitalistic system (2) a willingness to modify extensively American laissez-faire economic practices (3) Fascist philosophy of economic and political regimentation (4) a timidity in dealing with the basic differences of the free enterprise system.

4. Franklin D. Roosevelt first gave his attention to what major problem? (1) Unemployment (2) bank failures (3) speculation in securities (4) farm relief.

5. The Civilian Conservation Corps did all *except* which one? (1) Hired older men for leaf-raking jobs (2) gave useful work and some discipline to young men (3) gave most of the pay of enrollees to their parents (4) promoted development of natural resources.

6. Roosevelt did all of the following for agriculture *except* (1) prevent farm mortgage foreclosures (2) reduce acreages in cultivation (3) increase the export market (4) raise farm prices.

7. Which was *not* a measure affecting agriculture under the New Deal? (1) The Resettlement Administration (2) the Federal Farm Board (3) the Bankhead-Jones Act (4) the Frazier-Lemke Act.

8. Which was *not* true of the NRA? (1) It discouraged unionization of labor (2) it reversed the purposes of earlier anti-trust laws (3) none of its features were rescued from the unfavorable Supreme Court decisions (4) it delegated law-making power to the president.

9. Private business opposed the Tennessee Valley Authority because (1) it was thought the lakes would soon be filled with silt (2) the project did not provide satisfactory protection against floods (3) electricity was produced and distributed (4) it called for regimentation of the farmers of the valley.

10. Which statement is *untrue* in regard to New Deal assistance in housing finance? (1) It was the first to provide federal home loans (2) the FHA operated mainly by insuring home mortgages (3) federal slum clearance began under the New Deal (4) loans were provided to refinance homes already built.

11. With regard to the regulation of issues of securities the SEC (1) supervises all except personal corporations (2) does not take cognizance of securities exchanges (3) seeks to require full disclosure of information (4) seeks to prevent losses through speculation.

12. Social Security (1) covers all persons in the United States (2) probably affects more persons than any other measure begun by the New Deal (3) does not cover persons incapacitated by injury (4) insured farmers from its inception.

13. The election of 1936 (1) reflected grudging national support for the New Deal (2) saw much debate over the Supreme Court issue (3) may not be described as a landslide victory for the New Deal (4) overwhelmingly endorsed the New Deal.

14. FDR's attempt to reform the Supreme Court (1) secured more decisions favorable to New Deal laws (2) was completely unsuccessful (3) was the first attempt to change the number of members of the Court (4) was endorsed by nearly all Democrats.

15. Full employment under Roosevelt was (1) not achieved until 1939 (2) not achieved until 1942 (3) realized by 1936.

16. On the labor front all the following happened during the 1930s *except* (1) separation of the CIO from the AF of L (2) sit-down strikes (3) passage of the Fair Labor Standards Act (4) rigid non-intervention by the federal government in labor disputes.

COMPLETION

17. Before becoming President, Franklin D. Roosevelt served as governor of _____ state.

18. The three goals of the New Deal were, in order, _____ , _____ , _____ .

19. Roosevelt's first legislation to deal with the economic crisis was the _____ .

20. The last and the most comprehensive of the New Deal unemployment relief agencies was the _____ .

21. In the devaluation of the American dollar the price of gold was increased to _____ an ounce.

22. In order to determine what prices farmers should receive for their produce the New Deal adopted the principle of _____ . The tax levied to raise money to finance the Agricultural Adjustment Act was called a _____ . When the AAA was declared unconstitutional it was replaced by the _____ . It was decided how much could be planted by each farmer by a system of acreage _____ and how much could be sold by a system of _____ .

23. Wind erosion in a particular drought-stricken area of the Great Plains created what was designated as the _____ .

24. To bring relief from too much competition and to raise wages in industry Roosevelt created the _____ ; those who found ways to evade its rules were called _____ ; it was declared unconstitutional in the _____ case. Its defunct Section 7a relating to labor was restored in the _____ .

25. The Wagner Act was administered by the _____ .

26. A national agency to help workers find jobs was created; it was the _____ .

27. A primary purpose of the Tennessee Valley Authority was to create a _____ to determine the cost of producing electric power. To bring electricity to farmers the _____ was created. Electric power holding companies were largely eliminated by the _____ clause of the _____ Act.

28. The Glass-Steagall Act created the _____ to insure bank accounts.

29. The radical Senator from Louisiana who criticized the New Deal was _____ and the Catholic priest who offered radical solutions was _____ .

30. To maintain a strong merchant marine _____ the was created.

31. In 1936 Roosevelt won every state except two _____ . In this election the _____ Poll successfully foretold the outcome while the _____ failed miserably.

32. After the election Roosevelt criticized the Supreme Court by calling its members the _____ . By the law finally passed justices were encouraged to retire with full pay after the age of _____ .

33. A let-up in relief and recovery expenditures brought on another severe recession in the year _____ .

MATCHING

34. John L. Lewis   a. Formerly governor of New York

35. Henry A. Wallace   b. Secretary of Labor

36. William L. Green   c. Helped create the National Labor

37. Alfred M. Landon   Relations Board

38. Franklin D. Roosevelt   d. Old age pension leader

39. Frances Perkins   e. Most aggressive recent labor leader

40. Cordell Hull   f. Ran against FDR

41. Senator Wagner   g. Secretary of Agriculture

42. George Norris   h. Sponsor of the reciprocal trade agreements

43. Charles Townsend   i. Secretary of the Interior

     j. TVA

     k. President of the AF of L

CHRONOLOGY / CHAPTER 20

1931   Japan invaded Manchuria.

1932   Stimson Doctrine of non-recognition of Japanese conquest of Manchuria.

1933   Good Neighbor policy announced.

Hitler became Chancellor in Germany.

1934   Platt Amendment abrogated.

Reciprocal Trade Agreements Act provided a means of tariff reductions.

Tydings-McDuffie Act provided for Philippine independence.

Nye investigation of munitions industry role in World War I.

1935   First neutrality law enacted. Revised again in 1936 and 1937.

Italy invaded Ethiopia.

1936   Germany reoccupied the Rhineland. Rome-Berlin Axis formed.

Spanish Civil War began.

1937   Japan invaded China.

Roosevelt delivered "Quarantine Speech" in Chicago.

1938   Mexico expropriated American oil properties.

Austria annexed by Nazi Germany.

Munich surrender permitted Germany to annex Sudeten region of Czechoslovakia.

1939   German-Russian nonaggression pact.

September 1, World War II began when Germany invaded Poland.

1940   Roosevelt reelected for third term; Willkie (Rep.) defeated.

Preparedness measures taken in United States; destroyer deal with Great Britain. Selective Service Act passed.

Germany overran Western Europe.

Chapter

20
THE BACKGROUND OF WORLD WAR II AND U.S. FOREIGN AFFAIRS, 1933–1941

> At first Roosevelt's attention was directed to domestic problems; he abandoned the London Economic Conference and the opportunity it provided for international cooperation. America's neglect of international problems helped the rise of nationalist dictatorships. When the aggressor powers threatened the security of independent countries, Roosevelt opposed them as vigorously as the isolationism and pacifism of America permitted.

PAN-AMERICAN RELATIONS

Roosevelt took positive steps in the Good Neighbor policy to promote good-will in the Western Hemisphere. Later hemispheric defense needs called for further cooperation.

❂❂❂ **The Good Neighbor Policy**—Roosevelt announced the "good neighbor" policy at his first inauguration. At the Montevideo (Pan-American) Conference in 1933, Secretary of State Cordell Hull agreed with the Latin-American nations that no nation has the right to intervene in the affairs of another nation. Roosevelt himself stated that the United States would oppose armed intervention.

In 1934 the United States and Cuba abrogated the Platt Amendment; when trouble broke out in Cuba the United States did not intervene as had been done before. Roosevelt continued the Hoover policy of withdrawing troops from Haiti. By 1935 the last troops were removed from Nicaragua. The right of intervention in Panama was given up by treaty in 1936. In 1940 the customs receivership in the Dominican Republic was terminated.

In 1938 Mexico expropriated more American oil properties under the Mexican constitution of 1917. The United States recognized Mexico's right of expropriation and insisted on fair payment to the owners. A joint commission in 1942 finally agreed upon the amount of compensation which Mexico was to pay.

✪✪ **Hemispheric Solidarity**—In the face of growing threats from Germany and Italy, the United States worked to achieve unity among the American states.

In the Buenos Aires Conference (1936) Roosevelt joined delegates from other American nations in reaffirming the principle of collective security. At the Lima Conference (1938) the nations again reaffirmed the agreement to join in common consultation. In 1939, after war began in Europe, a conference at Panama City declared a safety zone around the Western Hemisphere in which the warring nations were advised to refrain from hostilities.

In 1940 in the Act of Havana the United States and the other American nations declared that an act of aggression against one state would be taken as an act against all. The Act of Havana provided for a committee of American nations to take over any European possessions in America in danger of transfer to another power. The other nations recognized the right of the United States or any other nation under the Monroe Doctrine to take necessary action to defend the continent against a foreign enemy. In effect this internationalized the Monroe Doctrine.

Reciprocal Trade Agreements Act (1934)—The tariff policy of the New Deal provided for the negotiation of tariff agreements with separate nations. Secretary of State Hull made trade agreements with many of the Latin-American nations as well as other countries. The treaties reduced tariff duties to promote trade and thereby helped combat economic nationalism.

✪✪ PHILIPPINE INDEPENDENCE

The Democratic policy of independence for the Philippines was implemented by the Jones Act (1916) in the Wilson administration. This act extended the degree of self-government and promised independence as soon as the Filipinos could carry the responsibilities. The Republican administration made no moves to grant independence. The influence of several groups in the United States, after the Democratic victory in 1932, brought action. These groups included sugar producers, dairy interests that sought to exclude the competition of coconut oil used in making oleomargarine, tobacco growers, labor opposition to Filipino immigrant workers, and isolationists.

The Hawes-Cutting Act was passed by a Democratic Congress in 1933 to provide independence, but the Filipinos rejected its terms.

In 1934 the Tydings-McDuffie Act was passed; it provided for independence after a ten-year period and gradual withdrawal of tariff concessions. On July 4, 1946, the Philippines were given independence under a treaty that permitted the United States to retain air and naval bases there.

AMERICAN REACTION TO AGGRESSION

The United States had cooperated with other nations in many ways but never took steps positive enough to prevent the rise of the aggressor nations of Japan, Germany, and Italy. When war broke out in Europe, Roosevelt led the nation as strongly as he dared to in a policy of intervention on the side of the Allies.

✪✪ **Aggression in Asia**—The Japanese began aggressive war in 1931 with the invasion of Manchuria. This action violated the Open Door, the Nine Power Treaty, the Kellogg-Briand Pact, and defied the League of Nations. When the Japanese set up the puppet government of Manchukuo, Secretary of State Stimson notified Japan and China in 1932 that the United States would not recognize territorial changes made by force or in violation of the Open Door (Stimson Doctrine). The League of Nations merely condemned Japan and it withdrew its membership.

In 1937 Japan invaded China in an undeclared war. The United States with other nations condemned Japan's aggression and disrespect for its treaty agreements. Japan soon occupied most of China's seacoast; the United States sold and transported war matériel to China over the Burma Road in 1938. Loans were also extended to China. In 1937 the Japanese challenged the United States deliberately by bombing the American gunboat *Panay* in China. Japan apologized but had demonstrated that she could get away with the attack. In 1938 Japan also repudiated the Open Door in China; the United States denied the legality of this unilateral abrogation of earlier commitments.

In July 1939, the United States gave the required notice of termination of her commercial treaty of 1911 with Japan. The Japanese imports of gasoline and scrap iron decreased as they came under more severe control. American consumers boycotted Japanese goods, and contributions were made for the relief of Chinese war sufferers. More loans were made by the United States; Roosevelt refused to apply the Neutrality Act since it would have stopped aid to China. The Japanese began to grow desperate as imports of American war matériel steadily dwindled.

✪✪ **Threats of Aggression in Europe**—Germany had always chafed under the severe terms of the Treaty of Versailles. When the worldwide depression hit Germany, dissatisfied elements began supporting the Nazi Party under the leadership of Adolf Hitler; he promised to overthrow the treaty and reassert German power. In 1933 Hitler gained control of Germany and began rearmament.

The response in the United States was to take steps to avoid entanglement in any war in Europe and to discourage aggression. The Nye Committee in 1934 investigated the munitions industry as a factor in American involvement in World War I. The committee showed that United States munitions makers had reaped enormous profits and hinted that pressure from financiers and arms manufacturers had led America into war. The committee's effect was to promote isolationism.

The Johnson Act, sponsored by Senator Hiram Johnson and passed in 1934, forbade the purchase of the securities of any government that had defaulted its war debts. This act prevented most European nations, except Finland, from raising loans in the United States to finance war.

○○ American Neutrality Legislation—The determination of the United States to avoid war caused Congress to pass the three neutrality laws of 1936, 1937, and 1938. Their provisions 1) prohibited the sale of war matériel to belligerents, 2) forbade the use of American ships to transport war matériel to belligerents, 3) and banned travel of Americans on belligerent ships. In this legislation Congress gave up the rights America had fought for in the War of 1812 and in World War I. Americans in the thirties believed the nation should have stayed out of World War I and were now strongly in favor of isolation. The neutrality legislation reflected the belief that the munitions business had helped pull America into World War I.

○○ Roosevelt's Policy—President Roosevelt repeatedly advocated preparedness. In 1934 Roosevelt asked Congress to increase the navy as far as treaty agreements would permit. It was 1938 before Congress authorized any large appropriation for naval construction.

Roosevelt delivered his "Quarantine Speech" in Chicago in the fall of 1937. He condemned the aggressor nations and asked for an international "quarantine" against them. Isolationists interpreted any positive action as a step toward war and protested. But Roosevelt had put himself on record as favoring collective security by cooperation with the Democracies.

○○ Background of World War II in Europe—In 1933 Hitler withdrew Germany from the League of Nations. In 1935 Germany legally annexed the Saar Basin by plebiscite, but in 1936 defied the League by the reoccupation of the Rhineland. In 1938 Austria was occupied and annexed to Germany. After this success Hitler began agitation for the return of the German inhabited Sudetenland border of Czechoslovakia. At Munich Prime Minister Chamberlain of Britain and Premier Daladier of France met Hitler and Mussolini in a policy of appeasement and asked Czechoslovakia to vacate the border lands to Germany. In March 1939, Hitler, in spite of his solemn promise at Munich, took most of the remainder of Czechoslovakia.

Hitler next began a propaganda campaign demanding the return of much of Poland and in August 1939 entered a nonaggression pact with Russia in preparation for the partition of Poland. The British and French promised all possible aid to Poland in case of attack.

Italy under the dictator Mussolini defied the League of Nations in 1935 and invaded Ethiopia. In 1936 Italy joined Germany in an alliance known as the Rome-Berlin Axis. When the revolt broke out in Spain under the Fascist Francisco Franco, Italy and Germany sent aid to Franco. Mussolini occupied Albania soon after Hitler took Czechoslovakia.

✪ The Outbreak of War in Europe and the American Policy— The Second World War began on September 1, 1939, when Hitler launched a blitzkrieg invasion of Poland. Russia occupied eastern Poland and then annexed the Baltic countries and made war on Finland at the same time. Britain and France on September 3 declared war on Germany.

In the United States public opinion favored the isolationists who organized the influential America First Committee. The internationalists led by the Committee to Defend America by Aiding the Allies favored all possible aid "short of war." Roosevelt took the side of the interventionists. He called Congress into special session and secured modification of the neutrality laws. Congress replaced the arms embargo with the "cash and carry" provision that permitted sales to the belligerents but by its nature would help the Allies only. The hemispheric solidarity agreements were negotiated in the Pan-American conferences as already noted.

✪✪ Preparedness Measures in the United States—The successes of the Nazis in Europe brought preparedness measures in America in the summer of 1940. Congress appropriated large sums to strengthen the military services. In September a Selective Service Act provided for the registration of men from 21 to 35 years of age. An Office of Production Management was created to mobilize industry for war. Roosevelt appointed two Republicans to his cabinet to help create a bi-partisan policy. Henry L. Stimson became Secretary of War and Frank Knox became Secretary of the Navy. In September Roosevelt also leased eight naval and air bases from Great Britain in the western Atlantic. For these he transferred to Britain 50 destroyers left over from World War I; Congress was not asked to approve the deal.

✪ Axis Successes in Europe—After the speedy occupation of Poland, the war in Europe settled into a stalemate, called the "sitzkrieg," along the Western front; the French felt secure behind their Maginot Line. The Germans had built their own Siegfried Line. In April 1940, the war became active again when Germany occupied Norway and Denmark. Immediately thereafter Hitler's troops quickly overran Holland, Belgium, Luxembourg, and France. At the Battle of Dunkirk the British managed to escape across the Channel to England with most of their men. Hitler also occupied the Balkans. In June 1941, he invaded Russia in great force.

✪ The Election of 1940—During these startling events in Europe another presidential election came up. The Republicans chose Wendell L. Willkie, a utility company head, a former Democrat, and a newcomer in politics. The Democrats chose Henry A. Wallace, Secretary of Agriculture, as Roosevelt's running mate. Both parties favored all aid to Great Britain "short of war"; the Republicans under the liberal Willkie accepted many of the New Deal reforms. Roosevelt won election and thereby became the first to break the anti-third term tradition. The Democrats strengthened their majorities in Congress. After the election Willkie called for national unity and support of Roosevelt's policy to aid Britain against the totalitarian dictatorships

✪✪ Aid to the Allies—Although a majority of Americans hoped to avoid war, they hoped the Allies would win. In March 1941, the Lend-Lease Act was passed to permit the United States to lend, lease, and otherwise transfer military goods and other aid to Britain. The President declared America to be the "arsenal of democracy," and the country now abandoned neutrality. Vast amounts of goods began flowing to the aid of Britain. By agreement with Denmark, the United States occupied Greenland in April 1941, and in July 1941 occupied Iceland to protect routes to England. When Hitler invaded Russia in June 1941, Roosevelt immediately extended lend-lease aid to her.

✪✪ The Atlantic Charter—Roosevelt and the British war leader, Prime Minister Winston Churchill, met in August 1941, and issued a joint generalized statement of their war aims called the Atlantic Charter. The leading statements made were that 1) neither nation sought territorial gains, 2) they would seek to give all nations access to trade and raw materials over the world, 3) all peoples had the right to choose their own forms of government, and 4) the Allies would support international cooperation to secure improvement of labor standards and social security. 5) Both supported complete freedom of the seas, and 6) both sought disarmament of the aggressors. 7) They would seek to promote "freedom from fear and want" throughout the world.

✪✪ Battle of the Atlantic—German submarines sought to prevent American aid reaching England by attacking freighters under British convoy in the Atlantic. President Roosevelt ordered sea and air patrols in the North Atlantic; positions of German submarines were reported to the British forces. In October 1941, the American destroyer *Reuben James* was sunk by a German submarine attack. Roosevelt then ordered the navy to shoot on sight. In November, Congress provided for the arming of merchant ships.

CHAPTER BOOK LIST

Adler, Selig, *Isolationist Impulse* (Collier). Survey of American isolationism from its beginning.

Barnes, H.E., ed., *Perpetual War for Perpetual Peace* (1953). Isolationist's viewpoint of America's entry in the two world wars.

Borden, Morton, ed., *America's Ten Greatest Presidents* (1961). Critical essays, the last about FDR.

Burns, J.M., *Roosevelt: The Soldier of Freedom* (1970).

Devine, Robert A., *Reluctant Belligerent: American Entry into the Second World War* (Wiley).

Feis, Herbert, *Road to Pearl Harbor, The Coming of the War Between the United States and Japan* (Atheneum).

Gunther, John, *Roosevelt in Retrospect* (Pyramid).

Hull, Cordell, *The Memoirs of Cordell Hull* (1948). Two-volume work by the Secretary of State.

Kelko, Gabriel, *The Politics of War* (Random House).

Perkins, Dexter, *New Age of Franklin Roosevelt: 1932–1945* (University of Chicago). Brief survey of FDR's Presidency.

Rauch, Basil, *Roosevelt: From Munich to Pearl Harbor* (1950). Pro-Roosevelt.

Roosevelt, James, and Roosevelt, Sidney S., *Affectionately, FDR* (Avon). By the sons of FDR.

Stimson, Henry L., and McGeorge, *Bundy, On Active Service in Peace and War* (1954).

Wiltz, J.E., *From Isolation to War, 1931–1941* (1968).

Wood, Bryn, *The Making of the Good Neighbor Policy* (1961).

REVIEW QUESTIONS

MULTIPLE CHOICE

1. The Platt Amendment was revoked in 1934. Which nation had it affected? (1) Santo Domingo (2) Cuba (3) Nicaragua (4) Mexico.

2. Probably the most important factor promoting more friendly relations with Latin America during the 1930s was (1) American policy of promoting democracy there (2) the threat of Argentina to American peace (3) economic pressure from Latin America (4) the threat of a second world war.

3. Reciprocal trade agreements (1) were negotiated first under Hoover (2) brought bilateral agreements to increase trade (3) applied only to Latin America (4) were the pet project of Henry Wallace.

4. Independence was finally realized by the Philippine Islands in which year? (1) 1932 (2) 1936 (3) 1944 (4) 1946.

5. The first notable violation during the 1930s of nonaggression treaties by the aggressor nations was the (1) attack on Ethiopia by Mussolini (2) invasion of Manchuria by Japan (3) German occupation of the Rhineland (4) Japanese invasion of China proper.

6. American neutrality legislation in the 1930s (1) gave up the rights that were fought for in World War I (2) reflected belief that the United States would go to war (3) was sincerely desired by Roosevelt (4) permitted Americans to travel on ships of belligerents.

7. Among others, Hitler annexed these lands: A. Austria, B. Poland, C. Czechoslovakia. Which below indicates the correct time order of these annexations? (1) A, C, B (2) B, A, C (3) C, A, B (4) C, B, A.

8. Before World War II Roosevelt's personal leadership was exerted to (1) preserve American neutrality (2) avoid war at all costs (3) aid the Allies (4) isolate China.

9. The United States traded destroyers for British territory in America because the United States (1) was afraid these particular bases would fall under German control (2) needed more bases to protect herself (3) needed additional missile launching sites (4) hoped to realize the full implications of the Monroe Doctrine.

10. The Atlantic Charter was (1) somewhat similar to the Fourteen Points (2) a military alliance with Britain (3) the announcement of an Atlantic Alliance (4) signed by America, Britain and France.

TRUE-FALSE
11. Under the Good Neighbor policy the United States withdrew troops from the Caribbean countries and restored good relations with Mexico.

12. In general trend the different Pan-American Conferences in the 1930s brought agreement that the United States would cooperate with rather than dictate to the Latin-American countries.

13. The Tydings-McDuffie Act is related to the agricultural depression in the United States.

14. Japan pretended to uphold the Open Door in China until 1941.

15. The effect of the Nye Investigation was to discourage isolationism.

16. Mussolini invaded Ethiopia after Hitler took Austria.

17. Roosevelt exerted his influence after 1938 to modify and weaken the neutrality laws.

18. In 1940 Wendell Willkie actually spoke out against aid to any belligerents in Europe.

19. The American navy was operating in cooperation with the British in the summer of 1941 against German submarines.

COMPLETION

20. Roosevelt's policy toward Latin America is known as the _____ policy; it was announced by the Secretary of State named _____ at the _____ Conference in 1933.

21. By the act of _____ the Monroe Doctrine was made multilateral so that other nations might have the right to enforce it.

22. In 1932 the Republican Secretary of State warned Japan under what came to be known as the _____ that the United States would not recognize territorial changes made by force.

23. The Japanese defied the United States in 1937 by sinking the gunboat _____ in China.

24. Adolf Hitler came to power under the Nazi or _____ Party.

25. The _____ investigated the munitions industry and blamed it for promoting war. The _____ Act forbade Americans to buy the securities of any nation that had defaulted her World War I debts.

26. Roosevelt sought to lead the nation in the strong stand against the aggressor nations in 1937 in his famous Chicago Speech calling for a _____ .

27. World War II began in September _____ when Hitler attacked _____ by a method of warfare called the _____ .

28. Americans opposing war to aid the Allies organized as the _____ .

29. Along the German border the French built an underground defense system known as the _____ ; opposing it the Germans built the _____ .

30. After Hitler's victories in Europe the British evacuated the Continent successfully at _____ .

31. In 1940 the Republicans nominated _____ to oppose Roosevelt.

32. In 1941 before the United States entered World War II aid was extended to the Allies by the _____ Act and Roosevelt declared America to be the _____ .

WORLD WAR II AND
THE FAIR DEAL, 1941–1953

CHRONOLOGY / CHAPTER 21

1941   Lend-lease Act passed to aid democracies. Atlantic Charter
      announced.
      Germany invaded Russia.
      December 7, Japanese attack Pearl Harbor. December 8,
      Congress recognized state of war with Japan and
      Germany.

1942   Battle of the Atlantic to keep sea lanes open.
      May, Corregidor, Philippines, surrendered after long siege.
      June, Battle of Midway.
      August, American invasion of Guadalcanal, first American
      offensive.
      September, Battle of Stalingrad stopped Germans in Russia.
      November, U.S. landings in North Africa.

1943   Successful American offensives in South Pacific theater.
      Allies won control of North Africa and invaded islands of
      Central Pacific.
      Germans defeated at Stalingrad.
      July, Sicily taken. Italy invaded in September.

1944   June 6, "D-Day" invasion in Normandy.
      September, Battle of Germany began.
      October, Philippines invaded by American forces.
      November, Roosevelt reelected for fourth term; Dewey (Rep.)
      defeated.

1945   February, Yalta Conference. Philippines reconquered.
      April, Roosevelt died; Truman became President.
         San Francisco United Nations Conference met. Okinawa
         invaded. United States and Russian forces met in
         Germany.
      May 8, V-E Day.
      July, Potsdam Conference for postwar occupation of
      Germany.
      August, atomic bombs dropped in Japan.
      September 1, V-J Day.

Chapter

21
THE U.S. IN THE SECOND WORLD WAR, 1941–1945

On December 8, 1941, Congress recognized the existence of a state of war with Japan. Germany and Italy declared war on the United States on December 11. The war ended in Europe with the surrender of Germany on May 8, 1945 (V-E Day). Japan surrendered September 1, 1945 (V-J Day). Allied strategy gave priority to the war against Germany.

The United States found itself in a difficult position from the sudden destruction of powerful units in the fleet and the important naval base at Pearl Harbor. After almost nine months the military services began, at Guadalcanal, the first important push to drive the Japanese back. Materials and manpower meanwhile were being prepared for the invasion of the occupied countries in Europe. In time America's overwhelming material resources and the development of the atomic bomb brought victory. The United States learned that it could not hope to avoid world wars in the future and now took the lead in organizing the United Nations Organization to work for the preservation of world peace.

THE WAR IN ASIA

For the United States the war began in Asia, with important engagements fought over the Pacific for almost a year before comparable action first occurred in the European Theater.

●●● **The Attack in the Pacific**—The demands of Japan and the United States were diametrically opposed in relation to the status of China in 1941. When General Tojo became premier in Japan in October, he sent a peace mission under Saburo Kurusu to Washington. During negotiations with Secretary of State Hull, Japanese planes carried out (December 7, 1941) the devastating attack upon American warships and military installations at Pearl Harbor in the Hawaiian Islands. At the same time Japanese forces began attacks at Guam, the Philippines, Hong Kong, and in the Malay Peninsula. Congress declared war on December 8 against Japan. Japan's allies, Germany and Italy declared war upon the United States three days later.

✪✪ **Japanese Victories**—The crippling of the American fleet was followed by sweeping Japanese victories over the Pacific. The Allied forces were defeated and the Japanese occupied Hong Kong, Guam, Wake Island, Singapore, and the Netherland East Indies and later Burma. Allied warships in the area were sunk. The Americans in the Philippines carried out a delaying action on Bataan Peninsula and at Corregidor but surrendered in early May 1942. The Japanese moved on into nearly all of New Guinea and into the Bismarck and Solomon Islands. The Japanese advance was extended into the Aleutian islands of Attu and Kiska.

✪✪ **First Defeats of the Japanese**—At first the American naval and air forces succeeded in thoroughly arresting the Japanese offensive in the naval battles of the Coral Sea off Australia and at Midway Island in June 1942.

The Americans began the counterattack against Japan at Tulagi and Guadalcanal Islands in the Solomon group. Allied forces supported the Americans in the various Pacific island conquests that followed.

The Japanese were pushed out of the various widely scattered islands in the Central Pacific where Admiral Chester W. Nimitz was in command. In the Southwest Pacific General Douglas MacArthur commanded the combined forces from Australia. Everywhere "leapfrog" tactics were used to bypass and leave concentrations of Japanese forces stranded as the Allied forces moved toward the north and west to force the Japanese back. Important bases captured included Saipan in the Marianas, Guam, and Iwo Jima.

In June 1945 Okinawa, on the outskirts of Japan, was captured. The taking of these advanced bases gave the Americans air strips for bombing Japanese bases and the homeland cities and industries of Japan.

Reoccupation of the Philippines, 1944-1945—In October 1944 General MacArthur's forces landed in the Philippines at Leyte Island. American naval forces in the Philippines campaign were commanded by Admiral William Halsey. The naval Battle of Leyte Gulf was actually three battles; the whole action combined was the greatest naval battle of all history. In January 1945, the largest of the Philippines, Luzon, was invaded by the American forces.

✪ **China During the War**—In 1942 when the Japanese overran Burma all the way to the border of India, they disrupted the flow of supplies over the Burma Road. The Chinese under Generalissimo Chiang Kai-shek managed to keep up the resistance against Japan. The Ledo Road from India and the airlift over the Himalayas brought further supplies to the Chinese. Allied forces in Burma made some headway there against the Japanese.

China received aid from the United States in the form of $500,000,000 in loans. The United States gave moral support by renouncing the rights of extraterritoriality and other special privileges in China. In 1943 China was given an immigration quota to replace the humiliating absolute exclusion. Reports of the dictatorship of Chiang Kai-shek and misuse of American wartime aid turned Americans against him.

✪✪✪ Defeat of the Japanese—The costly fighting at Okinawa, where the Japanese on land fought from caves and used scores of kamikaze (suicide) planes against American ships, threatened to make the occupation of Japan costly indeed. The unconditional surrender of Japan, however, was won by dropping two atom bombs on the two cities of Hiroshima and Nagasaki. As terrible as it was, the mass slaughter cost fewer lives than would have been lost in prolonged war of American air attacks upon the Japanese cities or a land invasion of the main islands. Russia declared war on Japan in August, 1945, in time to lay claim to the spoils of war in the Far East. The Japanese formally surrendered on September 2, 1945, when they signed the articles of surrender aboard the battleship Missouri in Tokyo Bay.

THE AMERICAN FORCES AGAINST THE AXIS IN EUROPE

Stalin pleaded to the Allies to attack in Europe and draw off part of the devastating German forces that had reached as far as Stalingrad. Even a year after the war began, the Americans were not prepared to launch an offensive of sufficient force directly against Europe. The attack was made in North Africa instead. Careful preparations made for the D-Day invasion of Europe ensured the defeat of Germany within the next 12 months.

✪✪ The War in North Africa—Axis forces in North Africa under General Rommel had been threatening for some time to push eastward beyond Cairo to take the Suez Canal and force all British shipping around the Cape of Good Hope, Africa. Victory in North Africa was needed to help protect shipping in the Mediterranean.

In November 1942, a huge British-American fleet occupied French Morocco and Algeria. A large German force in Tunisia was surrounded or driven across the Mediterranean. The Germans surrendered in Tunisia in May 1943.

✪ The Invasion of Italy—In July 1943 the forces in Africa under Eisenhower moved into Sicily. During this invasion Mussolini was overthrown by an Italian revolt and Italy surrendered, but the Germans there took control and continued to resist. The invasion of Italy itself followed in September. The whole Allied effort in Italy proceeded slowly and

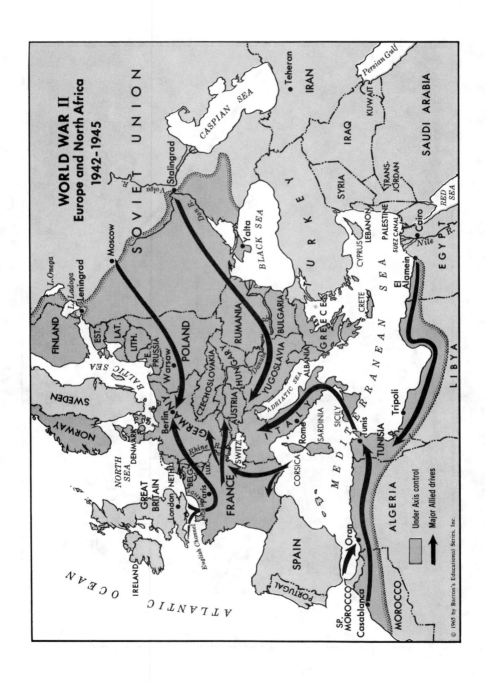

WORLD WAR II
Europe and North Africa
1942–1945

Under Axis control
Major Allied drives

© 1965 by Barron's Educational Series, Inc.

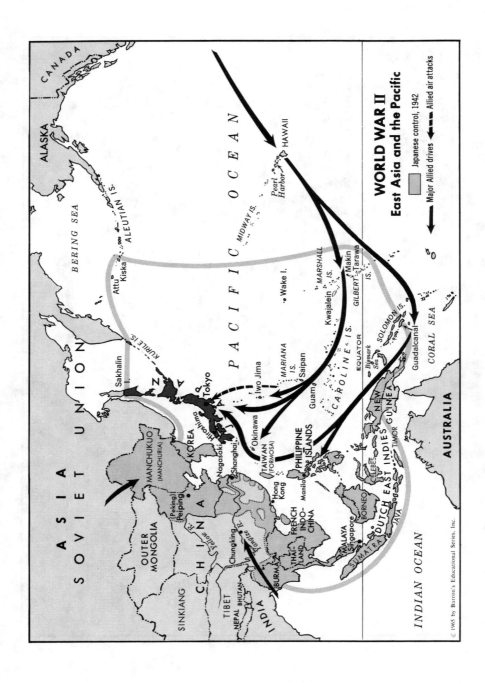

proved costly. The war against Germany was won in the main attack in France and in Germany itself.

✪✪✪ **The Early War Against Germany**—Air bombings of Germany by Britain and the United States from English bases grew steadily from the beginning of the war until the Allies had won air supremacy. American flying fortresses bombed industrial centers in western Germany. The larger cities in Germany suffered enormous damage. The armies of Russia made large gains against the German invaders during winter campaigns. By the summer of 1944 Russia had re-won their own territory and other large areas on the eastern front. The battle in the Atlantic against the German submarines was won in 1943. After that time forces were built up rapidly in Britain for the opening of the second front.

✪✪✪ **The Battle of France**—This large campaign began with the "D-Day" invasion on June 6, 1944, by American and British forces in Normandy. Supreme Commander Dwight D. Eisenhower directed the invasion forces. Two million American troops were transported into France during the summer invasion. The landings were preceded by air and naval bombardment of the landing area to open beachheads for the landings. Paris was liberated August 25. Just before this, landings were made on the Mediterranean coast in southern France. In October mopping up of the enemy all over France was completed.

The last major offensive of the Germans occurred in December, 1944, in the area of Belgium and Luxembourg, the Battle of the Bulge. This last desperate, surprise offensive threw the Allied troops off balance, but the German bulge was pressed back by the end of January, 1945.

✪✪ **The German Surrender**—The Russians mounted an offensive in the east with five armies in January 1945. On March 7 the Allied troops crossed the Remagen Bridge across the Rhine southeast of Cologne. In six weeks the American and Russian troops made contact on the Elbe River. The advance of the Allied armies in the next two months cleaned up pockets of German forces. Hitler and other high officials committed suicide or went into hiding. On May 7 a German official made the "unconditional surrender" and May 8 was proclaimed V-E Day. Allied forces were now free to concentrate for the final victory over Japan.

THE HOME FRONT

World War II was won by industrial production as well as by manpower and strategy. America enjoyed a great advantage in her resources of raw materials and manufacturing capacity.

✪ **Production for War**—Soon the vast industrial capacity and labor forces of the United States were directed into the production of materials to win the war. The War Production Board under Donald M. Nelson directed industry. This Board allocated materials into the most essential war production and prepared factories for the production of tanks, airplanes, and shipbuilding. The War Labor Board tried to fix wages and managed labor relations without much loss of production from labor disputes. Wage earnings almost doubled, partly because labor put in more overtime. The Office of Price Administration (OPA) fixed prices on consumer goods and rationed certain items so that the needs of the military could be satisfied.

The farmers produced bumper crops in spite of a lack of labor and of machinery. The enormous need for foodstuffs was adequately met for the American forces and the Allies. A War Manpower Commission directed men and women into work where they were needed most. The railroads performed their job so efficiently that the government had no need to take them over as had been done in World War I. The Office of Defense Transportation directed the movement of troops and supplies. A War Shipping Board directed the construction of merchant shipping to overcome the heavy losses from submarine attacks.

✪ **War Financing**—War financing increased the national debt to $250,000,000 in 1945. Bonds of all kinds were sold to the public in seven large drives. The government paid a larger proportion of the war cost by current levies of taxes than in any previous war. Tax rates were increased to new highs. A pay-as-you-go system of income taxes was put in effect by withholdings from individual wages and salaries. Taxes took the form of higher individual and corporate income levies, the excess profits tax on corporations, and luxury taxes on consumer goods. Lend-lease provided billions in aid to the Allies without leaving an irritating war debt problem.

✪ **Election of 1944**—In spite of the serious illness of President Roosevelt, he was renominated and won his fourth term. The vice-presidency was contested between Secretary of Agriculture Wallace and Senator Harry S. Truman of Missouri. Truman won on the second ballot with Roosevelt's support. The Republicans chose a middle-of-the-road candidate, the efficient Thomas Dewey of New York, instead of the liberal Willkie. Again there was no great disagreement in either foreign or domestic policy. The Democrats claimed a need to continue the wartime leadership to make a secure peace. In the Electoral College Roosevelt won 432 votes to 99 for Dewey.

CHAPTER BOOK LIST

Blum, John M., *V Was for Victory: Politics and American Culture During World War II* (1976).
Churchill, Winston, *The Grand Alliance* (1950).

Congdon, Don, *Combat: European Theater-World War II* (Dell). Eye-witness accounts.

Congdon, Don, *Combat: Pacific Theater-World War II* (Dell). Eye-witness accounts.

Davis, K.S., *Experience of War: The United States in World War II* (1968).

Divine, R.R., Second Change: *The Triumph of Internationalism During World War II* (Atheneum).

Eisenhower, Dwight, *Crusade in Europe* (Dolphin). Biographical survey of World War II.

Feis, Herbert, *Churchill, Roosevelt, and Stalin* (Princeton).

Greenfield, K.R., *American Strategy in World War II* (1963).

Haworth, David, *D-Day* (Pyramid).

Langsam, W.C., *Historic Documents of World War II* (Anvil).

Morison, S.E., *The Two-Ocean War* (1963).

Stemson, H.S., and McGeorge, *Bundy, On Active Service in Peace and War* (1954).

Toland, John, *Battle: The Story of The Bulge* (New American Library) .

Wilmot, Chester, *The Struggle for Europe* (1952). Excellent one-volume account.

Wright, Gordon, *The Ordeal of Total War* (1939–1945) (Harper & Row).

REVIEW QUESTIONS

MULTIPLE CHOICE

1. Friction between the United States and Japan after 1905 was due mainly to   (1) aggressive actions by Japan against China   (2) American possession of Pacific islands   (3) Japanese "picture brides"   (4) the whole question of Japanese immigration.

2. Excluding the Asian mainland, the Japanese expansion reached its peak in the Pacific Area in   (1) August, 1942   (2) May, 1942   (3) February, 1942   (4) January, 1943.

3. The United States aided China in World War II by all means *except*   (1) extending loans   (2) renouncing special rights in China   (3) landing troops in China   (4) supplying war matériel.

4. The invasion of North Africa in 1942 was made for all reasons *except* the   (1) pleadings of Stalin for relief from German pressure   (2) need to prepare a base for the attack on Europe   (3) need to protect shipping in the Mediterranean   (4) safety of the Suez Canal.

5. During World War II the earnings of laborers   (1) nearly doubled   (2) increased by 50 percent   (3) gained only slightly   (4) declined in terms of real wages.

6. The Allied campaign in Italy in World War II (1) brought the surrender of Mussolini (2) made the least progress of any invasion in the European theater (3) made encouraging progress most of the time (4) was allocated few men and materials.

7. Which part is *not* true? Only Franklin D. Roosevelt (1) served as President for more than 8 years (2) was elected four different times (3) served more than 12 years (4) served four full terms.

8. World War II was financed differently than World War I in that (1) excess profits taxes were levied (2) income taxes were levied (3) more of the cost was raised by taxation (4) the withholding tax was not used.

TRUE-FALSE

9. The naval Battle of Leyte Gulf was the greatest naval battle of all history.

10. Before the war was over the Japanese cut all overland roads by which supplies could be transported into China.

11. The United States refused to give up any of its special rights in China during the war.

12. The last major offensive of the Germans in Europe against American forces was in southern France.

13. The War Labor Board prevented any advance in wages during the war.

14. In World War II the railroads did their job so well it was not necessary for the government to take charge of them.

15. The withholding system of income tax collection began in World War II.

COMPLETION

16. The last American strongholds in the Philippines to be captured by the Japanese were at _____ and _____ . In the Aleutian Islands the Japanese advance reached as far at Attu and _____ and, in the direction of India, the nation of _____ was occupied.

17. The Americans first halted Japanese expansion in the battles of Coral Sea and _____ ; American counterattack began at _____ in the Solomon Islands.

18. Admiral _____ commanded American forces in the Central Pacific while General _____ commanded forces in the Southwest Pacific Theater.

19. In the reoccupation of the Philippines Admiral _____ headed the American naval fleets.

20. _____ was the Chinese leader in World War II.

21. After the Philippines, the United States invaded _____ and the Japanese fought back in suicide or _____ attacks.

22. The United States dropped atom bombs first on the city of _____ and next on _____ ; President _____ made the decision to do so.

23. The first American invasion in the European Theater was in _____ , the next in the island of _____ , then in _____ . The D-Day invasion of Europe occurred in the French province of _____ in the year _____ under the supreme command of General _____ .

24. During the war on the "Home Front" prices were fixed and rationing enforced by the _____ .

25. In 1944 Roosevelt won a fourth term by defeating the Republican nominee _____ .

CHRONOLOGY / CHAPTER 22

1945   January, Yalta Conference.
April 12, Roosevelt died; Truman became President.
April, UN meeting at San Francisco.

1946   Rapid demobilization of American forces. Peacetime conscription adopted.
Prolonged strikes and severe inflation.
Atomic Energy Commission created.
Republicans gain control of Congress in midterm elections.
Veterans receive generous benefits after discharge from service.

1947   Taft-Hartley Act for regulation of labor unions.
Presidential Succession Act passed.
Department of Defense combined Army and Navy Departments.

1948   Truman elected in surprise victory over Dewey.

1949   Eleven leading Communists imprisoned under Smith Act.

1950   McCarran Act passed against subversives.

1952   McCarran-Walters Act revised immigration laws.

22
THE TRUMAN ADMINISTRATION, 1945–1953

On April 12, 1945, President Roosevelt, who had been in declining health for several months, died of a massive cerebral hemorrhage. Harry S. Truman succeeded to the Presidency. It became his duty to carry out the postwar plans made by Roosevelt; he proved faithful to the policies that had won reelection for the Democrats. His administration was chiefly concerned with demobilization, the challenge of the Soviet Union, and the enactment of the Fair Deal.

INTERNATIONAL COOPERATION

Frequent conferences between the heads of the Allied nations during the war not only helped to coordinate the war effort but gave hope that agreement might help maintain peace and promote international cooperation afterwards.

✪✪✪ **The High Level Conferences**—At the Casablanca Conference in North Africa in January 1943, Roosevelt and Churchill announced that only "unconditional surrender" would be accepted from the Axis powers.

In the Moscow Conference, Hull and British Foreign Secretary Eden met Molotov of the Soviet Union in October 1943, and agreed that an organization of the nations of the world would be established after the war for the purpose of maintaining peace and preventing aggression.

At the Cairo Conference in November 1943, Roosevelt and Churchill met Chiang Kai-shek and promised the restoration to China of territory taken by Japan since World War I. Immediately afterwards, Roosevelt and Churchill met Stalin at Teheran to announce their general accord and intention to cooperate for victory and peace.

At Yalta, the most important of the wartime conferences, the Allied leaders met on the Russian Black Sea coast in January 1945. Agreements regarding Germany were: 1) the occupation of Germany by the United

States, Britain, Russia, and France; 2) the destruction of Nazism and militarism; 3) the disarmament of Germany and control of her industry to prevent rearmament; 4) punishment of all war criminals; and 5) that some reparations would be exacted. Agreements regarding Asia were: 1) that Russia would enter the war against Japan, 2) southern Sakhalin Island and the Kurile Islands would be restored to Russia, 3) certain rights would be accorded Russia in Manchuria that would give Russia domination there. Other agreements provided: 1) that Russia would have three votes in the Assembly of the UN; 2) for the grant of the veto power to members of the Security Council of the UN; 3) for the establishment of democratic government in Poland and Yugoslavia; 4) that delegates would meet at San Francisco to draft the charter for the UN.

THE UNITED NATIONS

In April 1945, the delegates of nations that had declared war on the Axis nations met at San Francisco to draw up the charter of the United Nations.

✪✪✪ **Organization**—It was agreed that 1) the Security Council would consist of five permanent members—the United States, Russia, Britain, France, and China. Six other members are chosen for two-year terms by the General Assembly. The permanent members each have the right of veto. The Security Council was given the power to enforce international peace and security. 2) The General Assembly was composed of representatives of every member nation, each nation having one vote. This Assembly could debate, make recommendations, and supervise the special agencies. When the veto in the Security Council brought deadlock the Assembly could act. 3) The Secretariat was to be headed by the Secretary-General, the leading official of the UN, with the responsibility of executing decisions of the organization and carrying on the routine work. Dag Hammarskjold of Sweden served to enlarge the powers of the Secretary-General. 4) The International Court of Justice of fifteen justices meeting at The Hague to settle disputes between nations became a part of the United Nations. Special agencies established include: 1) the Economic and Social Council, 2) the United Nations Education, Scientific and Cultural Organization (UNESCO), 3) the Food and Agricultural Organization (FAO), 4) the International Labor Organization (ILO), 5) the World Health Organization (WHO), 6) the International Monetary Fund to help nations stabilize their currencies and increase international trade, and 7) the Trusteeship Council to supervise the colonies taken from Japan.

✪ **Some Achievements of the UN**—In several instances the UN helped materially in restoring peace. The protest of Iran to the Security Council led to the withdrawal of Russian troops in 1946. War broke out in Palestine between the Jews and Arabs when England gave up its control of Palestine in 1948. Dr. Ralph Bunche, UN mediator from the United States, brought an end to the war there. In Indonesia the Security Council stopped a war between the East Indies and the Dutch, a war that led to independence of the Republic of Indonesia in 1949. Fighting between India and Pakistan over Kashmir was stopped. The war in Korea beginning in 1950 and the war against Egypt in 1956 were settled by UN intervention.

DOMESTIC PROBLEMS UNDER TRUMAN

When Harry Truman succeeded to the Presidency in April 1945, he seemed humbled by the weight of his sudden responsibilities but after a time proved to be both decisive and confident.

✪ **Truman: Career and Character**—Harry S. Truman was born in Missouri and served as an artillery officer in France in World War I. He went into politics and studied law at evening school in the early 1920s. In his career in politics he was associated with the notorious Pendergast political machine in Kansas City but personally stayed clear of all corruption. He held an important county judgeship for nine years, then served as United States Senator from 1935 to 1945 when he became Vice President. He won the nomination for the Vice Presidency for his vigorous prosecution at the head of the Senate committee investigating corruption in war contracts. In the Presidency Truman frequently exhibited an undignified scrappiness by writing hot-tempered letters and by intemperate statements about his critics. However, he proved to be a decisive leader in critical situations and vigorously worked for the measures he advocated. Truman eventually cast off the cabinet officials he had inherited from Roosevelt. He showed a strong pro-labor bias.

✪ **Rapid Demobilization**—Demands at home for the return of the servicemen and demonstrations at many army establishments abroad compelled the government to carry out a hasty release of the men and abandonment of bases and materials all over the world. The first peacetime draft, in 1946, conscripted replacements for the discharged troops. The liberal veterans legislation paid unemployment benefits until veterans could find jobs, made home loans available to them, and gave free education in vocational schools and in colleges.

Consumer annoyance with scarcities and manufacturers' demands for removal of price controls caused a brief period of decontrol during which prices jumped about 20 percent. Inflationary price rises continued to the harassment of returned veterans while organized labor went out on a series of long strikes. These strikes resulted in settlements that gave workers the same earnings as in wartime but without their having to work overtime. Each succeeding year saw new labor negotiations with increased wages or equivalent benefits. After a while only rents remained under control. In several years after the war the thrifty and patriotic investors in war bonds found that their money had lost half the purchasing power it had at the time it had been saved during the war.

The sudden dismantling of the American war machine left the nation in a weak bargaining position in opposing Russian grabs for advantage and power. The ownership and production of fissionable materials and atomic research was placed under the Atomic Energy Commission in the Atomic Energy Act in 1946.

✪✪✪ The Taft-Hartley Act (1947)—In the mid-term election of 1946 the Republicans regained control, in the 80th Congress, for the first time since 1930; people were tired of the deprivations of the war effort. Unauthorized strikes during the war, particularly by John L. Lewis's coal miners, antagonized the public and convinced a majority that labor had now grown too strong under the Wagner Act. To restore the balance between labor and management the Republican Congress passed the Taft-Hartley Labor Relations Act in 1947.

Leading provisions of the Taft-Hartley Act 1) permitted employers to sue unions for breaking contracts or for damages suffered from jurisdictional strikes; 2) prohibited the closed shop but permitted the union shop under certain conditions; 3) provided that the government might secure an injunction to postpone serious strikes; 4) prohibited certain unfair practices, such as "featherbedding"; 5) forbade contributions by unions to political campaigns; 6) required union officials to take a non-Communist oath in order to secure the benefits of government mediation of disputes. Unions began demanding the repeal of the act.

✪✪ Presidential Succession Act—In 1947 Congress changed the line of succession to the presidency at Truman's request. After the vice president the Speaker of the House was placed next in line and followed by the president *pro tempore* of the Senate; after that the cabinet officials followed in the order of rank which in turn is based upon the date of creation of their respective departments.

The Twenty-second Amendment passed Congress in 1947 and was ratified in 1951; this anti-third term amendment, a slap at Roosevelt, forbade future presidents to take office for a third term.

✪ The Department of Defense (1947)—Congress reorganized the military services by combining the Army and Navy Departments into a single Department of Defense. The air force was given equal status with the army and navy within the new department. The act still did not satisfactorily solve the problem of interservice rivalry nor prevent the waste of money by duplications of all kinds.

✪✪ The Election of 1948—The Republican congressional victory in 1946 was interpreted as a certain indication that the party would capture the presidency too in 1948. The Democrats could not induce General

Eisenhower to accept the nomination and accepted Truman somewhat reluctantly. President Truman's strong advocacy of civil rights to prevent discrimination because of race, color, or creed alienated conservative Southern Democrats; they nominated Governor J. Strom Thurmond of South Carolina. The Democratic extremists on the left who favored a friendly policy towards Russia organized a Progressive Party, nominated Henry Wallace, but suffered from Communist support.

The Republican Party nominated Governor Dewey of New York and Governor Earl Warren of California. Overconfident of victory, especially because of the splintering of the Democratic Party and the predictions of the pollsters, the Republicans made few commitments and talked in generalities. Almost alone Truman believed he could win and fought a "give-'em-hell" campaign in which he made specific promises to the voters to support social legislation and farm price supports. In the most surprising upset in American presidential campaign history, Truman won by a large electoral vote.

TRUMAN'S FAIR DEAL

Truman called his program the "Fair Deal" since he favored an extension of the New Deal. One of Truman's early acts was to execute, under the authority of Congress, the recommendations of the Hoover Commission to consolidate and reorganize various agencies of government. His main program, however, was his Fair Deal.

○○ **The Fair Deal Program**—The Fair Labor Standards Act was amended to increase the minimum wage from 40 to 75 cents an hour. A huge program for slum clearance and low-rent housing was passed. The Social Security Act was extended to cover an additional 10,000,000 persons and benefit payments increased. Agriculture was given high supports for commodity prices.

○○ **The Conservative Coalition**—The Republican and conservative Southern Democratic opposition formed an alliance that defeated Truman's program to repeal the Taft-Hartley Act and to pass a national health insurance program. A filibuster of Southern Democrats defeated the civil rights program. The Republicans further strengthened themselves in Congress in the election of 1950 and ended hope of extending the Fair Deal program.

○○ **Internal Security**—When international Communism resumed its drive after World War II to communize the world, steps were taken to protect the nation against subversives. Publicity given to Soviet espionage during and after the war and the trial and conviction of Alger Hiss aroused the nation to the new threat to internal security. Eleven leading Communists were imprisoned in 1949 under the Smith Act (1940), which had made it a crime to advocate overthrow of the government by force or to belong to a group advocating it.

Congress passed the McCarran Act in 1950 over Truman's veto. This act required the registration of Communists and of their organizations. It also required the deportation of Communist immigrants and forbade the immigration of persons who had previous membership in totalitarian organizations.

Immigration—The McCarran-Walter Act (1952),opposed by Truman and by many liberals, essentially a revision of the immigration laws, ended the principle of racial discrimination by giving Asian countries a quota of about 100 each year. It gave preference to persons with important skills and those having relatives in the United States. This law restricted the immigration and naturalization of Communists and made it easier to deport undesirable aliens and newly naturalized citizens.

CHAPTER BOOK LIST

Barth, Alan, *The Loyalty of Free Men* (1951). Critique of the anxiety of the Truman years.

Benedict, M.R., *Farm Policies of The United States, 1790–1950* (1953). Best survey of farm problem.

Bernstein, B.J., and Matusow, Allen J., *The Truman Administration: A Documentary History* (Harper & Row).

Bohlen, Charles, *Witness to History* (1973).

Cooke, Alistair, *A Generation on Trial* (1950). The Hiss Case.

Daniels, Jonathan, *The Man of Independence* (1950). Friendly account.

Doublas, William O., *Almanac of Liberty* (Dolphin).

Goldman, Eric, *The Crucial Decade, 1945–1960* (Vintage). Interesting recent history.

Madison, C.A., *Critics and Crusaders* (Ungar). Reformers throughout American history.

Truman, Harry S., *Memoirs* (Two vols., 1956).

REVIEW QUESTIONS

MULTIPLE CHOICE

1. The decision to require unconditional surrender of the enemy was made in 1943 at (1) Cairo (2) Moscow (3) Yalta (4) Casablanca.

2. At Yalta the Allied leaders agreed upon all *except* (1) the denazification of Germany (2) the establishment of a democratic government in Poland (3) Russia entering the war against Japan (4) details of the occupation of Germany.

3. Before becoming Vice President, Truman's most important government position was as (1) Governor of Missouri (2) a federal judge (3) congressman (4) United States Senator.

4. Demobilization after World War II (1) proceeded cautiously (2) ignored the needs of veterans (3) was too hasty (4) provided fewer benefits for veterans than in World War I.

5. The term "open shop" refers to a plant or business where (1) only unionized workers are hired (2) either union or non-union workers are hired (3) employees must join a union after six months (4) only non-union workers are hired.

6. The Taft-Hartley Act (1) imposed unusual restrictions on employers (2) gave labor greater power than ever (3) was opposed by the Republicans (4) sought to curb the power of unions.

7. The popularity of President Truman in 1948 was due to (1) his direct and forthright statement of his position on public issues (2) his correct, tactful behavior on all occasions (3) his conservative position during the period of postwar reaction (4) the intellectual quality of his television appearances (5) the dramatic stage appeal of Margaret Truman.

8. Most of Truman's Fair Deal program (1) was passed by a combination of liberal Republicans and Northern Democrats (2) met defeat at the hands of a coalition of Republicans and Southern Democrats (3) was defeated by filibuster (4) was enacted after long debate.

TRUE-FALSE

9. One of the most important agreements made at Yalta was that Russia would enter the war against Japan.

10. UN intervention in many instances has brought settlement of international wars.

11. Truman has never been found implicated in any case of corruption in spite of his association with the Pendergast political organization in Kansas City.

12. Before becoming Vice President Truman was governor of Missouri.

13. The sudden dismantling of the war machine of the United States in 1946–47 strengthened the United States by proving its peaceful intentions.

14. The 22nd Amendment was intended partly as a slap at Roosevelt.

15. The split in the Democratic Party in 1948 made the Republicans overconfident.

COMPLETION

16. At the _____ Conference it was agreed that Russia might control the northern Chinese province of _____ after the war.

17. The UNO was organized at _____ in the year _____; just before the conference met _____ died. At San Francisco it was agreed that the Security Council would consist of _____ permanent members, each having the right of _____ . The other two main branches of the UNO are the _____ and the _____ , or permanent working force.

18. Before becoming Vice President Harry Truman was _____ from _____ .

19. The provision of the Taft-Hartley Act especially resented by labor leaders was the requirement they take a _____ oath.

20. The Presidential Succession Act of 1947 places the _____ next in line after the _____ .

21. The Anti-Third Term Amendment is numbered _____ .

22. In 1947 the Army and Navy Departments were combined in the _____ .

23. Truman's program of domestic reform was known as the _____ .

24 The _____ Act of _____ requires the registration of Communists and deportation of Communist immigrants.

25. The most recent major law relating to immigration was the _____ Act of 1952.

THE COLD WAR, 1945–1989

CHRONOLOGY / CHAPTER 23

1945   Potsdam Conference provided terms for occupation of
        Germany.
        Military government established in Germany by four Allied
        powers.
        Beginning of American military government in Japan under
        MacArthur.

1946   Nuremberg war crimes trials in Germany.
        Disagreements start between Russia and other Allies.

1947   Peace treaties with minor powers signed.
        Truman Doctrine brought aid to Greece and Turkey.
        Marshall Plan for long range economic recovery of Europe.
        Rearmament begun in the United States.

1948   Russian blockade of Berlin thwarted by American airlift
        in 1949.
        Truman defeated Dewey for Presidency.
        Communists take control in Czechoslovakia.

1949   Federal Republic of West Germany formed.
        North Atlantic Treaty signed by twelve nations.
        Point Four program begun by Truman.
        Russians exploded their first atomic device.

1950   Communists complete control of China.
        June, Korean War began with invasion of South Korea.
        November, Chinese troops attack UN forces in North Korea.

1951   Peace negotiations begun in Korea.
        General MacArthur recalled from Korea.
        Peace treaty signed with Japan.

1952   Gen. Eisenhower (Rep.) elected President over Stevenson
        (Dem.).
        Agreement with West Germany ended Allied occupation.
        ANZUS Treaty signed.

1953   Korean armistice signed.

Chapter

23
FOREIGN AFFAIRS UNDER TRUMAN, 1945–1953

> During the war ample evidence existed that the common war effort did not evoke the same cooperation and trust from Russia as existed among the other Allies. At the end of the war and after Truman became President, the Russians shifted to independent and antagonistic policies. This rivalry of the Soviet Union came to be the dominant problem in foreign relations under Truman.

EARLY POSTWAR PROBLEMS

The nation's most weighty postwar problems related to foreign affairs. The Cold War with Russia, with its accompanying crises, taught Americans after some time to accept such problems as the normal course of events. Truman continued the internationalist policies of Roosevelt and displayed considerable ability and decisiveness in meeting the challenges as they arose.

✪✪✪ **The Occupation of Germany**—During the war the Allies agreed at Yalta to divide Germany into four zones of military occupation under the leading allies—the United States, the Soviet Union, Great Britain, and France. The German capital of Berlin was similarly divided into separate occupation zones. Communist Russia schemed to gain control of Germany. After much quarreling with Russia, the Allies united their three zones and the Russians withdrew from the Allied control council. In an effort to gain control of all Berlin, the Russians began a land blockade of the city. The Allies, to prove that they would support their friends, began an airlift in 1948 that transported all necessary supplies to Berlin by cargo planes. In May 1949, the Russians discontinued the blockade. The Western Allies proved that they would not be driven out of Berlin. In 1949 the Federal Republic of West Germany was formed under a new constitution adopted there; Bonn became the capital. Allied troops remained in Germany but military government was terminated. West Germany was assisted in her economic recovery, and limited rearmament was permitted as it became apparent the Allies needed a stronger ally in Germany.

✪✪ **The Occupation of Japan**—An Allied Council, with members from the United States, Russia, England, and China, was established in Japan, but the real power in the reconstruction of Japan was assumed by General Douglas MacArthur. Japan in 1946 drew up a new constitution that provided for democratic elections and the breakup of large land holdings and business monopolies.

In 1952 a peace treaty between the Allies and Japan became effective; the treaty was negotiated without the agreement of the Soviets. The United States received the right to maintain military forces in Japan but military government came to an end.

✪ **The War Crimes Trials**—The United States wished to establish the precedent that individuals could be held responsible for violating international law and could be tried and punished by international courts. At Nuremberg, Germany, in 1946, trials of the accused wartime leaders of Germany were conducted by an International Tribunal. Justice Robert H. Jackson of the United States Supreme Court headed the prosecution; 11 of the high Nazis were found guilty and executed; others were given prison sentences; three were acquitted. Less important offenders were tried by German denazification courts.

In the same way Japanese militarists were tried and sentenced soon after the war. Premier Tojo received the death sentence and was hanged. Trial of minor war criminals continued for some time afterwards.

✪✪✪ **The Peace Treaties**—In 1945 at the Potsdam Conference the Allies agreed to establish a Council of Foreign Ministers to draft peace treaties. The first treaties were drawn up with the minor powers of Finland, Hungary, Bulgaria, Romania, and Italy. The peace conference met in Paris in 1946 and the treaties were signed in 1947. These defeated countries all lost territory and had to pay large indemnities. The treaty with Japan in 1952 had to be drawn up without Russian consent. In 1955 a treaty with Austria was concluded with Russian participation. No peace treaty was drawn up with Germany.

FOREIGN AID AND ALLIANCES

As a friendly gesture during the war the Communists dissolved the Comintern, the world propaganda agency. In 1947 the Communist countries revived this agency by organizing the Cominform. The United States was forced to meet the new aggressiveness of Russian Communism.

✪✪ **The Truman Doctrine (1947)**—In 1947 the British announced that they did not have the financial resources to maintain the conservative government they had established in Greece. Communist guerrillas in Greece were receiving aid from their Communist neighbors to the north. If Russia could control Greece she could outflank the entrance to the

Black Sea and the Suez Canal. At the same time Russia began a campaign of intimidation against Turkey; the USSR demanded territory and military bases and a subordination of Turkish foreign policy to Russia.

President Truman at this point took a positive stand against the Russian threat. He asked Congress to vote $400,000,000 economic aid to Greece and Turkey. He declared it to be the policy of the United States to support "free peoples who are resisting attempted subjugation by armed minorities" within or from outside pressure. This policy became known as the Truman Doctrine. The funds given were used so effectively to strengthen the military forces that the Communist danger soon became negligible in these two countries.

✪✪✪ **The Marshall Plan (1947)**—Soon after aid had been voted for Greece and Turkey, Secretary of State George C. Marshall recognized the need to support economic recovery in Europe to preserve democratic governments there and announced that the United States would give aid to countries that would cooperate.

Congress soon voted 5 billion dollars and established the European Cooperation Administration to administer the European Recovery Plan. European nations drew up plans, as suggested, that provided for cooperation with each other as well as with the United States to promote the recovery of all of Europe. The aid had the immediate result of winning an election victory over Communists in Italy.

By 1949 economic recovery in Italy and France had restored almost normal conditions. The Marshall Plan funds were kept under American control rather than being administered by an international agency. The plan superseded other earlier funds for European recovery and rehabilitation. The Marshall Plan set in motion widespread continuing economic cooperation among the nations of Europe. It promoted basic industries, such as water power development and fertilizer plants, that would lift living standards. After a few years Europe had more than recovered the production records of the prewar days.

✪✪✪ **The North Atlantic Pact**—In 1949 the United States joined the friendly countries of Western Europe in a military alliance—the first membership by the United States in a peacetime military alliance with European powers since the alliance with France after the American Revolution. The threats of aggression by Russia, which could not be prevented by the UNO, needed to be countered by a firm military alliance ready to oppose Russian attack and thereby prevent it.

Twelve nations signed the North Atlantic Treaty (1949). In it they agreed that all would defend an attack against any signatory power. To implement the alliance the North Atlantic Treaty Organization (NATO) was formed to integrate the military forces of the democracies. The United States Congress voted large sums for the rearmament of our allies; President Truman made General Eisenhower supreme commander of the military forces of the Western nations. In 1957 the NATO representatives agreed to stockpile nuclear missiles.

○ **The Point Four Program**—In 1949 Truman urged Congress to appropriate money for giving technical and scientific aid to underdeveloped countries over the world to raise their living standards. The program began work in 1950; its purpose was to make such countries more immune to Communist appeals.

WAR IN ASIA

Communist revolution in Asia led to the takeover of China and an attempt to take South Korea behind the Bamboo Curtain. Frustrated by the "war without victory" in Asia, U.S. voters turned against the Democrats in the election of 1952.

○○ **China After the War**—The turn of events in China after World War II brought deep frustration to Americans. The war with Japan began in support of China and of its friendly government, but the military victory over Japan was accompanied by a Communist victory in China and the loss of China as a powerful ally in Asia. The Nationalist government of Chiang Kai-shek was characterized by incompetency, inflation, corruption, and a failure to bring much needed social reform to the Chinese people. The Chinese Communists in North China, with Russian aid, exploited the situation and rapidly gained Nationalist territory. The American people were looking forward to demobilization, and the administration did not wish to become involved in a large-scale, apparently hopeless, civil war in China in support of the corrupt and harsh government of Chiang Kai-shek. The able General George C. Marshall, sent to China in 1946, failed to secure the necessary cooperation of Chiang Kai-shek in plans to limit Communist advances in China by introducing reforms.

As time passed and conditions grew worse in Nationalist China, the Chinese Communist leader Mao Tse-tung, with Russian support, gained power and influence. Communist armies made steady gains until they had brought all of China under Communist rule in 1950. The Chinese Nationalists took refuge on Formosa.

○○○ **The Korean War**—Independent Korea, which had been absorbed by Japan after the Russo-Japanese War in 1905, regained its independence in 1945. For purposes of military occupation Russia and the United States divided Korea along the 38th parallel pending the establishment of a united Korean Republic. In 1948 Russia set up a Communist government in North Korea instead of leaving the question of government to be determined by free elections throughout Korea. In South Korea Syngman Rhee, a Korean patriot, headed a government recognized by members of the United Nations. In 1949 American forces were withdrawn from Korea, but Rhee's government was left without military preparation to defend itself.

In late June 1950, North Korean troops with Russian training and equipment invaded South Korea. The United Nations' Security Council met and declared North Korea as an aggressor and urged the restoration of peace. President Truman made a quick decision to support the United Nations resolution and ordered sea and air forces to defend South Korea; from Japan American ground troops were sent in. The Communist attack was a challenge to the willingness of the United Nations to take action against an aggressor in order to preserve peace. The United States recognized that if the Communists went unchallenged, they would resort to aggression in other countries.

In the course of the invasion the North Koreans, at first highly successful, occupied most of South Korea except for the Pusan perimeter in the southeast. From Pusan the UN forces under General Douglas MacArthur rallied and steadily drove the enemy back into North Korea until three fourths of North Korea was occupied in November 1950. Late in November Chinese Communist troops, coming in large numbers from across the Yalu River, attacked and sent the UN forces reeling back across the 38th parallel. Again the UN forces stopped the enemy, regained the offensive, and this time stabilized the battle front somewhat north of the 38th parallel when truce teams began their discussions to end the war. The peace negotiations began in June, 1951; it soon became apparent the North Koreans were in no hurry to end the war. The talks bogged down in the question of repatriation of prisoners of war; the UN asked that prisoners be free to decide for themselves whether or not they would return to the country they had been fighting for. Determination of the new boundary also held up the negotiations which were concluded under Eisenhower.

○ **The Recall of MacArthur**—After the Chinese "volunteers" entered the war in North Korea, General MacArthur began demanding the right to carry the war into Communist China. He disagreed strongly with the policy of the Truman administration which was seeking to fight a limited war and to appease American allies. In short, MacArthur was attempting to influence policy, which properly belonged to the civilian authorities. For what was essentially insubordination, President Truman relieved MacArthur of his command. MacArthur returned to the United States in an attempt to make political capital of his removal and discredit the Democratic administration. In this he succeeded at first in appealing to a large minority of Americans who wished to take stronger action in the war but did not thoroughly understand that a democracy must keep the military subordinate to the civilian government.

○ **Decline of Truman's Popularity**—Several factors combined to bring a decline in the popularity of President Truman within two years after his election victory. Basically the postwar rise in conservatism accounts for the change. In writing scolding letters and in personal rejoinders in public, Truman displayed a tactlessness reminiscent of Andrew Johnson. Truman's decisive stand against the Communists in the Korean War won public applause, but as the war dragged on and MacArthur was dismissed, Truman suffered increasing criticism. A combination of Southern conservatives and of Republicans in Congress stalled the liberal Fair Deal program Truman sought to pass. The Democrats were blamed for American frustration in the Cold War, especially the loss of China. At home the administration was criticized for an alleged softness toward Communist influence in government and for considerable corruption in various federal departments. Truman in 1952 confiscated the steel industry when it had been closed down by a strike. Truman's error was revealed when the Supreme Court ordered return of the properties to management.

○○ The Election of 1952—President Truman chose not to run for the Democratic nomination in 1952 even though the Twenty-second Amendment limiting the tenure in the presidency did not apply to him as the incumbent. Governor Adlai Stevenson of Illinois apparently was drafted for the nomination, but Senator Estes Kefauver worked eagerly for the prize.

As for the Republicans, Dwight D. Eisenhower, the popular hero of the war in Europe, finally announced himself as a Republican and admitted his willingness to accept the nomination. Senator Robert A. Taft of Ohio vigorously sought the nomination; the conviction among many delegates that the conservative Senator could not win gave the nomination to Eisenhower.

Stevenson, in the campaign, had the enthusiastic support of the liberals in his party. Stevenson promised the repeal of the Taft-Hartley Act, supported civil rights, and endorsed the New Deal reforms. His speeches revealed unusual literary skill, but his voice and seemingly stilted sense of humor did not win the masses as did the broad smile and friendly personality of the less articulate Eisenhower. The Republicans criticized the Democrats for corruption, softness toward Communism, extravagance, and for involvement in the Korean War. Just before election Eisenhower promised that if elected he would "go to Korea."

Eisenhower won by a landslide vote but the victory in the House was thin and in the Senate Republican control depended upon the support of conservative Democrats. The victory was an Eisenhower victory rather than a party victory.

CHAPTER BOOK LIST

Acheson, Dean, *Present at the Creation* (1969).
Ambrose, Stephen, *Rise to Globalism: American Foreign Policy* (1976).

Barth, Alan, *The Loyalty of Free Men* (1951).

Bowles, Chester, *American Politics in a Revolutionary World* (1956).

Coyle, Davis Cushman, *The United Nations and How It Works* (Mentor). Clear statement of various aspects of the UN.

Feis, Herbert, *The China Tangle* (1953).

Goldman, Eric F., *Rendezvous with Destiny* (Vintage). Reform movements brought up to date.

Halle, Lems J., *The Cold War as History* (Harper & Row).

Hersey, John, *Hiroshima* (Bantam). Brief.

Le Feber, Walter, *America, Russia and the Cold War 1945–1975* (Third ed., 1976).

Price, H.L., *The Marshall Plan and Its Meaning* (1955).

Russell, Ruth B., *A History of the United Nations Charter* (1958).

Spanier, John W., *The Truman-MacArthur Controversy and the Korean War* (Harvard).

Ulam, Ann, *The Rivals: America and Russia Since World War II* (Viking).

REVIEW QUESTIONS

MULTIPLE CHOICE

1. The basic cause of disagreement between Russia and the other Allies was (1) Russia's attempt to dominate all of Germany (2) conflicts between France and the United States (3) German desire to join the Russians (4) faulty Allied occupation policies.

2. Japan after her surrender was occupied by American forces under which general? (1) Wainwright (2) Eisenhower (3) Clay (4) MacArthur.

3. The Truman Doctrine was (1) announced in 1951 (2) was the first step in the American policy of giving military aid to help nations resist Communism (3) called for the unification of the occupation zones of West Germany (4) required the nations saved from German aggression to adopt democracy.

4. America's most significant foreign aid program has been executed through the (1) Point Four Program (2) NATO (3) Marshall Plan (4) Truman Doctrine.

5. The North Atlantic Pact represented a great departure in American foreign policy because it (1) established a military alliance in peacetime (2) was organized outside the UNO (3) was a step against communism (4) gave American military aid to the Allies.

6. The greatest significance of the Korean War is that it showed that (1) Korea was hopelessly divided (2) China had again become a major power (3) the United States would go to war to stop Communist aggression (4) MacArthur would never win the Presidency.

7. MacArthur was recalled by President Truman because (1) MacArthur was a Republican (2) American Allies demanded his recall (3) MacArthur committed acts of insubordination (4) MacArthur was losing the Korean War.

8. Truman's popularity and that of the Democrats had declined by 1952 because of all *except* (1) the personality of the President (2) the frustrations of the Korean War (3) a strong reaction against Fair Dealism (4) numerous cases of corruption.

9. Eisenhower was elected in 1952 because (1) of a strong surge of conservatism reflected in many places by Republican victories (2) personal popularity which enabled Eisenhower to win many votes from Democrats (3) the extreme corruption of the Truman administration (4) he promised to be even more liberal than the Democrats.

TRUE-FALSE
10. While President, Truman showed much decisiveness and ability in meeting the international problems of his time.

11. The peace treaty with Japan was signed with the agreement of the Soviets.

12. Truman's seizure of the steel industry during the strike in 1952 was ruled unconstitutional by the Supreme Court.

13. A strong reaction against the liberal policies of the Democrats was chiefly responsible for their defeat in 1952.

14. The main difficulty in the peace negotiations in Korea after 1952 were over the procedure for repatriation of prisoners of war.

COMPLETION
15. The Allies agreed to divide Germany into how many occupation zones? _____ .

16. The Russian attempt to blockade Berlin in 1948 was broken by the Allied _____ .

17. The Truman Doctrine was applied first in _____ and _____ .

18. In 1949 Truman began a program to give technical aid to underdeveloped countries; this was called the _____ program.

19. The North Korean attack drove the UN forces as far south as the _____ perimeter before they were turned back north.

20. Chinese Communist forces entered the war by crossing the _____ River.

MATCHING

21. Douglas MacArthur	a. Leader in Formosa
22. George C. Marshall	b. In charge of occupation of Japan
23. Robert H. Jackson	c. Ordered troops to Korea
24. Mao Tse-tung	d. Originator of the ECA
25. Adlai Stevenson	e. Korean patriot
26. Chiang Kai-shek	f. Chinese Communist leader
27. Syngman Rhee	g. Democratic nominee in 1952
28. Harry S. Truman	h. Prosecutor in war crimes trials
29. Robert A. Taft	i. Leader of North Koreans
	j. Lost the Republican nomination in 1952

CHRONOLOGY / CHAPTER 24

1952 Eisenhower elected President on basis of personal popularity.

1950s Reciprocal Trade Agreements Act renewed from time to time;
Republicans pursue policy of tariff reduction.

1953 Business recession.
McCarthyism became active.

1954 *Brown v. Board of Education of Topeka* ruled against racial
segregation in public schools.
St. Lawrence Seaway project approved by Congress.

1955 Guaranteed annual wage became goal of labor unions.
AF of L and CIO merged.
Dixon-Yates contract canceled.

1956 Eisenhower defeated Stevenson a second time.
Agricultural Act of 1956 included "soil bank" to idle farm
lands.

1957 Federal troops sent to Little Rock in school segregation
trouble.
First civil rights law passed since 1875.

1958 Recession and unemployment.
Alaska admitted.
National Defense Education Act passed.

1959 Landrum-Griffin Act passed to curb labor union abuses.
Hawaii admitted.

1960 Kennedy defeated Nixon for Presidency, by very narrow
margin.
Civil Rights Act of 1960.
African Americans organized "sit-ins" against segregation at
lunch counters.

Chapter

24
THE EISENHOWER
ADMINISTRATION, 1953–1961

As a moderate Republican, President Eisenhower pursued many policies in domestic affairs that coincided with or differed little from those of the New Deal and Fair Deal. The conservative minority in the President's party were disappointed with this acceptance of certain features of the welfare state that the Democrats had enacted into law.

Eisenhower: Career and Policies—Dwight D. Eisenhower, born in Texas to humble parents, grew up in Kansas. As a West Point graduate his entire career was that of a professional army officer until after World War II. After the outbreak of the war Eisenhower won rapid promotion for his administrative talents. His remarkable abilities of leadership caused him to be chosen as commander of the Allied forces in the invasion of Europe. From the war he emerged as a popular and highly respected leader. He became the first professional military hero chosen for the Presidency since Grant.

As President, Eisenhower avoided strong partisanship or militant leadership in politics; he set an example of dignity and restraint in politics and sought the support of moderates of both parties. Eisenhower's philosophy of government was opposed to the concept of strong presidential leadership. He failed to provide strong moral, intellectual, or political leadership to fight for the policies he professed to favor. His lack of political experience and shortcomings in spoken and written communication also made him less effective. His skill was in delegating authority to subordinates and in getting people to work together.

❂❂ **Eisenhower's Cabinet and Appointees**—Eisenhower's acceptance of the principles of the Republican Party made him receptive to the influence of business interests; unlike his Democratic predecessors he favored businessmen in making his appointments to office rather than choosing career politicians or academicians. Critics said his cabinet included "nine millionaires and a plumber." John Foster Dulles became Secretary of State. The administration created the new cabinet position of Secretary of Health, Education, and Welfare and placed it under Oveta

Culp Hobby of Texas. Sherman Adams, the leading presidential assistant, exercised considerable power as the President's chief agent. Charles E. Wilson of General Motors Corporation became Secretary of Defense.

Farm Program—The nation's chronic peacetime ailment of crop surpluses and agricultural depression awaited the ministrations of the Eisenhower administration. Farm prices fell at the same time that farmers had to pay more for the things they had to buy. The administration abandoned its campaign pledge of 90 percent of parity for Secretary of Agriculture Ezra Benson's flexible plan with lower support prices. The Agricultural Act of 1956 made a new attack on the problem of farm surpluses known as the "soil bank"—farmers were paid to leave farm lands idle in addition to lands idled by the acreage quotas of farm laws already in effect.

The Public Utility Issue—In the development of hydroelectric power the administration opposed federal expansion in favor of development by private utility companies or by local government. Water power development in the West was relinquished to private corporations. In the Dixon-Yates contract the administration aroused determined opposition by a contract to buy electric power from a privately owned utility company. Electric power generated at several dams on the St. Lawrence Seaway was placed under the authority of the state of New York. However, Eisenhower by his veto refused to exempt natural gas producers from federal regulation.

✪ Labor—Under the Eisenhower administration organized labor continued to improve its status relative to other groups in the national economy. Substantial wage increases were won year after year and added an inflationary bias to the economy. The "guaranteed annual wage" became a leading achievement of the labor movement after 1955. In the same year the two major labor organizations, the AF of L and the CIO, were united in a loose merger. Minimum wages were raised to one dollar an hour.

✪✪✪ Integration of the Public Schools—The 14th Amendment provides that no state may deprive citizens of their privileges nor deny them "equal protection of the laws." In the case of *Plessy v. Ferguson* in 1896 the Supreme Court held that "separate but equal" public facilities for African Americans did not violate the Constitution; this decision permitted segregation of African Americans but schools and other facilities were normally inferior instead of being equal.

In 1954 the Supreme Court by unanimous vote under Chief Justice Earl Warren, a liberal Republican, recognized the inequality, perpetuated by segregation, in the case of *Brown v. Board of Education of Topeka*. The Court held that "separate educational facilities are inherently unequal." Thus 17 states were found in violation of the Constitution.

In 1955 another Court decision ordered the states to terminate segregation with "all deliberate speed" and designated Federal District Courts as agents for deciding if local authorities were complying with the decision. In other cases the ban on segregation was applied to public recreation and transportation facilities.

❍ **Extent of Desegregation**—The first steps toward ending segregation were taken in six of the border states where there was little public opposition to obeying the Court's decision. Six other states of the South gave token acceptance but there was much public opposition. In the states of the Deep South, with a larger percentage of African Americans, various measures were taken to obstruct the enforcement of the decision. Laws were passed empowering local schools to assign pupils upon various bases by which segregation could be maintained. State funds were denied schools that integrated and laws passed to abolish public schools in favor of private schools. Court decisions often required reopening of such schools on the basis of integration. When the governor of Arkansas used the Arkansas National Guard to prevent integration at the Little Rock High School, Eisenhower ordered federal troops to protect African American pupils in 1957–1958.

❍❍ **McCarthyism**—The Cold War, the loss of China to the Communists, the Alger Hiss conviction, the Korean War, and other similar developments created a national anxiety regarding the threat of Communism. Senator Joseph R. McCarthy of Wisconsin rose to prominence on this wave of fear by making unsubstantiated, loose accusations of Communism against prominent persons. Loyalty oaths were required by state legislatures over the country and investigations conducted in Congress and by the state legislatures. When McCarthy's crude and unfair tactics were observed on television by the nation, the public turned against him and his methods. Finally, he was censured by the Senate, in a bipartisan resolution, for conduct unbecoming a senator.

St. Lawrence Seaway (1954)—For a half century plans were advocated for deepening and widening the St. Lawrence River to permit ocean-going vessels to sail from the Atlantic into the Great Lakes. Dams that could be used for the production of hydroelectric power were to be a part of the project. The approval of the project had been long delayed by opposition of Atlantic seaports, Eastern railroads, and private utilities. Canada strongly favored the project and all the presidents since Wilson had requested Congress to act. In 1954 Eisenhower urged construction as a measure of military security and Congress finally consented. The project was completed all the way to Lake Superior in 1959 when it was officially opened.

❍ **Election of 1956**—In this campaign Eisenhower and Stevenson, as in 1952, opposed each other as nominees of their respective major parties. For the Vice Presidency the Republicans named Richard Nixon and the

Democrats chose Estes Kefauver. The Republicans asked for voter support on a basis of the peace and prosperity of Eisenhower's first term. The Democrats criticized the administration of a lack of imagination in conducting foreign relations and for favoritism toward big business. Eisenhower's heart attack and a later intestinal operation were cited by Democrats to show that the President was too much incapacitated to serve vigorously. The outbreak of the Suez Crisis helped Eisenhower to win reelection by an even greater popular vote than in 1952. However, the Democrats increased their strength in both houses of Congress.

❍❍ **Eisenhower's Second Term**—Although Eisenhower continued to hold the respect of the nation, the Republican administration was criticized more and more for various reasons. Farm surpluses continued to accumulate but the agricultural policy of support prices, crop allotments, and the soil bank remained substantially unchanged, and farmers' incomes remained low. In the rest of the economy mild but persistent inflation continued. A recession in 1958 brought unemployment to a critical level, and the Republicans were blamed for not doing enough to stimulate the economy. The presidential assistant, Sherman Adams, was found guilty of accepting substantial rewards for favoring the textile manufacturer Bernard Goldfine, but Adams's assistance to the President was so necessary that Eisenhower waited unduly long to dismiss him.

The Landrum-Griffin Act was passed in 1959 to end certain labor abuses; it required labor unions to report their membership and finances, outlawed secondary boycotts, outlawed certain types of picketing, and gave the states greater regulatory authority over unions.

Alaska was admitted to the Union in 1958 and in 1959 Hawaii became the fiftieth state.

A new development in federal promotion of education was the National Defense Education Act of 1958 to provide loans and graduate fellowships for students.

The failure of Congress in 1960 to pass legislation to increase the minimum wage to $1.25, to provide medical care under Social Security for the aged, to expand public housing, and to give increased federal aid to public education in the states—these failures gave the liberal Democrats campaign issues in 1960.

❍❍ **The Civil Rights Act of 1957**—After the failure of Reconstruction, the Southern states succeeded in evading the intent of the 14th and 15th Amendments by segregation of African Americans and by discrimination against them in various ways. Southern senators in Congress defeated civil rights bills year after year by filibuster. In 1957 Eisenhower asked Congress to pass a broad civil rights law. After its provisions were weakened considerably by Southern Democrats in the Senate, it was passed—to become the first civil rights bill to pass Congress since 1875. The law

1) created a Commission on Civil Rights with the duty of investigating denial of voting rights based on unfair discrimination and 2) gave the Department of Justice certain powers of enforcement.

When Southern officials obstructed the enforcement of the act, the Commission investigated denial of the vote to African Americans. The Commission made further recommendations, and Congress responded with the Civil Rights Act of 1960. This law provided federal penalties for anyone resorting to violence to obstruct the Civil Rights Act and placed restrictions on election officials to help secure the enforcement of voting rights.

In February 1960, African Americans organized "sit-ins" at restaurants and lunch counters where discrimination was in force. These demonstrations ended segregation at lunch counters in many Southern cities.

❍ **Tariff Policy**—President Eisenhower continued the reciprocal trade program begun by the New Deal. Congress granted short extensions of the program. A four-year extension in 1958 gave the administration power to reduce tariffs as much as 20 percent below existing rates. Tariff reductions negotiated with other nations under the modern Republicanism of Eisenhower represented a departure from the traditional policy of the Republican Party. It was consistent with the nation's recognition of the necessity of international cooperation.

CHAPTER BOOK LIST

Alexander, Charles C., *Holding the Line: The Eisenhower Era, 1952–1961* (1975).

Childs, Marquis, *Eisenhower: Captive Hero* (1958). Critical of Eisenhower for the influence of conservative advisers.

Donovan, Robert J., *Eisenhower: The Inside Story* (1956). Accurate and friendly.

Howe, Irving and Coser, Lewis, *American Communist Party: A Critical History* (Praeger).

Judd IV, G.P., *Hawaii: An Informal History* (Collier). Well-told story.

King, Jr., Martin L., *Stride Toward Freedom* (Ballantine).

Martin, J.B., *Stevenson of Illinois* (1976).

Mason, Alpheus, T., *The Supreme Court from Taft to Warren* (1958).

Parmet, Herbert S., *Eisenhower and the American Crusade* (1972).

Rogin, M.P., *McCarthy and the Intellectuals* (1967).

Rovere, R.H., *Senator Joe McCarthy* (Meridian). Sophisticated account of a "gifted demagogue."

Satin, Joseph, *1950s: America's "Placid Decade"* (Houghton Mifflin).

White, Theodore, *The Making of a President 1960* (Atheneum).

REVIEW QUESTIONS

MULTIPLE CHOICE

1. All of the following were true of Eisenhower *except* (1) he had always been thought of as a Republican (2) he was the first professional military man to become President since Grant (3) in many policies he differed little from the moderate Democrats (4) he rejected the philosophy of strong presidential leadership.

2. The farm program of Eisenhower (1) included the essential provisions of the Brannan Plan (2) provided flexible price supports (3) put in effect rigid price supports (4) was never realized because of Democratic control of Congress.

3. The basis of the Supreme Court's decision against desegregation in 1954 was (1) an act of Congress passed by the Eisenhower Republicans and Northern Democrats (2) an act of the Democratic Congress under Truman (3) the civil rights provision of the Fourteenth Amendment (4) Article IX of the Bill of Rights.

4. The term "McCarthyism" refers to (1) the practice of making unsubstantiated, militant charges of communism (2) blind loyalty to one's country (3) any strongly reactionary political beliefs (4) challenging the honesty and character of respectable persons.

5. In the election of 1956 (1) Eisenhower won a weaker victory than in 1952 (2) a candidate's health was not an issue (3) national prosperity was not a factor (4) the same presidential candidates opposed each other as in 1952.

6. In Eisenhower's second term all occurred *except* (1) the Reciprocal Trade Agreements Act failed to be renewed (2) the first civil rights bill passed since 1875 (3) Sherman Adams was dismissed for accepting favors (4) unemployment reached a critical level.

7. The tariff policy of the United States in the 1950s was one of (1) reciprocal trade agreements only (2) strictly protective tariffs (3) continuing the pursuit of free trade.

COMPLETION

8. President Eisenhower's farm program to reduce acreage in cultivated crops included an innovation called the _____ .

9. Under Eisenhower a much publicized controversy related to the TVA was the _____ contract.

10. A leading achievement of the labor movement after 1955 was the

    _____ .

11. In 1955 the two great labor organizations were joined by a loose

    _____ .

12. Eisenhower ordered troops to the high school at _____ , Arkansas, to enforce racial integration.

13. Two new states admitted under Eisenhower were first _____ and next _____ .

14. An act of Congress in 1959 to prevent abuses by labor unions was the _____ Act.

MATCHING

15. Eisenhower   a. Secretary of State
16. Ezra Benson   b. Democratic presidential nominee in
17. John Foster Dulles   1956
18. Oveta Culp Hobby   c. Grew up in Kansas
19. Sherman Adams   d. Leading presidential assistant
20. Estes Kefauver   e. Senator from Wisconsin
21. Adlai Stevenson   f. Flexible farm price supports
22. Joseph R. McCarthy   g. Formerly governor of New York
23. Earl Warren   h. Resigned as Secretary of Health,
24. Charles E. Wilson   Education, and Welfare
                              i. Democratic Vice Presidential nominee
                              j. Eisenhower's Secretary of Defense
                              k. *Brown v. Board of Education of Topeka*

CHRONOLOGY / CHAPTER 25

1953   Armistice signed in Korea.

Stalin died. Cold War thaws somewhat.

1954   War in Indo-China concluded; North Vietnam left with Communist government.

Mutual Security Treaty with Nationalist China on Formosa.

Paris Agreement recognized sovereignty of West Germany.

SEATO created.

1955   Geneva Summit Conference met in effort to promote peace.

Austrian peace treaty signed.

1956   Uprising in Hungary crushed by the Soviet Union.

Nasser seized Suez Canal.

Suez Crisis ended by American and Russian pressure.

Eisenhower reelected.

Stalin denounced in Russia.

1957   Eisenhower Doctrine announced readiness to use armed forces to aid Middle East nations threatened by Communist aggression.

Sputnik I satellite orbited by Soviets.

European Common Market organized.

1958   War threatened with Communist China over Quemoy and Matsu.

American troops sent to Lebanon at request of Lebanese president.

First American satellite orbited.

Democrats gain further strength in Congress.

1959   Castro's control of Cuba completed.

Economic aid voted for Latin America.

Khrushchev visited United States.

1960   U-2 incident.

Chapter

25
FOREIGN AFFAIRS UNDER EISENHOWER, 1953–1961

Over the long run, changes in the leadership of both the United States and Soviet Russia brought little practical change in the rivalry between them. The Korean War was succeeded by other outbreaks of violence that threatened to flare into a major conflict during the Eisenhower Presidency. At first, after the death of Stalin in 1953, there was some easing of tension, but after Khrushchev came to power new crises in the Cold War perpetuated it in varying degrees of intensity. Most American foreign relations were strongly affected by the Cold War.

PROBLEMS IN ASIA

The Communists exploited the strong tide of nationalism that swept the peoples of Asia after World War II. The Communist regime in China encouraged other such movements in the nations of Asia.

❂❂ **Korea**—Eisenhower's visit to Korea showed that America desired to end that war. Truce negotiations at Panmunjon dragged out for many months over the question of exchange of prisoners. In July 1953, a truce was signed. The border between North and South Korea was redrawn so that South Korea was slightly favored and provisions agreed to for the return of prisoners of war. The death of Stalin earlier and the possibility of an all-out war against China had made the Communist negotiators more conciliatory.

❂ **Indo-China**—A long war in Vietnam was finally concluded in 1954 in a conference of nineteen nations at Geneva. A boundary was established that conceded North Vietnam to a Communist government; South Vietnam became a republic.

❂ **Alliances in Asia**—Just as NATO was formed to contain the Communist aggression in Europe, alliances were concluded by the United States in Asia. In 1952 Australia, New Zealand, and the United States signed the ANZUS treaty to make plans for mutual defense. In 1954 a mutual security treaty was signed with Nationalist China for the defense of Formosa and of the Pescadores Islands. In 1955 the South East Asia Treaty Organization (SEATO) was created with Great Britain, France, Australia, New Zealand, Pakistan, the Philippine Republic, and Thailand; these nations agreed to cooperate for mutual defense. In 1958 agreement with Nationalist China threatened to involve the United States in another struggle with Communist China when the offshore islands of Quemoy and Matsu were shelled from the Chinese mainland.

THE SUMMIT CONFERENCE AND EUROPEAN RELATIONS

Since the beginning of the Cold War in Europe, the Allies had found it necessary to relax the restrictions upon Germany and to permit preparations for self-defense. In 1954 the Paris Agreement recognized the sovereignty of West Germany and the nation was integrated with NATO.

The more conciliatory attitude of Russia under Bulganin, Stalin's immediate successor, encouraged Eisenhower to call the much-heralded Geneva Summit Conference in July 1955. France and England joined the United States and Russia. Eisenhower offered a general disarmament plan calling for aerial inspection, but the Russians refused to accept this plan. The conference created a better feeling and offered the possibility that agreements might be worked out later.

Restlessness of the peoples behind the Iron Curtain in 1956 aroused the hope that Russian control might be thrown off there. Demonstrations in Poland won an increased degree of self-government for the Poles.

A violent uprising in Hungary brought massive retaliation by Russian invaders; world opinion turned against the Soviets in this demonstration of their willingness to use force to crush the national aspirations of other peoples.

CRISES IN THE MIDDLE EAST AND OTHER CHALLENGES IN FOREIGN RELATIONS

Russia, long ambitious to expand and to extend her influence in the Middle East, has been thwarted there by the British and French since the Crimean War (1856). After World War II only the United States had the necessary power to prevent Russian domination. The strongly nationalistic Arab nations sought to profit from the rivalry of Russia and the United States. American and Russian rivalry also manifested itself in the space race and in the Castro revolution in Cuba.

○○ The Suez Crisis—In the rivalry between the United States and Russia, the American Secretary of State, Dulles, promised Egypt financial aid in building the Aswan Dam on the upper Nile. In 1956 the request of the

Egyptian President Nasser for a loan was refused because Egypt had been importing arms from Russian dominated satellite nations. Nasser struck back by seizing the Suez Canal (September 14, 1956) in order to obtain its revenues for financing the dam.

Israel took advantage of the British and French anger at Egypt's seizure of the canal by invading Egyptian territory (October 29, 1956). Britain and France demanded that both nations withdraw from the canal. When Egypt refused, Britain and France invaded her territory in cooperation with Israel. Acting through the UN, the United States and the Soviet Union both strongly demanded a withdrawal and cease fire in the war zone. On November 30, UN forces began to replace troops of the belligerents.

◐◐ The Eisenhower Doctrine—President Eisenhower, to prevent Russian aggression in the Near East, in January 1957, asked Congress 1) for power to use armed forces to resist Communist aggression in the Near East and 2) for funds for military and economic assistance to Middle East nations. The resolution passed both houses strongly after some debate.

American Troops in Lebanon—When the President of Lebanon requested the United States to protect his country against internal subversion, Eisenhower landed troops there in July, 1958. At the same time the British landed troops in Jordan; both Western powers asked the UN Security Council to deal with the crisis. When the Soviet Union vetoed the proposal, the matter was taken up in a special session of the General Assembly. A resolution was eventually passed with the support of the Arab nations for the restoration of stability under the UN, and the American and British troops were withdrawn.

◐◐ The Weapons Race—When the United States successfully exploded the world's first atomic bomb in Japan in 1945 it enjoyed an enormous lead in weapons development over any other power. But in 1949 Russia succeeded in exploding her first atomic bomb and in 1952 England followed suit. Subsequently the United States and Russia greatly increased the destructive power of their atomic weapons with the development of hydrogen bombs. The atomic bombs, essentially super-bombs capable of destroying large cities, superseded the powerful explosives used in the blockbusters of World War II.

Threatening to completely supersede manned aircraft in the delivery of bombs—now with atomic warheads—are the recently developed rocket-propelled missiles. These were rapidly being perfected by German scientists toward the end of World War II. With the aid of captured German scientists, the United States and Russia proceeded to develop, in both size and purpose, a whole range of missiles. The most dangerous missile developed so far, the intercontinental ballistic missiles (ICBMs), were being perfected in the late 1950s; with these missiles, either rival could soon develop enough high-speed, accurate, long-range projectiles to shower each other thoroughly and with little possibility of interception of the other's missiles.

✪✪ **Satellite Launching**—In 1957 the Soviet Union put in orbit *Sputnik I,* the first man-made satellite in history. This achievement proved that the Russians had surpassed the United States in the scientific advancements necessary for this particular accomplishment. The Russians naturally derived much advantage in propaganda from this. The Russian success shocked Americans profoundly; much soul-searching took place in the effort to understand how this kind of leadership had passed to the rival power. The United States reacted by speeding up its own missile and satellite programs. In January 1958, the army orbited the first American satellite and others were sent up since then. In August 1958, Congress passed the National Defense Education Act to provide funds for the states and to aid individuals in the study of science, mathematics, and foreign languages. The whole nation reexamined its educational philosophy and goals with a resulting emphasis upon educational achievement.

✪✪✪ **Castro in Cuba**—American foreign relations since victory in World War II neglected Latin-American nations, but billions of dollars were lavished upon European countries considered more vulnerable to Communist inroads. Policies that approved of dictators to the south offended liberals there. Communist propaganda took advantage of the accumulated resentment. In Cuba, Fidel Castro, a Communist who did not at first reveal his true loyalties, came into power (Jan. 1, 1959) by overthrowing dictator Fulgencio Batista and by denouncing the Yankee imperialists. In 1961 the United States broke diplomatic relations with Cuba. Castro confiscated most American investments in the island. He entered into trade agreements with Russia and China and received enough Communist arms to become the strongest military power among the Latin Americans. The United States managed to secure a condemnation of Communist infiltration in America from the Organization of American States. Eisenhower got Congress to appropriate a half billion dollars for a "Marshall Plan" for economic assistance to Latin America. The Communist victory in Cuba set to work to "export" its revolution to its neighbors; the Communist foothold represented a serious blow to American prestige in the Cold War.

CHAPTER BOOK LIST

Beal, J.R., *John Foster Dulles: A Biography* (1957). Journalistic.
Crossman, Richard, ed., *God That Failed* (Bantam). On Communism.
Graebner. N.A., *The New Isolationism* (1956).
Kennan, George F., *Russia, the Atom, and the West* (1957). The problem of the Cold War.
Lippmann, Walter, *The Communist World and Ours* (1959).

Mills, C.W., *Listen, Yankee!—The Revolution in Cuba* (Ballantine). Controversial.

Rees, Davis, *Korea: The Limited War* (1964).

Schwarz, Urs., *American Strategy* (1966).

Spanier, John W., *American Foreign Policy Since World War II* (Second ed., 1962).

Stebbins, R.P., *The United States and World Affairs* (Vintage).

Williams, T. Harry, *Americans at War.* The Development of the American Military System (Collier). Brief survey; tells present significance of our military history.

REVIEW QUESTIONS

MULTIPLE CHOICE

1. In foreign policy the Eisenhower administration (1) was much less internationalist than the Democrats had been (2) opposed attempts at reconciliation with Russia (3) differed little in essentials from Democratic policy (4) attempted to rescue nations from Russian control.

2. During the Eisenhower administration no agreement was reached with Russia on the control of atomic weapons chiefly because (1) Russia insisted upon an agreement providing adequate inspection of atomic projects (2) the United States insisted upon adequate inspection (3) neither side believed adequate inspection was feasible (4) the United States would never give up experimental atomic explosions.

3. The Suez Crisis in 1956 was settled by (1) the United States acting unilaterally (2) Russia and the United States acting through the UN (3) British and French victory and withdrawal (4) an Israeli defeat.

4. The orbiting of Soviet Sputnik I in 1957 had the following consequences in the United States *except* (1) it caused a vigorous reexamination of the system of public education (2) it led to the Defense Education Act (3) enactment of comprehensive federal aid to education (4) more emphasis was given to American missile and satellite programs.

5. In the election of 1960 all occurred *except* (1) debates between the candidates for the Presidency (2) a promise of vigorous leadership by Kennedy (3) Kennedy won a weaker victory than his party (4) a military crisis.

COMPLETION

6. At first, after the death of the Russian dictator _____ relations improved with Russia, but after _____ won control in Russia the Cold War continued as before.

7. Similar to the NATO were two new mutual security pacts related to Asia and which were organized in the early fifties; they go by the abbreviations _____ and _____ .

8. A summit conference was held between Russia and the United States at _____ in 1955 where Eisenhower offered a general disarmament plan to be enforced by _____ inspection but it was not accepted by the Russians.

9. A war between Egypt and Israel broke out in _____ after Nasser seized the _____ .

10. The Eisenhower Doctrine resembles very closely the _____ Doctrine. Under the Eisenhower Doctrine troops were landed in _____ to prevent Communists from seizing control there.

11. In 1959 Fidel Castro came into power in Cuba by overthrowing the dictator named _____ ; Castro received aid from both Russia and _____ .

12. Elected Vice President under Kennedy was _____ .

13. During the 1960 campaign Kennedy criticized the Republicans for alleged lack of military preparedness by talking much about "the _____ gap."

CHRONOLOGY / CHAPTER 26

1930s Decade of severe and prolonged Great Depression; great changes in American economic attitudes.

1939 *Grapes of Wrath* by Steinbeck called attention to Dust Bowl conditions, sharecroppers, and migrant labor.

1940s Full employment in war industries, large migration to the cities, decline of farm population, and increased marriage and birth rate.

War-stimulated economy brought shortages, increase in individual incomes, and wartime economic controls.

1946 Full Employment Act recognized responsibility of federal government in nation's economy. Postwar depression failed to materialize.

1947 Television introduced to American homes.

1950s Heavy migration of Americans to West and South. Growth of suburbia and decline of rural America recognized.

Postwar farm depression causes increases in subsidies to farmers.

Decade of prosperity in United States.

Growth of middle class in America.

Airlines become main mode of public transportation.

Defense-related research accelerates advance of science.

1958 National Defense Education Act. Realization of deficiencies in American education.

1960s United States population reached 180 million.

Concern over world "population explosion."

Airlines converted to jet-propelled planes.

College education booms.

Atomic energy becomes competitive with fossil fuels.

○○○ GREAT SIGNIFICANCE
○○ IMPORTANT TOPICS
○ SECONDARY IMPORTANCE

26

SIGNIFICANT SOCIAL AND ECONOMIC DEVELOPMENTS SINCE THE DEPRESSION, 1933–1964

After 1941, war and the postwar prosperity brought a huge migration to the cities everywhere and to the regions of the South and the West. Beginning with the war and accelerating with the return of peace, came also a great increase in population. The Great Depression revolutionized the American economic philosophy of "rugged individualism," introduced the present philosophy of economic regulation, and brought approaches to the "welfare state." These changes, instead of being reversed by the prosperity of the fifties, were only slowed. Instead of resting on past achievements, advances in science and technology accelerated.

CHANGES IN POPULATION AND CLASS STRUCTURE

The permanent westward shift in the geographical center of the nation's population was accelerated by World War II. After the war, population growth in the United States was greater than in any other nation of the western world. Notable population trends in evidence were from the farm to city, from city centers to suburbs, from lower to middle class, and from Protestant to Catholic.

○ **Population Growth and Composition**—In 1940 the population of the United States had reached approximately 131,000,000. The American birth rate had been in a declining trend since the twenties when smaller families had become fashionable. From this background forecasters projected a steadily declining birth rate, one that would in a few decades leave the nation with a stable population. The coming of the Second World War greatly altered the outlook. Increased wartime and postwar marriages at earlier average ages and the popularity of larger families caused a sudden, rapid increase in the birth rate. By 1960 the American population had vaulted to 180 million. Although in 1958 the birth rate began an annual decline from the numbers registered since about 1940, large annual increases in absolute numbers remained almost as high as ever. In the early 1960s population experts repeatedly called attention to the American as well as to the world "population explosion" and the consequent threat of food shortages in the future.

As for immigration, after 1945 the annual number of immigrants increased several times over the low figures of the years of economic depression and of World War II but totaled only about 4,000,000 from 1946 to 1963. The nation's population was about 95 percent native born. The two outstanding recent immigrant groups, reminiscent of the less assimilable impoverished immigrants of a half century earlier, were the Puerto Ricans and Mexicans.

The constantly diminishing death rate, due especially to improvements in medical care and advances of medical science, increased life expectancy and consequently the proportion of "senior citizens." The increased birth rate at the same time enlarged the proportion of children and youths.

○ **Population Shifts**—Remarkable shifts in population took place since the beginning of the Great Depression. The depression caused many farm-born to return temporarily to the security of the land. The return of somewhat improved job opportunities in industry in the later thirties saw a resumption of the centuries-old migration from country to city. The rate of migration to the urban centers vastly increased with full employment during World War II and increased job openings during most of the years following the war. America has become about as much urban-industrial as any other nation of the western world.

Regional shifts in population brought great changes in the national pattern of population distribution. During the thirties and forties the states of the Great Plains area gave up much of their population to the cities and towns of the West Coast. The Dust Bowl refugees, as depicted soon afterwards by John Steinbeck's great crusading novel, *The Grapes of Wrath,* became the symbol of this migration. During and after the war many African Americans of the South, as well as whites, moved to cities of the North and West. In the South, however, Texas and Florida continued to make outstanding gains in population. The largest increase by any state during these years fell to California. During the single decade of the fifties California's population increased 50 percent. Americans everywhere became more and more migratory as job opportunities and improved status caused more moving from one home to another within local areas. As percentage of total population, Catholics continued to increase over Protestants. With a membership approaching 43,000,000 Catholics were more than two thirds as numerous as the 64,500,000 Protestants.

⊙ **Movement to the Suburbs**—After World War II, sociologists made much of the large movement of the urban middle classes from the larger cities to their suburbs, a movement made possible by the increasing use of automobiles for commuting to jobs. The growing middle classes could afford to move to suburbia to escape the congestion, the automobile fumes, and problems of the decaying residential parts of the cities in order to gain fresh air, space, modern homes, and status.

In the suburbs the monotonous, dated home architecture of the twenties gave way to the white, unadorned, boxlike economical houses of the thirties which in turn were superseded by the single-story, wide-eaved ranch houses of the postwar period. Better incomes and status-seeking required that these new homes have two-car garages (usually gaping at the street) and the large picture window displaying the large decorative lamp of the living room.

⊙ **The Decline of Rural America**—The fact that the agricultural depression of the twenties resulted from overproduction forced the New Deal to pursue policies which in various ways curtailed the existing over-expansion of land under cultivation. Acreage limitations and marketing quotas reduced agricultural production. Soil exhaustion as well as wind and water erosion forced thousands off the farms of the South and the Great Plains. The administration of the agricultural programs motivated many owners to expel their tenants, and the continued rapid mechanization of agriculture as well as New Deal-initiated agricultural programs caused farmers to buy out and consolidate adjoining farms into larger units. Falling prices of farm staples after World War II even accelerated the tendency to larger farms as more land had to be worked to yield sufficient incomes for the remaining farmers. Jobs in the cities attracted younger people from rural towns as well as from the farms. The total effect brought not only a relative but even an absolute decline in population in the agricultural counties and towns. The decline of rural life was visible to any passing motorist and statistics confirmed the obvious. By 1960 only about one person in ten lived on the farm. The proportion of population in town and country had been reversed from what it had been in 1800.

Just as efficiency increased output per worker in industry, so it did on the farm, but twice as fast. The exodus of population from the farm brought millions to work in industry and trade where they produced goods and services that helped raise national living standards. Agricultural output increased with fewer workers and upon fewer acres in cultivation. During the 1950s the number of agricultural workers declined by about 2,600,000, a decrease of 37 percent. The number of acres in farm crops in 1962 fell to the lowest figure since 1909—with surpluses so great as to require federal expenditures of as high as six billion dollars annually to keep them off the market. Higher production per acre was realized by use of better varieties, more fertilizer, and better methods of cultivation.

○ **Improved Living Standards**—The dreaded return of the economic depression, so fully expected following the war, never materialized. Instead, most Americans enjoyed ever-increasing prosperity. One of the more prominent, rising economists, John Kenneth Galbraith, dealt with this surfeit of private possessions in America in a popular book, *The Affluent Society*. America's prosperity as compared with the rest of the world was becoming almost embarrassing until Europe enjoyed a startling recovery in the mid-fifties when the Marshall Plan took full effect.

The impetus given the economy was a consequence of the war which created a great increase in money in circulation and postponed the rising demand for consumer goods. As the goods became available (after the postwar wave of industrial strikes), people spent wartime savings, their increasing incomes, and used installment financing to buy still more. The postwar boom in residential construction absorbed much of the spending. Where one car had been a necessity before, now a great many families seemed to require two cars. Rapid family formation after the discharge of the servicemen created a huge demand for all kinds of household furnishings and gadgets. Television aerials sprouted from every rooftop while movie attendance sharply declined.

After the immediate postwar demand for goods was partially satisfied, people began to spend more for services of all kinds, including education, entertainment, and medical care. Travel and all kinds of sports boomed with the increase in leisure time and in disposable incomes. Leisure time increased because of the shorter work week and longer vacations. More people came to own their own homes. In travelling, people shifted from trains and busses to private automobiles and airplanes. Investors in common stocks increased at an annual rate of about 850,000 new stockholders during the fifties and increased more rapidly in the early sixties as more investors looked to stocks as a hedge against inflation.

○○ **Class Structure**—Class differences in American society decreased as the twentieth century advanced, mainly because opportunities increased for individuals to move upward. But it can be said that the total effect was a greater leveling possibly than America had ever seen. This may be explained by the following factors: 1) More families achieved the symbols of middle class status as incomes rose—a result of the unionization of labor and the earnings of working wives who numbered more than ever before; 2) steeply graduated income taxes reduced the effect of differences in large and small incomes, as did 3) the absence of the conspicuous consumption flaunted earlier by moneyed classes. 4) The upward mobility of earlier immigrant and minority racial groups was increased by opportunities for education and the lessening discrimination against minorities. At the same time there was a sharply reduced immigration of the people who had augmented the lower classes. 5) The standardization of consumer goods ranging from food, clothing, and automobiles to housing made it more difficult for moneyed families to set themselves apart and the desire to do so declined. The fluidity of social classes was erasing so much of the immobility that maintained class structure that sociologists were forced to discover new criteria for distinguishing lower, middle, and upper classes and their sub-classes.

ECONOMIC CHANGES

The change from conditions of economic depression to those of war- and postwar-prosperity was undoubtedly the swiftest that the nation has ever experienced. As the coming of depression in 1929 raised the curtain on abrupt change so did the sudden outbreak of war in 1941 catapult the nation into another era. American economic philosophy underwent its greatest change since the time of Adam Smith and the departure from mercantilism.

✪✪✪ **Effects of the Depression**—The onset of the depression brought the decade of the flippant twenties to an abrupt close. The social and psychological effects of unemployment and other economic distress upon individuals was as tragic as war itself. Unemployment brought loss of skills, loss of pride, and serious want to individuals and families. Idleness represented a deplorable national waste of labor productivity that could never be regained. As many as 12,000,000 workers were without jobs at the depth of the depression in 1932–1933. Starvation mostly showed up in the form of nutritional diseases but also in felt hunger. At the same time farmers were being foreclosed because they could not sell foodstuffs for enough to meet all expenses incident to their production. In parts of the Midwest farmers resorted to violence in attempts to prevent the movement of produce to markets.

Somehow the laissez-faire economic system had ceased to work when left alone. Older adolescents hitchhiked over the nation in large numbers looking for work or adventure. "Hoover-towns" made of scrap tin and boxes flourished on the edges of most cities. Births and marriages declined in the face of economic uncertainty and want. Political radicals, such as Huey Long, appealed to large followings of discontented but for the most part without disturbing consequences. The depression strengthened the Progressive tradition and resulted in the enactment by the New Deal of some unrealized parts of the Progressive program for limiting private gains over social well-being.

✪✪ **Economic and Social Effects of World War II**—As the Great Depression abruptly rang down the curtain on an era, so did the attack at Pearl Harbor. The war stimulus to the economy ended the problems of depression, and individuals now sought to find their place in the new wartime environment. Unemployment gave way to large-scale movement of people into the armed services and into jobs in war and other industries. More women worked in industry than ever before. Conservation of rubber and stoppage of automobile production ended most automobile traffic except for economic purposes. After a time surpluses turned to shortages of many items of food and clothing; rationing had to be instituted to conserve goods for military services and lend-lease to the Allies. The movie industry boomed as more people found other forms of recreation unavailable. The economy came under extensive controls like those of a thoroughly planned economy. Higher wages, higher farm prices, and wartime deficit financing multiplied earnings and greatly increased the money supply. Much of the increase in purchasing power was absorbed by bond-selling campaigns, the repayment of debt, and increased savings accounts. Nevertheless, the resulting inflation was only postponed by these factors, by rationing, and by popular heed to patriotic appeals. Labor was asked to forego the right to strike but received increased wages that brought a net rise in living standards except for goods in short supply. Taxes were increased and income levies were withheld at the source. Shipbuilding and aircraft industries expanded most of all.

Incomes of farmers increased relatively more than did other incomes since they started from a lower base. Much of the production of foodstuffs went into the wartime black market to evade price controls and rationing. Farm production increased by 15 percent in spite of shortages of machinery and a drop in farm population of 17 percent.

In its social effects the war caused a large increase in juvenile delinquency as home life was neglected by working parents. African Americans migrated from the South as they found job opportunities elsewhere. Roosevelt created the Fair Employment Practices Commission to prevent discrimination by whites resentful of the improved lot of African Americans, an improvement that was to be permanent. Propaganda and outright advertising by government and industry "sold" the war to the people. The Office of War Information organized these propaganda efforts.

○ **The Economy After the War**—There was almost universal expectation of a return to prewar conditions of depression upon the cessation of hostilities. Even before the war had ended, urgent needs for war production plants had been met and sufficient munitions and weapons had been produced to last beyond the probable end of the fighting. Many war workers returned to their prewar occupations. The unemployment accompanying the end of the war was, for the most part, a result of friction in readjustment to a peacetime economy rather than to any basic economic failure.

The postwar economic readjustment was far from smooth. Trouble arose due to overly rapid dismantling of the military services, the debate over ending price controls, and successive nationwide strikes by labor unions. That the readjustment did not bring economic collapse is due to several conditions. Popular preparation for economic slack by repayment of debt, the accumulation of savings, and the lack of over-optimism by farmers and businessmen prevented excesses that would require later correction. Pent-up demand for civilian goods and postponed modernization of commercial and industrial facilities created a backlog of economic demand. The application of various Keynesian countervailing measures by the federal government helped sustain the demand for consumer goods.

The Cold War necessitated a program of national rearmament and renewed military aid to the Allies that provided the economy with a continuing stimulus similar to but much less than that of wartime demands. Price supports prevented a serious depression among farmers. The adoption of the Marshall Plan and other new forms of foreign aid helped sustain the export market (the decline of foreign demand had been a major cause of the severe primary postwar depression in 1921). A recession in 1949 began to lift even before the Korean War brought a sudden stimulus in July 1950.

The demands of the Korean War forced a revival of some of the earlier wartime economic controls over industry. In 1953 another recession occurred but again failed to bring extensive unemployment. With revival of the economy in 1954 came a capital goods boom that lasted into 1957. The necessity of apparently permanent foreign aid and the lesson of successive war threats and crises in the fifties demonstrated the need to modernize and maintain the military establishment.

✪✪ **Changed Attitude Toward the Role of Government in the Economy**—When the national economy failed to recover, as promised, from the initial effects of the panic and subsequent depression in 1929 and 1930, people began to lose faith in the adequacy of the economic philosophy of "rugged individualism" of the past. It soon became apparent from the sufferings of the unemployed, the farmers, and small-businessmen that the self-regulating economy required some form of government intervention. Even Hoover himself took considerably greater action than presidents had taken earlier in times of depression. After the New Deal came to power, the already prolonged, deep depression required drastic countermeasures that only the federal government could administer. As business leadership was discredited by various disclosures, the country was ready to accept the advice of academic and other specialists and permit political action for extensive modifications of the free enterprise system.

At first, makeshift measures were taken by the New Deal to bring government relief for victims of the depression; in earlier depressions such action had not been taken or had been left to private initiative. Reform legislation soon afterwards brought permanently increased activity by the federal government in banking, securities regulation, agriculture, credit of various kinds, public utilities, and labor relations. The need to adjust federal taxation and spending to stimulate the economy was accepted. The federal government undertook to provide and enlarge individual economic security through unemployment insurance, insurance for dependents of wage earners, security in old age, and other security benefits. While these measures originated largely with the Democratic Party, they came to be accepted by a majority of the Republicans.

After World War II, the Full Employment Act of 1946 provided for a Council of Economic Advisers to assist in economic planning. These changes in the economic role of the national government had their important beginnings with the Populists. They represented also the influence of the British economist John Maynard Keynes and a sharp modification of the philosophy of the influential classical economist Adam Smith who had previously influenced American economic thought so profoundly.

These revolutionary changes gave not only security to individuals but contributed a large measure of stability to help prevent another such depression. Another depression would find the federal government better prepared to meet the emergency in innumerable ways with little time wasted in allowing the disease of economic stagnation to run its course.

⬧ **Chronic Economic Problems**—A worrisome problem of chronic unemployment dogged both Republican and Democratic administrations after World War II. In 1958 as high as seven percent of the national working force was idled. In some regions, as in the coal mining towns of Pennsylvania and the textile mills of New England, whole communities stagnated from loss of payrolls. Labor leaders and the liberal organization Americans for Democratic Action (ADA) urged increased federal spending or other government remedies and blamed the Eisenhower administration for both the economic slack and failure to stimulate a faster rate of economic growth. Actually the unemployment was due to the greater efficiency of labor in America—made possible by machines that often did the work of two or more employees in other countries.

In spite of economic slack, wage rates, incomes, and prices of consumer goods generally continued to advance so that there was much concern over the persistent annual average decline of about two percent in the purchasing power of the dollar. The Republicans claimed credit for not being panicked into administering further artificial and inflationary stimulants to the economy. Federal budgetary deficits recurred from time to time in spite of promises and efforts to halt the growing national debt; Congress raised the limit on the debt as needed.

Heavy annual appropriations of several billion dollars had to be made to support farm prices; the cost of storage of surplus farm produce alone required a billion dollars a year after 1958. The efficiency of agricultural production continued to pile up unrelenting surpluses while farmers were caught in a squeeze between prices paid and prices received.

Transportation—In transportation the trends already established in the twenties continued. Auto transport in private cars, busses, and by trucks carried a larger and larger proportion of passengers and freight. Pipelines took an increasing proportion of petroleum transportation away from the railroads and from oceangoing tankers. Both pipeline construction and air travel grew during and after World War II. Increased efficiency of the railroads enabled them to carry more freight but actual mileage of tracks declined after 1945 as did the number of freight cars which might be needed for a national emergency. Air freight began to grow more rapidly about 1950. The airlines replaced piston-engine planes with higher-speed jet-powered craft in the late 1950s. An expensive ten-year program of national highway building was authorized in 1956 by Congress. This program provided a stimulus to the economy, improved roads for possible defense transport, and provided safer, faster roads for autos and trucks. The growth of barge traffic on inland waterways reduced rail rates further by the competition they offered.

CULTURAL AND SCIENTIFIC ADVANCES

Among Americans the depression years brought a greater awareness of cultural values relative to material possessions. The requirements of business and the professions extended the years of schooling required, and education expanded to meet these needs. America kept her place at the forefront of technological advance, and more effort went into research and innovation than ever before.

✪ **Culture in America**—The old image of America as a materialistic society having little interest in the fine arts was receding in the face of an increased interest in painting, classical music, local symphony orchestras, drama, the dance, and the growing market for books. In 1963 more people engaged in painting as a hobby than in fishing, classical recordings outsold jazz, and the growing number of publishers who were issuing paperback books brought a larger sale of books than ever before—in spite of the distraction of television. In literature there was no remarkable postwar renaissance as that following World War I.

Television in the fifties became the most popular of all sources of entertainment and had repercussions greater than radio had ever had. There was much justifiable criticism of the poor quality of most programs and of their effects upon children. Nevertheless, television brought cultural opportunities and entertainment never before so cheaply and easily available to the masses. Advertisers made the most of the new medium and politicians now had to meet the requirements of favorable appearance on TV screens.

⊙ **Education**—Every American postwar period has seen accelerated progress and change in education; post-World War II was no exception. The immediate postwar boom struck the colleges first after the GIs were released and took advantage of the liberal opportunities for free education in colleges and vocational and high schools. The college boom quickly subsided as the flood of veterans exhausted their benefits or went to work, but the baby boom of earlier years produced an ever-increasing crowd for the grade schools. Taxpayers were called upon to contribute more to finance buildings and to raise salaries enough to relieve the scarcity of adequately trained teachers. College enrollments resumed their growth in 1956, a growth that accelerated a few years later when the war babies began to reach college age. The percentage of high school and college students both, relative to the population, greatly increased. In 1960 a college education came to be the requirement for jobs and status that a high school diploma had been 40 years earlier. Many more students were finishing college and more were going on to take graduate degrees as professional and vocational standards were raised.

The problem of financing education at all levels required larger private and public contributions than before, but with larger incomes people had more ability to finance education just as they had more for recreation and luxury. Still the burden was hard for many public schools and colleges to finance.

In Congress advocates of federal aid to all levels of education were stymied year after year by fear, as in the South, that federal aid would bring federal control. Congressmen with Catholic constituents opposed federal aid which would be refused to parochial schools of all denominations under the principle of separation of church and state.

Many conservative-minded citizens after World War II became critical of the public schools for lack of emphasis upon such fundamental studies as spelling and mathematics. Instead, schools had adopted methods and courses that were intended to develop the whole person, especially in social skills. The reaction set in abruptly when Russia put her first Sputnik in orbit in 1957. The schools responded to public demand by emphasizing scholastic achievement, especially with emphasis upon mathematics, the sciences, and languages. Federal scholarships, loans, and grants were voted more liberally for the colleges under such acts as the National Defense Education Act (1958) to subsidize defense-related subjects.

⊙⊙ **Scientific Advances**—Research and the application of its findings made spectacular advances in America after 1940. Subsidies by the federal government and large increases in research expenditures by industry made possible this accelerated technological progress. The most startling developments came in the application of atomic physics. The development of the hydrogen bomb increased a thousandfold the destructive power of the earlier uranium bombs. Atomic energy, for many years considered uneconomical in generating electric power, by 1963 was considered competitive enough with the fossil fuels—coal, oil, and gas—that profit-minded utility companies were starting plans to build nuclear-powered generating plants, in addition to plants already operating for experimental production of electric power. Atomic energy came to be used extensively for exploration for oil, for fighting insects, in electronics, in medicine, and in various sciences.

Growing out of defense needs was still another technological achievement that was finding innumerable applications in industry, in government, and in scientific research—the construction of high-speed electronic computing and data-processing machines. These machines solve mathematical problems beyond the grasp of the human mind, or, in hours, find answers that require weeks of time of many persons. These devices are used also in conjunction with automation of large factories.

Another defense-related field of scientific research was that of space exploration. Aside from the aspects of military advantage and national prestige, space exploration promised dividends in the prediction of weather, communication by satellite, and scientific data. After 1950 the cost of desalination and other purification of water was being reduced enough that such water was coming into economic use in large quantities for residential, industrial, and even for irrigation use. There was a prospect that research would soon reduce the cost of ocean water enough to make it competitive in many more areas with fresh water obtained by the traditional methods. Several different processes were under study in large-scale operating plants largely financed by the federal government. New sources and the conservation of existing supplies of water were needed because of real or threatening shortages in many places, especially to the west of the Mississippi.

CHAPTER BOOK LIST

Allen, F.L., *Big Change* (Bantam). Entertaining survey of social change since 1900.

Becker, C.L., *Freedom and Responsibility in the American Way of Life* (Vintage).

Brooks, John, *The Great Leap* (Harper & Row).

Davis, J.P., *Corporations* (Capricorn).

Degler, Carl N., *Out of Our Past. The Forces that Shaped Modern America* (Colophon). Thoughtful interpretative survey of our history.

Galbraith, J.K., *New Industrial State* (Second ed., 1971).

Galbraith, J.K., *The Affluent Society* (Houghton Mifflin). Widely read discussion of American prosperity by a Harvard economist.

Hacker, L.M., *American Capitalism: Its Promise and Accomplishments* (Anvil). Another useful Anvil survey with readings.

Halberstam, D., *The Fifties* (1993).

Konefsky, Samuel, *Legacy of Holmes and Brandeis: A Study in the Influence of Ideas* (Collier). About two outstanding liberals on the Supreme Court.

Lerner, Max, *America as a Civilization: Life and Thought in the United States Today* (1957). Left-wing view.

Lubell, Samuel, *The Revolt of the Moderates* (1971).

Miller, Herman P., *Rich Man, Poor Man* (1971).

Miller, J.A., *Fares, Please! From Horsecars to Streamliners* (Dover). Popular history of recent transportation.

Mills, C.W., *White Collar: The American Middle Classes* (1951).

Pessell, Glen, and Rees, Leonard, *The Retreat from Riches* (1973).

Silberman, Charles E., *Crisis in Black and White* (1964).

Stover, John F., *American Railroads* (University of Chicago). Survey of railroads.

Vatter, Harold G., *The United States Economy in the 1950s* (1963).

Warmer, W. Lloyd and Abegglen, James, *Big Business Leaders in America* (Atheneum). Sociological study.

Whyte, Jr., W.H., *The Organization Man* (1956). Sociological study of conformity in a business society.

REVIEW QUESTIONS

MULTIPLE CHOICE

1. Which statement is *untrue?* (1) The birthrate declined in America in the twenties and thirties (2) the birthrate increased in the forties and fifties (3) immigration decreased after World War II (4) after 1958 the birthrate began to decline but population continued at a rapid increase.

2. Since 1940 all of the following net shifts in population in the United States occurred *except* which one? (1) From rural to urban (2) from Middle West to the East (3) to the West (4) from urban center to suburb.

3. Which change in population did *not* occur after 1940? (1) Increase in the middle class (2) rapid movement from rural areas (3) increase in mobility of residence (4) increase in Protestants relative to Catholics.

4. After 1940 (1) there was an absolute decline in the population numbers in rural areas (2) the decline in rural population was only relative (3) production efficiency decreased on the farms (4) farming units decreased in size.

5. Which change in the standard of living did *not* occur after 1945? (1) People spent more for services after the demand for goods had been satisfied (2) postwar depression reduced living standards (3) people had more leisure time (4) more money was invested in common stocks.

6. After World War II class differences greatly decreased because (1) all classes became affluent (2) of increased opportunities for formerly depressed classes (3) unemployment had been eradicated (4) social classes were becoming less fluid.

7. As a result of the Great Depression (1) many parts of the program of the earlier Progressives were enacted into law (2) moral standards were elevated (3) people developed a greater respect for material values (4) political radicalism declined.

8. Which was *not* an economic effect of World War II? (1) Except for scarce goods people lived better than during the Depression (2) people repaid debts rapidly (3) farm production decreased because of labor shortages (4) many economic controls had to be applied by the government.

9. Immediately after World War II the economy suffered most from (1) a shortage of labor (2) successive nationwide strikes by organized labor (3) reduced incomes (4) over-optimism and speculation.

10. After World War II and up until about 1957 the American economy was stimulated by all *except* (1) foreign aid programs (2) rearmament and war demands for goods (3) price supports and social security payments (4) prosperity among the farmers.

11. After 1933 the economic policies of government reflected most of all the (1) reaction against Communism (2) return to rugged individualism (3) influence of Keynesian economics (4) persistence of laissez-faire philosophy.

12. Which economic problem did not exist in the United States during the fifties? (1) General price deflation (2) anxiety regarding levels of unemployment (3) an increasing federal debt (4) farm depression.

13. As for modes of transportation from 1930 to 1963 (1) trends in effect since the twenties continued (2) water transportation declined (3) no notable changes were evident (4) railroads became less efficient than ever.

14. Culture in America from 1930 to 1963 (1) reflected mostly crass materialism accelerated by wartime influences (2) showed a remarkable increase in popular appreciation of the media of culture (3) showed a great renaissance in literature after 1945 (4) showed little change from the twenties.

15. Probably the greatest change in education since 1945 has been in the (1) increased need for and emphasis upon college education at the various levels (2) percentage of population attending grade schools (3) increase in federal aid to public school education (4) increase in teachers' salaries.

TRUE-FALSE

16. The percentage of persons over age 65 in the population has increased in recent decades.

17. Federal programs to increase incomes of farmers have accelerated the exodus from the rural areas.

18. The unionization of labor has prevented more workers from achieving middle class incomes.

19. The range in cost of consumer goods in America offers greater opportunity than ever to exhibit class status.

20. Social classes in America since World War II have been generally harder to distinguish than ever before.

21. During the 1930s there was no actual starvation or malnutrition due to the Great Depression.

22. The New Deal represented a resumption of the goals of Progressivism.

23. During World War II incomes of farmers continued their slow decline.

24. Possibly the worst social evil growing out of World War II has been the increase in juvenile delinquency.

25. Foreign aid proved to be a deflationary factor in the American post-war economy.

26. The philosophy of "rugged individualism" has remained dominant in the thinking of a majority of Americans.

27. Much of America's high percentage of unemployment, as contrasted with Europe, is due to the greater output of individual American workers who use more machines than ever.

28. Popular pursuit of artistic interests has increased in America in spite of television and spectator sports.

29. The federal government in the fifties voted more federal aid to education than ever before and in spite of controversies over federal aid.

30. Technological and scientific advance in America are slowing down.

COMPLETION

31. The outstanding immigrant groups that proved difficult to assimilate in the forties and fifties came from _____ .

32. Refugees from a drought-stricken area known as the _____ were the subjects of _____ novel, *The Grapes of Wrath.*

33. After World War II the strongest population movement within the cities was to the _____ .

34. Give the name of the author of *The Affluent Society* _____ .

35. Groups of houses thrown up during the Depression on the outskirts of most cities were nicknamed _____ .

36. To prevent discrimination against African Americans in war jobs Roosevelt created a watchdog agency named the _____ .

37. The most influential world economist in recent times has been _____ .

38. To promote the economy, sustain employment, and counteract the depression expected to follow World War II, Congress passed the _____ .

39. An emphasis upon science and mathematics in education occurred after Russia put her first _____ in orbit.

CHRONOLOGY / CHAPTER 27

1961 Kennedy inaugurated as President.
United States broke relations with Cuba.
"Bay of Pigs" invasion failed in Cuba.
Peace Corps authorized.
Russia erected wall to separate its sector of Berlin.
"Alliance for Progress" instituted in Latin America.

1962 Kennedy took action against price increase by steel industry.
Stock market crash in April and May.
Glenn became first American astronaut.
Federal troops sent to integrate African Americans at
 University of Mississippi.
American troops sent to aid South Vietnam against
 Communist guerrillas.
American-Russian confrontation over missiles in Cuba.
Democrats made gains in midterm elections.

1963 Test ban treaty concluded between United States and Russia.
Kennedy visited West Berlin and proclaimed "Ich bin ein
 Berliner."
Civil Rights leader Medgar Evers was assassinated; death
 sparked demonstrations.
Freedom March on Washington drew 200,000 people.
 Dr. Martin Luther King, Jr. told crowd "I have a dream."
November 22, Kennedy assassinated; Johnson succeeded to
 Presidency.

1964 Twenty-fourth Amendment to the Constitution, the abolition
 of the poll tax, was ratified.
Johnson won enactment of Civil Rights Act of 1964.
Congress gave Johnson military approval to intervene in
 Vietnam as a result of Gulf of Tonkin incident.
Three civil rights workers murdered in Mississippi.
Warren Commission report released; no conspiracy found.
Republicans chose Barry Goldwater to oppose Johnson for
 President.

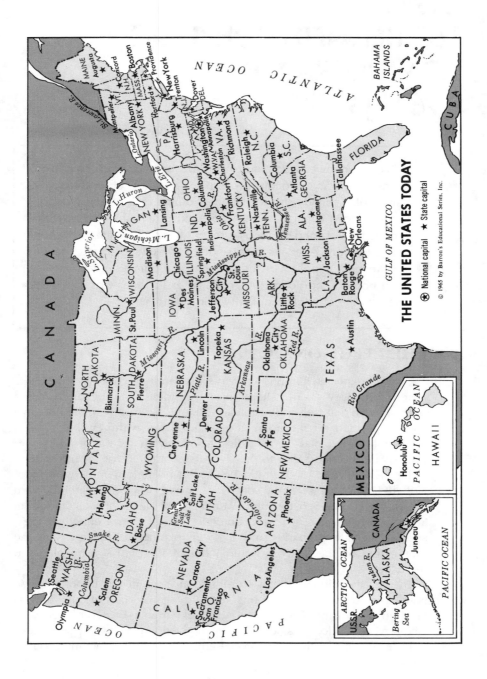

THE UNITED STATES TODAY

⊛ National capital ★ State capital

© 1965 by Barron's Educational Series, Inc.

Chapter

27
THE KENNEDY-JOHNSON ADMINISTRATION, 1961–1965

> While Eisenhower's administration had been liberal Republican, Kennedy's administration proved to be that of a moderate Democrat. Kennedy showed firmness on the face of Soviet expansionism, gave strength to the space program, signed the Trade Expansion Act, and vigorously fought for civil rights and school desegregation. After his assassination, President Johnson continued Kennedy's policies. During Johnson's administration, a very large body of legislation was enacted, a fact that was overshadowed by the escalation of the war in Vietnam.

✪✪✪ THE ELECTION OF 1960

As was expected Eisenhower gave his cautious endorsement to the Nixon candidacy for the Republican presidential nomination. When polls showed that Nelson Rockefeller, Nixon's nearest rival, did not have enough support for the nomination, Rockefeller withdrew but refused to accept second place on the ticket. Instead Henry Cabot Lodge, Jr., United States Ambassador to the UN was nominated for Vice President.

It was not clear who would be the Democratic nominees. Senator Hubert Humphrey of Minnesota was an early threat. Senator Lyndon Johnson of Texas, Senator John F. Kennedy of Massachusetts, and Adlai Stevenson were the leading contenders. However, Kennedy's great success in state primaries and his well planned campaign won the nomination on the first ballot and Johnson accepted second place on the ticket.

In the campaign Kennedy's Catholicism became an important side issue and swayed many voters for and against him. Kennedy was charged with being too youthful and inexperienced as compared with Nixon who, as Vice President, had been given important responsibilities in his grooming for the succession. Kennedy's youth, vigor, and promise of strong leadership in foreign affairs and in fighting the current recession appealed to the voters who now had tired of the part-time, unaggressive leadership of Eisenhower. Studies showed that America's prestige in world affairs had dipped with the successes of Russian satellites, victory in Cuba under Castro, and the apparent "missile gap" in America's defense. Nixon was unavoidably associated with the Eisenhower administration. Nixon's much publicized "kitchen debate" with Khrushchev in Moscow in 1959 was cancelled out by the better impression made by Kennedy in the nationally telecast face-to-face television debates. The effect of these debates and the current recession were the crucial factors upon which the outcome turned. Kennedy won a strong electoral majority but by a popular lead of only 113,957 of nearly 69,000,000 votes, the smallest lead of any victorious candidate since Harrison in 1888. Both houses of Congress went strongly Democratic; Kennedy's youthfulness and religion apparently kept him from winning the same strong endorsement that his party won.

DOMESTIC AFFAIRS

In domestic affairs Kennedy might have led Congress down a more liberal path to his "New Frontier" but conservative Democrats of the South often nullified the promises of the Democratic platform by voting with the Republican minority. Without vigorous support, the President was unable to "move forward" with spending plans for the "public sector" of the economy to the extent that had been promised. All in all, the young President conducted the administration with sufficient industry, vigor, and modesty to increase or at least maintain his popularity enough to cause prognosticators to forecast his reelection short of some unexpected mistake or event.

○○ **Kennedy: Career and Policies**—John F. Kennedy was the third generation of his family to be active in politics in America. His father, Joseph P. Kennedy, who accumulated by speculation a fortune of many millions, served as Ambassador to England just before World War II. The President, a Harvard graduate and author, had first attracted national attention to himself in investigating labor union abuses in Congress and in sponsoring legislation for their correction. John F. Kennedy had served heroically and had been wounded as a PT boat commander in the deadly fighting in the Solomon Islands. Upon taking office at the age of 43, he became the youngest man ever elected to the office and the first Catholic President.

Although Kennedy during the campaign had promised vigorous presidential leadership in the tradition of the strong presidents, including Franklin D. Roosevelt, there was no such emergency to be met as in 1933. Consequently, the President had little success in two significant projects promoted by the liberals, free medical service to the aged under the Social Security system and federal aid to education. The President positively endorsed liberal government spending and opposed budgetary surpluses, but Congress kept a careful watch to check any great increase in spending. No new solution could be found for the farm problem.

The promise of vigorous and imaginative solutions in foreign relations was for the most part delayed until the crisis over Russian missiles in Cuba arose in October 1962. Defense preparations were stepped up and the President maintained firmness in the face of Russian attempts to force the Allies out of Berlin. Such difficult problems as Communist infiltration in Southeast Asia and atomic testing and disarmament were no easier to resolve than under the preceding administration. Kennedy's able handling of televised press conferences won him much popular support.

⊙ **Cabinet and Other Appointments**—To head the Department of State Kennedy chose Dean Rusk (New York). Douglas Dillon, originally from a New York investment banking firm and holder of high office under Eisenhower, was chosen as Secretary of the Treasury in a move that appealed to the business community. Robert S. McNamara (Michigan) became Secretary of Defense. Robert F. Kennedy, the President's younger brother, was chosen as Attorney General and became his most influential adviser. The Postmaster General's job was given to J. Edward Day (California); Stewart L. Udall (Arizona) was made Secretary of the Interior; Orville L. Freeman (Minnesota) became Secretary of Agriculture; Luther H. Hodges (North Carolina) became Secretary of Commerce. Arthur J. Goldberg (Illinois) served as Secretary of Labor until he was appointed to the Supreme Court late in 1962; W. Willard Wirtz succeeded him. Abraham A. Ribicoff (Connecticut) served as head of the Department of Health, Education, and Welfare until he won election to the United States Senate in 1962 and was succeeded by Anthony J. Celebrezze (Ohio).

Kennedy was assured of a liberal majority in the Supreme Court by the appointment of Byron White and, later, Arthur Goldberg. Adlai Stevenson won appointment as the United States Representative to the United Nations. Walter W. Heller became the Chairman of the Council of Economic Advisers. Nearest to the role of Sherman Adams as a leading assistant to the President was Theodore C. Sorenson (Nebraska) in the office of Special Counsel to the President; Sorenson served as the President's alter ego and speech writer. Pierre Salinger, in charge of White House press relations, was influential. Like Franklin D. Roosevelt, Kennedy favored Harvard scholars with appointments; among them were two liberals, the historian Arthur Schlesinger, Jr., as Special Assistant to the President, and the economist John Kenneth Galbraith, made Ambassador to India.

○○ Space Exploration—In February 1962, the United States, in making its first earth orbit, rocketed astronaut John Glenn three times around the world in a space capsule and recovered him without harm. The launching was postponed many times until optimum conditions prevailed. Glenn received wild acclaim with the same modesty that Lindbergh had shown in 1927, and it was expected that his flight was an introduction to further progress in space exploration by America in the race with Russia to demonstrate what each political system could accomplish. However, the Russians were earlier, for in 1961 they had orbited two separate, manned craft; the Russians also consistently rocketed heavier space vehicles than did the United States. Many short flights, both failures and successes, had been carried out during the intense preparation for Glenn's successful flight. In May 1962, Scott Carpenter completed three orbits. After him Walter Schirra, America's third astronaut, made a nearly faultless six-orbit flight in October 1963.

Many unmanned space shots were made for various exploratory purposes. As the first step in a global communications system, the Telstar satellite was put in orbit in July 1962. The most distant space exploration was made by the Mariner 2; on December 14, 1962, it had reached its nearest point to Venus in a flight of 35,000,000 miles.

○ National Defense—The "missile gap," that the Democrats had talked of so much during the campaign of 1960, was admitted to be much less serious than the Democrats had represented it during the campaign, but spending for defense was substantially increased. Late in 1963 one authority showed that the United States had several times as many ICBMs as Russia and many more surface naval vessels and long range bombers. Russia had the lead in men in the armed services, conventional submarines, and in armored tanks. Kennedy secured liberal appropriations from Congress for a build-up of conventional weapons so as to avoid too much dependence upon nuclear weapons which could not be used in local wars triggered by the enemy.

○○ Testing of Nuclear Weapons—The apprehension of public opinion in America and over the world regarding the threat to peace from the race between Russia and the United States to develop atomic weapons was reinforced by fears of the effects on health of radioactive strontium-90 released in the atmosphere by hydrogen bomb tests. It was hoped that an international agreement might bring an end to further tests. However, atomic scientists disagreed as to the extent of danger from such radioactivity in the atmosphere.

Russia scored propaganda gains by announcing a unilateral suspension of nuclear tests in April 1958. The Western Powers could not give up their lead in atomic weapons; subsequently, the West demanded the condition that a system of inspection and control be established to enforce the test ban and that steps be taken toward disarmament in conventional weapons. Discussions, with some concessions, continued between the United States and Russia with both clinging substantially to their original positions. After three years, the United States and Russia both resumed testing to prevent the other from gaining a lead in the contest to develop better atomic weapons. Discussions continued at Geneva in efforts to reach agreement to ban further tests.

In July 1963, talks were begun at Moscow upon Kennedy's initiative. In ten days the Soviet Union, the United States, and Great Britain did reach agreement to prohibit nuclear testing in the atmosphere, in outer space, and under water, but there was no prohibition on underground tests. The agreement, ratified in September, resulted in further easing of tension.

⚙ **Kennedy, the Steel Industry, and Labor**—In April 1962, the steel industry, during a time of rising economic indices, undertook to post price increases. Kennedy some months previously had asked steel officials to absorb the cost of a new round of wage increases forced upon the industry by organized labor; he understood that the industry leaders had agreed. When the price increases were announced, the President immediately denounced the steel corporation officials and quickly and efficiently mobilized almost every conceivable weapon that big government could muster to force a cancellation of the increases. One step was the threat of an antitrust suit against United States Steel which had taken the lead in the price increase. The increases were quickly rescinded.

Kennedy, in this affair, in the role he had cast for himself during the election campaign, used the big stick policy of other strong presidents. His purpose apparently was to stop the monotonous succession of almost annual price increases by industry. These increases had maintained a steady erosion of the purchasing power of the dollar, threatened to price American goods out of the world market, and increased the drain on gold reserves. A month later Kennedy addressed the United Auto Workers and took a stand against wage increases in excess of increases in the productivity of labor.

Kennedy's course followed that of Truman in using the power of government as a strong third force in regulating relations between labor and industry. Many hoped that the interest of consumers and of the nation would thus be protected against the monopolistic practices of both big labor and big business and the recurring cycles of wage increases and price increases.

Minimum wage rates were raised by Congress under Kennedy. The administration intervened actively to settle labor disputes quickly, in contrast with the usual hands-off policy of Eisenhower.

The Stock Market Panic and Decline—The stock market had enjoyed several successive rises to new high levels since 1950 and had come to evaluate stocks at prices higher than ever before. When Kennedy took measures to force the steel industry to rescind its price increases, the investing public decided the administration was anti-business. Stock prices, already topping out, reacted by going into a sharp downturn in April 1962. Much of the rise had been predicated upon chronic inflation. The President's action suggested the possibility that inflation might be halted and that stocks would no longer offer their past attraction as a hedge against indefinite inflation. The decline became a panic on May 28 but the market rallied in a few days. However, in June, stock prices dropped more deliberately to still lower averages; in the average percentage drop in value, stocks experienced their worst decline since 1937. By the end of the year stocks had recovered half their decline from the peak and the panic had still failed to tailspin into the depression that former President Hoover read into it in expressing his sympathy for Kennedy. By 1963 the decline seemed to be only a correction of gross overvaluations, especially in the exaggerated vogue of growth stocks that had been nourished by brokers.

Agriculture—Only small changes occurred in federal policy toward agriculture, since Kennedy only slightly modified the policies inherited from previous administrations. Farmers continued to increase their efficiency to the embarrassment of efforts at production limitation and price-fixing. The expensive program of storing surpluses and supporting farm prices was maintained.

The new Food and Agriculture Act of September 1962, passed after eight months of wrangling in Congress, afforded about the same level of payments but lower price guarantees. A new experimental feature provided direct subsidies to maintain incomes of wheat and feed grain producers without supporting grain prices. This feature recalled the controversial Brannan Plan, a plan to support farmers' incomes without price supports. The Brannan Plan, proposed under the Truman administration, failed enactment at that time. Another new feature provided government price supports for only a limited number of bushels instead of offering price support to all produced on an allotted acreage. Acreage allotments were maintained, however. The soil bank and other leading provisions of earlier laws were retained.

The Money Problem Again—The easy money policies favored by the Democrats could not easily be followed in the prevailing economic environment. The main difficulty was the outflow of gold from the United States and the declining gold reserves. Interest rates receded only slightly; they needed to stay high relative to rates in other countries to prevent an outflow of capital to foreign nations. Besides, inflated prices in America were causing both Americans and foreigners to buy foreign goods in preference to American goods, with a consequent drain on the American money supply and gold balances. The Kennedy administration continued measures to reduce this outflow of gold; the problem had begun under Eisenhower. Kennedy gave repeated assurances in 1962 that the dollar would not be devalued; he won the cooperation of Allied nations in assuming part of the burdens of international aid, of resistance to Communism, and of giving support to the American dollar.

The administration introduced departures from the policy of hoarding silver bullion as a backlog for silver certificates. In 1961 Treasury Secretary Dillon halted sales to industry of silver from the Treasury's silver hoard, kept to redeem $1, $5, and $10 silver certificates; the certificates were likewise being withdrawn and Federal Reserve notes backed by the gold reserve began to take their place. In 1963 Kennedy requested and was granted congressional authority to permit issuance of $1 Federal Reserve notes. It was planned that the retirement of silver certificates would permit the Treasury to free its hoard of silver bullion to be used for coins and that no more silver would be bought by the Treasury. The purpose was to release silver output of domestic mines for important industrial uses.

✪✪✪ **Civil Rights and School Desegregation**—The President and Attorney-General Robert Kennedy took vigorous steps to realize the goal of civil rights for African Americans. Also, African Americans and white sympathizers pursuing tactics of nonviolence rode "freedom buses" into the South to break the customary segregation of African Americans in public transportation there. Signs indicated that many communities in the South would follow their more responsible leaders and move more rapidly toward terminating the various segregation practices. The crusaders for equality also undertook "sit-ins" at public lunch counters in drug and department stores, to force management to serve all persons regardless of color. This tactic won desegregation in many towns, but in some instances led to minor violence. Late in 1962 the administration, by executive order, banned racial discrimination in renting or buying FHA-assisted housing.

The forced enrollment of James H. Meredith, an African American, at the University of Mississippi in September 1962 led to a showdown between state and federal authorities similar to that at Little Rock in 1957. Over 10,000 federal troops were sent in to protect the African American student in attendance at University classes. Two persons were killed in the rioting when Meredith enrolled.

In spite of resistance offered to desegregation in parts of the deep South, African Americans were steadily and quietly winning innumerable victories. These gains made available to them, for the first time, the right to vote, to hold white collar jobs, to attend integrated schools, to use desegregated transportation facilities, and to live in desegregated housing.

✪ **Midterm Elections, 1962**—The Democrats showed unexpected strength in the off-year congressional elections in 1962. The Democrats gained four seats in the Senate and suffered a loss of four seats in the House, but there were more liberals among the newly elected Democrats. This was the best demonstration of strength since 1934 by the majority party in Congress in a midterm election. Another outcome was that voters had leaned toward moderate candidates rather than favoring extremists. Every congressional candidate member of the reactionary John Birch Society suffered defeat.

The beginnings of a return to the Reconstruction and pre-Civil War two-party system in the South made further headway as several Republicans won seats in Congress. More of the Southern conservative voters in several states turned to Republican candidates to serve as their spokesmen.

✪ Trade Expansion Act of 1962—This measure, which has been appraised as possibly the most significant act of the administration, was enacted in response to the European Common Market. By this measure 1) Congress granted the President greatly increased authority to reduce tariff duties in return for concessions by other nations. 2) Federal aid was provided for business firms and workers hurt by competition from imports. The intent of the act is to increase foreign trade and thereby open markets for American exports. The actual significance of this reciprocal trade law remains to be proved but its potential is great. It could bring much closer economic ties between America and Europe. De Gaulle's veto of Britain's membership in the Common Market was a hard blow to these hopes of trade expansion.

✪ Civil Rights, 1963—The African American civil rights movement gained some further momentum in 1963. In the South, Tulane University and Clemson College quietly admitted African Americans, and a show of force brought the admission of three African Americans to the University of Alabama. The civil rights movement in the South aimed to desegregate public facilities and business places and to register voters. In the North and elsewhere the goals were job equality, de facto school integration, and housing desegregation. Opposition to African American demands often took forms of lawlessness and violence. Three outstanding cases of violence were the killing of a white integration marcher in Alabama and of an African American leader in Mississippi. In September, four African American girls were killed in the bombing of a church in Birmingham. There were cases of mass arrests; police dogs and clubs were used against demonstrators. In Congress, Southern Democrats were joined by some Republicans who regarded enforced integration of business places as a violation of property rights.

To win recognition of their rights, African Americans and white sympathizers conducted meetings, held peaceful demonstrations, marches, "sit-ins," and exercised their legal rights. They received encouragement from the political climate as political leaders recognized the African American's voting strength. Better incomes for African Americans provided funds as did contributions by religious and reform groups. Independence of the African American republics of Africa gave moral support. President Kennedy and his brother Robert, the Attorney-General, were most active in using the executive power of the federal government; for example, the Interstate Commerce Commission ordered an end to segregation in bus terminals. The federal courts handed down orders to desegregate schools and permit registration of voters. Federal troops were employed three times in Alabama disputes.

President Kennedy twice called for civil rights legislation. After his assassination, President Johnson asked for legislation as a memorial to his predecessor. Leading provisions of proposed legislation called for protection of rights to vote, equality of job opportunity, desegregated schools, and use of privately owned public accommodations. Federal powers and police enforcement were asked in order to make these provisions effective. The 1963 demonstrations reached a climax in August in a civil rights march on Washington staged by 200,000 persons who gathered peaceably at the Washington Monument and marched to the Lincoln Memorial. Addressing the crowd, Dr. Martin Luther King, Jr. spoke of his hopes and dreams in his now famous speech, "I have a dream…"

○ **Legislation in 1963**—Congress, in December 1963 enacted important legislation to aid education. 1) Over $2 billion was provided for vocational education for persons unemployable because of lack of skills and for job retraining for those who had lost jobs in declining industries or by technological change. 2) Further appropriations were made for loans to college students and for aid to school districts with federal installations. Federal aid for public elementary and high schools failed to pass during the year. 3) Probably the most significant educational measure was the appropriation of over a billion dollars to aid colleges in meeting construction costs for needed expansion for a new wave of increased enrollments. This law provided aid for both public and private schools, including church-related institutions.

Earlier, the Senate ratified a treaty that returned the Chamizal area of El Paso, Texas, to Mexico; the long-standing dispute had arisen from a change in course by the Rio Grande that had thrown the disputed area to the American side of the stream.

Congress continued to postpone action on Kennedy's tax reduction bill even after most of its reform provisions were dropped; many members opposed tax reduction in the face of a federal budget growing at the rate of about $5 billion a year and a steadily rising national debt. Other administrative measures were not passed. The plan to provide hospital care for the aged under the Social Security system and expanded aid to depressed areas, such as the coal-mining communities of West

Virginia, did not pass, nor did aid for urban mass-transit systems. Congress reflected increasingly the popular resistance to nonmilitary foreign aid. Thus in 1963 Kennedy met the same resistance to several of his leading measures as he had had from Congress during his first two years in office. The conservative coalition of Republicans and Southern Democrats functioned frequently enough to defeat several of the leading proposals of the administration.

⊙ **Assassination of Kennedy**—On November 22, 1963, while riding in the open presidential automobile in a motorcade in Dallas, Texas, President Kennedy was killed by a rifleman firing from a building overlooking the street. When the news broke, there were rumors that extreme rightists were somehow guilty and there was also apprehension that a foreign enemy might have been responsible. But evidence indicated that it was the act of an unbalanced individual, Lee Harvey Oswald, who himself was soon shot while in the hands of the Dallas police. Vice President Johnson, who was touring with the Kennedy motorcade, took the oath of office as President. In an emotional speech to the nation, the new President pledged to continue Kennedy's policies.

FOREIGN RELATIONS

Foreign policy, in spite of new phrases, new promises, and mutual criticisms by the two major parties, changed little through the Truman, Eisenhower, and early Kennedy years. The United States adhered to the course of international cooperation and assumed the world leadership that World War II had compelled the nation to take. Foreign policy had to take into account certain fundamental conditions arising from the war: the predominance of Communist influence in a large part of Eastern Europe and Asia, the rise of Russia as an opposing power armed with atomic bombs and other advanced technology in weaponry, the decline of Britain and France, the revolt against colonialism, and the rise of nationalism among the peoples of Asia and Africa. In the face of profound forces they could neither escape nor control, Americans had to learn to live in crisis and frustration.

⊙⊙ **The Berlin Crisis**—Kennedy inherited the problem of a disunited Germany; from this arose the crises centering in Berlin. Premier Khrushchev fully tested the will of the new administration to resist his pressures to squeeze the Western powers out of the former German capital. West Berlin constituted a painful thorn in the side of the Communists. The prosperity there contrasted with the drabness of Communist Germany and at the same time offered an easy escape route for Germans fleeing East Germany. The Soviets threatened to unilaterally turn the whole problem over to Ulbricht's Communist regime in East

Germany, a government that the United States had never recognized and one that might not permit continued access to Berlin. This Soviet course might lead to greater danger of war being precipitated by the East German regime. The Communists defiantly built a wall across Berlin in August 1961 to seal off the border traversing the city. On numerous occasions gunfire and tear gas bombs were exchanged across the wall. Khrushchev prevented the ultimate crisis by postponing the time for signing and agreement with East Germany. President Kennedy visited West Berlin and, in a symbolic gesture, told a cheering crowd that he considered himself a citizen of the besieged city saying "Ich bin ein Berliner."

○○ **Cuba**—Cuban refugees, coming to the United States in large numbers in 1960, brought reports of widespread dissatisfaction with the Castro regime there and gave rise to predictions of an imminent uprising that would remove the Communists from power. The Central Intelligence Agency (CIA) under Eisenhower began plans with Cuban refugees for an invasion of Cuba. During the election campaign of 1960 Kennedy freely criticized Eisenhower for taking no action against Castro in Cuba. In the early months of the Kennedy administration many newspaper reports told of the coming invasion of Cuba. Castro had such knowledge of the coming invasion that his forces greeted the poorly prepared invaders at the Bay of Pigs in April 1961, and rounded up all of them soon after the landings. The invasion, made with American cooperation, turned into a complete fiasco. Only the joint responsibility of the preceding administration prevented Republicans from capitalizing upon the miserable bungling that brought American prestige to a new low.

○ **"Alliance for Progress" in Latin America**—The same threat of Communist revolution in Europe that had given rise to the Marshall Plan spurred the United States to take more vigorous countermeasures in Latin America. In the Declaration of Punta del Este, adopted in August 1961, Kennedy and the American government started a $20 billion program of foreign aid with an initial pledge of a billion dollars to stimulate economic and social rehabilitation and reform in Latin America. After more than a year the results were disappointing; turmoil in some countries and the failure to vigorously pursue reform retarded the program. Lack of cooperation by the governments of recipient nations provoked Congress into applying various restrictions on the use of funds. Many nations failed to draw up long-range plans for use of the American funds and failed to levy higher taxes on the wealthy or to divide huge estates among impoverished peasants. Yet, in 1964, important beginnings sustained hope. Training programs were preparing thousands of students to teach improved farming techniques. Tax reforms were started in several countries; it would take more time for the program to prove itself.

✪✪ Cuban-Soviet Missile Crisis—From the beginning of the Castro regime, Russia and Communist China both exploited Cuba as a base for promoting Communism in Latin America. In the summer of 1962 American senators warned that Cuba was being turned into a missile base against the United States, and reports followed of Russian technicians and troops in Cuba. In October, when our surveillance proved that Russian offensive missiles were in Cuba, Kennedy took the initiative in the Cold War by ordering a blockade of Cuba to prevent further Soviet arms shipments there. The most serious crisis since the Korean War reached its climax when Russian ships steaming toward the American blockading ships were recalled or submitted to blockade regulations.

The President's decisiveness and successful confrontation of Russia had the effects of 1) greatly raising the hitherto sagging national morale and 2) increasing the popularity of the Kennedy government at home and American prestige among the European Allies and Latin American nations.

The ban on almost all trade with Cuba, begun in February 1962, remained in effect as the most effective action against the Castro regime.

✪ The Peace Corps—This agency, begun in March 1961, and headed by Sargent Shriver, was created to provide teachers and technicians for underdeveloped nations in Africa, Asia, and Latin America. Largely manned by idealistic youth, the Corps helped foreign governments meet urgent needs for skilled workers; it helped offset Communist influence begun earlier by similar use of technicians in backward nations. After 18 months about 5,000 volunteers, at an average age of about 24, were in training or at work in 40 different countries; these voluntary workers received only living allowances but were to receive about $75 a month severance pay. It was an inexpensive form of foreign aid that would benefit everyone involved. The workers, made up of teachers, engineers, technicians and skilled building tradesmen, taught high school subjects and modern techniques in agriculture, health protection, and various other skills.

✪ The Common Market—A development in Western Europe that had come to take on much significance to American businessmen and the government in the early sixties was the further integration of Europe in the Common Market. It had its beginnings in the Marshall Plan which made American economic aid contingent upon economic cooperation among the nations of Europe. The organization of the Benelux Customs Union, the European Payments Union, the Coal and Steel Community, and Euratom were steps toward the creation in 1958 of the European Common Market, officially known as the European Economic Community (EEC). The EEC began the elimination of tariff duties and other trade barriers among its members. Several legislative, executive, and judicial bodies of the EEC provided its machinery of government and a step toward European unification. Members of the EEC are Belgium, the Netherlands, Luxembourg, France, Italy, and Germany. Because Great Britain at first did not wish to join the Common Market, she organized a similar customs union called the Outer Seven (Britain, Sweden, Denmark, Norway, Switzerland, Portugal, and Austria). The Common Market increased European prosperity and opened new opportunities for American businessmen to participate in the larger market. It could evolve into a United States of Europe.

○ **New Nations of Africa and Asia**—In its leadership in the United Nations and in the Cold War struggle since World War II, the United States has often been faced with problems created by the independence movements of colonial peoples. In Africa and Asia the aspirations of subject peoples for freedom from control of Western imperialism were encouraged by the weakness of Europe made evident by Japanese conquests during the war. The Cold War distractions created the opportunity for these nations to strike for freedom and to play the United States and Russia against each other. In these colonial struggles, several of which resulted in bloody wars, the United States usually supported the independence movements either morally or through United Nations intervention to restore peace. But America's position was often difficult because of her ties with the colonial powers of Great Britain, France, Holland, Belgium, and Portugal. Russia, without such alliances, was in a better position to support the new nations and to work to form diplomatic and economic ties with them. The new nations, however, became "uncommitted nations" in the Cold War. The alignment of the United States with one faction in local wars within or between these nations and of the Soviet or the Chinese Communists with an opposing faction often created conditions that could lead to World War III. In Korea, Vietnam, Laos, and the Congo, serious wars did occur.

The admission of these new states to the United Nations created a large voting bloc in the Assembly. By January 1964, the number of nations in the African-Asian bloc had increased to 58. Voting together, these nations outnumbered the 55 nations of the rest of the world, nations that did not vote as a bloc. Twenty-five years after the formation of the United Nations, its member nations had increased from 50 to 113. African members grew from 3 to 34 and Asian from 9 to 24. In the General Assembly, Zanzibar, about one third the size of Delaware, had one vote, the same as the United States.

○ **Changes in International Relations**—In 1963 the appearance of further disunity among the Communist nations offered the possibility of a significant easing of tension between Russia and the United States. The main rift was between Moscow and Peking. Soon after the Communists took control of China in 1949, observers predicted eventual friction with Russia. The Korean War in 1950 soon created tension.

Tension increased with Khrushchev's denunciation of Stalin in 1956, Moscow's criticism of Red China's People's Communes in 1958, Soviet neutrality in China's invasion of Native American border lands in 1959, and the withdrawal of Soviet technicians from China in 1960. In 1960 the Chinese criticized Khrushchev's policy of peaceful coexistence with the West. Albania took the side of China, and Yugoslavia became more friendly with Russia. Khrushchev believed Communism could win the world by peaceful competition, but China favored a course of promoting strife. China criticized Khrushchev's retreat from Cuba in 1962. A Chinese-Soviet meeting in Moscow in mid-1963 made the ideological split more evident instead of healing it. Peking next criticized the nuclear test ban agreement as a Moscow betrayal of the Communist world.

At home Russia's position was further weakened by failure of her wheat crop, which forced it to import huge quantities of grain and to take up negotiations with the United States for a large wheat purchase. There was some evidence that Soviet relations in other parts of the world were far from perfect. The new nations of Africa accepted Russian aid and technicians but did not intend to blindly follow Moscow. In December 1963, demonstrations by hundreds of African students in Red Square, in spite of Soviet police, showed that Africans regarded Russia as guilty of racial discrimination.

In the West there was disagreement also. The greatest discord here originated with President Charles de Gaulle's pursuit of French grandeur. De Gaulle refused an American offer to share control of its nuclear weapons by the formation of a NATO Polaris missile surface fleet made up of mixed crews of member nations. Earlier De Gaulle vetoed the admission of Britain to the Common Market, an action that offended other Common Market nations. Evidently De Gaulle's aim was the restoration of French leadership on the Continent.

PRESIDENT JOHNSON

Lyndon Baines Johnson was the descendent of early settlers in the "hill country" ranching section of west central Texas. As head of the National Youth Administration in Texas, his identification with the New Deal started at an early age. In 1937 he won election to Congress and later to the United States Senate. His voting record in Congress was that of a moderate liberal; prior to his nomination on the Kennedy ticket, he demonstrated such energy and force as to become recognized as an outstanding Senate leader.

An early course of action by Johnson was the reduction of defense and other expenditures. Such action was taken to win the assent of Congress to tax reduction that was given early priority in Congress in January, 1964. Johnson pursued the Kennedy decision to take up tax reduction before civil rights but emphasized his desire for action on civil rights legislation. The new President expressed his endorsement of the congressional enactments to aid education and emphasized his desire for an "attack on poverty."

○○ JOHNSON'S DOMESTIC PROGRAM

After assuming the Presidency upon the death of President Kennedy, Lyndon Johnson exercised successfully his ample powers of leadership upon the members of Congress to bring enactment of measures that Kennedy had sought. Johnson, large in physique and equally energetic, loved his work and spared neither himself nor his assistants.

Early Victories—Johnson soon won enactment of the income tax reduction that Congress had been delaying. He won the support of business by reducing the budget to demonstrate his economy-mindedness. Defense expenditures were reduced but more was spent upon education, health, and welfare. He settled a threatening railroad strike by unions fighting to save the jobs of featherbedding firemen no longer needed on diesel engines. In his State of the Union message in January 1964, he began to take a stance independent of the Kennedy program but not contradictory to it. He called for a war on poverty and secured enactment of the Economic Opportunity Act eight months later. The program established a domestic peace corps (VISTA), vocational training, part-time employment for youth and federal funds to the states to fight poverty.

In June 1964, the Senate for its first time voted to end a filibuster to bring passage of Kennedy's Civil Rights Act of 1964. In substance the bill strengthened provisions to secure voting rights for African Americans, sought to prevent discrimination in employment and in the use of public accommodations (hotels, public facilities, amusement parks, etc.). The Civil Rights Act would help to alleviate the poverty that prevailed so much more among African Americans than whites.

CHAPTER BOOK LIST

Burns, James M., *John Kennedy: A Political Profile* (1960).
Caidin, Martin, *Man Into Space* (Pyramid).
Carr, W.H.A., *JFK: An Informal Biography* (Lance).
Goldman, Eric F., *The Tragedy of Lyndon Johnson* (Dell).
Heath, Jim F., *Decade of Disillusionment: The Kennedy-Johnson Years* (1975).
Kennedy, J.F., *Profiles in Courage* (Pocketbooks). About courageous and patriotic political leaders.

King, Jr., Martin Luther, *Stride Toward Freedom* (Ballantine).

Novak, Robert D., and Evans, Jr., Rowland, *Lyndon B. Johnson: The Exercise of Power* (1966).

Schlesinger, Jr., Arthur, *A Thousand Days* (Houghton Mifflin).

Sorenson, Theodore C., *Kennedy* (Harper & Row).

Viereck, Peter, *Conservatism from John Adams to Churchill* (Anvil). Survey of conservative thought in America and Europe.

Walton, Richard J., *Cold War and the Counter-revolution* (1972).

White, Theodore, *The Making of the President* (1964) (Atheneum).

Wills, Garry, *Nixon Agonistes: The Crisis of the Self-made Man* (1970).

REVIEW QUESTIONS

MULTIPLE CHOICE

1. Kennedy's inability to secure passage of his legislative recommendations was due to (1) a combination of Republicans and conservative Democrats (2) a lack of legislative experience on the part of the President (3) distractions of foreign problems (4) a Republican majority in one or both houses of Congress.

2. All of the following statements are true of Kennedy *except* (1) the first Catholic President (2) the youngest President ever elected to office (3) first President from New England since Franklin Pierce (4) he came from a family that had long been interested in politics.

3. Which of these policies did Kennedy oppose in practice? (1) Federal aid to education (2) budgetary surpluses (3) medical care for the aged under Social Security (4) foreign aid.

4. In space exploration up to 1963 the United States did all the following *except* (1) rocket heavier space vehicles than the Russians did (2) sending as many as three manned spacecraft in orbit (3) orbit a communications satellite (4) undertaking deep space exploration.

5. The main obstacle to atomic disarmament and the suspension of atomic testing was (1) refusal of the United States to reduce conventional weapons (2) positive refusal by the Russians (3) lack of Russian agreement to adequate inspection to insure compliance (4) American disinterest.

6. In labor-management relations Kennedy followed a policy of (1) less intervention than the previous administration (2) relatively active intervention (3) enactment of a more stringent labor law (4) enactment of a more liberal labor law.

7. In his legislation dealing with the farm problem Kennedy did all of the following *except* (1) retain the soil bank program (2) retain the main features of earlier programs (3) revise price supports radically (4) try certain new experimental devices.

8. In monetary policy Kennedy (1) urged abandonment of the gold standard (2) showed no interest in the heavy gold outflow (3) greatly reduced interest rates (4) initiated a change in silver policy.

9. During the Kennedy administration up to 1963, tactics employed to end discrimination included all *except* (1) "sit-ins" at public lunch counters (2) African American violence (3) use of federal troops (4) "freedom riders" on public transportation.

10. The mid-term election of 1962 (1) showed a strong swing toward the Republicans (2) gave the majority party in Congress an unusually strong vote in an off-year election (3) brought victories to John Birch candidates (4) elected a majority of Republican representatives from several Southern states.

11. American foreign policy from 1947 to 1963 (1) showed little fundamental change through three different Presidents (2) showed strong differences between Truman and Kennedy (3) showed strong contrast between Kennedy and Eisenhower (4) softened toward Russia during this time.

12. Both the most persistent and serious controversial spot in American-Russian relations from 1946 to 1961 was in (1) China (2) Korea (3) Germany (4) Cuba.

13. In its first two years the Alliance for Progress in Latin America (1) made remarkable progress (2) failed to win eager cooperation in many countries (3) brought numerous democratic revolutions (4) elicited concerted resistance by a majority of the Latin-American nations.

14. The most serious crisis in foreign affairs under Kennedy before the midterm elections in 1962 was (1) in Berlin (2) in Cuba (3) in Vietnam (4) with Britain.

TRUE-FALSE

15. Two outstanding legislative measures in which Kennedy had little early success were in federal aid to education and in promoting medical care for the aged under Social Security.

16. Space and military achievements in Russia were achieved at a greater sacrifice of consumer living standards than in America.

17. The "missile gap" of the 1960 campaign proved less critical soon after the inauguration of the new administration.

18. There was almost universal agreement among scientists that radio-activity had surpassed dangerous levels by 1962.

19. Russia outwardly never unilaterally suspended nuclear testing.

20. Kennedy asked industry to forego price increases without asking labor to sacrifice wage increases in excess of productivity increase.

21. Much of the increasing public investment in common stocks could be attributed to the belief inflation would endure.

22. The outflow of America's gold was partly due to the increasing demand for foreign goods.

23. In spite of the publicity given to civil rights enforcement little progress was being made in the fifties and early sixties toward achieving equality.

24. The wall across Berlin was built during Kennedy's administration.

25. The outcome of the Cuban missile crisis in 1962 increased public support of the administration and raised public morale.

COMPLETION

26. The label given by Kennedy to his announced program to promote economic and social progress in the United States was the _____ .

27. President John F. Kennedy took office at the age of _____ .

28. Kennedy appointed _____ as Secretary of State and _____ as Attorney-General.

29. America's first astronaut to orbit the earth was _____ ; next after him was _____ .

30. In national defense the emphasis in the fifties changed from manned aircraft to _____ .

31. Agreement to discontinue nuclear testing and achieve atomic disarmament has been stalled by Russian refusal to allow adequate _____ .

32. In 1962 in the desire to prevent continued price inflation Kennedy clashed with the _____ industry.

33. The stock market panic in May of 1962 brought on the worst decline in security prices since the year _____ .

34. Kennedy hoped to replace silver certificates in circulation with _____ notes.

35. In the first two years of Kennedy's administration the worst crisis in the enforcement of school integration occurred in the state of _____ .

36. An extremist reactionary group active in the American political scene in the early sixties was the _____ society.

37. In the early sixties the leader of the Communist world was the Russian premier _____ .

38. The abortive invasion to overthrow the Cuban dictator in 1961 occurred at the _____ .

39. The program of economic aid in Latin America was given the name _____ .

40. A Kennedy-created agency to send young technicians and teachers to give aid in underdeveloped countries was named the _____ .

CHRONOLOGY / CHAPTER 28

1964   Johnson elected President in landslide vote.

1965   Great Society program enacted. Covered civil rights,
        Medicare, anti-poverty, and aid to education legislation.
        Vietnam War escalated; sparked peace demonstrations.
        Black Muslim leader Malcolm X assassinated.
        African Americans rioting in Watts caused extensive damage.

1966   New cabinet positions approved: Housing and Urban
        Development and Department of Transportation.
        War in Vietnam escalated; new bombing of Hanoi.
        Supreme Court ruled on self-incrimination procedures.

1967   More troops sent to Vietnam; air attacks continued; anti-war
        demonstrations spread.
        Summit held in U.S. between Johnson and Kosygin.
        Worst race riot in U.S. history took place in Detroit.
        Thurgood Marshall sworn in as first African American
        Supreme Court Justice.
        Six-Day War between Israel and Egypt.

1968   Tet Offensive in Vietnam turned public opinion against war;
        peace talks began in Paris.
        Pueblo seized by North Korea.
        Johnson withdrew from race for president.
        Martin Luther King, Jr. and Robert Kennedy assassinated.
        Nuclear Proliferation Treaty signed.
        Nixon and Humphrey faced each other in presidential election.

Chapter

28

THE LYNDON JOHNSON ADMINISTRATION, 1965–1969

Lyndon Johnson's long experience in the United States House of Representatives and afterwards in the Senate prepared him unusually well for working with members of Congress. Most presidents earlier had entered office with backgrounds of executive experience. Johnson's legislative experience bore fruit in a large number of laws enacted as the Great Society program and others projected earlier by his forerunner. Johnson's preoccupation with domestic reform contrasted strongly with the distractions from domestic affairs of foreign involvements during the preceding administrations. There were so many new programs to promote domestic reform that it took specialists to keep track of them. Only too soon the war in Vietnam drew off resources from social programs and divided the nation as to its advisability.

●● **The Election of 1964**—The extremists of the right wing of the Republican party wrested control of the physical and political machinery of the national convention in San Francisco and nominated the conservative Senator Barry Goldwater of Arizona for President and the equally conservative but little-known William Miller of New York as a running mate. The liberal wing had failed to roll up enough support to nominate either Governor Nelson Rockefeller of New York or Governor William Scranton of Pennsylvania. Johnson won the Democratic nomination without a struggle and chose the active, well-known liberal Senator Hubert H. Humphrey of Minnesota as his running mate in preference to Robert Kennedy. Goldwater made tactless, bumbling remarks in his speeches advocating escalation of the war in Vietnam while Johnson opposed enlargement of the war. Johnson traveled strenuously to meet the people but did not feel a need to discuss specific issues. The ouster of Khrushchev in the USSR created a foreign uncertainty that favored the President. The Goldwater defeat was devastating; he won in his home state and in five states of the South. In the popular vote Johnson won 42 million to Goldwater's 26 million votes. The Democrats gained additional seats in Congress.

✪✪✪ **The Great Society**—Johnson's great victory enabled the Democrats under his leadership to enact, beginning in 1965, a flood of legislation unprecedented since the early days of the New Deal. The Civil Rights Act of 1965 authorized the Attorney General to send federal registrars to register voters where fewer than 50 percent of the people of voting age had voted in 1964. The war on poverty was accelerated with expansion of the Economic Opportunity Act, aid to depressed areas, and aid to youth. Public schools for the first time were given large-scale federal funds, including parochial schools, under a formula that gave aid according to the number of needy children in a district. Aid to higher education, including grants of scholarships, was increased. The Medicare program of health insurance for those over age 65 finally became law after a 20-year struggle. Other legislation provided aid to medical education and research and funds to fight water and air pollution.

The Department of Housing and Urban Development was created and the first African American to serve in a cabinet position was appointed in 1966 as its first Secretary, Robert C. Weaver. Also a Department of Transportation was created to coordinate the federal relations with the various modes of interstate transportation. A new immigration law changed fundamentally the basic immigration law of 1924 with its discriminatory quota system. The national quotas were dropped; now immigrants qualified on a basis of education and skills or because of having relatives in the United States.

In January 1966, President Johnson proposed further legislation to Congress, but the cost of the war in Vietnam began to compete strongly for funds and Congress resisted some of his requests. Urban rehabilitation received more money and financing provided for continuing earlier programs. In February 1967, ratification of the Twenty-fifth Amendment to the Constitution providing for presidential disability and succession was completed.

In 1968 Congress passed an open-housing law forbidding discrimination in about 30 percent of sales and rentals and billions of dollars were voted for low-income housing.

The nation was straining itself financially as reflected in the increasing rate of inflation which reached an annual rate of 6 percent by 1969. The outflow of gold threatened the soundness of the dollar. President De Gaulle of France attempted to force the United States to devalue the dollar, but the strain caused France later to devalue her own franc and the retirement of De Gaulle himself in 1969. Unemployment remained at an irreducible minimum and prosperity was greater than ever except for the unemployable and the unskilled in the ghettos.

❂ The Great Society Falters—Factors related to the Vietnam War ended the expansion of the Great Society. The competition of domestic demands with military pressures strained the national resources. Prices and wages rose faster than in any time since the Korean War. Rationing and price fixing did not seem necessary, but the President's great persuasive powers did not quite do the job. The election of 1966 brought more conservative Democrats to Congress; they often combined with the Southern wing to vote with the Republicans. There was criticism that the Great Society was trying to do too much too soon. Money was distributed through 170 separate programs, requiring specialists to keep up with the different sources of federal funds. Much of the money expended failed to achieve what had been expected. Riots made ghettos in large cities throughout the country resemble battlefields and brought a "white backlash" which hurt the administration. Demonstrations of doves, peaceniks, hippies, and followers of the New Left protesting the Vietnam War weakened the Democrats.

The ambitions of the Kennedy clan, with Robert Kennedy now as its head, split the ranks of the Democrats. Kennedy had advised his brother to send the first large body of troops to Vietnam but now found openings to criticize Johnson's part in the war. The intellectuals, overlooking the nature of a democracy, criticized the President for "lack of style" (which they had admired in John Kennedy) and the President's common background in Texas. Some states of the Deep South resented the gains of the African Americans. The social accomplishments and the long prosperity brought by the administration were taken for granted.

AFRICAN AMERICAN UNREST

The frustration of the African American with ghetto life in the cities of the North and the West Coast expressed itself in radicalism and violence beginning in 1964. Until then nonviolence as practiced by Martin Luther King, Jr. and the leaders of the National Association for the Advancement of Colored People had characterized African American demonstrations.

❂❂ Remaining Frustrations of African Americans—Northern African Americans encountered a bewildering frustration because of de facto segregation in the cities. African Americans attended inferior schools in slums to which they were confined by selling practices of realtors and discrimination by landlords. Others were locked in by low incomes; these African American slums came to be called ghettos. To overcome these handicaps African Americans demanded that their children be "bused" to schools in other parts of town and demanded open housing laws. African Americans picketed and boycotted businesses to force employers to hire more African Americans in all kinds of jobs. In the Deep South school integration had hardly begun. On the television screens the discrepancy between white and African American living standards was apparent to all. Though frustration continued, much actual progress had been made in meeting the needs of the African Americans. For example, the number of African Americans employed in responsible, well-paid jobs had doubled.

⊙ **The Advocacy of Violence and Radical Solutions**—Most of the violence attending the Black Revolution up to 1965 originated with whites. Beginning in 1964 African American leaders came forward in the North to repudiate nonviolence. The best known group among African American militants was the Black Muslims, led by Malcolm X, who advocated Black Nationalism and separateness. In 1966 the Black Power concept caught on among African Americans tired of the slow change in attitudes of whites. Black Power meant, among other things, the cooperation of African Americans among themselves to gain economic and political power; to some it also meant threats and resort to violence and guerrilla warfare. In the "long hot summer" of 1964 riots erupted in African American sections of many large cities in the North. In 1965 the Watts riot in Los Angeles resulted in the death of 34 people and the destruction by fire of $35 million in property. In the summers of 1966 and 1967 a great many more riots broke out, many of them of major proportions. Commissions, such as the Kerner Commission, were appointed to study the causes of the riots. They recommended job opportunities, better transportation, more hospitals, improved housing and more social services. However, the expenses of the war in Vietnam and the "white backlash" to this violence caused even the curtailment of antipoverty programs. In April 1968, the assassination of Martin Luther King, Jr., advocate of nonviolence, was followed by African American looting and arson in the cities all over the nation. Congress immediately passed the Civil Rights Act of 1968 providing for open housing. In the summers of 1968 and 1969 African American riots were greatly reduced. In 1969 the Nixon administration advocated a go-slow policy in integration in public schools and visibly slackened the enforcement of the recently enacted civil rights acts.

⊙⊙ **The Supreme Court**—The Warren Court remained activist during the Johnson years, responding to civil rights protests and continuing to set precedents in the area of civil liberties. The court decided in the *Heart of Atlanta* case that the Civil Rights Act of 1964 was legal and that segregation of public accommodations was unconstitutional. In 1966 the Court declared in the *Miranda* case that a suspect's fifth amendment rights were extended to include what has become known as "Miranda rights." Separation of Church and State was clarified in the *Epperson* case, in which the court struck down the right of a state to restrict the teaching of evolution. This decision for the first time set a national standard since the Scopes trial. In addition, Johnson had the opportunity to appoint the first African American Supreme Court Justice, Thurgood Marshall, in 1967. In an historical irony, Marshall was the young lawyer who argued the *Brown v. Board of Education* case before the court in 1954.

THE VIETNAM WAR

American involvement in Vietnam began in a small way during World War II when nationalists in Indo-China sought freedom from France. In 1964 American involvement escalated rapidly into a major war. In terms of such statistics as cost, duration, tonnage of bombs dropped, and American casualties, it became one of the major wars of the United States, outranking the Korean War. The nation became deeply divided as the more radical advocates of peace agitated for precipitate withdrawal of American forces from South Vietnam.

✪✪✪ **American Involvement**—The United States became involved in Vietnam after the French had been driven out by the Japanese during World War II. When the French attempted to restore colonial rule over Indo-China (which was made up of Vietnam, Laos, and Cambodia), Ho Chi Minh's Communist-led Vietminh and other nationalist Vietnamese groups were determined to win independence. Ho announced the formation of the independent Democratic Republic of Vietnam and the French recognized it conditionally "as a free state within the French Union."

Misunderstandings between the French and the Vietnamese broke into open warfare in December 1946. In July 1949, the French gave support to the ex-Emperor of Vietnam Bao Dai in forming the State of Vietnam with its capital in Saigon. The United States in 1950 recognized this new state and dispatched to it a military advisory mission. Later in the same year the United States signed a Mutual Defense Agreement and nine months later agreed to provide economic aid. But in 1954 the French made the mistake of choosing Dienbienphu as the site of a decisive battle with the Communist forces of North Vietnam. President Eisenhower considered resorting to massive air raids to aid the beleaguered French but did not find sufficient agreement among other leaders in the United States and Great Britain to do so.

After the fall of Dienbienphu, the Western Allies met at Geneva (1954) to discuss Indo-China with Russia, the states of Indo-China, and Communist China. The conference agreed to partition Vietnam temporarily into North Vietnam and South Vietnam along the 17th parallel until elections could be held to "bring about the unification of Vietnam." The French now finally recognized the complete independence of the states of Indo-China. The United States and South Vietnam did not sign the agreement. There was no agreement as to whether the conference intended to make South Vietnam a separate state nor was anyone bound to enforce the agreements.

The United States now offered economic and military aid to South Vietnam and organized the Southeast Asia Treaty Organization (SEATO) to guarantee the security of member nations and of South Vietnam. The corrupt leaders in South Vietnam failed to make needed reforms there. North Vietnam capitalized upon dissatisfaction among some of the many diverse elements in South Vietnam and organized bands of Vietcong guerrillas against the government of the premier of South Vietnam, Ngo Dinh Diem. The United States pledged continued aid to South Vietnam. In December 1960, the National Liberation Front (NLF) was organized under the influence of North Vietnam. North Vietnam and the Vietcong received military aid from Russia and China. In 1961 the Kennedy administration signed a treaty of friendship with South Vietnam and continued to give aid. In December 1962, the United States had only 4,000 men in Vietnam; a year later there were 15,000; however, it was not until late 1964 that the United States began major increases in troop assignments to South Vietnam.

✪✪✪ **Escalation of the War**—On August 2, 1964, a United States destroyer that had been patrolling in conjunction with South Vietnamese vessels was attacked by three North Vietnamese PT-boats in the Gulf of Tonkin. American planes then bombed North Vietnamese PT-boat bases. Congress in a few days passed the Gulf of Tonkin Resolution giving the President power to "take all necessary measures to repel any armed attack against the forces of the United States and to prevent further aggression." A Vietcong mortar attack on the American air base at Pleiku was followed by United States bombing raids over North Vietnam. It was hoped the raids would force North Vietnam to the conference table.

In March 1965, the buildup of American air and ground forces accelerated. As the President reacted to developments in Asia the air strikes and ground action continued to increase. North Vietnamese regulars entered the war in large numbers. North Vietnam increased its aid to the Vietcong. Red China and the Soviet Union maintained their supplies of munitions to North Vietnam. United States forces by mid-1968 had reached well over a half million. In June 1968, the war had lasted over six years and by then had exceeded the length of the longest previous war of the United States, the American Revolution. From time to time the United States halted air strikes and made other efforts to initiate negotiations to end the war, but the North Vietnamese usually replied to the effect that the United States must stop all bombings and withdraw unconditionally from the south. The North Vietnamese used holiday truces to accelerate the flow of men and materials to the south. In October 1969, United States casualties exceeded 40,000 killed and 255,000 wounded.

The American justification for the war by the hawks was the containment of Communism. The Administration justified the war according to the domino theory. This theory held that if South Vietnam should become Communist then one after another the countries of Southeast Asia would be taken over until the United States would be forced to resort to defending itself through full-scale war. Also the United States felt it had to demonstrate the credibility of its promises to aid friendly nations withstand Communist aggression.

✪✪ Opposition to the War—As early as 1965 the escalating war increased the casualties as well as the protests. In August of that year there were already close to 1,000 war-related deaths, over 3,000 wounded, and close to 50 soldiers missing in action. The first organized nationwide anti-war demonstration was held in October. Draftees and "doves" burned their draft cards and rallies were held. Congress responded by passing a law making it a violation to destroy a draft card. At the end of the year close to 25,000 people marched on the nation's capital, the first of many Washington demonstrations.

Increasing inflation set in, but Congress delayed granting a ten percent increase in income taxes to curb it and to finance the war. A gold pricing system was established to halt U.S. outflow of gold. The war strained relations between the U.S. and its allies. Demonstrations were held overseas.

By 1966 the escalation of the war resulted in the beginning of massive air strikes on North Vietnam, more U.S. soldiers being sent to the front, the bombing of North Vietnam's capital, Hanoi, and its main harbor, Haiphong, and the bombing of the demilitarized zone. Because of the draft deferment system, American soldiers comprised a disproportionate number of minorities, which further tarnished the image of the government. Schooled to fight nuclear wars with sophisticated weaponry, the U.S. military never adapted to the guerrilla tactics of the Vietcong.

In 1967 over 250,000 people demonstrated in New York City, marching from Central Park to the United Nations. Events in 1968 brought the opposition of the war to a peak. Since it was an election year, candidates from both political parties campaigned to end what was becoming the longest war in American history. Even African American activists like Martin Luther King, Jr. took up the cause. The year began with the largest North Vietnamese attack, the Tet Offensive. Though the United States withstood the massive assault, evening newscasts showing attacks on Saigon and a key marine base in South Vietnam shocked the American people. Democratic Senator Eugene McCarthy, who had declared his candidacy for the presidency and promised a quick end to the war, surprised President Johnson when he captured almost 40 percent of the vote in the New Hampshire primary. New York Senator Robert F. Kennedy quickly entered the race and it became apparent to Johnson that he would have a difficult time retaining the Presidency. Thus, in a broadcast to the nation, he announced that he would not seek his party's nomination and that he would order a partial halt to the bombing in Vietnam to speed up the peace talks. The Republicans nominated party faithful Richard Nixon, who promised he would "Vietnamize" the war. Peace demonstrators pledged they would make a statement at the conventions.

AMERICAN FOREIGN RELATIONS

In 1965 President Johnson ordered American troops into Santo Domingo, where the conservatives were in danger of defeat by opposition forces. There were dangers of a Communist takeover and the President was determined to prevent the establishment of another Castroite base in the Caribbean. Soon the Organization of American States (OAS) authorized the establishment of an Inter-American Peace Force which served under a Brazilian general. A year later after the election of a moderate president in Santo Domingo the peace force was withdrawn. However, considerable hostility to the United States had been aroused in Latin America by the American intervention. Cuba actively engaged in training guerrillas to aid and abet revolutions in Latin America.

The United States was threatened again with being drawn into war in the Middle East in June 1967, when Israel occupied the Sinai Peninsula in an overwhelming defeat of the Egyptian forces in the Six-Day War. The Egyptians and their Arab allies refused to accept the verdict of the war, including the loss of territory, and after a time attacks across the Suez Canal continued to threaten the peace. Many Americans demanded armed support of Israel.

In July 1968, the United States and Russia signed the Nuclear Proliferation Treaty, along with 63 other nations, to prevent the further spread of nuclear armaments. In August, Russian tanks occupied Czechoslovakia to suppress an independently liberal nationalist regime there; it was evident the United States would not become involved.

In Latin America the Alliance for Progress made only slow progress in solving problems of poverty, the need for tax and land reform, and the lack of industrial production. In 1964 riots occurred in Panama and she broke off diplomatic relations with the United States and demanded a new treaty relating to the Canal Zone. Early in 1968 the North Koreans captured the American intelligence vessel *Pueblo* in international waters; its crew was held in prison for over 11 months while negotiations for their release slowly proceeded. American military presence in South Korea was still being maintained.

○○ **The Moon Landings**—A scientific and engineering achievement on par with the explosion of the first atomic bomb occurred with the first landing of men on the moon in July 1968. Three American astronauts—Neil Armstrong, Edwin Aldrin, Jr., and Michael Collins—flying in Apollo 11, under the eyes of television viewers over the world, took part in the successful landing and return. Apollo 11 blasted off July 16 and splashed down in the Pacific on July 24. Although the moon voyage elevated the national prestige, aided defense technology, satisfied man's spirit of adventure, and gained much information valuable to science, many believed that resources had been diverted from social needs. A second manned spacecraft mission achieved another American moon landing only four months later. Both missions brought back samples of lunar rocks. The moon landing program, begun under President Kennedy in May 1961, was a culmination of many costly preparatory flights.

CHAPTER BOOK LIST

Abrams, Charles, *The City is the Frontier* (Colophon).
Alsop, Stewart, *The Center: People and Power in Political Washington* (1968).
Buttinger, Joseph, *Vietnam: A Dragon Embattled* (Two vols., 1967).
Cater, Douglas, *Power in Washington* (Vintage).
Commager, Henry S., ed., *The Struggle for Racial Equality* (Torchbooks).
Conot, Robert, *Rivers of Blood, Years of Darkness* (Bantam).
Goldman, Eric F., *The Tragedy of Lyndon Johnson* (1969).
Grant, Joanne, ed., *Black Protest: History, Documents, Analyses* (1968).
Gross, Bertram M., ed., *A Great Society* (1968). Poverty problem.
Heath, Jim F., *Decade of Disillusionment: The Kennedy-Johnson Years* (1975).
Hull, Roger, and Novgorod, John, *Law and Vietnam* (1968).
Lasky, Victor, *Robert F. Kennedy: The Man and the Myth* (1968).
Malcolm X, *Autobiography* (Grove).
Novak, Robert D., and Evans, Jr., Rowland, *Lyndon B. Johnson: The Exercise of Power* (1966).
Pike, Douglas, *Viet Cong.* (MIT Press).
Sidney, Hugh B., *A Very Personal Presidency* (1968).
Trager, Frank N., *Why Viet Nam?* (1968).
White, Theodore B., *The Making of the President: 1964* (1965). On the campaign.
White, William S., *The Professional* (1964). On Johnson as a politician, favorable.
Wicker, Tom, *JFK and LBJ* (1968). On Johnson's loss of consensus over Vietnam.

REVIEW QUESTIONS

MULTIPLE CHOICE

1. Which enactment of the Johnson administration represented a victory where several preceding presidents had failed? (1) Aid to public housing (2) open housing for minorities (3) VISTA (4) Medicare.

2. Which civil rights legislation did *not* begin during the Johnson Administration? (1) Open housing (2) integrated public accommodations law (3) voting rights.

3. In the election campaign of 1964 the outstanding occurrence was (1) the nomination of Hubert Humphrey (2) the overwhelming vote for Johnson (3) the nomination of Nelson Rockefeller (4) the defeat of Richard Nixon.

4. The most important change in immigration policy in the 1960s was (1) the elimination of the quota system (2) admission of Asiatics for the first time (3) reducing the quota of northern European nations (4) provisions to encourage immigration of Latin Americans.

5. African Americans who wished to do so felt they could not escape the generally stunting environment of the ghettos unless (1) the right to vote was guaranteed (2) open housing was assured (3) their children could be bused to white schools (4) Black Power succeeded in establishing African American operated businesses.

6. With regard to Vietnam, the Western Allies at Geneva in 1954 agreed (1) to unite the northern and the southern parts immediately (2) to hold free election to determine if all of Vietnam would become Communist or non-Communist (3) to make South Vietnam a separate non-Communist state (4) generally speaking there were no unanimous, definite agreements for the permanent settlement of the Vietnam question.

7. Escalation of the American involvement in the Vietnam War began soon after (1) the fall of Dienbienphu (2) the Geneva meeting of 1954 (3) the attacks in the Bay of Tonkin (4) the Tet Offensive.

8. Which justification for the American war effort in South Vietnam was offered most strongly? (1) That Communism must be suppressed everywhere (2) that America must demonstrate she would always come to the aid of free governments (3) that the Communist takeover of South Vietnam would be followed by Communist power grabs in neighboring countries of Southeast Asia.

9. Which was *not* a consequence of the Vietnam War? (1) Loss of good-will abroad (2) inflation (3) increase in taxes (4) sharp division of public opinion at home (5) creation of SEATO.

10. In which crisis was the American response the strongest and quickest? (1) Santo Domingo (2) Panama (3) Six-Day War (4) Czechoslovakia (5) *Pueblo* capture.

11. Most responsible for beginning the moon landing program was (1) Truman (2) Eisenhower (3) Kennedy (4) Johnson (5) Nixon.

COMPLETION

12. The name Johnson gave to his administration's program of reform was the _____ .

13. Johnson appointed Robert C. Weaver as Secretary of the newly created Department of _____ and _____ _____ .

14. Johnson's domestic peace corps was known by the name _____ .

15. African American separateness was advocated by a group known as the _____ .

16. The name of the guerrilla opponents of Americans in South Vietnam was _____ .

17. The most notable race riot in the African American protests occurred in the _____ district in the city of _____ .

CHRONOLOGY / CHAPTER 29

1968   Nixon elected President in race with Humphrey.

1969   Nixon inaugurated.
Burger succeeded Warren as Chief Justice of the Supreme Court.
American astronauts landed on moon in Apollo 11.
Massive protests against war in Vietnam; troop withdrawals began.
Nixon established wage and price controls to combat inflation.

1970   Drastic declines in securities markets; interest rates peak; increases in unemployment.

1971   Nixon announced his "New Economic Policy" of wage and price controls.
First Nixon devaluation of the dollar.
Communist China admitted to the United Nations.

1972   Nixon visited Communist China.
Nixon visited Moscow and signed Strategic Arms Limitation Treaty.
Twenty-sixth Amendment ratified—reduced voting age to 18.
Nixon re-elected President.

1973   The United States signed Vietnam ceasefire agreement in Paris.
Second Nixon devaluation of the dollar.
Native American militants occupied hamlet of Wounded Knee.
Successive shocking revelations in Watergate scandal in 1972 election.
Vice President Agnew resigned.

1974   Nixon resigned as President. Ford became President.
Ford pardoned Nixon.
Ford granted amnesty to Vietnam draft dodgers.

1975   South Vietnam surrendered to North Vietnam.
Mayaguez seized.

1976   Nuclear Test Pact limiting underground tests signed.
United States celebrated nation's bicentennial.
Koreagate investigation aimed at lobbyist who influenced congressman and other government officials.

Chapter

29
THE NIXON-FORD
ADMINISTRATION, 1969–1977

> The Nixon administration pursued moderately conservative Republican policies. It is usually characterized as pragmatic rather than doctrinaire in its approach to national problems. In neither house of Congress did Nixon enjoy the support that a Republican majority would have given him in his first six years in office, but the enormous powers of the presidency enabled him to carry out his positive policies in foreign affairs and for the most part his rather negative policies in domestic affairs. He sought to make his most compelling record in foreign affairs. At home he terminated and curtailed many of the programs of his predecessor but made no really outstanding changes of his own.

DOMESTIC AFFAIRS

Without the support of a majority in Congress Nixon could do little by way of legislating, but he was able to use the presidential powers of veto and threat of veto, appointment, and impoundment of funds appropriated by Congress, to end or weaken many of the social programs of the Great Society, which had lost public support anyway. Nevertheless, considerable progress was made toward equality for African Americans. Nixon gained stature during his first term and won reelection overwhelmingly in 1972. Soon after the beginning of his second term, the Watergate scandal and other revelations of wrongdoing unfolded. Nixon's forced resignation in 1974 left his Vice President, Gerald Ford, to complete the two terms of Republican rule before the Democratic Party once again regained the presidency.

● ● **Nixon: Career**—Richard M. Nixon grew up in a lower-middle-class Quaker family in southern California, was graduated from Whittier College in 1934, was graduated from Duke University Law School in 1937, entered the Navy in World War II, and was elected to the House of Representatives in 1946 and 1948. On the House Un-American Activities Committee he was chiefly responsible for the perjury conviction of Alger

Hiss. He continued to gain political following as an anti-Communist when he defeated Democrat Helen Gahagen Douglas in a bitter congressional contest in which he accused her of being "soft on Communism." He then served two terms as Vice President under Eisenhower, in which capacity he kept himself in prominence by active service to the administration. His political career, however, seemed ended after he lost the presidential race to John F. Kennedy in 1960 and the governor's race in California in 1962. But he devoted himself so assiduously to rebuilding the Republican Party and his own public image that he won the presidential nomination again on the first ballot in the campaign of 1968.

✪✪✪ **The Election of 1968**—Both the Vietnam War, with its related issues of inflation and the draft, and the Black Revolution and its subsequent "white backlash" created a background of discontent in 1968. The election year was one of violence and the surprise elimination of one of the candidates for the presidential nomination: Senator Robert Kennedy was assassinated by a disgruntled immigrant from the Middle East, Sirhan Sirhan, as he was making great progress toward winning the Democratic nomination for President. (Although his death was not related to the election, the greatest of the African American leaders, Martin Luther King, Jr., also died by assassination; African American violence followed in most of the larger American cities.) Mob violence raged near the Democratic National Convention in Chicago where the city police clashed with young demonstrators of such New Left groups as the Students for a Democratic Society (SDS).

Vice President Hubert H. Humphrey, representing the Johnson administration, won the Democratic nomination on the first ballot. Senator Edmund Muskie of Maine was nominated for Vice President. As for the Republican Party, the Presidential nominee Nixon chose as his running mate, in a "Southern strategy," was Governor Spiro T. Agnew of Maryland.

Domestic discontent at the continuance of the Vietnam War outweighed the public satisfaction with the booming economy. The results of political polls and the failure of Humphrey to catch on with the voters indicated that Nixon had a strong chance of winning. Consequently, he conducted a guarded campaign and avoided a strongly partisan role. The Southern and reactionary viewpoint found a spokesman in the candidacy of ex-Governor George C. Wallace of Alabama of the new American Independent Party. As in the 1962 election, results were close. Nixon's popular lead was less than one percent of the vote, but Nixon won a strong majority in the electoral college. Wallace won five states of the Deep South. The Republicans gained seats in Congress, but the Democrats held a strong nominal majority of both houses. The Republicans further strengthened their party in the South.

✪ **Early Nixon Policies**—Rather than seeking radical changes through legislation, appointments, or administrative policy, President Nixon took a quiet approach to problems facing the nation. He generally took a middle-of-the-road stance and a pragmatic position. There were no attempts to dramatize issues, and demands for solutions were met with the appointment of study commissions. His cabinet appointees were all Republicans and generally of moderate views.

Near the end of his first year Nixon signed an income tax reform law that sought to close some of the well-publicized loopholes by which much income of the wealthy had escaped taxation. Notable among the changes was the reduction of the depletion allowance of oil companies. Nixon sought to encourage private industry to employ more workers from minority groups and to promote "Black Capitalism."

Nixon did not assert himself as a strong leader of Congress in spite of his own experience there. As for the problem of crime, statistics everywhere showed growing rather than reduced rates. Congress reduced many items of expenditure in the Johnson budget in the fields of education, health care, and social services. Nevertheless, much progress was made in the integration of public schools and in the percentages of African American students remaining in high school and going on to college. Vice President Agnew made news from time to time expressing bluntly what were administration views in attacking anti-war protesters and "biased" television news coverage of the administration. The Twenty-sixth Amendment, proposed and ratified in 1972, lowered the voting age to 18 in federal elections. The states in turn reduced their voting age to 18 in state elections.

○○ **The Supreme Court**—In the Supreme Court Chief Justice Earl Warren retired in 1969. Warren had handed down many liberal decisions relating to civil rights, reapportionment of representation, and the protection of the rights of persons accused of criminal acts. Nixon named a little known judge of a lower federal court, Warren E. Burger, as Warren's successor. Burger had a reputation as a strong advocate of "law and order." In October 1969, Burger's court ended the "deliberate speed" timing for public school desegregation and called for immediate (within months) integration. The policy went into effect in Mississippi in January 1970.

By 1973 the shape of the Nixon Supreme Court had become fairly well delineated. The four conservatives on the Court, chosen by Nixon as "strict constructionists," were Chief Justice Burger and Justices Lewis F. Powell, Jr., Harry Blackmun, and William Rehnquist. Three holdover liberals from the Warren Court were Justices William O. Douglas, William Brennan, and Thurgood Marshall. Two other holdovers, Justices Byron White and Potter Stewart, were moderates who frequently provided swing votes on important decisions. A big swing to the right did not occur even after the last two Nixon appointees took their seats.

Several important decisions since 1972 controverted Nixon's positions: the Court struck down the death penalty, restricted electronic bugging, and nullified aid to church-related schools. In the landmark decision of *Roe v. Wade,* the Court affirmed a woman's right to have an abortion in the first trimester of her pregnancy. Instead of reversing the famous bold decisions of the Warren Court, the Nixon Court limited their expansion in such areas as rights of criminal suspects, equal rights for the poor, and legislative reapportionment. After Justice Burger, Nixon's next appointment was that of Harry Blackmun of Minnesota. Then to fill a new vacancy he nominated successively two Southerners both of whom the Senate predictably refused to confirm because they were not regarded as qualified. In December 1971, the Senate confirmed Nixon's nomination of Lewis F. Powell, a Virginian. Powell was the first Southern conservative to be approved for the top Court since the appointment of James F. Byrnes in 1941. Also in December the Senate confirmed the appointment of William H. Rehnquist of Arizona. Powell and Rehnquist filled vacancies left by Justice Hugo N. Black and John Marshall Harlan, both of whom had resigned due to ill health.

○ **The Distress of Inflation**—The economy under Nixon suffered from both unemployment and inflation. For two and one-half years Nixon pursued a doctrinaire hands-off policy toward inflation, relying upon a highly restrictive monetary policy, including high interest rates to rein in the inflationary economic boom. Interest rates reached new highs for a period going back as far as the Civil War. Federal spending was substantially curbed except for defense expenditures. But in August 1971, Nixon gave in to pleadings of economists and businessmen and proved himself a pragmatist by adopting a "New Economic Policy" of wage and price controls. Phase I began with a wage-price-rent freeze and ended convertibility of the dollar into gold. In Phase II, November 1971, Nixon tried a return to voluntarism by lifting controls except in certain problem areas of food, health care, and construction. In Phase III, January 1973, Nixon terminated mandatory wage and price controls, but the termination had been ordered too soon. Therefore, in June 1973, Nixon ordered a 60-day price freeze ("Phase III½") to give time to prepare Phase IV wage-price policies.

In preparation for the election of 1972 the administration had pursued a policy of reduced interest rates and massive increases in the money supply in order to stimulate the economy for election year. After the election the supposedly independent Federal Reserve Board was permitted once again to resume tight money policies and high interest rates. Interest rates rose month after month until the high levels of 1970 brought back the falling security markets of 1969–1970. But consumer prices rose more sharply than at any time since the Korean War after Phase III of Nixon's decontrol went into effect. Employment also reached new highs; nevertheless many jobs went unfilled in spite of a five percent rate of unemployment. Prices of meat and other agricultural commodities increased sharply during the first half of 1973 so that Nixon began to put in effect curbs on certain exports. In February, the dollar was again devalued, this time by ten percent. (The first devaluation, of 8.57 percent, occurred in December 1971.) It was hoped that devaluation, making American dollars cheaper in terms of other currencies, would promote exports, discourage imports, and end deficits in the United States balance of payments.

❍ **Social Developments**—The struggle of African Americans for social and economic equality set an example of radical protest that was followed to a lesser degree by other groups. Among these were the women's liberation movement, equal rights for Mexican-Americans (Chicanos), Puerto Ricans, Native Americans, and homosexuals. There were movements for penal reform and ecological controls. College students were especially active in many of these movements. Radical demonstrators like the Chicago Eight were tried on charges of conspiracy to incite riots at the Democratic National Convention in 1968. During the trial, one of the defendants, African American leader Bobby Seale, disrupted the court and was ordered bound and gagged. He and the other defendents were convicted.

During the Nixon administration protesting Native Americans occupied several federal properties, including Alcatraz Island in San Francisco Bay. A few hundred Native American militants led by activists of the American Indian Movement (AIM) occupied the Bureau of Indian Affairs headquarters building in Washington, DC, in November 1972. This was in protest against treaties broken by the federal government and in particular by the Bureau of Indian Affairs. In February 1973, about 200 armed supporters of the American Indian Movement seized control of the hamlet of Wounded Knee (site of the final defeat of the Sioux) on the Oglala Sioux reservation in South Dakota to dramatize demands for a Senate investigation of Native American problems. Nixon renounced the policy of "termination" (began under Eisenhower) of special federal treatment for Native Americans. Instead, federal aid was expanded and the policy of Native American self-determination was recognized.

FOREIGN AFFAIRS

It was in foreign affairs that Nixon believed he had the most to offer to the American people. He continued the policy of deliberate reduction of American ground forces in South Vietnam and the "Vietnamization" of their defense. The Nixon Doctrine stated that Asian nations must assume the greater part of the burden of their defense against Communist aggression. Nixon won national acceptance by the "silent majority" of his policy of deliberate, not precipitate, reduction of the American ground forces in Vietnam. In November 1969, Nixon renounced biological warfare and ordered the Defense Department to destroy its germ weapon stockpiles. He reaffirmed American policy against the first use of lethal chemical weapons.

✪✪ **Vietnam**—In July 1969, President Nixon began the withdrawal of troops and in November announced the intention of eventually withdrawing all United States ground combat forces—this in response to the mounting mass demonstrations of peace advocates. The Nixon plan called for ultimate "Vietnamization" of the war by replacing American troops with those of South Vietnam. By the end of 1969 over 100,000 men had been withdrawn from Vietnam and this policy of scheduled withdrawals was continued, but peace advocates called for immediate, complete, and unconditional withdrawal, trusting that the adversaries would reciprocate by releasing American prisoners of war. In May 1970, the President ordered a temporary invasion of Cambodia to destroy Vietcong sanctuaries. New unprecedented protest demonstrations occurred all over the nation, especially on college campuses. Rioting students were killed in confrontations with police at Kent State University in Ohio and Jackson State College in Mississippi. Nixon promised that ground troops would be withdrawn in six weeks from Cambodia. American opposition to the war was increased by widespread use of hard drugs among American troops, by South Vietnamese atrocities, and murder of civilians by American soldiers, such as a massacre in the remote hamlet of My Lai. Lt. William Calley was later relieved of his duties and court-martialed as a result of his involvement in the incident.

After a breakdown of secret peace talks in Paris between Henry Kissinger, Nixon's special representative and the delegates from North Vietnam, the United States resumed massive bombing of North Vietnam in late December. Peace talks resumed near Paris on January 8, 1973. On January 27 a cease-fire agreement was signed in Paris to end the war. The truce was eventually extended to Laos and was to be extended to Cambodia. Hundreds of violations of the agreement occurred on both sides so that another cease-fire agreement had to be negotiated in June (to be followed by new, but decreased, violations). Pressure mounted in Congress to cut off funds for the continuation of the bombing in Cambodia, and Congress and the President agreed that such funds would be terminated in August 1973. The South Vietnamese fought until April 30, 1975 when they surrendered to the North. The Vietnamese war was the longest in American history. From 1965 to 1972, the United States dropped more than three times as many bombs on Vietnam as on Germany and Japan in World War II.

✪✪✪ **China**—By 1969 conclusive evidence of the breakdown of monolithic world Communism led by Russia or China made it possible for Nixon to move toward friendly relations with both China and the Soviet Union.

In 1969 Nixon relaxed the embargo of American purchases of Chinese goods, as a first step. On November 15, 1971, Communist China made her entry into the United Nations. Later China invited a United States table tennis team to visit Peking ("ping-pong diplomacy") and admitted Western newsmen to cover the event. In April Nixon eased relations with China by relaxing a 20-year trade embargo. In July Nixon announced to a surprised American public that he would visit China the next year to confer with her leaders about normalizing relations between the two countries. The trip was arranged in a secret meeting in Peking between Henry A. Kissinger and Premier Chou En-lai. In February 1972, Nixon arrived in Peking for a visit that concluded with a joint communiqué pledging both powers to work for "a normalization of relations."

OO The Soviet Union—As the first United States President to visit Moscow, Nixon arrived in May 1972 for a week of summit talks which produced a landmark arms pact to head off a nuclear missile race between the two nuclear giants. A Strategic Arms Limitation Treaty (SALT), later ratified by the Senate, limited defensive antiballistic missile systems to 200 ABM interceptor missiles in each country. An executive agreement froze offensive missile arsenals at roughly existing levels. Adherence to the treaty could be verified by spy satellites. Other agreements on health, science, and trade reflected the beginning of a *détente* from the Cold War and a new era of cooperation between the two great powers. In May 1972, Nixon and Soviet Premier Kosygin signed the United States-Soviet Agreements in Space Exploration and Science and Technology. In July the Soviet Union agreed to a purchase of an estimated $1 billion of wheat and other grains from the United States.

NIXON'S SECOND TERM AND THE SUCCESSION OF FORD

During the campaign, negotiations for peace in Vietnam proceeded slowly but steadily through the efforts of Henry Kissinger. The withdrawal of nearly all American troops from South Vietnam had almost eliminated the issue of war. The public felt that the policy of deliberate withdrawal was the most honorable. In the campaign Nixon played the role of an on-the-job President and delegated the campaigning to others.

OOO The Election of 1972—The Republicans renominated Nixon and Agnew. The Democrats at Miami Beach nominated George S. McGovern of South Dakota for President. McGovern's nomination was the result of the adoption by the Democratic Party of a quota system of choosing delegates to the nominating conventions. Consequently delegates were heavily weighted with quotas representing dissident minorities of women,

African Americans, Chicanos, and Native Americans. Many old-line Democratic politicians and representatives of the middle class and of average Americans were actually excluded from the convention. The American TV-viewing public took note of this. After his nomination McGovern hastily chose the young and unknown Senator Thomas F. Eagleton of Missouri. Eagleton soon had to be dropped when it became known he had had psychiatric therapy at three different times. At first, McGovern indicated he would retain Eagleton but was forced to drop him in favor of Sargent Shriver, brother-in-law of former President Kennedy. This created a credibility gap for McGovern, who had been stressing morality as a campaign issue.

George Wallace, founder of the American Independent Party, had to drop out of the race. He was confined to a wheelchair, recovering from four bullet wounds inflicted by a would-be assassin in May at a shopping center where he was campaigning in Laurel, Maryland. Wallace had been winning by larger vote totals than had been expected. In the Democratic primaries Wallace had moved up to second place among contenders for the Democratic nomination, having won by May 17, 323 delegates to McGovern's 405. He remained paralyzed from the waist down.

The election results on November 7 gave Nixon and Agnew every state except Massachusetts and the District of Columbia. Nixon won 521 electoral votes to 17 for McGovern, 97 percent of the total and 60.83 percent of all votes cast. Only 55 percent of eligible persons voted, indicating a lack of strong appeal of either ticket. Nixon received 45,901,204 votes to McGovern's 28,419,009. Public opinion polls all along had forecast an overwhelming victory for Nixon. Democrats retained majorities in both houses, gained two seats in the Senate and lost twelve in the House and thus retained strength to continue influencing legislation and domestic policy. Democrats increased their margin of control in state houses to 31–19. Nixon won strongly in the South and with the Catholic and blue-collar voters. The youth vote did not come through for McGovern as expected. McGovern lost his home state of South Dakota. The voting public was tired of demonstrations, racial discord, and wasteful spending for poorly designed antipoverty programs. The reaction against the revolutionary aims of the sixties was in full-swing.

The campaign was undoubtedly the most rotten in all American experience with respect to the calculated employment of unethical and illegal practices. The burglary of Democratic offices in the Watergate complex was revealed by subsequent investigations to be only the tip of an iceberg of massive, well-organized, highly financed, and well-planned employment of falsehood, espionage, sabotage, secret funds, special interest deals (dairy industry and ITT campaign contributions), and criminal activity by persons associated with the Committee to Re-Elect the President and serving as the closest subordinates to the President.

Nixon was chosen as the alternative to encouraging more unfulfillable expectations on the part of minorities and the poor. The nation wanted more "law and order" and less libertarianism, more restraint and less crime, and more civility and less dissidence.

○ **Nixon Cabinet Changes**—Nixon's cabinet appointees of his first term may be characterized as rather modest men from moderate and conservative Republican ranks. William P. Rogers was retained as Secretary of State. Melvin R. Laird had served as Secretary of Defense but retired and was replaced by HEW Secretary Elliott Richardson. Some of the appointees and second-term changes may be noteworthy. Earl G. Butz succeeded Clifford M. Hardin as Secretary of Agriculture. Walter J. Hickel was followed by Rogers C. Morton as Secretary of the Interior. Henry A. Kissinger retained his position as adviser on national security affairs. Nixon's controversial "law and order" law partner, John N. Mitchell, was the first of four Attorney Generals during his administration. Kissinger became Secretary of State in August 1973.

○ **The Imperial Presidency**—The powers of the presidency were brought to a new peak by Richard Nixon in his second term. This concentration of power and the conduct of the office under Nixon came to be referred to as the "imperial presidency." The authority of the office had begun to magnify with Theodore Roosevelt, increased with Wilson, and was greatly multiplied by Congress with the enactment of statutes giving Franklin Roosevelt innumerable special and emergency powers to deal with economic depression and war. The popularity of John Kennedy, the political skills of Lyndon Johnson, and the failure of Congress to terminate any of this accumulation of power all prepared the way for Nixon's unscrupulous exercise of indiscriminate power. He believed he had the right to impound funds appropriated by Congress for social purposes he himself disapproved. Nixon asserted the executive privilege of withholding information from Congress. The President surrounded himself with imperious aides, and ceremonial trappings of office were adopted to emphasize the majesty of the office. Through the bombing of Cambodia, he exercised war powers without the approval of Congress. Under the cloak of national security, he justified the disregard of criminal statutes by his appointees. Millions of citizens regarded him as a Tory and a tyrant. In handling the sordid Watergate crisis, Nixon's unscrupulous abuse of power reached its peak.

○○○ **The Watergate Affair**—This scandal began with the arrest of five men who had gained illegal entry into Democratic National Committee headquarters in the Watergate building in Washington, DC, on the night of June 17, 1972. James McCord, a former CIA operative and then a security officer for the Committee to Re-Elect the President, as well as four others, were working apparently under the direction of aides closest to the President. Police confiscated "bugging" and photocopy equipment from the burglars. The intruders were seeking information regarding the activities of Nixon's antiwar opposition; the President's justification for these illegal activities was that national security was endangered by anti-war activists. But the Watergate entry was only the tip of the iceberg. Nixon had authorized a host of measures such as the opening of mail, the monitoring of telephones, and the use of undercover agents on college campuses. Earlier, in 1971, Nixon set up an extralegal unit within his staff to gather information regarding the activities of Daniel Ellsberg, anti-war activist who published the *Pentagon Papers* with their damaging revelations regarding the Vietnam war.

The trial and conviction of the Watergate intruders brought exposure of the scandal. Newspapermen's investigations and confessions of participants seeking reduced sentences brought out the shocking criminal activities authorized by Nixon. In the Congress in 1972, hearings conducted by Senator Sam Ervin of North Carolina brought confessions from public officials and undercover men. The discovery that the President had bugged his own offices to record conversations led Judge Sirica, who conducted the trials, to subpoena the tapes. The President refused to yield them. After several months the tapes were released to a special prosecutor by order of the Supreme Court in the historic case *Nixon v. United States*. The tapes revealed the clear responsibility of the President for ordering the illegal activities as well as his lying to the public to deny and cover these activities. By 1975 over 30 presidential agents were indicted or found guilty, including Attorney General Richard Kleindienst and ex-Attorney General John Mitchell. For their part in the affair, three key administration officials resigned on April 30: H. R. Haldeman, John D. Ehrlichmann, and John W. Dean. These were the three closest aides to the President.

The Watergate scandal severely crippled conduct of the executive branch for months; it weakened public confidence in government and the office of the President. Congress reasserted itself against the executive branch; it enacted several measures limiting the president's war powers and enacted a law to force government agencies involved in international affairs to furnish information to Congress.

✪ Agnew's Resignation—Vice President Spiro Agnew, in October 1973, was fined $10,000 and was placed on probation for income tax evasion in connection with acceptance of about $100,000 in graft money when he was Governor of Maryland. His resignation made him the second Vice President to resign. (In 1832 John C. Calhoun resigned in protest against President Jackson's actions.) President Nixon made an appointment to fill the vacancy. He selected Gerald R. Ford, prominent Republican Congressman from Michigan, as Agnew's successor. Ford inspired confidence because of his reputation for being straightforward and open in contrast to Nixon's reputation for being secretive and pretentious.

✪✪✪ **Nixon's Resignation**—The White House tapes, when finally released, revealed Nixon's guilt of felony in the Watergate coverup. They revealed the sordid, vulgar conversations and amorality of the President and the men he employed. Not only Democrats, but conservative Republicans, whose party had been badly besmirched by their leader, demanded his resignation. The House Judiciary Committee recommended three articles of impeachment for the Watergate coverup, for the abuse of presidential powers, and for refusal to be subpoenaed by the Committee. From Republican leaders in Congress he learned of his certain impeachment. He resigned on August 9, 1974, and returned to his home in San Clemente, California.

Nixon was succeeded by his own appointee, Gerald Ford. Nixon was the first President to resign from office. Ford was the first President not chosen by national election; in effect, Nixon chose his successor.

FORD AS PRESIDENT, 1974–1977

Congressman Gerald R. Ford, whom Nixon had appointed Vice President after Agnew resigned, served the remainder of Nixon's second term after Nixon resigned. His first major appointment, which followed the dictates of the Twenty-fifth amendment to the Constitution, was the selection of New York's former Governor, Nelson A. Rockefeller, as Vice President. His first major act as President was to pardon former President Nixon for any crimes he may have committed while in office. Ford inherited a country facing difficult economic conditions. He also had the task of completing the negotiations to end the war in Vietnam.

✪ **Gerald R. Ford**—Ford was elected to the House of Representatives from Michigan and served for 25 years. He rose to the position of House minority leader and became known as an obstructionist, fighting Democratic sponsored legislation. He was a combative conservative and an effective and influential party spokesman. Ford was also considered an open-minded individual who liked people and who possessed a sense of humor. Popular television poked fun of Ford's horrendous golf game and his awkwardness.

When he became President, he retained most of the members of the Nixon cabinet, including the architect of Nixon's foreign policy, Secretary of State Henry Kissinger. Ford maintained the conservative stance of Nixon on economic and social issues. In the area of foreign policy he was an old cold-warrior and believed in increasing the defense budget. Ford used the veto frequently to curb the liberal spending habits of the Democratic-controlled Congress, especially in areas of welfare and education. He worked to reduce the regulation of business by the federal government, establishing the WIN program to combat inflation. He appointed a mild conservative, John Paul Stevens III, to the

Supreme Court after liberal Justice William O. Douglas resigned. Like Nixon, Ford allowed large budget deficits in order to combat high unemployment. This resulted in inflation, which increased to a high of twelve percent. An assassination attempt on Ford in 1975 by a deranged woman failed.

○○ Ford's Pardon of Nixon—A firestorm of criticism greeted President Ford's pardon of former President Richard Nixon just a month after he announced his resignation. Ford felt that he had to close on one of the saddest chapters in American history. He announced he was pardoning Nixon for any crimes Nixon may have been involved in while serving as President. The pardon short-circuited the investigation by the Watergate special prosecutor who was about ready to indict the former President. A week after the pardon, Ford announced he was also issuing an amnesty proclamation to thousands of Vietnam draft resisters and military deserters. Ford's attempt to bring the country together by the pardon of Nixon and limited clemency of anti-war activists failed. Even political reforms initiated after Watergate were soured after the "Koreagate" incident, which involved revelations of unlawful campaign contributions and the investigation of a Korean lobbyist. Only during the celebration of America's bicentennial two years later did the country seem to unite in purpose.

○ Domestic Policy—With inflation increasing to double digits, President Ford decided to get support from the American people by creating the WIN program (Whip Inflation Now). Ford pushed government deregulation of business as a solution to the economic problems, but also insisted that the defense budget receive increased appropriations. The President vetoed inflationary spending programs such as the Education Appropriation Act of 1976, and a federal jobs bill. Unemployment increased, but benefits declined. Big cities were facing a loss of federal funds and were threatened with bankruptcy. (A headline in a New York City daily proclaimed "Ford to New York—Drop Dead.") Even with a continuing energy crisis and increased gas prices at the pumps, Ford refused to impose gas rationing or develop a government program designed to foster energy conservation.

○ Foreign Policy—Though Ford was an arch anti-Communist and advocated a strong military, he continued the détente with the Communist powers. He visited the Soviet Union and People's Republic of China, and reached a five-year agreement to sell American grain to the Russians. In the Middle East, the United States, almost single-handedly, maintained support of Israel against the Arabs despite the importance of Arab oil on America's economy. For the first time since the end of World War II and Korea, there were no international wars threatening the country. The United States completely withdrew from South Vietnam in 1975 and North Vietnam immediately completed its takeover of the once divided country. In Africa colonialism practically came to an end in 1975 when Portugal gave up Angola. In Latin America the U.S. continued to support right wing anti-Communist leaders and funnelled military aid to bolster their regimes. A nuclear test ban treaty that limited underground nuclear testing was signed in 1976.

○○ **The *Mayaguez* Incident**—In May of 1975, the Cambodian Communists seized the American merchant ship *Mayaguez*. Brief, unsuccessful negotiations failed to set its 35 crew members free. In a dramatic strike ordered by Ford, American ground, sea, and air forces freed the captured Americans. However, the toll was great—38 Americans were killed and even though many anti-war politicians supported the action, others claimed it was in direct violation of the 1973 War Powers Act. In addition, Cambodia claimed they only captured the ship because they felt it was a spy vessel, and complained that they had been ready to release the Americans before the attack.

CHAPTER BOOK LIST

Alexander, H.E., *Money in Politics* (1972). A standard work.

Anson, R.S., *McGovern* (1972). Good campaign biography.

Bernstein, Carl, and Woodward, Bob, *All the President's Men* (Simon & Schuster).

Dutton, F.G., *Changing Sources of Power* (1971).

Evans, Rowland, and Novak, Robert D., *Nixon in the White House* (1971).

Falk, R.R., Kolko, Gabriel, and Litton, R.J., eds., *Crimes of War* (Random).

Fulbright, J.W., *The Pentagon Propaganda Machine* (Random).

Galbraith, J.K., *The New Industrial State* (Rev. ed., New American Library).

Hickel, Walter, *Who Owns America?* (1971). View of one who became disillusioned.

Kissinger, Henry, *White House Years* (1979).

Lubbell, Samuel, *The Hidden Crisis in American Politics* (Norton).

Lukas, Anthony, *Nightmare: The Underside of the Nixon Years* (1976).

Magruder, Jeb Stuart, *An American Life: One Man's Road to Watergate* (1974).

Mazo, Earl, and Hess, Stephen, *Nixon, A Political Portrait* (1968).

Novak, R.D., *Nixon in the White House: A Critical Portrait* (1971).

Safire, William, *Before the Fall* (1975).

Schlesinger, Jr., A.M., *Imperial Presidency* (1973).

Taylor, Telford, *Nuremberg and Vietnam* (Quadrangle).

White, Theodore H., *Breach of Faith* (1975).

White, Theodore H., *The Making of the President, 1968* (1969).

Wills, Garry, *Nixon Agonistes: The Crisis of the Self-made Man* (1970).

Witcover, Jules, *The Resurrection of Richard Nixon* (1970).

Witcover, Jules, *White Knight: The Rise of Spiro Agnew* (1972).

REVIEW QUESTIONS

MULTIPLE CHOICE

1. Which was not true of the election of 1968? (1) The Democrats were badly divided. (2) Nixon won by a large majority in the electoral college. (3) Humphrey lost overwhelmingly in the popular vote. (4) Democrats retained control of both houses of Congress.

2. Which action did Nixon take during his first year as President? (1) appointed an African American cabinet member (2) created the Department of Transportation (3) asked for a drastic reform of the welfare system (4) reduced interest rates.

3. Which were not offices held by Nixon in his political career? (1) Secretary of State (2) Vice President (3) Congressman (4) U. S. Senator

4. The candidate running against Nixon on the Democratic ticket in the election of 1968 was (1) Robert Kennedy (2) Adlai Stevenson (3) Edmund Muskie (4) Hubert Humphrey (5) George McGovern.

5. Leading protest movements during Nixon's first term were against (1) war in Vietnam (2) broken Native American treaties (3) discrimination against African Americans (4) pollution of the environment

6. Possibly the most tangible immediate gain of the African Americans after Nixon came into office was (1) widespread adoption of the Philadelphia plan (2) busing of African American students to predominantly white schools (3) generally strict enforcement of civil rights laws (4) a Supreme Court decision calling for immediate desegregation of schools in the South.

7. With regard to Nixon's policies, his Supreme Court (1) acted as a rubber stamp (2) proved even more conservative than Nixon (3) mainly expressed conservatism by limiting expansion or contracting decisions of the Warren Court (4) flatly reversed liberal decisions of the Warren Court.

8. Which was not the subject of a reform movement during the Nixon administration? (1) women (2) Irish-Americans (3) Native Americans (4) inmates of penal institutions

9. Nixon's friendship with the two great Communist powers was explained chiefly by (1) a shift in Nixon's political philosophy (2) the dissension among Communist powers (3) a strategy to promote war between mainland China and the Soviet Union (4) a desire to improve the American foreign trade position

10. What was especially reprehensible about the Watergate affair was that (1) it represented subversive action against the American political process (2) the President was the known leader of a burglary ring (3) Democrats exaggerated the scandal and caused a lack of

confidence in the political system (4) it was justified by action of radicals in the Democratic Party

COMPLETION

11. Nixon advanced his early political career by making a reputation as
    a foe of those whom he accused of being "soft on _____ ."

12. Nixon's choice of Agnew as his running mate was known as his
    " _____ strategy."

13. The greatest discontent with the Nixon administration was aroused
    by his action with regard to _____ ?

14. On the economic front Nixon's greatest problem was _____?

15. AIM militants in 1973 occupied the battlefield hamlet of
    _____ .

16. The United States finally agreed to a cease-fire in Vietnam in the
    year _____ .

17. The outstanding scandal of the Nixon administration is known by
    the name of _____ .

MATCHING

18. Spiro T. Agnew
19. George C. Wallace
20. Hubert H. Humphrey
21. Warren Burger
22. Martin Luther King, Jr.
23. Henry A. Kissinger
24. George S. McGovern
25. William P. Rogers
26. John Mitchell
27. Maurice Stans

a. Nixon's "law and order" Attorney
     General
b. Attacked news media for biased
     political coverage
c. Democratic nominee for President
     in 1968
d. Nixon's special representative
     in foreign affairs
e. Leader of black separatist movement
f. Leader of American Independent Party
g. Brought defeat to his party in
     1972 election
h. Leading African American advocate
     of non-violent demonstrations
i. Nixon's Secretary of State
j. Nixon's appointee as Chief Justice
     of the Supreme Court
k. Pentagon Papers

CHRONOLOGY / CHAPTER 30

1976 Carter elected President in close race with Ford.
America celebrated bicentennial.

1977 Carter began crusade for human rights abroad.
Carter pardoned Vietnam War resisters.
Department of Energy created.
U.S. and Soviet Union implemented SALT I Agreement.
Senate ratified treaty to return Panama Canal Zone.
National Women's Conference called for passage of Equal
Rights Amendment.

1978 Camp David Accords brought peace between Egypt and
Israel.
Supreme Court ruled in *Baake v. U.S.* that affirmative action
was allowable.
United States and China started full diplomatic relations.

1979 Department of Education created.
American embassy personnel in Teheran held hostage by
Iranians; rescue mission failed in 1980.
Meltdown at Three Mile Island nuclear plant raised concerns
over nuclear energy.

1980 Inflation reached record high rate; nation was in grip of a
recession; Reagan raised economy as campaign issue.
U.S. announced boycott of Moscow Olympics; Carter
canceled grain to Soviet Union as a result of Afghanistan
invasion.

✪✪✪ GREAT SIGNIFICANCE
✪✪ IMPORTANT TOPICS
✪ SECONDARY IMPORTANCE

30
THE CARTER ADMINISTRATION, 1977–1981

Carter promised new style, ethical conduct, and innumerable reforms if elected. He was the first President from the Deep South since Zachary Taylor, was a "born again" Baptist, and called himself a "populist." He promised something different from the old political atmosphere in Washington. During his Presidency, it was largely a time of peace and of little social turmoil; the problem of inflation predominated.

DOMESTIC DEVELOPMENTS

On the domestic front, President Carter failed to realize most of the promises he had made so freely during the campaign. His lack of familiarity with the ways of politicians in Washington proved a handicap. He changed the style of the presidency to a casual and familiar one.

✪✪ **The Election of 1976**—At the beginning of the election campaign of 1976, no one Democratic candidate clearly led the dozen aspirants. Most prominent among them were Senator Henry Jackson of Washington and Governor George Wallace of Alabama. Least known among the runners was Jimmy Carter, former Governor of Georgia. He started campaigning two years early by shaking hands and talking to groups over the country. Early primary victories in Iowa, then in New Hampshire, and later in Florida demonstrated his appeal. He promised moral conduct and freedom from ties to the old politicians of Washington, DC. He promised reorganization of the federal government, reform of the income tax, a curb on inflation, and full employment. In fact, there seemed to be no promise he did not make. His openness, his sincerity, his promise—"I will never lie to you"—gave credence to his other promises. His politician's strategy was to deny being a politician—not an unusual strategy on the American scene in times when politicians are distrusted. Carter won the nomination of the Democratic Party on the first ballot; he named Senator Walter Mondale of Minnesota as his running mate.

The Republicans nominated the incumbent President, Gerald Ford. Ford's reputation with the public and his party had not improved greatly, so that the former Governor of California Ronald Reagan seriously threatened to take the nomination. Reagan appealed to the more conservative elements of his party. After winning the nomination, Ford chose Senator Robert Dole of Kansas, another conservative, as his vice-presidential partner.

In the campaign, Ford definitely began as the underdog, but he busied himself at the White House to exhibit a presidential image. Carter campaigned actively, spoke frankly of his sexual impulses in an interview for *Playboy* magazine, and labeled himself a "populist." Many thought he had a way of straddling the issues, but his piety contrasted with the image people had of Nixon. Ford's standing began to improve, but in a series of three televised debates, Carter proved himself to be more articulate and better informed. Existing high inflation and a degree of unemployment hurt Ford.

In the election, Carter won all states of the South, except Virginia, and several large states of the Middle Atlantic region. Ford won all states of the West and Southwest except Texas. Carter lost California, largely because its Governor, Jerry Brown, opposed Carter for the nomination and did not work for him in his home state. Ford's pardon of Nixon was a key factor to the outcome of the election. Carter's base of voters included African Americans, labor, large cities and the South, the traditional Democratic bloc of voters. Voter turnout was extremely low, with only 53 percent of the electorate going to the polls. The popular vote difference was only two percent and the electoral vote was 297–240. A shift in one or two of the key industrial states would have meant a Ford victory. The Democrats maintained a strong majority in both houses of Congress.

✪ **Carter as President**—After the inauguration ceremony, Jimmy Carter symbolized his populist values by walking down Pennsylvania Avenue with his family to the White House. One of his first acts in office was the pardon of about 10,000 Vietnam War draft evaders living in Canada.

Carter's cabinet appointments came from Washington insiders, the corporate world, and personal friends. Key advisers Bert Lance, head of the Bureau of the Budget, Attorney General Griffin Bell, Chief of Staff Hamilton Jordan, and Press Secretary Jody Powell all came from Georgia. Lance soon became embroiled in an ethics scandal that forced him to resign. Business leaders such as Secretary of State Cyrus Vance and Secretary of Defense Harold Brown gave a clear signal to the American people that Carter was not as much of a populist as he tried to symbolize. Minority representation was missing from Carter's cabinet.

Even though there was a solid Democratic majority in Congress, Carter ran into early conflicts with party leaders. In fact his inability to get along with Congress, along with congressional veto overrides, became significant features of his administration.

Early legislation by Congress included authority to reorganize the federal bureaucracy. Congress created a new Department of Energy in 1977 and Carter appointed Nixon's Secretary of Defense, James Schlesinger, as the department's first head. Immediately the new cabinet department ran into difficulty with Congress. Instead of promoting government regulation, Carter proposed an increase in oil production and a reduction of oil consumption. Congress did not pass a proposed 10 cents a gallon gas tax. The Three Mile Island nuclear reactor meltdown in 1979 caused great public concern over the future potential use of nuclear energy as a substitute for oil.

Congress also rejected Carter proposals to reform the welfare system, the electoral college, and campaign financing. It imposed restrictions on Carter's ability to formulate the federal budget through provisions of the 1974 Budget Act.

There were early legislative victories when Congress approved Carter's proposal to reorganize the federal bureaucracy. Jobs for the unemployed were created, taxes were nominally reduced, minimum wages were raised (even though this act certainly increased inflation), and Social Security payroll taxes were increased to try to offset some of the inflationary spending increases. Another cabinet position, the Department of Education with Shirley Hufstedler as first head, was created in 1979.

✪ **The Energy Crisis**—Ever since the Arab oil embargo of 1973 ended, American importation of foreign oil increased for many years. This dependence on foreign oil, predominantly from the Arab states, conflicted with the policy of support to Israel. The OPEC nations established a cartel to control production and raise oil prices, thus creating a trade deficit for the United States. This resulting foreign trade deficit, coupled with inflation, steadily eroded the value of the dollar. The American economy temporarily became hostage to Arab oil producers. As time passed, no resolution of the energy problem was achieved— either the President lacked strong leadership, or the nation could not face up to the fact of oil shortages at home and abroad.

✪ **The Economy**—Oil prices were skyrocketing and so was U.S. inflation. In 1979 the country saw inflation increase to double-digit levels. Besides the energy crisis, the country was also facing a more severe trade imbalance. The federal deficit increased continuously and Carter was unable to balance the federal budget. A recession was declared in 1980 and became a key issue in the 1980 campaign.

The Carter Family—The interest of the news media in the doings of the President's younger brother, Billy, doubtless brought embarrassment to the President. Billy figured on marketing his opinions and talents as a political observer as being more profitable than minding his gasoline service station in Plains, Georgia. He collected fees for his appearances at various public events, where he shared his wit and wisdom nurtured by his surroundings in Georgia. His name was exploited in selling for a time a product labeled as "Billy Beer." The public-spirited mother of the President, "Miss Lillian," who once has served creditably in the Peace Corps, was interviewed by journalists from time to time for her plain-spoken blunt language. One of the President's sisters was a fundamentalist evangelist. His active wife Rosalynn once tried her hand as a diplomat in a mission to Brazil, but made an undiplomatic remark to the embarrassment of all. The most serious embarrassment to the President came in 1980 from Billy's work as a hired agent of the Libyan government. For his services to Libya, he admitted to receiving more than $220,000. Billy's relations with his brother and Libya were investigated, and the President was exonerated.

FOREIGN DEVELOPMENTS

Carter emerged early in his administration as a crusader for human rights. He called for reform in the dictatorial governments of Cuba, Uganda, Ethiopia, and Argentina. He appointed Andrew Young, an African American Southern Congressman, as Chief United States Delegate to the United Nations. Unfortunately, Young embarrassed the administration with bold pronouncements regarding human rights. He was later replaced because of his unauthorized contacts with the Palestinian Liberation Organization (PLO). Carter called for free emigration of Jews from the Soviet Union, as well as other human rights declarations which came from the Helsinki Accord of 1975 and the International Declaration of Human Rights. The Soviets rejected Carter's crusade claiming that the United States, too, had a record of minority mistreatment.

✪✪✪ **The Hostage Crisis in Iran**—An almost unprecedented violation of the diplomatic immunity of embassy personnel occurred in November 1979, when the Ayatollah Ruhollah Khomeini's followers seized the American embassy building in Teheran and its personnel and held them as prisoners. Iranian revolutionary discontent, long and harshly suppressed, had succeeded (in January 1979) finally in overthrowing the Shah Mohammed Reza Pahlevi. The Shah had been supported by the United States and now was given refuge in America. The American embassy personnel, about 50 in number, were held hostage while the Iranians demanded the return of the sick Shah to Iran for trial. President Carter took economic, diplomatic, and, at first, other measures short of military intervention to help bring their release. But in April 1980, Carter launched a number of planes to the vicinity of Teheran to stage a raid to rescue the hostages. The mission was withdrawn after a sandstorm.

and mechanical failures in several helicopters—failures that cost the lives of eight Americans in a collision of a helicopter with a transport plane. The excruciating hostage situation extended through the election campaign of 1980, and after the death of the Shah, the UN condemned Iran for taking the hostages.

In 1980 Iraq attacked Iran. At the beginning of a long war between the two countries, the oil consuming nations lost their fuel supplies coming out of the Persian Gulf. Finally, in January 1981, the 52 American hostages were released and flown to freedom at the end of the long, tedious negotiations.

✪ **SALT Talks**—The Strategic Arms Limitation Talks agreement came up for negotiation in 1977, but the Soviets did not wish to reduce greatly their long range bombers and missiles. They did, however, agree to continue to observe the 1972 agreement, which resulted in a ceiling on some nuclear weapons.

Carter was a strong believer in achieving a second SALT agreement. In 1979 he signed a new treaty with Soviet President Leonid Brezhnev. The terms of the treaty called for major Soviet reduction of existing missiles, a limitation of nuclear warheads, and the future reduction of new missile systems by the Soviets. Carter made an emotional plea to Congress for ratification of the treaty. Presidential politics and anger over the failure of the Carter administration to achieve a release of the hostages doomed the treaty. A further source of friction with the Soviets developed from Cuban-Soviet activities in parts of Africa, such as Angola and Ethiopia.

✪ **Afghanistan**—In December of 1979, Moscow sent 5,000 troops to Afghanistan as further aid to the pro-Soviet regime in that country that was attempting to suppress Muslim insurgents. Carter condemned the invasion and announced a U.S. boycott of the 1980 Olympics to be held in Moscow. In addition he announced the cancellation of grain shipments to Russia. The United States sought NATO support of its position.

✪ **The Panama Canal Zone**—Panama had long been demanding the return of the Panama Canal Zone, and treaties drafted were being debated by the United States Senate. Conservatives opposed the ratification of these treaties. However, a treaty to maintain the neutrality of the canal won approval in 1978 by only two votes, only after an amendment was passed conceding the right of American armed intervention if it became necessary to ensure the continuing operation of the canal. In October of 1979, Panama took control of the Canal Zone and was promised total control of the canal at the turn of the century.

✪✪✪ **The Camp David Agreements**—Perhaps Carter's greatest foreign policy achievement came in 1978 when he hosted a series of meetings at Camp David between Israeli Prime Minister Menachim Begin and Egyptian President Anwar Sadat. Under a cloud of potential warfare in the Middle East, Carter was able to convince both sides to sign the first peace treaty between Israel and another Middle Eastern country. Carter's popularity was bolstered but later plummeted because of his inability to attain release of American hostages in Iran.

✪✪ **Relations with China**—Even though President Nixon urged full diplomatic relations with China, he was not able to achieve it during his administration. Carter, too, believed it would be in the best interests of the U.S. to recognize the Asian Communist giant. On January 1, 1979, Carter announced full diplomatic recognition of China. As a result, all standing treaties with Taiwan were cancelled and China was admitted into the United Nations shortly thereafter.

ECONOMIC CHANGES IN THE SEVENTIES

In the seventies, growing scarcities of natural resources slowed the earlier rapid rise in real incomes in America, and leaders began to speak of an era of limits. American petroleum reserves were no longer being discovered as rapidly as they were being consumed. Inflation followed the Vietnam War and persisted as the most serious economic problem, while the American dollar declined in value relative to several other currencies, mainly the German mark and the Japanese yen. High military budgets helped defense industries and high technology companies to prosper. Transistors and microcircuitry brought innumerable applications of electronic technology. Computers, first developed in the mid-forties, brought a revolution not only in the information industry but came to be hailed as the cause of another industrial revolution. Laser applications began to expand rapidly in the late seventies and held promise of changes proportionate to the introduction of transistors in the 1950s. Farming utilized machine production so successfully that only four percent of the United States population produced foodstuffs for the nation and for export of large surpluses. Land idled by the "soil banks" was planted once again. White collar and service industry workers continued to grow in proportion to other workers. Although many of them organized unions, the percentage of workers belonging to unions declined and with this, the political power of organized labor. Living standards increased despite inflation, but poverty and unemployment persisted.

SOCIAL CHANGES OF THE SEVENTIES

The struggle for equality of African Americans ("Black Revolution") was one of the most notable of the social changes of the sixties and set an example for other suppressed groups to demand more opportunity and recognition. Among these were Hispanics, Native Americans, women, and the aged. Significant population changes occurred, too.

○ **African Americans**—The main struggle for African American opportunity centered in efforts to integrate public schools, particularly in the North where segregation occurred according to residential distribution of people. Courts ordered busing of pupils to achieve a mixture of African American and white in the classrooms; busing consequently became a political issue. Affirmative action programs brought protests from white students who charged "reverse discrimination" since minorities were given preferred admission to colleges and financial aid. The *Bakke* decision of the United States Supreme Court upheld the claims of Alan Bakke that he had been denied admission to medical school because of "reverse discrimination." General admissions quotas were judged constitutional since various factors had to be considered.

○ **Spanish Americans**—Along with African Americans, Spanish-speaking Americans suffered discrimination. Most numerous among these were the Mexican Americans who began to refer to themselves as *Chicanos;* they were concentrated most in the states bordering Mexico. Many were migrant workers, employed particularly in agriculture. Chicano demands brought in the use of Spanish language, along with English, in education, in the ballot, and in public services. In California, Cesar Chavez arose as the leader of farm workers through his leadership of the United Farm Workers in 1963. Puerto Ricans and Cubans increased the Spanish-speaking population in the cities of the East. "Brown Power" defended rights of more than 11 million, the second largest racial minority and the fastest growing.

○ **Native Americans**—The Native Americans, the most isolated and disadvantaged of all minorities, suffered from underemployment and low incomes. Too much federal money supported bureaucrats and suffocated Native Americans with regulations. Reservation lands were exploited by corporations that leased them. Wishing to go further than the concessions to Native American culture of the Wheeler-Howard Act of 1934, more radical leaders organized the American Indian Movement (AIM). Members, in the seizure of the Bureau of Indian Affairs (BIA) building in Washington in 1972, carried off bundles of documents damning to the BIA. In addition to the occupation of the hamlet of Wounded Knee, still another Native American group later occupied Alcatraz Island in San Francisco Bay. Native Americans learned to employ lawyers to enforce treaty rights and to gain compensation for lost tribal lands. They began to use corporation charters to conduct their communal business enterprises.

○ **Women's Movement**—The women's movement considered their gender in need of liberation. Impetus from the enlargement of women's rights drew inspiration from Betty Friedan's *The Feminine Mystique* (1963). In 1966, middle-class women organized the National Organization for Women (NOW). NOW began a long struggle for an equal rights amendment, but other women opposed it as a threat to certain special treatment. Women did not receive equal pay for equal work and held only a small percentage of top level positions. The Supreme Court ruled in 1974 that women must be paid equally with men for equal work. Along with other suppressed groups, women began to receive preferential consideration for jobs—to make up for past discrimination in public and corporate life. Women raged against "sexism" and "male chauvinism." Women as well as minorities benefited from "affirmative action" requirements of the federal government in industry, education, and in public service jobs. In addition, feminists advocated the ratification of the Equal Rights Amendment (ERA), which would have guaranteed all women the constitutional rights of equality not specified in the Bill of Rights. This measure failed to obtain the number of state votes needed for passage.

○ **Gray Power**—The lengthened life expectancy due to better health practices and medical techniques increased the proportion of elderly and retired persons. The median age rose toward forty in the late 1970s, and one in nine persons reached the traditional retirement age of 65. Such groups as the Gray Panthers organized to work for more favorable treatment and recognition of the special needs of older persons. The mandatory retirement age of 65 was abolished in 1978 by Congress. Social Security taxes on wages had to be raised to forestall the eventual bankruptcy of the system as more liberal benefit payments grew, including benefits to the disabled, benefits to dependents of decreased members, and payments to college students. Retired persons needed protection against inflated prices for necessities; automatic cost-of-living adjustments and the passage of Medicare helped ease this erosion of living standards.

Population Changes—The "baby boom" following World War II leveled off in the 1960s, and by 1972 zero population growth had almost been reached except for large numbers of immigrants, legal and otherwise. After 1970, absolute declines in the number of children led to school closings and less employment for persons prepared as teachers. The post-war babies of the fifties entered the job market in the seventies, and in the late seventies their demand for housing brought on inflated prices for homes. In the seventies, younger people no longer wanted large families, and improved birth control techniques and legalized abortion enabled them to limit the number of births more successfully.

The "sunbelt" rather than the "frostbelt" benefited from population growth after World War II and, if anything, the movement accelerated in the seventies as the cost of energy for home heating rose. California, Florida, Arizona, and Texas received the largest numbers of newcomers looking for jobs and retirement homes. Many African Americans returned to the South, where discrimination had greatly decreased.

The Family—In the 1970s divorces occurred more than half as frequently as marriages. More women working meant that more children were dropped off at schools and more day-care centers were formed.

More couples lived together without benefit of license, and premarital sex became more common. Many younger people joined communes as the kind of extended family living arrangement.

CHAPTER BOOK LIST

Adler, Bill, *The Wit and Wisdom of Jimmy Carter* (1977).
Chafe, William H., *The American Woman: Her Changing Roles* (1972).
Fey, H.E., and McNickle, D'Arcy, *Indians and Other Americans* (Harper & Row).
Fink, Gary M., *Prelude to the Presidency* (1980).
Franklin, John Hope, *From Slavery to Freedom* (4th ed., Knopf).
Gordon, Mitchell, *Sick Cities* (Macmillan).
Hertzberg, Hazel W., *Search for American Indian Identity* (1971).
Hyatt, Richard, *The Carters of Plains* (1977).
Jordan, Hamilton, *Crisis: The Last Year of the Carter Presidency* (1980).
Kreps, Juanita, *Sex in the Marketplace* (Johns Hopkins).
Meier, Matt S., and Rivera, Feliciano, *The Chicanos* (Hill & Wang).
Mercer, Charles, *Jimmy Carter* (1977).
Miller, Herman P., *Rich Man, Poor Man* (Crowell).
Miller, William, *Yankee from Georgia* (1978).
Mollenhoff, Clark R., *The President Who Failed* (1980).
Moore, Joan, and Cuellar, Alfred, *Mexican-Americans* (Prentice-Hall).
Roszak, Theodore, *The Making of a Counter-culture* (Doubleday).
Shoup, Laurence H., *The Carter Presidency and Beyond* (1980).

REVIEW QUESTIONS

MULTIPLE CHOICE

1. Leading foreign problems in the Carter administration centered in which part of the world? (1) Panama (2) the Middle East (3) Africa (4) Southeast Asia.

2. Least known among the early contenders for the Presidential nomination in 1976 was (1) George Wallace (2) Edward Kennedy (3) Henry Jackson (4) Jimmy Carter.

3. A Southern state Carter failed to win was (1) Virginia (2) Texas (3) Alabama (4) New Mexico.

4. The largest contributor to the high rate of inflation was (1) imports of oil (2) high farm commodity prices (3) high building costs (4) budget deficits.

5. In the Middle East which leader made the most unusual demands upon American restraint: (1) Sadat (2) Begin (3) the Shah of Iran (4) Khomeini.

6. Which persistent economic problem finally vanished in the 1970s? (1) Farm surpluses (2) deflation of the dollar (3) unemployment (4) high welfare costs (5) all of above (6) none of above.

7. Which population change did *not* occur in the 1970s? (1) increase in the average age (2) increase in movement to the Sunbelt (3) increase in divorces (4) increase in family size.

COMPLETION

8. Early during his administration Carter and Congress created a new Department of _____ .

9. Probably the most serious domestic problem of Carter was _____ .

10. In foreign affairs Carter began first with a crusade for _____.

11. The above crusade was based on an international agreement known as the _____ .

12. In the Americas, Carter's most prominent diplomacy related to what country? _____ .

13. Andrew Young had to resign from his office because of his unauthorized talks with what unfriendly association? _____ .

14. Mexican Americans fighting for minority opportunities called themselves _____ .

15. The Washington agency blamed by Native Americans for neglect and abuse was the *(abbreviate)* _____ .

16. Federal health insurance for persons over the age of 65 is known as _____ .

17. Federally sponsored measures to achieve better employment opportunities for various minorities formerly underprivileged were known as _____ action programs.

MATCHING

18. Cesar Chavez	a. American ambassador to the UN
19. Betty Friedan	b. Lead negotiations for Egypt-Israel peace
20. Andrew Young	c. Conservative Israeli leader
21. Alan Bakke	d. Gerald Ford's running mate
22. Robert Dole	e. Successor to the Shah of Iran
23. Walter Mondale	f. Chicano leader in California
24. Jimmy Carter	g. Leading Republican conservative
25. Gerald Ford	h. Vice President
26. Ronald Reagan	i. Reverse discrimination decision
27. Anwar Sadat	j. Egyptian President
28. Menachim Begin	k. *The Feminine Mystique*
29. Ruhollah Khomeini	l. Never elected to office of president

CHRONOLOGY / CHAPTER 31

1980   Reagan elected President; Carter defeated.

1981   Iran hostages released.

Reagan proposes New Federalism; works to cut size and scope of federal government.

Space Shuttle era began.

Assassination attempt on Reagan fails.

Sandra Day O'Connor appointed to Supreme Court.

Anwar Sadat assassinated.

Polish Solidarity movement began.

1982   Reagan budget calls for increased deficit.

Equal Rights Amendment fails.

U.S. Marines land in Beirut as peacekeeping force.

1983   Terrorist attack on U.S. marines in Lebanon

U.S. Invades Grenada.

Congress votes aid to Contras.

Sally Ride, first woman astronaut, named to *Challenger* crew.

Federal Holiday for Martin Luther King, Jr. established.

1984   Reagan visits China.

Withdrawal of marines from Beirut; U.S. embassy bombed.

Walter Mondale nominated for President by Democrats; Geraldine Ferraro named first female Vice Presidential candidate.

U.S. economy strongest since 1951.

Deficit Reduction Act passed by Congress.

Reagan elected in landslide.

AIDS virus identified.

Chapter

31
THE REAGAN ADMINISTRATION, 1981–1985

Ronald Reagan's inauguration in 1980 reflected the hope and optimism of the American electorate. Hope that the American hostages held by Iran for 444 days would be released and optimism that the economy, mired in double-digit inflation, would recover. The newly elected President expressed his prayers for the safe return of the hostages, whose release was timed by Iran to coincide with Reagan's inauguration in a last act of defiance to Carter. Domestically, Reagan promised a New Federalism, a downsizing of government spending, and a decrease in government programs. His Presidency ushered in the most reactionary conservative administration since the Republican era of Harding, Coolidge, and Hoover. Virtually the same problems that had confronted the Carter administration in both domestic and foreign affairs challenged Reagan, but these were met with different responses.

✪✪✪ **The Presidential Election of 1980**—In the election of 1980 the nation voiced a demand for change from the tired liberalism, the expansion of federal functions, and the growth of debt and inflation. Last but not least, the election repudiated the failures and unfulfilled promises of the Carter Presidency. The campaign for the presidency was contested in both parties. Even though the Democratic President, Jimmy Carter, was an incumbent, he was challenged by Massachussetts Senator Edward Kennedy. It was Kennedy's last hurrah and he was easily defeated in the primaries by Carter. The Republican field embraced a conservative host of candidates including former Governors Ronald Reagan of California and recently turned Republican John Connally of Texas, Director of the Central Intelligence Agency George Bush, and Senator Robert Dole of Kansas. Former President Gerald Ford hoped to emerge as a consensus candidate. In the end, Reagan received the Republican nod. A serious third party candidate, Representative John Anderson from Illinois, entered the race on the Independent Party line, but in the end only received seven percent of the vote. The American people, tired of a failing economy and embarrassed by Iran's refusal to release the hostages, gave Carter very low approval ratings. Televised debates gave the impression that Reagan had a presidential style and he became known as "the great communicator." Much of his success was attributed to the fact that he had experience as a Hollywood actor. The results of the election gave a clear signal that traditional party loyalties were beginning to change. Carter's southern base had vanished and a new breed of "Reagan Democrats" was born. Winning in 43 states in a landslide victory, Reagan became the first candidate to defeat an incumbent President since the Franklin Roosevelt victory over Herbert Hoover in 1932. Anderson finished a distant third. In addition, the Republicans wrested control of the Senate from the Democrats who, though weakened, retained a majority in the House.

✪ **The First Family**—Ronald Wilson Reagan, forty-ninth President of the United States and the oldest to serve in the office, was born February 6, 1911, in Tampico, Illinois. He graduated from Eureka College in 1932 and then worked for five years as a sports announcer. He began his film career in 1937, starred in numerous B-movies and later in television shows until the 1960s. He served as president of the Screen Actors Guild from 1947 to 1952 and in 1959. After divorcing screen actress Jane Wyman, he married Nancy Davis. Maureen, a daughter from his first marriage, was outspoken during the Reagan years. He also has an adopted son, Michael, and children from his second marriage, Patricia and Ron. Critics of Nancy accused her of influencing her husband and of bringing a Hollywood lifestyle to the White House.

At first a liberal Democrat, Ronald Reagan became active in Republican politics in the 1964 presidential campaign of Barry Goldwater. He was elected Governor of California in 1966 and was reelected in 1970. After retiring as governor, he became the leading spokesman for the conservative wing of the Republican Party. He ran for President unsuccessfully in 1976, but was gracious in his concession to Gerald Ford.

DOMESTIC POLICIES

✪✪✪ **Reagan as President and His Philosophy of Government**— Calling for "an era of national renewal" and claiming that "government is not the solution to our problem, government is our problem," Reagan's New Federalism reflected a conservative philosophy. He used this approach to attack the major domestic problems facing the country—inflation, recession, unemployment, and increasing deficits in the federal budget. Ironically, he called for a decrease in federal programs and a decrease in personal income taxes, yet he consistently asked for major increases in defense spending. Although he was not able to balance the federal budget, he called for a constitutional amendment to achieve it. His first act was to order a hiring freeze to trim the federal work force of nearly five million people. He called for the dismantling of the Department of Energy and threatened to abolish the Department of Education. Both attempts failed. His conservative approach extended to his Supreme Court nominations. During his first term, Reagan made the historic appointment of Sandra Day O'Connor to the Court, the first of three Reagan appointments. Ultimately his Supreme Court nominations created one of the most conservative courts in U.S. history. One of his strongest messages to organized labor was the firing of air traffic controllers after they went on strike. Reagan was committed to a continuation of the space program and the Shuttle was initiated under his administration. Reagan's strongest character trait, his ability to communicate with the American people, was unfortunately lacking when it came to dealing with members of his own administration and his own political party.

✪✪ **Reagan's Appointments**—American corporate business supplied much of the personnel for leadership in the new administration. For the Secretary of the Treasury post came Donald T. Regan, chairman of Merrill Lynch and Company, and for the Secretary of Defense position came Caspar W. Weinberger from Bechtel Power Corporation. Alexander M. Haig, Jr., retired Army general, came from United Technologies Corporation to head the State Department. James G. Watt, lawyer, became Secretary of the Interior. In addition, Reagan appointed Margaret Heckler as Secretary of the Health and Human Services Department. Many of Reagan's appointments ran into serious moral, ethical, and legal problems. Others left over policy differences. Haig resigned in June, 1982, stating that the administration had departed from a foreign policy course it had laid out earlier. George P. Schultz, Nixon's Secretary of the Treasury, replaced him. David Stockman, head of the Office of Management and Budget and architect of Reagan's economic program, resigned in 1982 after he admitted that the mixture of spending cuts and tax cuts would lead to large budget deficits. More than 100 appointees were accused of crimes or had to resign over a question of ethics. His Housing and Urban Development Secretary, Samuel Pierce, had to take the Fifth Amendment while testifying before a congressional committee.

✪ **The Assassination Attempt**—On March 30, 1981, in Washington DC, Reagan was shot in the chest by John W. Hinckley. His Press Secretary, James Brady, was seriously injured and required years of rehabilitation. Brady became later a strong advocate of gun control legislation. As a result of the assassination attempt, Reagan's popularity rose and he was able to set an economic agenda after an address to Congress on April 28.

✪✪✪ **Reaganomics**—Consistent with his philosophy of downsizing government, Ronald Reagan proposed an historic program of tax cuts and reductions in federal expenditures. By the end of July he was able to secure passage of a program of large cuts in the budget and in taxes. In achieving this, perhaps his greatest legislative victory, Reagan proved to be a skilled politician. Because of these tax cuts, the program to limit federal spending, and high interest rates, the country experienced a deflationary economy which was popularly known as Reaganomics. The deficits, though, continued to mount. In 1982 economists and politicians were alarmed over the rising deficit with accompanying unemployment, the highest since 1940. The most severe critics characterized Reaganomics as "Voodoo Economics." In 1981 the national debt limit was raised until it exceeded the trillion dollar mark. Congress passed the Gramm-Rudman Act, which set limits for the deficit over a five-year period. However, because of the many loopholes, the deficit mainly went unchecked. The country was in the middle of a recession, yet individual wealth and personal spending were at an all-time high. The rate of inflation kept falling and, by early 1983, reached less than four percent. There was a significant rise in family income. However, unemployment reached almost 11 percent of the work force by January 1983, even though 13 million jobs were created between 1981–1986.

FOREIGN DEVELOPMENTS

Ronald Reagan had a basic mistrust of the Soviet Union. In fact, he described it as the "Evil Empire." After the hostage crisis ended with Iran, Reagan's foreign policy centered on three major world hot spots: Latin America, the Middle East, and the Soviet Union and its Eastern Bloc satellites. The administration took a hard line toward the Soviet Union—particularly in view of the invasion of Afghanistan. Reagan supported substantial increases in military spending to improve the national defense and to back up the bargaining posture vis-a-vis the Soviets. He called for the production of 100 B-1 bombers and deployment of 100 MX land-based missiles. Détente became a policy goal, though not a reality until Reagan's second term. There was a visit to China in 1984. The administration held out the olive branch to the Soviets by ending the ban on grain exports to them. Only after internal Soviet strife was Reagan able to move towards détente. Unfortunately, the foreign policy initiatives in the Middle East were more reactive than proactive. While a war raged between Iraq and Iran, U.S. forces landed in Lebanon and soon experienced one of the worse terrorist incidents in U.S history when a marine barracks was bombed with great loss of life. In Latin America, the United States attempted to aid revolutionaries in Nicaragua, gave aid to dictators, and committed U.S. forces to the tiny island of Grenada. Reagan took the side of Great Britain in its war against Argentina over the Falkland Islands, which eventually was ended through a peace conference.

✪✪✪ The Middle East—A cease-fire arrangement in Lebanon ended April 1, 1981, when clashes between Syrian troops and Christian militiamen began. Israeli jets bombed guerrilla positions in southern Lebanon and clashed with Syrian planes. In August of 1982, 800 U.S. marines landed in Beirut as part of a United Nations peacekeeping force. They were withdrawn and later returned after Lebanon made a request for assistance. The United States Congress reaffirmed the War Powers Act of 1973 in allowing the marines to remain in Lebanon. Terrorist attacks reached a peak in 1983 when two bombings took place. In April, the United States embassy was attacked by a car-bomb that killed 17 Americans and 46 foreigners and resulted in the destruction of the embassy. One of the most successful attacks on American forces occurred when a suicide truck bomber rammed into the marine compound killing 241 marines and navy personnel. By 1984 Reagan announced the withdrawal of U.S. troops from Lebanon. The terrorists continued their campaign, again bombing the U.S. embassy.

✪ Israel—Israel's relationship with the United States and the rest of the Arab world caused major unrest. In June of 1981, Israeli warplanes destroyed a Iraqi atomic reactor near Baghdad. Israel charged that the plant would have enabled Iraq to produce atomic weapons. The UN Security Council strongly condemned the attack, and the United States threatened an arms embargo against Israel. On December 14, 1981, Prime Minister Menachem Begin secured the consent of the Israeli Knesset to annex the Golan Heights, a strategic zone along the Syrian border. The UN Security Council voted unanimously a resolution branding the annexation illegal. In June of 1982, Israeli armed forces invaded southern Lebanon claiming retaliation for the attempted assassination of the Israeli ambassador to Great Britain. They advanced to Beirut as President Reagan called upon Israel for a cease-fire, but in August the Israelis had entered Beirut. After the U.S. sent marines to occupy Beirut, Lebanese Christian militiamen massacred over 300 Palestinians in refugee camps near Beirut. World opinion was highly critical of both the Lebanese Christians and the Israeli-approved attack.

✪ Egypt—On October 6, 1981, President Anwar Sadat of Egypt was assassinated by a group of Islamic fundamentalists in military uniforms during a parade near Cairo. He was succeeded by Vice-President Hosni Mubarak, who later was elected President and pledged to continue Sadat's policies. The Camp David Accords were recognized by Mubarak and peaceful relations continued between Egypt and Israel after Sadat's death.

✪ Iran-Iraq War—The war began in 1981 in a dispute over the Shatt al-Arab waterway in the nearby oil-rich region, and the conflict quickly escalated. Lasting over seven years, the fighting centered around oil-refining facilities. Oil exports from both nations ceased, causing a rise in oil prices. Chemical warfare was used by Iraq and the world watched as the death toll for both sides rose. Even though the United States was publicly neutral, secret aid to Iraq was given. The byproduct of the aid was ultimately used by Iraq against the United States during the Persian Gulf War. The war also influenced President Reagan to pursue an arms-for-hostage deal with Iran, leading to what became known as the Iran-Contra Affair during Reagan's second administration.

✪✪ **The Soviet Union and Eastern Europe**—The Soviet Union went through a series of political crises as a result of a lack of stable leadership. Leonid Brezhnev died in 1982, followed by Yuri Andropov, who died in 1984. Konstantin Chernenko was selected as General Secretary but died in 1985. President Reagan insisted that the best response to the Soviet Union would be an increase in the defense budget. Sanctions were taken against the Soviet Union in 1983, after the Russians shot down a South Korean passenger airliner killing all 269 aboard.

This instability gave Lech Walesa, leader of Poland's Solidarity Movement, an opening. He was jailed and released after 11 months. Continual food shortages and other economic, political, and social crises perpetuated unrest year after year. Strikes and threats of strikes continued to dominate the news, with the distinct possibility of Soviet intervention. In 1981 Poland proclaimed a state of martial law and closed the doors of the Solidarity Trade Union. The United States pledged its support of Walesa. It took the failure of Communism to ultimately enable Solidarity to succeed.

✪✪ **Latin America**—United States policy in Latin America during the Reagan administration can be described as aiding all countries or revolutionaries, whether democratic or dictatorial, provided they opposed Communism. In El Salvador, guerilla fighting supported by outside Communist sources brought American aid to the existing right-wing government under the leadership of José Duarte. Similar unrest in Guatemala threatened the right-wing regime there. Poverty and politics in Haiti sent refugees to the United States. In Nicaragua, U.S. aid to the right-wing Contra rebels against the leftist Sandanista government was a source of debate in Congress.

✪ **Grenada**—Perhaps in an attempt to redeem the loss of the marines in Lebanon, President Reagan sent 4,600 troops to this small republic in the Caribbean. Action was taken after a coup led by Cuban Marxists, ostensibly to protect the 1,000 American students studying there. The U.S. prevailed and after three days restored democratic government. Reaction by the American press and public was negative, and again the question of unilateral military action by a president without the consent of Congress was raised.

CHAPTER BOOK LIST

Bogarsky, Bill, *Ronald Reagan* (1981).
Cannon, Lou, *Reagan* (1982).
Dye, Thomas R., *Who's Running America?* (1983).
Evans, Rowland, and Novak, Robert, *The Reagan Revolution* (1981).
Gartner, Alan, et al., eds., *What Reagan Is Doing to Us* (1982).
Kirkpatrick, Jeane, *The Reagan Doctrine and United States Foreign Policy* (Heritage Foundation).
Knelman, F.H., *Reagan, God and the Bomb* (Prometheus).
Krieger, Joel, *Reagan, Thatcher and the Politics of Decline* (OUP).
Lees, J.D., et al., *Reagan's First Four Years: A New Beginning* (Manchester Press).
Reagan, Ronald, *The Creative Society* (1982).
Sandez, Ellis, and Gabb, Cecil, *Election Eighty-four* (NAL-Dutton).
Weintraub, Sidney, and Goodstein, Marvin, eds., *Reaganomics in the Stagflation Economy* (1983).
White, Clifton F., and White, Gill, *Why Reagan Won* (1982).

REVIEW QUESTIONS

MULTIPLE CHOICE

1. What was unique about Reagan's inauguration? (1) He called for a bold new government spending program (2) Iraq released American hostages after he took the oath of office (3) Iran released American hostages after he took the oath of office (4) he announced a peace initiative with the Soviet Union in his inaugural address.

2. Who was *not* a contender for the presidential nomination in 1980? (1) Senator Edward Kennedy (2) George Bush (3) Senator Robert Dole (4) George Wallace.

3. What term was given to a new breed of Republican voters? (1) New Republicans (2) Turncoats (3) Reagan Democrats (4) Southern Democrats.

4. Ronald Reagan's political career can be described as one in which he was (1) always a conservative (2) first a conservative, then a liberal, then a conservative (3) always a liberal (4) first a liberal, then a conservative.

5. The outstanding first act of President Reagan was to (1) trim the federal work force (2) begin negotiations with the Soviet Union (3) get the Israelis out of Lebanon (4) reduce the federal deficit.

6. Reagan called for the abolition of which federal agency? (1) The Department of Education (2) the Agriculture Department (3) the Interior Department (4) the Department of Housing and Urban Development.

7. What action did Reagan take against organized labor? (1) He dismissed striking air traffic controllers (2) he called for federal legislation prohibiting closed shops (3) he sent federal troops to stop a postal strike (4) he criticized the collective bargaining process.

8. Reagan's appointments came mostly from (1) the public sector (2) former congressmen (3) corporate business (4) lawyers.

9. Reagan's economic program was described as "Reaganomics." It was characterized by (1) low interest rates and high inflation (2) high interest rates and high inflation (3) high interest rates and a program to limit federal spending (4) high unemployment and a low federal deficit.

10. The Reagan administration took a hard line against the Soviet Union because of their (1) invasion of Afghanistan (2) stand on human rights inside the Soviet Union (3) continuing buildup of nuclear weapons (4) all of the above.

COMPLETION

11. The philosophy of government of the Reagan administration was branded with the term _____ .

12. Terrorists attacked and killed 241 U.S. marines in which Middle Eastern country? _____ .

13. In 1981 Israel annexed what strategic zone along the Syrian border? _____ .

14. What element in Lebanon was friendly to the Israelis? _____ .

15. The Iran-Iraq war began as a result of a dispute over _____ .

MATCHING

16. George Bush	a. First woman appointed to the Supreme Court
17. Donald T. Regan	b. First Secretary of State under Reagan
18. Edward Kennedy	c. Solidarity leader
19. Alexander M. Haig	d. Reagan's leading adviser on the budget
20. Sandra Day O'Connor	e. Succeeded Sadat
21. David Stockman	f. First woman Secretary of Education
22. Hosni Mubarak	g. Sought to win the Democratic nomination for Carter
23. Lech Walesa	h. Second Secretary of State under Reagan
24. Caspar W. Weinberger	i. Appointed as Secretary of Defense
25. George Schultz	j. Secretary of Treasury for Reagan
	k. Sought Republican nomination for president

CHRONOLOGY / CHAPTER 32

1985 Terrorism on the rise; *Achille Lauro* hijacked.
Bush acting President during Reagan surgery.
Summit held between Reagan and Gorbachev.
Record federal deficit; U.S. became debtor nation.

1986 Space shuttle *Challenger* exploded after taking off.
New immigration law passed.
U.S. air strike aimed at Libya.
Landmark income tax revision passed.
Iran-Contra affair uncovered; Congress held hearings.

1987 Black Monday—stock market recorded largest one-day loss.
More Americans taken hostage in Middle East.
Nuclear Arms Treaty signed after Washington Summit.
Homeless problem caused great concern.
Free trade with Canada established.

1988 Panama's General Noriega indicted for illegal drug dealings.
Japanese Americans received compensation for World War II
internment.
Welfare Reform Act passed.
Withdrawal of Soviet troops from Afghanistan.
Bush defeated Dukakis in presidential election.
Reagan and Bush subpoenaed in Oliver North trial.
Gorbachev met with Reagan and Bush in New York City.
United States opened talks with PLO.
Terrorists bombed a Pan Am passenger plane.

32
THE SECOND REAGAN ADMINISTRATION, 1985–1989

Ronald Reagan's reelection was a foregone conclusion because of an expanding economy. The country seemed at ease with him, age notwithstanding. Events of the past four years convinced most Americans that they would be better off with Reagan as President. Little did they know that the nation would face the worst stock market crash since the Depression, increased deficits, and the Iran-Contra scandal. These events would taint the Reagan Presidency. He became known as "the Teflon President" because negative events never seemed to stick to him, as most Americans supported him.

A new and frightening disease, AIDS, was largely ignored by the government, though the drug AZT was approved in 1987. Homelessness became part of the city landscape. The space shuttle *Challenger* disaster left a lasting impression on young and old alike. A new conservative Supreme Court threatened to reverse many of the landmark decisions of the past. Abroad, such foreign terms as *glasnost* and *perestroika* became Anglicized. Suddenly, the USSR, the "Evil Empire," was joining with the United States in significant and historic arms agreements. By the end of the second term, Ronald Reagan, at age 77, retained the support of the majority of the American people and polls indicated that if there had not been a constitutional amendment, a third term would have been a distinct possibility.

✪✪✪ **The Presidential Election of 1984**—For the Democrats, the election posed a dual dilemma: Achieving a united party and making people believe that keynote speaker New York Governor Mario Cuomo's vision of America was correct. Two candidates emerged as frontrunners—former Vice President Walter Mondale and Senator Gary Hart. For the first time in American history, a viable African American candidate,

Jesse Jackson, made a serious run for the presidency. His Rainbow Coalition gave minorities hope and many African Americans and Hispanics registered to vote for the first time. After Mondale was nominated, he asked Geraldine Ferraro, a three-term congresswoman from New York, to be his vice-presidential candidate, a milestone in American politics.

Reagan had no opposition and kept his Vice President, George Bush, on the ticket, leaving no doubt who his successor would be. The campaign was never in question. The economy played into Reagan's hands. Appearing on a televised debate, Mondale repeated to the American people a statement he had made during his inaugural speech that he would have to raise taxes to combat the deficit. Reagan, the more effective speaker, asked the people to decide whether they were better off now than they were during the Carter years. The election gave the clear answer. Reagan won in an electoral landslide, receiving 525 votes and capturing every state except Minnesota and the District of Columbia.

DOMESTIC DEVELOPMENTS

The economy emerged again as the major concern of the second Reagan administration. In 1984 the economy expanded 6.8 percent, its best showing since 1951, and personal income rose 6.8 percent. Three years later the stock market crashed. The United States became a debtor nation for the first time since World War I, and the deficit continued to rise at record levels. Deregulation of the Savings and Loan Associations in the end resulted in a massive government bailout that continued during the Bush administration. However, Americans continued to prosper, with family income rising over 10 percent. A landmark tax reform law was passed in 1986. In the last year of the Reagan Presidency, unemployment was at it lowest since 1974.

Social issues, such as abortion rights, continued to split the nation. The religious right in the form of televangelists attempted to become the moral conscience of the country. The presidential disability constitutional amendment was used by George Bush when Reagan was successfully operated on for colon cancer. New appointments to the Supreme Court were rejected and a new chief justice, William Rehnquist, set the future course of the Court.

✪✪✪ **The Deficit**—Two key pieces of legislation had a major impact on the ever-increasing deficit, the Gramm-Rudman Act and the landmark Income Tax Reform Act of 1986. The Gramm-Rudman Act aimed to eliminate the federal deficit by 1991 by imposing mandatory government spending reductions if Congress did not meet them through the budget process. However, in 1986 the Supreme Court found certain provisions of the act unconstitutional although it did leave in place a requirement that Congress limit spending. An attempt at a balanced budget constitutional amendment failed to gain Senate passage. The Income Tax Act of 1986 was the first major revision of the tax codes since the 1940s and compressed the number of tax brackets. The laws, critics claimed, gave an unfair tax advantage to the wealthy, since the top rate was lowered from 50 percent to 38 percent, though the amount of taxes collected was to be the same, as many tax shelters favored by the rich were eliminated.

✪ **The Stock Market Crash**—In 1985 the bulls took control of the stock market. Wall Street set a record in December 1985 when the Dow Jones closed at 1553. The market continued to rise through the first three quarters of 1987, peaking at 1800. One day "glitches" in the bullish trading occurred when the market recorded a one-day loss in June 1986 of 46 points and broke that record in September, falling over 88 points in one day, and setting a record volume of trading. The largest one-day fall of the stock market since the Great Crash of 1929 took place on October 19, 1987. The Dow Jones Industrial Average fell over 500 points—a decline of almost 25 percent of the market and nearly double the decline of 1929. The computerized trading system and a shaky international market were the culprits. As a result, the Securities and Exchange Commission imposed computer trading restrictions, automatically shutting down computerized trading after a set decline. Even though the market recovered marginally, "paper profits" were almost wiped out for many investors. Ironically, the national economy as a whole fared much better than the market for the year.

✪ **The *Challenger* Disaster**—A tragedy with great visual impact occurred on an atypically cold day in Cape Canaveral, Florida. Following on the heels of a long delayed launch of its sister shuttle, *Columbia,* the space shuttle *Challenger* exploded shortly after lift-off. All seven crew members, including the first teacher/astronaut, Christa McAuliffe, were killed. A government investigation placed the blame on a faulty seal on one of the shuttle's solid-fuel booster rockets. The report indicated that NASA was previously warned about the problem. Congress debated the funding of the program, but in the end, the space program continued.

✪✪ **The Legislative Agenda**—Even with Republican control of the Senate in 1985, Reagan's legislative successes were minimal. In 1986 the Democrats regained control of the Senate and maintained control of the House. They even had enough votes to override vetoes on three important bills, The Clean Air Act of 1988, Mass Transit Act of 1988, and the Civil Rights Restoration Act of 1998. The Immigration Act of 1986, a bill Reagan supported, placed new restrictions on aliens and on employers hiring them. It also defined how aliens illegally living in the United States could gain legal status. In 1988 Congress passed a law, and President Reagan signed it, which paid $20,000 to descendants of Japanese Americans who were placed in internment camps during World War II. Another major piece of legislation passed was the Welfare Reform Act of 1988, which made it necessary for single parents on welfare with children over three years old to get jobs or enroll in a job training program.

✪✪✪ The Supreme Court—One of Ronald Reagan's historical legacies was his judicial appointments, both on the lower federal courts and the Supreme Court. Nowhere was it more apparent that a highly conservative philosophy was behind his Court choices. In fact, many believed that a "litmus test" (single criterion) on issues such as abortion, criminal rights, separation of church and state, and affirmative action was used. It was well into his second term when his Supreme Court designees established a solid conservative majority. After appointing the first woman to the Court, Sandra Day O'Connor, Reagan had to bide his time before the Burger Court started changing. After Burger announced his retirement in 1986, Reagan nominated the highly respected conservative William Rehnquist as chief justice. His second appointment, Antonin Scalia, was even more conservative and became the Court's "intellectual" when it came to writing the majority opinion. Even with these appointments, however, the Court's balance was still not defined.

It took the resignation of Lewis Powell in 1987 and Reagan's fourth appointment to set the Court on a truly conservative course. The fight over this justice pointed out the emotional climate of the country and the importance of the nominee as a swing vote. Reagan first sent to the Senate the name of Robert Bork, an intellectual who was characterized as a strict constructionist. The Senate Judiciary Committee grilled Bork before a national television audience and ultimately created enough doubts that the Senate rejected the nomination 58–42. The next nominee put forth by Reagan was Douglas Ginsburg, another outspoken conservative. His admission that he had once smoked marijuana doomed his nomination. Finally, Anthony Kennedy, though conservative, but appearing more independent than Bork, was approved. Through the remaining Reagan years and into the Bush years the Rehnquist Court made significant inroads into the judicial activism of the Warren-Burger Courts, especially in the areas of civil liberties and abortion. The Court gave the police greater power in obtaining evidence and in a series of decisions allowed restrictions to be placed on women's right to obtain abortions.

REAGAN'S FOREIGN POLICY

Reagan's first term was characterized by a defensive foreign policy and an absolute distrust of the Soviet Union. His second term would be remembered for his five summit meetings with the new Soviet leader Mikhail Gorbachev, and the frustration Reagan encountered over the lack of success in the Middle East and Latin America. The major legacy of this failed foreign policy would surface in the Iran-Contra affair.

⚙️ Terrorism on the Rise—While attempting to develop a Mideast policy that would protect American interests and maintain a balance of power, the United States had to be concerned about terrorists attacks and the release of hostages. In 1985 terrorist attacks resulted in the deaths of 17 Americans. Over 90 planned incidents were detected by the government. In June 1985, a TWA jetliner was hijacked in Athens by Shiite Muslims. The plane was forced to land in Lebanon and 39 Americans were held hostage for over two weeks. That same year, the Italian cruise liner *Achille Lauro* was hijacked on the open sea by the Palestinian Liberation Front. The report that an American citizen, who was in a wheelchair, was thrown overboard outraged the nation. In 1986 a terrorist bombing of a TWA jet flying from Rome to Athens killed four American citizens.

Another terrorist bombing in 1986, supported by Libya, in a West Berlin disco injured 60 Americans. In 1987 three American hostages were abducted in Lebanon, joining five others. Perhaps the most vicious terrorist attack took place at the end of Reagan's term. On a Christmas flight in 1988 terrorists planted a bomb on a Pan Am flight from Frankfurt, West Germany. It exploded over Lockerbie, Scotland, killing all aboard, mostly Americans, including 35 students.

⚙️ Libya—Closely aligned with terrorist groups, the military leader of Libya, Colonel Muammar al-Qaddafi, became a United States target. As a result of terrorist actions in 1985, the United States imposed economic sanctions against Libya early in 1986. All citizens of the United States were ordered home and Libyan assets were frozen. In March 1986, the United States Navy, in a show of force, held military maneuvers near Libyan waters. Libya protested and, in response to the bombing of the West German disco that was linked to Libyan terrorists, the United States launched an air attack on Libyan missile sites, also hitting the home of the Libyan leader and killing members of his family.

⚙️ Latin America—The administration's basic Latin American policy of protecting the area against Communist influence continued during Reagan's second term. Hotspots again were Haiti, Honduras, El Salvador, and Nicaragua. Staunch support of the Duvalier regime in Haiti continued even though, as a right-wing dictator, he stifled democracy. Military aid was given to Honduras because of a perceived Nicaraguan threat against Contra bases outside of Honduras. In 1988 American troops were sent there as a warning to Nicaragua who allegedly attacked Contra bases there. Continued support of a right-wing military regime in El Salvador was tempered by Congress, which made human rights reforms by the government of El Salvador criteria for aid. In Panama, General Manuel Noriega was indicted for drug trafficking in 1989. Panama's President attempted unsuccessfully to remove him.

By far, the most controversial Latin American policy revolved around aid to the Contras, a revolutionary group, fighting the pro-Communist Sandinista government in Nicaragua. This regime had been accused by the United States of aiding other Communist rebel groups in Latin America and its overthrow by the Contras became a priority of the Reagan administration. Utilizing the CIA, aid and training was given to the Contras in safe havens in Honduras and Costa Rica. Initially, Congress gave $100 million in aid to the Contras in August 1986. However, the aid was earmaked for humanitarian purposes and a ban on all direct military support to the Contras was imposed by the Congress. It was this ban that thrust Reagan into a credibility crisis during the last two years of his presidency.

✪✪✪ **Iran-Contra Affair**—Ranking a close second to the Watergate scandal, the Iran-Contra affair paralyzed the Reagan administration during its last two years. Impeachment of the President was short-circuited because there was no direct proof that Reagan knew about the affair. Two subordinates, Lieutenant Colonel Oliver North, Deputy Director of Political-Military Affairs for the National Security Council, and his superior, Admiral John Poindexter, eventually took the responsibility for the planning and execution of the arms-for-hostage negotiations.

The affair began in 1985 when Reagan approved the sale of arms to Israel. These arms would then be sold by Israel to Iran in return for release of American hostages. A number of hostages were released, but new hostages were taken throughout the remainder of the Reagan administration.

Since Iran was paying exorbitant prices for the arms, the Middle East middlemen convinced the CIA and National Security Council to use the profits to aid the Contras. Congress, through the Boland Amendment, prohibited any direct military aid to the Contras. Director of the CIA William Casey, working closely with North, felt that using the profits, totalling over $48 million, did not violate the letter of the law. In July 1987, the Senate held hearings after the Tower Commission the previous February, was critical of the President and his Chief of Staff Donald Regan. Regan resigned as a result of the report. In November of that year the official report of the Congress directed major criticism at the President, stating that he bore "the ultimate responsibility" for his aides. Indictments were handed down against North and Poindexter and, even though they were convicted of obstruction of Congress, their sentences were overturned on appeal.

✪ **The Philippines**—United States support of the right-wing President, Ferdinand Marcos, changed as a result of the assassination of his opponent

Benigno Aquino. Aquino's widow, Corazon, assumed her late husband's candidacy but lost the election. She eventually became the country's leader in 1986 after Marcos was forced into exile. The Reagan administration worked to support Aquino and, despite a series of coup attempts, she remained as a democratic leader with full support of the United States.

❖❖❖ **The Soviet Union**—With the selection of Gorbachev as its leader in 1985, the Soviet Union began a policy of easing tensions with the West. Partly as a practical means of dealing with its own deteriorating domestic affairs, and partly to redirect its own arms expenditures, Gorbachev and Reagan met in a series of summits. The first meeting, held in Geneva in 1985, established a rapport between the two world leaders and gave a clear direction for future meetings. The atmosphere was not so cordial at the summit meeting in Reykjavik, Iceland. An icy impasse occurred when Reagan insisted that the United States would not abandon its Strategic Defense System (the so-called Star Wars strategy), an outer space anti-missile system that was only in the initial planning stages. Many observers felt that Reagan's tough stand convinced Gorbachev that Russia would eventually have to make concessions in order to obtain arms limitation agreements.

The first Strategic Arms Limitation Treaty (SALT) was signed by Reagan and Gorbachev in Washington in December 1987. This agreement resulted in the destruction of over 2,500 United States and Russian medium and short-range missiles. Verification procedures were also approved. The Senate ratified the treaty the following year. In another show of good faith, the Soviet Union withdrew its troops from Afghanistan in 1988. Notwithstanding, the fourth summit, held in Moscow, failed to achieve any further movement in this area. However, it did set the stage for the successful completion of SALT II by the Bush administration. Reagan was able to leave office knowing that the "Evil Empire" was moving toward true détente with the West.

CHAPTER BOOK LIST

Barrett, Laurence, *Reagan in the White House* (1983).

Blumenthal, Sidney, and Byrne Edsall, Thomas, *Reagan Legacy* (Pantheon).

Blumenthal, Sidney, *Our Long National Daydream: A Political Pageant of the Reagan Era* (1988).

Boyer, Paul, *Reagan as President: Contemporary Views of the Man and His Policies* (Elephant Paperbacks).

Davis, Patti, *The Way I See It: An Autobiography* (1992).

Hall, David, *The Reagan Wars: A Constitutional Perspective on War Powers and the Presidency* (1991).

Mayer, Jane, and McManus, Doyle, *Landslide: The Unmaking of the President 1984–1988* (Schocken).

Reagan, Ronald, *Ronald Reagan, An American Life, An Autobiography* (Pocket Books).

Reeves, Richard, *The Reagan Detour* (Simon & Schuster).

Stockman, David, *The Triumph of Politics: The Inside Story of the Reagan Revolution* (1987).

REVIEW QUESTIONS

MULTIPLE CHOICE

1. The election of 1984 was significant for the following *except* (1) the Democrats nominated a woman, Geraldine Ferraro, for vice-president (2) an African American, Jesse Jackson, ran for president (3) Reagan won every electoral vote (4) Mondale indicated that he would have to raise taxes to combat the deficit.

2. The Gramm-Rudman Act was passed in order to (1) limit the president's ability to develop a budget (2) create mandatory government spending reductions (3) create a test case for the Supreme Court to decide the legality of the Reagan budget (4) increase the amount of money in the federal budget.

3. Congress passed the Income Tax Act of 1986 in order to (1) overhaul the tax brackets (2) give tax cuts to the middle class (3) eliminate tax shelters for the rich (4) all of the above.

4. The Stock Market crashed in 1987 because (1) the Federal Reserve Board started a panic over interest rates (2) it was announced that the Consumer Price Index rose significantly the past quarter (3) the computerized trading system triggered massive selling (4) the international market announced new trade restrictions.

5. As a result of the Stock Market crash (1) the Securities and Exchange Commission instituted reforms (2) the United States entered into another great depression (3) the market did not recover for that year (4) international markets were unaffected.

6. What legislation did Reagan sign that dealt with the issue of Japanese relocation during World War II? (1) a law that reaffirmed the Koramatsu decision (2) a law that made it illegal for the United States to create new relocation centers for other ethnic groups (3) a law that only apologized to Japanese Americans (4) a law that apologized with a $20,000 indemnity to descendants of Japanese Americans who were in relocation centers.

7. The Immigration Act of 1986 (1) opened the doors to immigrants of Eastern Europe (2) placed new restrictions on illegal aliens (3) created provisions for boat people to enter the country (4) placed strict quotas on immigrants from Southeast Asia.

8. All of the following are true of Reagan's appointments to the Supreme Court *except* (1) Reagan appointed only one new chief justice during his second administration (2) Reagan believed in a litmus test for his appointees (3) two of Reagan's nominees were never confirmed by the Senate (4) the make-up of the new court was conservative.

9. A shift in Reagan's foreign policy occurred in which area? (1) relations with the Soviet Union (2) relations with Libya (3) relations with Israel (4) a move towards isolationism.

10. The Iran-Contra affair involved all of the following *except* (1) an arms for hostage deal with Iran (2) using Israel as a middleman (3) blame by Reagan on his subordinates Oliver North and William Casey for the affair (4) a congressional hearing that placed the responsibility for the affair on the President.

TRUE-FALSE

11. Reagan and Gorbachev agreed to a reduction of nuclear arms in return for an abandonment of the Star Wars defense system.

12. The Senate never ratified the Strategic Arms Limitation Treaty causing an embarrassment for the Reagan administration.

13. An active policy of research of AIDS was pursued by the Reagan administration.

14. The Rainbow Coalition's major accomplishment was to register minority voters.

15. The Republicans were able to capture control of the Senate during the Reagan administration.

COMPLETION

16. General Noriega of Panama was indicted for _____ by the United States.

17. America retaliated against Libya for terrorist acts by bombing the home of Libyan leader _____ .

18. American troops were sent to Honduras in 1988 as a warning to what Latin American country _____ ?

19. The United States supported the right-wing government of _____ in the Philippines.

20. _____ became the new leader of the Philippines after Marcos fled the country.

MATCHING

21. Lewis Powell
22. William Rehnquist
23. Robert Bork
24. Antonin Scalia
25. William Casey

a. New chief justice
b. Associate justice who resigned
c. New associate justice
d. Director of CIA
e. Failed to get Senate approval

THE UNITED STATES AND NON-COMMUNIST EUROPE

CHRONOLOGY / CHAPTER 33

1989 Unemployment at 5.3 percent; 14-year low.
Bush supported Savings and Loan bailout.
Exxon Valdez oil spill worst in Alaska's history.
Poland and Hungary rejected Communism.
Berlin Wall fell.
United States invaded Panama; captured Noriega.
Bush and Gorbachev declared Cold War over.

1990 Communism ended in Soviet Union.
Unemployment up sharply; United States moved toward
   recession. Bush agreed to tax hike.
Iraq invaded Kuwait.
East and West Germany united.
South Africa freed Nelson Mandella.

1991 Persian Gulf War started; United States forces crushed Iraq in
   100 hours.
Middle East talks started between Israel and Arabs.
Coup fails to oust Gorbachev. Boris Yeltsin emerged as new
   leader of Russia after Gorbachev resigned.
Soviet republics gained independence.
Clarence Thomas approved to Supreme Court.

1992 Recession slowed United States economy.
Riots erupted in Los Angeles.
Senate passes Strategic Arms Pact.
William Clinton defeated George Bush in presidential
   election.

Chapter

33
THE PRESIDENCY OF
GEORGE BUSH, 1989–1993

George Bush became the first incumbent Vice President since Martin Van Buren in 1836 to be elected president of the United States. If any Vice President was able to ride the coattails of an outgoing president, it was George Bush. Even with Ronald Reagan's Iran-Contra problems, he still left office as one of the most popular Presidents in modern history. It was ironic that Bush's popularity at the height of his Presidency was close to 90 percent of the American public, more than Reagan ever achieved. Yet at the end of his administration his popularity plummeted, along with the economy, and ultimately he joined the ranks of one-term presidents.

○ The Campaign of 1988—If the election of 1984 was a foregone conclusion, the election of 1988 was up for grabs. For the Democrats, even though some of the party leaders declined to throw their hats in the ring, seven viable candidates emerged. They represented the various interests of the Democratic Party and included also-rans Jesse Jackson and Gary Hart. Unfortunately for Hart, the media uncovered blatant evidence of an extramarital affair, forcing Hart to withdraw from the race. The media also torpedoed Senator Joseph Biden's campaign when they discovered that he had plagiarized a speech. The race narrowed between a Northern liberal, Governor Michael Dukakis of Massachusetts, and a Southern moderate, Senator Al Gore of Tennessee. After his victories in the primaries made him the clear frontrunner, the convention turned to Dukakis and he picked another southerner, Senator Lloyd Bentsen of Texas, to be his running mate.

Even though George Bush had served President Reagan loyally, the Republicans also had a field of candidates. They included Senate Minority Leader Robert Dole of Kansas, former Buffalo Bills quarterback and Congressman Jack Kemp of New York, televangelist Pat Robertson, and former Secretary of State Alexander Haig. Even though Dole won the Iowa Caucus, Bush won in New Hampshire, proving he could be a satirical and cutting debater. He won a decisive victory on Super Tuesday primary day, winning 16 primaries. The convention was marked by two significant events: Bush made a pledge during his acceptance speech, which four years later would come back to haunt him, stating "Read my lips, no new taxes." Second, he chose a 41-year-old who was unknown on the national level, Senator Dan Quayle from Indiana, to be his running mate. This choice gave his Democratic opponent an opening for attack because of Quayle's lack of experience and media scrutiny of the manner in which he joined the National Guard and thus avoided Vietnam War combat duty.

✪✪ **The Election of 1988**—With the media and public opinion polls playing a significant role, the election of 1988 was one of the dirtiest in modern presidential history. Dukakis came out of the convention with a 17-point lead in the polls. Instead of continuing his campaign, he let the Republicans regain the spotlight at their convention, and Bush never lost the momentum or lead. Images of Dukakis awkwardly riding a combat tank and accusations that he was soft on crime crippled his candidacy. Peace and Prosperity were the buzzwords of the Bush campaign. The word "liberal" became perjorative and the American people, though giving Bush an electoral landslide (426–112), turned out only 50 percent of voters. The Republicans maintained their hold on the South and won enough of the big industrial states to ensure Bush of an easy victory. The Democrats maintained control of Congress, yet over the next four years Bush would be able to successfully veto 35 out of 36 bills.

✪ **George Herbert Walker Bush**—Born on June 12, 1924, George Bush was the son of Connecticut Senator Presscott Bush. Both he and his wife Dorothy decided to send George to the prestigious prep school Phillips Academy before George joined the Navy during World War II. After the war Bush attended Yale, and in 1945 he married the former Barbara Pierce. He then moved to Texas and started an oil business where he earned his fortune. Deciding to enter public office, Bush became a congressman from Texas. Though he lost Senate and presidential bids, he served as Ambassador to the United Nations and Director of the Central Intelligence Agency under Richard Nixon. Reagan selected him as a more moderate running mate and, even though Bush was highly critical of much of Reagan's philosophy, at one time calling his economic program "Voodoo Economics," he served him for both administrations. Mrs. Bush was one of the most charming and popular First Ladies and was often described as a matriarch. In fact, she was a mother of four boys and a girl and a grandmother to 10 children. Her campaign for literacy was very successful and illustrated her genuine concern for people.

✪ **The Cabinet**—Unlike Reagan's selection of primarily businessmen, Bush's choices had more political experience. Other than the rejection of John Tower of Texas for Secretary of Defense because of Tower's admission of drinking and his lobbying for defense industries, Bush's appointments sailed through the Senate. After Tower's rejection, Bush selected former congressman Dick Cheney as his replacement. He also chose his campaign opponent Jack Kemp as Secretary of Housing and Urban Development. His primary opponent's wife, Elizabeth Dole, was named Secretary of Transportation. Former Reagan cabinet officials Nicholas Brady, Secretary of the Treasury, and Dick Thornburgh, Attorney General, were asked to continue their duties. James Baker, former Reagan Chief of Staff and close friend of Bush, was named Secretary of State. He, along with Cheney, played a crucial role in foreign affairs during the Bush administration. An African American, Louis Sullivan was named Secretary of Health and Human Services. With the exception of cabinet members who assumed campaign roles in 1992, the Bush cabinet was cohesive and created stability for the administration. Bush's White House Staff included former Governor of New Hampshire, John Sununu, as Chief of Staff. Brent Scowcroft was named National Security Adviser and his chief economic adviser heading the Office of Management and Budget was Richard Darman.

DOMESTIC DEVELOPMENTS

It was obvious that George Bush had an affinity for foreign policy; his Presidency received wide public support in this area. If Bush had concentrated and succeeded domestically, he probably would have been a two-term President. Even though Bush subscribed to Reagan's downsizing of government philosophy, the Democratic-controlled Congress attempted to create its own legislative program. Bush was successful in vetoing 35 bills, including many that were socially progressive, like the Family Leave Bill. The major problem dominating the Bush domestic agenda was the economy. He signed a bailout for the failed Savings and Loan Associations. A deep recession set in and Bush's campaign promise not to raise taxes was broken. Though he wanted to be known as the President who expanded the space program, who won the war on drugs, and who reformed the educational system, his legacy will certainly be in the area of foreign policy. Forced to break his campaign pledge, he compromised with Congress and signed a tax increase midway through his Presidency. Once the "R" word was spelled out and the independent economic agencies declared that the country was in a recession, Bush's last two years were characterized by public erosion of his domestic policies. Riots in Los Angeles over the verdict of a police brutality trial involving the beating of an African American man heightened the perception that Bush was a weak domestic president.

✪ **The S & L Bailout**—Within a month after his inauguration, President Bush proposed to close or sell financially troubled Savings and Loan

Associations. Over 350 banks would receive a government bailout of over $50 billion over a ten-year period, covered by government bonds, payable by both the banks and the taxpayers. In August 1989, Congress passed legislation that was signed by the President providing over $150 billion over a ten-year period to close or merge Savings and Loan Associations. Most of the cost would be picked up by taxpayers. Many of these banks had already closed and, without the bailout, more would have declared bankruptcy. The law established the Resolution Trust Company, which became the chief financial agent for the failed thrift institutions. By May 1990, the Treasury Secretary informed that the early reports of initial costs were too low. He estimated that real cost could rise to over $100 billion. In addition, the President's son, Neil, who was a director of a failed bank, testified before a congressional committee regarding a possible conflict of interest. The younger Bush denied the allegations. In September he was sued by the Federal Deposit Insurance Corporation for "gross negligence." Adding to the problems facing the banking industry, former S & L owner, Charles Keating, was indicted for criminal fraud in California. The S & L bailout symbolized the laissez-faire approach of the Reagan administration despite the failure of a significant number of banks. Finally, Bush had no choice but to support a government bailout, further increasing the nation's deficit.

○ **The Legislative Program**—Bush's battles with Congress centered around the legislature's attempt to pass social legislation versus the President's strong philosophy that government had no business in this area. Compromise was difficult to attain. Where there was agreement, laws did not resemble the original bills proposed. One area Bush was adamant about was abortion funding. In October 1989, Congress sent a bill to the President that reinstated federal Medicaid funding for abortions because of rape and incest. The bill was vetoed. Bush said he would only support funding if the mother's life was in danger.

Even though it was reported in March 1990 that the AIDS epidemic had reached a peak in the United States, rising around 10 percent in 1989, the Bush administration did not offer any AIDS related research or treatment legislation. In July 1990, Congress passed, and the President signed, the Americans with Disabilities Act. The major thrust of the legislation was to end discrimination against disabled Americans. It also provided coverage for AIDS victims who were being treated. The President appointed NBA basketball star Magic Johnson, who revealed that he had been diagnosed as HIV positive, to serve on an AIDS commission. Johnson later resigned, citing frustration over a lack of funds for research.

Another example of Bush's antithesis toward social legislation came when he vetoed an historic civil rights act, which would have rectified recent Supreme Court decisions that weakened anti-discrimination practices by employers. Citing affirmative action provisions of the bill, Bush refused to sign it. In 1991 Congress passed a weaker version of the bill, which Bush agreed to sign into law.

Two major pieces of legislation President Bush did sign were the 1991 Immigration Act and the Clean Air Act. The immigration law dramatically reformed immigration policy. It shifted the balance of immigration to Europe and aimed to attract trained workers. It also made it more difficult to exclude aliens because of political beliefs. The Clean Air Act of 1990 set overall sulfur dioxide standards and attempted to deal with the acid rain problem by cutting down nitrogen oxide emissions. Cities would have to reduce emissions that would deteriorate the ozone layer. Oil companies were required to develop cleaner burning fuels and tighter emission standards were imposed.

OO **The Supreme Court**—If Ronald Reagan began the conservative revolution in his Supreme Court appointments, George Bush completed it—and the decisions of the Court reflected the results. Bush's first opportunity to fill a vacancy occurred when Justice William Brennan resigned. Wanting to avoid a public debate over a controversial choice, Bush selected a mildly conservative New England judge, David Souter. Little was known about Souter's views on abortion and the Senate confirmed him. Ultimately, Souter became a moderate voice on the court and along with O'Connor became the surprise swing vote in a decision that affirmed *Roe v. Wade*. Bush's second appointment ran into a rocky road. Attempting to fill the "black seat" vacated by Thurgood Marshall, Bush nominated Clarence Thomas, head of the Equal Employment Opportunity Commission and a known conservative. His nomination was opposed by many legal groups and the NAACP. The confirmation hearings turned into a public spectacle when it was revealed that a African American professor, Anita Hill, charged Thomas with sexual harassment. The male-dominated Judiciary Committee came under public criticism for its treatment of both Thomas and Hill in televised hearings. In a narrow vote, the Senate confirmed Thomas.

The Court reflected a tenuous conservative majority in areas such as criminal rights, church-state relations, free speech, and abortion. There were, however, narrow victories for judicial activists. In two decisions, the Court affirmed the right of individuals to burn the American flag as symbolic speech. The Bush administration failed in its attempt to get Congress to pass a constitutional amendment prohibiting such an exercise of free speech. In the area of separation of church and state, the Court decided that it was a violation of that concept to allow clergy to recite prayers at school graduations. In the area of criminal right to appeal, the Court established a standard that made it more difficult for death row prisoners to appeal their sentences. It was the area of abortion that caused the most controversy. In a narrow 5–4 decision in the case of *Planned Parenthood of Pennsylvania v. Casey,* the Court affirmed the constitutional right of abortion established in *Roe v. Wade* but also established the right of states to impose restrictions such as a 24-hour waiting period and minors having to notify their parents.

○○ **The Economy**—By 1991 the country was teetering dangerously on the brink of a recession. Inflation and unemployment rose in 1990 to a three-year high of 6.1 percent. Consumer prices recorded the highest percentage hike since 1981. Following the invasion of Kuwait in August 1990, oil prices rose significantly. Even though the stock market recorded its second highest one-day gain, the overall outlook was bleak. The gross national product had declined in the last quarter of 1990, and by the middle of 1991 a recession had been declared by the Federal Reserve Board. Even though the stock market was bullish, the leading economic indicators reflected a sluggish economy. Other factors did not improve the picture. The trade imbalance grew larger as did the deficit, which grew to record proportion as a result of the Gulf War. Trying to reverse the trade imbalance with Japan, Bush went to Japan to try to pressure the Japanese to accept more American goods. In what became a symbol of the futility of the visit, Bush became ill at a reception and, to make matters worse, no agreement was reached. The only hopeful sign regarding the trade issue was a treaty negotiated with Canada and Mexico. The North American Free Trade Agreement (NAFTA) called for a free flow of trade between the United States and its hemisphere neighbors. Critics felt that higher unemployment would result.

FOREIGN POLICY

During his four years on the foreign policy front, Bush was at the right place at the right time. He was given credit for contributing to the fall of Communism and he declared an end to the Cold War, calling for a "New World Order." The first victim of this philosophy was Iraq after it defied the United Nations resolutions calling for Saddam Hussein to withdraw from Kuwait.

○○○ **The Fall of Communism**—During the first two years of the Bush administration, the face of the world changed. If the Cold War thawed during the Reagan years, it disappeared during the Bush years. The quiet diplomacy of the United States was certainly not directly responsible for the changes. However, Bush's experience in foreign affairs created a climate that allowed these dramatic events to occur.

Soviet leader Mikhail Gorbachev, the other player in this remarkable series of events, allowed the satellite nations of Eastern Europe to pursue a course of political independence. At home, Gorbachev had serious problems with his own republics. The economy of Russia was so bad that hard liners began planning an old fashioned coup d'état. Populist Boris Yeltsin was elected President of the Russian Republic and quickly became Gorbachev's major critic.

Perhaps the most visible symbol of the Cold War was the Berlin Wall. In October 1989, after the leader of East Germany, Erich Honecker, stepped down, its border with West Germany was opened. Thousands of East Germans fled to the West. Within a month, the Wall came tumbling down and, more than any other event, this showed the world that Communism was on its way out in Eastern Europe. In 1990 unification was completed. During the same time, demonstrations took place in Poland, Czechoslovakia, Hungary, and Romania. Lech Walesa was elected President of Poland. In Romania, the hated Communist leader, Nicolae Ceausescu, was executed. And in Czechoslovakia, without any violence, a dissident playwright, Vaclav Havel, became the new President. Hungary held free elections in 1990 and the Communist Party received less than 10 percent of the vote. Yugoslavia became embroiled in an ethnic civil war. Only in Bulgaria did the Communist hard liners succeed in maintaining power. The four last bastions of Communism, Cuba under the leadership of Fidel Castro, The People's Republic of China, Vietnam, and North Korea, did not succumb to the winds of change, though a massacre of civilians in China who were demonstrating for democracy in Tiananmen Square caused a cooling of relations with the United States.

The last attempt by the hard liners to save Communism came when a group of inept Party leaders placed Gorbachev under house arrest while he was on vacation. Boris Yeltsin, along with thousands of Russian citizens who barricaded the Kremlin, broke the coup attempt. By the end of 1991, Gorbachev resigned and Yeltsin orchestrated an agreement among the Russian republics to join a loose confederation.

✪✪ Summit Meetings—President Bush met with Gorbachev four times. It became apparent that both leaders and their wives truly developed a close relationship as opposed to the relationship that was said to have existed between the Gorbachevs and the Reagans. Substantively, the meetings resulted in an era of cooperation between the nations. Both countries agreed to troop reductions in Europe as well as reductions in conventional and nuclear weapons. Agreement was also reached to cease production of chemical weapons. The most significant agreement between the two former enemies was a treaty that would reduce strategic intercontinental nuclear weapons and destroy other nuclear weapons. The Senate passed this treaty in 1992. After Yeltsin became President, Bush also met with him and both leaders pledged international cooperation.

✪ The Invasion of Panama—Frustrated by the failure to force Manuel Noriega from power, President Bush authorized 20,000 American troops to invade Panama and arrest the Panamanian general on charges of drug trafficking. Even though Noriega was aided by the CIA to help keep him in power when Bush was its director, Bush wanted to stop the flow of drugs and send a clear message to the drug cartel. American casualties were extremely low and the mission was successful. Noriega was placed on trial in Miami and, after being convicted on all counts, he was sentenced to life imprisonment. The media and some members of Congress were critical of the invasion because Bush failed to obtain congressional approval. The foray also worsened U.S.- Panamanian relations.

✪✪✪ **The Gulf War**—The origins of the Gulf War actually go back to Iraqi perceptions about the United States. Knowing that the United States withdrew from Vietnam and Lebanon gave Iraqi leader Saddam Hussein confidence that he could annex Kuwait without opposition. He also felt that Iraq's Arab neighbors would never invite American forces to use their land as staging bases. In addition, American public opinion regarding the Iran-Contra affair and media criticism of presidential forays into foreign lands strengthened Hussein's belief that he would be able to withstand United Nations pressure to withdraw from Kuwait.

Little did he know that the response by the world community would be fast and decisive. Within a day after the August 1990 invasion of Kuwait, the United States announced it would increase its naval forces in the area. It also froze all Iraqi assets. The following week President Bush announced he would begin sending troops to Saudia Arabia. The rest of the world community, including every Arab nation except Jordan and Libya, supported a series of United Nations resolutions demanding the immediate and unconditional withdrawal of Iraq from Kuwait. The United Nations also imposed an economic boycott utilizing an air and naval blockade. Iraq responded by arresting foreign hostages and using them as bargaining chips. In announcing Operation Desert Shield, President Bush outlined a timetable of increased pressure on Iraq, an escalated announcement of troop and military deployment to Saudi Arabia, and a deadline of January 17, 1991 for Iraq to agree to follow the United Nations resolutions.

At home, Americans strongly supported the President's actions. There was debate in Congress as to whether or not they had to actually declare war on Iraq, but in the end, both houses overwhelmingly voted to support the United Nations resolutions. This action gave the signal to the world that the United States was prepared to lead an allied offensive against Iraq. On January 17, 1991, President Bush announced that Operation Desert Storm had begun. The most massive air attacks in military history pounded Baghdad and the rest of Iraq day after day. Immediately gaining air control, the allies attacked other strategic targets. Saddam Hussein countered by attacking Israel with SCUD missiles. Israel agreed not to enter the war, and the United States provided Patriot missiles to the Israelis. Though there were minimal civilian casualties in Israel, the threat of chemical warfare by Iraq turned world opinion against Hussein.

Led by the brilliant American general, Norman Schwartzkopf, allied forces led a ground attack on Iraq and Kuwait in February 1991. Within 100 hours every objective was met and Kuwait was liberated. In a final act of defiance, Hussein ordered all of Kuwait's oil fields to be set on fire. Thick black smoke covered the countryside in what was described as an environmental nightmare.

Though Iraq was humiliated, Saddam Hussein remained in power and took out his wrath against the rebel Kurds. At home, President Bush's popularity rose to around 90 percent according to public opinion polls. Maintaining an embargo on Iraq, President Bush was not successful in forcing Hussein out. In 1993 Iraq supported an attempt on former President Bush's life when he visited Kuwait to accept the country's thanks. The United States responded by attacking Iraq's intelligence headquarters as a reminder that terrorism would never be tolerated.

OO The "New World Order"—Victory in Iraq led by the United States signaled the start of what President Bush called a "New World Order," in which the U.S. would accept the role of world policeman. The United Nations would play a supporting role and could offer peacekeeping troops and resolutions to pressure countries to abide by world opinion. Three examples of the application of this principle took place in Somalia, the embattled former Yugoslavia republics, and in the Middle East.

In Somalia, a tragic power struggle was taking place among the country's tribal war lords. As a result, a large percentage of the population was caught in the middle. Starvation was rampant and UN supplies never reached the population. In late 1992 President Bush authorized a United States-led invasion of Somalia. Dubbed Operation "Restore Hope," the invasion was covered live on television. With minimal resistance, the Marines established control of the countryside. President-elect Bill Clinton fully supported the operation and by early 1993 a small contingency of U.S. troops joined a UN peacekeeping force in Somalia.

The situation in Bosnia-Herzegovina was just as tragic. A devastating ethnic civil war broke out between the Serbs and Bosnian Muslims. Media reports clearly showed that Serbia was supporting a policy of "ethnic cleansing," methodically killing Muslim civilians. Though the United States and United Nations imposed an economic blockade on Serbia, the fighting continued. President Bush was at the end of his term and could not achieve a negotiated peace between the warring republics.

In the Middle East, a state of war technically still existed between Israel and the Arab states. The question of PLO recognition and the issue of a Palestinian homeland further complicated the issue. President Bush initiated a Unites States-sponsored Middle East peace conference. Supported by Russia and the United States allies, the peace conference took place in 1992. For the first time in modern history, Israel sat down face to face, not only with Arab nations, but with the PLO. Little substantive progress was made at the initial talks, but, symbolically it signalled a start to a possible end of decades of hostility between Israel and her Arab neighbors.

CHAPTER BOOK LIST

Bjork, Rebecca, *The Strategic Defense Initiative: Significant Containment of the Nuclear Threat* (1992).
Freedman, Laurence, and Karsh, Efram, *The Gulf Conflict* (1993).
Green, Fitzhugh, *George Bush* (1989).
Hinckle, Warren, and De Antonino, Emile, *The George Bush Dilemma* (1989).
Ridley, Matt, *The Man Who Would Be Bush* (Penguin).
Slevin, Jonathan, and Wilmsen, Steven, *Chameleon: The Unauthorized Biography of George Bush* (1992).
Stinnett, U., *George Bush: His World War II Years* (Brasseys).
Weed, Doug, *Conversations with the President: George Bush in His Own Words* (1992).

REVIEW QUESTIONS

MULTIPLE CHOICE

1. The election of 1988 was influenced by the media because (1) it gave slanted coverage to Democrats (2) it uncovered marital infidelity and plagiarism of two candidates (3) it gave slanted coverage to the Republicans (4) it uncovered personal indescretions of Republican candidates.

2. All of the following were candidates for the Democratic nomination for President in 1988 *except* (1) Jesse Jackson (2) Gary Hart (3) Ted Kennedy (4) Michael Dukakis.

3. All of the following were candidates for the Republican nomination for President in 1988 except (1) Gerald Ford (2) Jack Kemp (3) George Bush (4) Pat Robertson.

4. In his acceptance speech George Bush pledged (1) to create a "New World Order" (2) to lower taxes for the middle class (3) to raise taxes for the middle class (4) not to introduce any new taxes.

5. The election of 1988 was characterized by (1) a record voter turnout (2) a narrow electoral victory by George Bush (3) a narrow popular vote victory by George Bush (4) a voter turnout of 50 percent of registered voters.

6. What legislative problem did George Bush face? (1) an inability to sustain vetoes (2) a split Congress—the house Democratic and the Senate Republican (3) Congress demanding passage of social legislation (4) congressional opposition to passing an S & L bailout.

7. The lesson learned from the bailout of the Savings and Loan institutions was (1) consumers should be careful investing their funds over the amount insured by the federal government (2) too much power was given to individuals in charge of managing S & L's (3) the problem was caused by a laissez-faire attitude of the Reagan-Bush administrations (4) all of the above.

8. One major piece of legislation George Bush vetoed successfully was (1) the Clean Air Act (2) the Family Medical Leave Act (3) the Immigration Act of 1991 (4) none of the above.

9. In a narrow decision by the Supreme Court, the longstanding right to abortion (1) was sustained (2) was reversed (3) was sent back to the lower courts (4) was turned over to the Congress to legislate.

10. In the area of foreign policy, Bush's major accomplishments were all of the following *except* (1) supporting the fall of Communism in Eastern Europe and the Soviet Union (2) supporting a military invasion of Panama (3) supporting a military invasion of Kuwait (4) supporting a military invasion of Bosnia-Herzegovina.

TRUE- FALSE

11. Bush's "New World Order" was adopted as a doctrine by the United Nations.

12. Civil war broke out in Bosnia-Herzegovenia between the Serbs and the Croatians.

13. The Bush administration was successful in bringing Israel and the PLO to the peace table.

14. Panama leader General Noriega was found innocent of drug trafficking charges.

15. Israel entered the Gulf war against Iraq after they were attacked by SCUD missiles.

COMPLETION

16. Unification of what European nation was completed in 1990? _____ .

17. The only Communist country in Europe that did not vote to democratize was _____ .

18. Major agreement was reached with the Soviet Union at summit meetings in the area of _____ .

19. The United Nations imposed what kind of boycott on Iraq prior to the Gulf War? _____ .

20. The United States military involvement in Somalia was given the name _____ .

MATCHING

21. John Tower

22. James Baker

23. David Souter

24. Anita Hill

25. Boris Yeltsin

a. Secretary of State, then Chief of Staff under George Bush

b. Accused Supreme Court nominee Clarence Thomas of sexual harassment

c. Nominated for Secretary of Defense; failed to get Senate approval

d. Russian leader who succeeded Gorbachev

e. Supreme Court appointee

CHRONOLOGY / CHAPTER 34

1992   The Clinton transition team took shape.

Twenty-seventh Amendment to Constitution ratified.

1993   William Clinton sworn in as the 42nd President.

Clinton held open house at White House.

New administration establishes its economic and social agenda.

Foreign policy problems in Bosnia, Iraq, and Somalia faced by Clinton administration.

New first lady, Hillary Rodham Clinton, named to head health care reform panel.

Clinton lifted the ban on gays in the military.

New President issued executive orders overturning abortion restrictions.

Clinton signed Family and Medical Leave Act.

Janet Reno confirmed as first woman attorney general after first two nominees withdrew.

Terrorist bomb closed down New York City's World Trade Center.

Congress passed budget resolution; job stimulus package defeated.

Clinton held summit with Boris Yeltsin.

U.S. attacked Iraq's intelligence headquarters in retaliation for plot against Bush.

Justice White resigned from Supreme Court; Ruth Bader Ginsburg confirmed.

North American Free Trade Agreement (NAFTA) signed into law.

1994   Clinton ended trade embargo against Vietnam.

34
THE PRESIDENCY OF WILLIAM CLINTON, 1993–

William (Bill) Clinton became the first "baby boomer" President, representing a generation born after World War II. Beset by character questions and a scandal that almost sank his campaign, Clinton became the self-proclaimed "comeback kid." Defeating incumbent President Bush, the election marked the first time the Democrats regained control of the White House since Jimmy Carter was elected in 1976.

Clinton promised an administration that would be marked by an "explosive" first hundred days. Instead, the country saw an administration that tried to tackle a host of social, economic, and foreign policy problems, never focusing on the central economic problems facing the country. Clinton's earlier reputation of changing his mind, popularly characterized as "waffling," came back to haunt him during the first weeks of his new administration. Though the Democrats maintained their majority in the Congress, there was enough Republican strength and Democratic opposition to his economic program that the specific deficit reduction program ended up in a congressional conference committee well past his first hundred days. It was in the area of foreign policy that Clinton achieved early high marks, as he held a successful summit with Russian President Boris Yeltsin. By the end of his first year in office, however, a foreign policy fiasco in Somalia and the resignation of his first cabinet member, the Secretary of Defense, raised serious questions about the New World Order and the role of the United States.

✪✪ **The Presidential Campaign of 1992**—Most Democrats felt that George Bush was invincible. Such notables as Governor Mario Cuomo of New York and Senator Bill Bradley of New Jersey decided not to make a run for President. Three candidates became the primary players vying for the Democratic nomination: Governor William Clinton of Arkansas, Senator Paul Tsongas of Massachusetts, and former Governor Jerry Brown of California. Each had a distinctive campaign style and a specific constituency. Tsongas attracted the more moderate Democrats and had a specific economic plan that gave him support. Brown tried to conduct a populist campaign, going so far as giving out an 800 telephone number for minimal campaign contributions under $100. Governor Clinton described himself as a new Democrat who would put people first. He emerged as the early frontrunner, but it then became obvious that character questions would haunt his campaign. Before the first primary, questions regarding Clinton's marital infidelity and his actions regarding the draft and Vietnam War were raised by the media. A letter was published that indicated that Clinton opposed the war in Vietnam and stated that he wanted to avoid the draft by joining the ROTC. Despite these allegations, he came in a strong second to Tsongas in the all-important New Hampshire primary. Calling himself "the comeback kid," Clinton achieved momentum. The turning point of the primary season came on Super Tuesday when Clinton emerged as the decisive victor. At the Democratic convention, held in New York City, the Democrats were the most unified in recent political history. Going against political school of thought, Clinton selected another southerner, Senator Al Gore of Tennessee, as his running mate.

The Republicans were greeted by an early announcement from syndicated columnist Pat Buchanan that he would be seeking the party's nomination for President. Because the country was sliding deeper into an economic recession, the New Hampshire primary revealed that President Bush would have serious problems in his own party. Buchanan received close to 40 percent of the vote. However, Bush was able to wrap up the nomination with a decisive victory in the Super Tuesday vote. At the Republican convention in Houston, the Republicans encouraged their conservative right wing to take the spotlight. The country saw speaker after speaker not only going after the Democratic nominee but attacking social issues like abortion. Bush kept Vice President Quayle on the ticket and left the convention trailing the Democratic team.

A viable third party candidate emerged. H. Ross Perot, a Texas self-made billionaire, appearing on a cable TV talk show, declared that, if the people wanted him to run for President and got his name on the ballots in all 50 states, he would be their servant and oppose the major political parties. His popularity rose to such a height that it appeared he could ultimately throw the election into the House of Representatives. He was a political novice with a lot of personal money to spend. His folksy style appealed to those voters who were politically demoralized. By the time the Democrats met, he had made serious blunders and announced he would not be a candidate, but that he would remain active in the campaign.

✪✪✪ **The Presidential Election**—Clinton started his campaign immediately following his nomination with a spectacular bus tour across the nation's heartland. He sustained the momentum of the convention and hammered on the issues of change and the faltering economy. The Democrats learned their lessons from the disastrous 1988 election and remained focused on the key issue facing the nation. On the other hand, George Bush's campaign lacked direction. He tried to go on the attack, raising the issues of trust and his opponent's character. He also tried to use his experience in foreign affairs as evidence that he was best able to lead the country. He blamed congressional gridlock for the nation's declining economy, announced the largest decrease in strategic nuclear weapons by Russia, and indicated that the country's children could finally go to sleep without worrying about the threat of nuclear warfare. Midway in the campaign, Perot announced he was reentering the race and introduced his running mate, highly decorated former Vietnam veteran James Stockdale. The three candidates appeared in a series of televised debates, the format of which helped Clinton, especially the one in which an audience of non-journalists asked the questions. Bush's popularity during the campaign hovered around 38 percent in opinion polls, a figure that would eventually reappear as the percentage of the popular vote that Bush received. The election saw the largest turnout of registered voters in recent political history, which was largely attributed to Jesse Jackson's campaign to register minority voters and the youth culture's voice, MTV (Music Television), conducting a "Rock the Vote" drive.

Trailing badly in the closing weeks of the election, Bush refused to give up. He told the American people he wanted to achieve a Harry Truman victory. Closing the gap in the last weekend before the vote, Bush's candidacy was mortally wounded when it was announced by the Iran-Contra special prosecutor that he had a letter indicating that Bush was present during the discussions that resulted in the arms-for-hostages deal. Exit polls, however, indicated that it was the economy and the public's lack of confidence in Bush's ability to improve it, that swung the election to Clinton. Bill Clinton ended up winning 370 electoral votes, but only received 43 percent of the popular vote. Women and minorities voted heavily for him. The Republican Southern strategy was upset and Clinton won in every section of the country. Though Perot did not receive a single electoral vote, his candidacy accomplished what no other recent third party candidate had ever achieved—almost 20 percent of the popular vote. Immediately after the election, Perot started a new political party, United We Stand. For George Bush it was the end of a distinguished career. For Bill Clinton, it was a chance to change the direction of America.

William Jefferson Clinton—Bill Clinton was born in Hope, Arkansas on August 19, 1946. His father, William Jefferson Blythe III, was killed in an automobile accident before his birth, and he took the last name of his stepfather, Roger Clinton. Clinton's interest in politics as a teen was fostered by a visit to Washington, DC, where he met

President John F. Kennedy. He became actively involved in politics in college, attending Georgetown University and majoring in international affairs. He was named a Rhodes scholar and spent his graduate years attending Oxford University in England. It was during this time period that he was accused of leading anti-draft/anti-Vietnam marches. After graduating from Yale Law School, Clinton married Hillary Rodham. He was elected governor of Arkansas in 1979 at age 32, the youngest in the nation. Clinton was defeated in his try for a second term. Learning from this defeat, he was reelected in 1982 and became more moderate in his views. As President, Clinton's philosophy can be described as moderately liberal. During his campaign, he promised a tax cut for the middle class, a reformed tax system that would tax the rich at a still higher rate, and a social agenda sounding like a mix of New Frontier and Great Society programs. The Clintons have one child, a daughter, Chelsea.

CLINTON'S FIRST HUNDRED DAYS

Ever since Franklin Roosevelt's New Deal, newly elected presidents have been judged by their performance in office during their first hundred days. Bill Clinton invited the scrutiny of the media stating that he would hit the ground running and that the first hundred days would be "explosive." Ronald Reagan's successes during his first three months in office became Clinton's model. Using campaign promises and stated goals as the criteria for evaluating Clinton, the media and public were quick to judge his performance.

Grades varied but, for example, the national newspaper *USA Today* gave Clinton an overall C plus. That mark correlated with a Gallup Poll that gave Clinton a consistent 55 percent approval rating. The significant aspect of that poll was that the disapproval percentage was higher than any other modern-day president. The report card was based on issues such as the economy, the federal budget deficit, health care policy, taxes, and foreign policy.

Style v. Substance—Clinton's inauguration symbolized, as did Jimmy Carter's, the arrival of a populist. Trying to emulate Andrew Jackson, Clinton held an open house the morning after he was sworn in. Hundreds of citizens had an audience with the President and First Lady, as well as the Vice President and his wife, Tipper. Clinton's first week symbolized the shotgun approach of the administration. Rather than keeping a campaign promise to "focus on the economy like a laser beam," Clinton made a series of executive orders. He lifted the ban on gays in the military. Then he had to modify that order because of opposition by the joint chiefs of staff and the Congress. The following summer a watered down version of the order was approved. Described as a "Don't ask, don't tell, don't pursue" compromise, it allowed homosexuals to enlist as long as they did not disclose the fact that they were gay. Clinton also lifted the ban on abortion restrictions. The gag rule that prohibited doctors working in federally funded clinics from discussing abortions as an option was cancelled. Experimentation on fetal tissues was reinstated, and Clinton directed the FDA to begin experimentation on the French abortion pill RU 486.

✪✪ **Clinton's Cabinet**—The President made a campaign promise to appoint a cabinet that would reflect the American people. Some interpreted this as bowing to special interest groups but the fact remained that there were more women and minorities in Clinton's cabinet than any previous president. Clinton nominated Democratic Party Chairman Ron Brown, an African American, as Secretary of Commerce, an Hispanic, Henry Cisneros, as Secretary of Housing and Urban Development, and the first female Attorney General, Janet Reno. It was the nomination to this office that caused the most negative backlash. Clinton was determined to appoint a woman to this position. His first attempt was to offer the position to Zoë Baird, a well-known corporate lawyer. During her background check, it was discovered that Ms. Baird had hired an illegal alien to take care of her young children. "Nannygate" brought down her candidacy as well as that of Kimba Wood, the second choice of the President. Reno's confirmation sailed through. She demonstrated that she would be a forceful law enforcement head when a religious fanatic took hostages and killed federal agents in Waco, Texas. Reno directed the government's response and, even though the incident ended tragically, with cult leader David Koresh setting fire to the compound and dying in the blaze along with 80 of his followers, including 17 children, most of the American people supported her actions. Although more minorities were represented than in previous administrations, Washington politicians and lawyers still dominated the cabinet. Texas Senator Lloyd Bentsen was designated as Treasury Secretary, Congressman Leon Pannetta was selected as Office of Management and Budget (OMB) Director, and Congressman Les Aspin received the Defense Secretary position. A carryover from the Carter administration, Warren Christopher, was named Secretary of State. Clinton was criticized for taking a long time to name a large number of sub-cabinet positions.

✪ **The First Lady**—A successful lawyer, Hillary Rodham Clinton symbolized for many Americans their vision of a truly activist First Lady. The President broke tradition when he appointed her to head the health plan reform panel. Giving Mrs. Clinton her own office in the White House, the President felt that his wife was the most qualified person to lead a task force and come up with a policy the nation would support. There was criticism regarding the fine line between giving a member of the first family a government position, which violated the law, and having a member voluntarily head a committee. Mrs. Clinton held meetings and issued a report that headed to the Congress in the fall of 1993.

✪✪✪ The Economy—If the Clinton administration was going to succeed, it would have had to effectively deal with the lagging economy and the tremendous budget deficit. President Clinton used his State of the Union address to Congress in February 1993 to outline his budget and economic proposal. Perhaps the first defining moment of the new presidency, Clinton was almost conversational in his approach to the problems facing the country. He proposed a deficit cutting plan that involved major tax increases on virtually all segments of the society. In addition, he offered a job stimulus spending program that was criticized by the Republicans as traditional Democratic "tax and spend" politics. He also made a commitment to develop a universal health plan that would cover every citizen. Prior to the address, he announced a 25 percent cutback in the White House staff. The speech received rave reviews and Clinton's popularity reached its peak the days following the speech.

✪ Congressional Legislation—The Democratic leadership realized they could not do to Bill Clinton what was done to Jimmy Carter early in his Presidency. By the end of March, both houses were able to pass a $1.5 trillion budget resolution, the earliest in recent years. However, a Republican filibuster prevented the job stimulus package from passing. The deficit reduction plan became embroiled in party politics over the summer of 1993—so much so that the final compromise plan, with $496 billion in deficit cuts over a five-year period, passed the house by two votes and needed Vice President Gore's vote to break a Senate tie.

Congress passed the Family Medical Leave Bill that had previously been vetoed by President Bush. Clinton signed the law that allowed employees to take unpaid emergency medical leave for themselves or their family. The President also pushed for a campaign finance bill that dramatically reduced special interest contributions. A Motor Voter registration law, enabling voters to register when they get their driver's license, was signed by Clinton. A law that extended unemployment benefits was also passed. A National Service Program for the nation's youth that gave college tuition in return for national service was signed. One of the most significant legislative battles, the debate over the North American Free Trade Agreement (NAFTA), was a turning point for the Clinton Presidency. The President received the endorsement of former Presidents Ford, Carter, and Bush, who urged Congress to pass the treaty. After Vice President Gore successfully debated former presidential candidate and NAFTA foe Ross Perot, Congress with bi-partisan support, passed the agreement opening a free trade market between the United States, Canada, and Mexico. One of the most dramatic pieces of legislation passed at the final meeting of the first session of Congress was the Brady Bill. Named after President Reagan's Press Secretary who was seriously injured in the assassination attempt, the law established a five-day waiting period for purchase of handguns. The law was opposed by the National Rifle Association (NRA), but because of public sentiment was approved by Congress and was signed by Clinton. In the end, though, the American people judged Clinton by the impact of his economic package, which became the economic blueprint of his administration. Because of the upswing in the economy and an impressive congressional record of passed legislation, Clinton's popularity soared to close to 60 percent approval rating in December 1993.

The World Trade Center Bombing—America held its breath when reports of a terrorist bombing of the New York City landmark World Trade Center were broadcast in February 1993. There were six casualties and thousands of injuries. Both buildings in the World Trade Center were closed for a month while the FBI investigated the incident. Ten individuals, of Middle Eastern origins, were indicted. After the incident, another planned plot to bomb New York City landmarks on July 4 was revealed. Public outcrys to tighten the existing immigration policies and restrict illegal aliens were heard in Congress. Shortly thereafter, Clinton tightened alien entry procedures.

CLINTON'S FOREIGN POLICY

President Clinton inherited from George Bush a world that no longer resembled anything like previous presidents had to deal with. The Cold War was over and a "New World Order" had been proclaimed. Yet, Russia was on the brink of economic disaster and the other Russian republics still had control of nuclear weapons; American troops were still in Somalia trying to restore peace among the tribal warlords; Bosnia was torn by civil war and world reaction began to create pressure to do something about the Serbian and Croatian atrocities; the Middle East peace talks were stalemated; and the arrogance of Saddam Hussein caused consternation in the United States and United Nations.

✪ **Relations with Russia**—During Clinton's first hundred days, Russia's President Boris Yeltsin had a great power struggle with the Russian Congress. After surviving a vote of confidence by the Russian people, Yeltsin met with Clinton in Vancouver in April 1993. Clinton pledged U.S. support of Russia, promising a $1.6 billion aid package. It was the first indication that the newly elected President of the United States could hold his own in the foreign policy arena. Yeltsin returned the favor when he supported the United States position urging the Serbs and Croats to agree to the United Nations peace plan. In the fall of 1993, opposition to President Boris Yeltsin resulted in the abolition of the Russian Parliament.

Yeltsin ordered martial law after the former Communist leaders declared that they were the new legitimate government and refused to leave the parliament building. Yeltsin ordered the army to attack the building and in a bloody battle ended the short-lived revolution. The Clinton administration offered Yeltsin public and private support. In December the Russian people passed a new constitution giving the Russian President increased powers, and also elected a new parliament. After a visit by President Clinton to Ukraine, he reached an agreement with the Ukrainian government to dismantle its nuclear arsenal in return for United States economic aid.

✪✪ **Bosnia and Serbia**—Daily reports of "ethnic cleansing" on the part of the Serbs against Bosnian Muslims angered the world community. President Clinton sent Secretary of State Warren Christopher to Europe in order to get support for a tougher United States response. After an attempt to airlift supplies failed, Clinton threatened Serbia with U.S. air strikes if they did not reach a negotiated agreement with Bosnia. The United States' allies were lukewarm to any American unilateral action. In the end, Clinton backed away from the plan and supported the United Nations initiatives.

✪ **Somalia**—President Clinton wanted to withdraw American troops from Somalia as soon as peace was restored. He agreed to incorporate a segment of U.S. troops to be part of a United Nations peacekeeping force. By the end of March 1993, a new UN force attempted to maintain the peace the United States had achieved. Unfortunately, one of the warlords stirred up trouble, killing and wounding UN troops. The United States led a retaliatory raid on the headquarters of the rebel war lord and relative peace returned to that war-torn country until the fall. The warlord ultimately sought revenge against the United Nations peacekeeping force. His supporters attacked United Nations troops as well as U.S. reinforcements and inflicted significant casualties. After intense Congressional pressure, Clinton promised to withdraw all American troops from Somalia by April 1994. His Defense Secretary, Les Aspin, became a casualty of this policy and resigned his position, becoming the first cabinet member to resign.

✪ **NATO**—Calling for a "partnership for peace," President Clinton urged the NATO alliance to allow the former Warsaw Pact countries to eventually join NATO. He obtained approval from both NATO and Czechoslovakia, Poland, and Hungry to start the process of total integration. The final step in this process may be the inclusion of Russia and the former Russian Republics.

✪ **North Korea**—The CIA reported that North Korea was on the brink of having nuclear capability. In a visit to South Korea, President Clinton promised that the United States would maintain its defensive posture with that country and press North Korea to allow United Nations inspection of its nuclear development sites. After much pressure, North Korea agreed to future site inspections. The United States also agreed to send Patriot missiles to South Korea to further bolster its defenses.

✪ **Vietnam**—President Clinton lifted the trade embargo against Vietnam in February 1994, which helped normalize the relations between the two countries. Even though many veterans' groups were opposed, this action symbolically ended the Vietnam War.

THE ADMINISTRATION'S AGENDA FOR THE FUTURE

At the end of Clinton's first year in office his critics were already predicting the early demise of the administration. However, "the comeback kid" surprised even his most severe critics by shaking up the White House staff and steering his economic package through a deeply divided Congress. He appointed former Reagan Communications Director David Gergen to head his communications office. He represented the United States at a trade summit in Japan and earned the respect of the other world leaders. Recognizing the plight of beleaguered Americans in the flood-ravaged Midwest and earthquake-torn Los Angeles, he made sure that federal aid was speedy and sufficient.

In his second State of the Union speech, Clinton firmly established the continuation of his legislative agenda, including measures still pending from the previous year. The first, developed by Vice President Gore, would "Reinvent Government" (REGO), by dramatically cutting bureaucratic waste. Legislation held up in conference committees such as a tough crime bill and a campaign spending reform bill were high on the agenda. But the centerpiece of Clinton's address was a call for adoption of a Health Care Plan. Following up his earlier dramatic speech in which he unveiled the long-awaited health care proposal and "health security card," Clinton again promised that before the turn of the century every American would be guaranteed universal health care. He even threatened to veto any legislation that did not include universal coverage. Offering new welfare reform legislation, Clinton urged Congress to fix a system characterized by generational dependency and other faults.

CHAPTER BOOK LIST

Allen, Charles P., *The Comeback Kid: The Life and Career of Bill Clinton* (1992).
Clinton, Bill, and Gore, Al, *Putting People First* (Time).
Levin, Robert E., *Bill Clinton: The Inside Story* (1992).

Michael, Nelson, *Election of Nineteen Ninety-Two* (Congressional Quarterly).

Perot, H. Ross, *United We Stand* (Hiperion).

Pomper, Gerald, et al, *Election of Nineteen Ninety-Two: Reports and Interpretations* (Chatton House).

REVIEW QUESTIONS

MULTIPLE CHOICE

1. The presidential election of 1992 marked the first time the Democrats regained control of the White House since the election of (1) Lyndon Johnson (2) Jimmy Carter (3) John Kennedy (4) Richard Nixon.

2. All of the following were involved in the Democratic primaries in 1992 *except* (1) Mario Cuomo (2) Bill Clinton (3) Jerry Brown (4) Paul Tsongas.

3. Clinton went against conventional wisdom by selecting Al Gore as his running mate because Gore (1) was an also-ran in the election of 1988 (2) was a "baby boomer" like Clinton (3) came from the South like Clinton (4) none of the above.

4. Even though President Bush was considered unbeatable, Pat Buchanan challenged Bush for the Republican nomination for all of the following reasons *except* Buchanan (1) disagreed with Bush's concept of the "New World Order" (2) felt that Bush was most vulnerable because of the lagging economy (3) wanted to establish himself as a possible contender in the 1966 election (4) wanted the Democratic candidate to win.

5. A truly viable third party candidate emerged in the 1992 presidential election because (1) Perot was a self-made billionaire who was willing to spend his own money (2) people were tired of the rhetoric of the two major parties (3) the people were impressed with Perot's folksy style (4) all of the above.

6. The results of the election of 1992 reflected (1) the largest voter turnout in recent elections (2) the smallest voter turnout in recent elections (3) a voter turnout about the same as recent elections (4) a decrease in the size of the youth vote.

7. After his inauguration Clinton issued an Executive Order that (1) lifted the ban on gays in the military (2) established a ceiling on the federal budget (3) prohibited women from having combat duty (4) lifted a ban on school prayers at graduation ceremonies.

8. Clinton's cabinet can be characterized as one that was made up of (1) mostly congressmen (2) mostly businessmen (3) a mixture of lawyers and minority representation (4) more women than men.

9. Hillary Clinton was given the responsibility of heading a panel to reform (1) the welfare system (2) campaign financing (3) abuses in federal hiring practices (4) the health care system.

10. Clinton's major economic thrust was to (1) increase social welfare spending (2) reduce the deficit (3) increase the taxes on the middle class more than the taxes on the rich (4) decrease the taxes on the middle class.

TRUE-FALSE

11. Clinton directed the FDA to begin experimentation on the French abortion pill RU 486.

12. Clinton lifted the gag rule that prohibited doctors in the federally funded clinics from talking to their patients about abortions as an option.

13. The United States sent troops to Bosnia in an attempt to end the civil war in Bosnia-Herzegovenia.

14. President Clinton received wide public support in the polls at the end of his first hundred days.

15. Clinton's job stimulus bill was approved by the Congress during the first hundred days of his administration.

COMPLETION

16. Congress passed the _____ Bill that had previously been vetoed by President Bush.

17. Terrorists bombed _____ that resulted in arrests of several illegal aliens from the Middle East.

18. Clinton promised Russian President Boris Yeltsin _____ aid at the Vancouver Summit.

19. Reports of _____ turned world opinion against Serbia in its civil war against the Bosnians.

20. The agreement initiated by President Bush and supported by President Clinton between the United States, Canada, and Mexico was called _____ .

MATCHING

21. Janet Reno   a. Secretary of Defense

22. Zoë Baird   b. First woman Attorney General

23. Warren Christopher   c. Clinton nominee who withdrew her name

24. Les Aspin   for consideration as Attorney General

25. Ruth Bader Ginsburg   d. Secretary of State

                                   e. First Supreme Court associate justice appointed by Clinton

ANSWERS TO CHAPTER REVIEW QUESTIONS

REVIEW QUESTIONS TO CHAPTER 1—PAGES 10–11

1. 3
2. 1
3. 3
4. 4
5. 2
6. 1
7. 3
8. 1

9. 1
10. 2
11. F
12. T
13. F
14. F
15. T
16. T

17. T
18. T
19. F
20. F
21. T
22. 1865, 1877
23. "Ten Percent Plan"
24. Monroe Doctrine

25. Napoleon III
    Maximilian
26. 1867
    Denmark
27. Thaddeus Stevens
    Charles Sumner
    "Conquered Provinces"
    "State Suicide"
28. "Black Codes"

REVIEW QUESTIONS TO CHAPTER 2—PAGES 20–22

1. 3
2. 3
3. 4
4. 2
S. 2
6. 4
7. 4
8. 2
9. 2

10. 1
11. T
12. T
13. T
14. F
15. F
16. T
17. T
18. F

19. T
20. F
21. F
22. T
23. T
24. T
25. T
26. Tenure of Office Act
27. Fourteenth

28. 1867
    Chief Justice Chase
    War
    Stanton
    One
29. Horace Seymour
30. Amnesty
31. Solid South

REVIEW QUESTIONS TO CHAPTER 3—PAGES 32–34

1. 4
2. 3
3. 2
4. 1
5. 2
6. 3

7. 2
8. 3
9. 4
10. 3
11. 4
12. 1

13. T
14. F
15. F
16. T
17. F
18. T

19. T
20. T
21. F
22. F
23. T
24. Black Friday

25. Tweed Ring
    Thomas Nast
    Samuel J. Tilden
26. Credit Mobilier
27. Whiskey Ring

28. Charles Sumner
    Hamilton Fish
29. Horace Greeley
    Liberal
    Republicans
    Grant

30. Jay Cooke and Company
31. Greenbacks
32. Resumption Act
    Greenback
33. Oliver H. Kelley

34. Tilden
    Hayes
    Tilden
    Hayes
    An Electoral Commission

REVIEW QUESTIONS TO CHAPTER 4—PAGES 42–44

1. 3	11. 3	21. Morrill	28. Andrew Carnegie
2. 4	12. T	22. 14	J. P. Morgan
3. 2	13. F	23. Ogden	United States Steel
4. 2	14. T	24. Union Pacific	Corporation
5. 3	15. T	25. Southern Pacific	29. George H. Bissell
6. 1	16. F	Santa Fe	Edwin Drake
7. 2	17. F	26. George Pullman	Pennsylvania
8. 1	18. F	27. Kelley	Benjamin Silliman
9. 2	19. F	Bessemer	John D. Rockefeller
10. 2	20. T		30. Armour, Morris, Swift

REVIEW QUESTIONS TO CHAPTER 5—PAGES 56–59

1. 1	15. 3	29. F	38. Dawes
2. 4	16. 1	30. T	1887
3. 3	17. F	31. T	Helen Hunt Jackson
4. 2	18. F	32. Pike's Peak	A Century of Dishonor
5. 3	19. F	Virginia	Ramona
6. 4	20. T	33. Vigilantes	1924
7. 1	21. F	34. Black Hills	39. Wheeler-Howard
8. 1	22. T	Deadwood	40. Abilene
9. 3	23. F	35. Stagecoach	41. Chisholm
10. 2	24. T	36. Sioux	42. Livestock Associations
11. 4	25. F	Nez Perce	1883
12. 2	26. T	Apache	43. Nesters
13. 3	27. T	37. Little Big Horn	44. Great Plains
14. 2	28. T		45. Joseph F. Glidden
			46. Bourbon
			47. Birmingham

REVIEW QUESTIONS TO CHAPTER 6—PAGES 75–79

1. 3	19. 3	37. T	47. Rebates
2. 2	20. 2	38. Ohio	Watered Stock
3. 3	21. T	1877	48. Interstate Commerce
4. 1	22. F	39. Senatorial	Commission
5. 1	23. F	Courtesy	49. Terence V. Powderly
6. 3	24. T	40. Resumption	50. Cleveland
7. 4	25. T	1879	51. Grand Army of the
8. 2	26. T	41. Bland-Allison	Republic
9. 3	27. T	42. Stalwarts	Grand Old Party
10. 1	28. F	Half-Breeds	52. e
11. 4	29. F	43. Chester A.	53. c
12. 2	30. T	Arthur	54. a
13. 3	31. T	Pendleton	55. h
14. 1	32. F	44. New York	56. i
15. 3	33. F	Maine	57. d
16. 4	34. T	45. Mills Bill	58. j
17. 2	35. F	46. Revenue	59. g
18. 1	36. F	Protective	60. b
			61. f

REVIEW QUESTIONS TO CHAPTER 7—PAGES 88–90

1. 1	11. 2	21. F	31. McKinley
2. 3	12. 3	22. F	Sherman Silver Purchase
3. 3	13. 1	23. T	Sherman Antitrust Act
4. 4	14. 4	24. F	32. Alliance
5. 2	15. 4	25. T	33. Australian
6. 1	16. 4	26. T	34. Wilson-Gorman
7. 2	17. F	27. F	35. Homestead
8. 3	18. F	28. F	Pullman
9. 4	19. T	29. F	
10. 2	20. T	30. Blaine	

REVIEW QUESTIONS TO CHAPTER 8—PAGE 95

1. 1	6. F	11. Marcus A. Hanna	14. Nebraska
2. 3	7. T	12. Cross of Gold	Three
3. 2	8. F	Populist	15. Dingley
4. 2	9. T	13. Tom Watson	
5. T	10. Coin's	Georgia	
	Financial		
	School		

REVIEW QUESTIONS TO CHAPTER 9—PAGES 105–107

1. 1	15. 2	22. Baltimore	
2. 1	16. F	Valparaiso	
3. 3	17. F	Indemnity	
4. 4	18. F	23. Pribilof	
5. 1	19. F	Bering	
6. 4	20. Liliuokalani	24. Maine	
7. 3	Cleveland	Havana	
8. 3	1898	25. Mahan, *Influence*	
9. 3	Joint	*of Sea Power;*	
10. 1	Resolution	Roosevelt, *Naval*	
11. 2	21. Pago Pago	*War of 1812*	
12. 4	Germany		
13. 3	Britain		
14. 4			

REVIEW QUESTIONS TO CHAPTER 10—PAGES 116–117

1. 2	12. T	21. Mary Baker Eddy	32. c
2. 2	13. T	22. Andrew Carnegie	33. e
3. 1	14. F	23. John Hopkins	34. b
4. 1	15. T	24. Eugene V. Debs	35. d
5. 1	16. F	25. Frederick J. Turner	36. i
6. 4	17. Blue-Sky	26. k	
7. 3	18. Carl Schurz	27. f	
8. 3	19. 1880	28. h	
9. 3	20. Fundamentalists	29. a	
10. T	*Origin of*	30. j	
11. T	*the Species*	31. g	

REVIEW QUESTIONS TO CHAPTER 11—PAGES 127–129

1. 3	12. T	21. Muckrakers	25. Mark Hanna
2. 4	13. T	Ida M. Tarbell	26. Taft
3. 1	14. T	Upton Sinclair	Bryan
4. 1	15. F	*The Jungle*	27. Hiram
5. 4	16. F	22. Big Bill Haywood	Johnson
6. 1	17. T	23. Employer's	28. 17th
7. 3	18. T	Liability or	Amendment
8. 3	19. New York	Workmen's	
9. F	Assistant	Compensation	
10. F	Secretary	24. Elkins Act	
11. F	20. Thorstein Veblen	Hempburn Act	

REVIEW QUESTIONS TO CHAPTER 12—PAGES 136–138

1. 3	11. T	20. Portsmouth	25. Gorgas
2. 1	12. T	1905	Goethals
3. 3	13. T	Indemnity	26. Big Stick
4. 3	14. F	21. Gentlemen's	27. Germany
5. 2	15. F	Agreement	Debt
6. 2	16. F	San Francisco	28. Roosevelt
7. 1	17. T	22. Root-Takahira	Corollary
8. 4	18. John Hay	23. Ferdinand	29. Algeciras
9. 3	19. Boxer Uprising	de Lesseps	Conference
10. F	Peiping	24. San Juan	
		Nicaragua	

REVIEW QUESTIONS TO CHAPTER 13—PAGES 144–145

1. 2	7. 1	13. T	19. Dollar Diplomacy
2. 1	8. 2	14. F	20. Mann-Elkins
3. 1	9. F	15. William H. Taft	21. Postal Savings
4. 4	10. T	16. Payne-Aldrich	System
5. 2	11. F	17. Ballinger	22. Labor
6. 4	12. T	18. George Norris	23. Bull Moose

REVIEW QUESTIONS TO CHAPTER 14—PAGES 155–157

1. 3	11. T	18. Underwood	20. Adamson Act
2. 3	12. F	Tariff	21. Smith-Lever
3. 2	13. T	Log-Rolling	Smith-Hughes
4. 4	14. F	Thirteenth	22. Madero
5. 4	15. New Freedom	19. Federal Farm	Huerta
6. 4	16. Princeton	Loan Act	Watchful
7. 4	Governor	Federal Farm	Waiting
8. 4	New Jersey	Commission	Pershing
9. T	17. William J. Bryan	Cease and	Francisco
10. T	Cooling-Off	Desist	Villa

REVIEW QUESTIONS TO CHAPTER 15—PAGES 167–170

1. 1	17. 1	30. Submarine	39. Influenza
2. 3	18. F	*Lusitania*	40. Colonies
3. 2	19. T	Britain	war-guilt
4. 3	20. T	31. Sussex	Reparations
5. 3	21. T	32. Theodore	41. Henry Cabot
6. 3	22. F	Roosevelt	Lodge
7. 1	23. F	33. Shipping Board	42. e
8. 4	24. T	34. California	43. i
9. 2	25. F	Hughes	44. b
10. 1	26. T	Hiram Johnson	45. a
11. 1	27. T	35. Belgium	46. c
12. 4	28. F	36. Herbert Hoover	47. h
13. 4	29. Archduke	Bernard M. Baruch	48. g
14. 3	Ferdinand	37. American Expedi-	49. f
15. 4	Austria-Hungary	tionary Force	50. d
16. 2		Doughboys	51. j
		38. Fourteen Points	

REVIEW QUESTIONS TO CHAPTER 16—PAGES 180–182

1. 3	11. 3	21. Denby	29. f
2. 2	12. T	Elk Hills	30. b
3. 3	13. T	22. Four-Power	31. j
4. 3	14. F	23. Solemn Referendum	32. c
5. 2	15. T	24. Muscle Shoals	33. a
6. 2	16. T	25. Dawes	34. d
7. 1	17. F	Young	35. g
8. 1	18. T	26. Dwight L. Morrow	36. k
9. 2	19. T	27. e	
10. 2	20. 1923	28. i	
	Alaska		

REVIEW QUESTIONS TO CHAPTER 17—PAGES 189–190

1. 2	6. 1	11. Farm Bloc	14. Sacco and
2. 4	7. 4	12. McNary-Haugen	Vanzetti
3. 2	8. 1	13. Democratic	15. William J.
4. 1	9. Henry Ford	21st	Bryan
5. 1	10. Charles A.	1933	16. Wright
	Lindbergh		

REVIEW QUESTIONS TO CHAPTER 18—PAGES 196–198

1. 3	9. F	16. Herbert Hoover	20. Reconstruction
2. 3	10. F	Al Smith	Finance Corporation
3. 1	11. T	17. Agriculture	Home Loan Bank
4. 4	12. F	Federal Farm Board	Norris-La Guardia
5. 3	13. T	18. Smoot-Hawley	21. Al Smith
6. 4	14. T	19. Stock Market	22. Interregnum
7. 2	15. T	1929	
8. 3		Just Around the	
		Corner	

REVIEW QUESTIONS TO CHAPTER 19—PAGES 211–214

1. 2	17. New York	25. National Labor	31. Maine and
2. 4	18. Relief, Recovery,	Relations Board	Vermont
3. 2	and Reform	26. United States Em-	Gallup
4. 2	19. Emergency Banking	ployment Service	Literary
5. 1	Act	27. Yardstick	Digest
6. 3	20. Works Progress	Rural Electrifica-	32. Nine Old Men
7. 2	Administration	tion Authority	70
8. 1	21. $35.00	Death Sentence	33. 1937
9. 3	22. Parity	Wheeler-Rayburn	34. e
10. 1	Processing Tax	28. Federal Deposit	35. g
11. 3	Soil Conservation	Insurance	36. k
12. 2	Act	Corporation	37. f
13. 4	Allotments	29. Huey Long	38. a
14. 1	Marketing Quotas	Father Coughlin	39. b
15. 2	23. Dust-Bowl	30. Maritime Commission	40. h
16. 1	24. National Recovery		41. c
	Administration		42. j
	Chiselers		43. d
	Schechter		
	Wagner Act		

REVIEW QUESTIONS TO CHAPTER 20—PAGES 222–224

1. 2	8. 3	15. F	21. Havana
2. 4	9. 2	16. F	22. Stimson Doctrine
3. 2	10. 1	17. T	23. Panay
4. 4	11. T	18. F	24. National Socialist
5. 2	12. T	19. T	25. Nye Committee
6. 1	13. T	20. Good Neighbor	Johnson
7. 1	14. F	Cordell Hull	26. Quarantine
		Montevideo	

27. 1939
    Poland
    Blitzkrieg
28. America First
    Committee

29. Maginot Line
    Siegfried Line
30. Dunkirk
31. Wendell Willkie

32. Lend-Lease
    Arsenal of
    Democracy

REVIEW QUESTIONS TO CHAPTER 21—PAGES 235–237

1. 1
2. 2
3. 3
4. 2
5. 1
6. 2
7. 4
8. 3
9. T
10. T
11. F

12. F
13. F
14. T
15. T
16. Bataan Peninsula
    Corregidor
    Kiska
    Burma
17. Midway
    Guadalcanal
18. Chester W. Nimitz
    Douglas Mac Arthur

19. William Halsey
20. Chiang Kai-Shek
21. Okinawa
    Kamikaze
22. Hiroshima
    Nagasaki
    Truman
23. North Africa
    Sicily
    Italy
    Normandy
    1944
    Eisenhower

24. Office of
    Price
    Administration
25. Thomas E.
    Dewey

REVIEW QUESTIONS TO CHAPTER 22—PAGES 244–246

1. 4
2. 4
3. 4
4. 3
5. 2
6. 4
7. 1
8. 2
9. T
10. T

11. T
12. F
13. F
14. T
15. T
16. Yalta
    Manchuria

17. San Francisco
    1945
    Roosevelt
    Five
    Veto
    General Assembly
    Secretariat
18. Senator
    Missouri
19. Non-Communist
20. Speaker of the
    House
    Vice President

21. 22
22. Department
    of Defense
23. Fair Deal
24. McCarran
    1950
25. McCarran
    Walter

REVIEW QUESTIONS TO CHAPTER 23—PAGES 256–258

1. 1	8. 3	15. Four	21. b	27. e
2. 4	9. 2	16. Airlift	22. d	28. c
3. 2	10. T	17. Greece	23. h	29. j
4. 3	11. F	Turkey	24. f	
5. 1	12. T	18. Point Four	25. g	
6. 3	13. F	19. Pusan	26. a	
7. 3	14. T	20. Yalu		

REVIEW QUESTIONS TO CHAPTER 24—PAGES 265–266

1. 1	8. Soil Bank	14. Landrum-Griffin	21. b
2. 2	9. Dixon-Yates	15. c	22. e
3. 3	10. Guaranteed Annual	16. f	23. k
4. 1	Wage	17. a	24. j
5. 4	11. Merger	18. h	
6. 1	12. Little Rock	19. d	
7. 3	13. Alaska	20. i	
	Hawaii		

REVIEW QUESTIONS TO CHAPTER 25—PAGES 272–273

1. 3	6. Stalin	9. 1956	12. Lyndon Johnson
2. 2	Khrushchev	Suez Canal	13. Missile
3. 2	7. Anzus	10. Truman	
4. 3	Seato	Lebanon	
5. 4	8. Geneva	11. Batista	
	Aerial	Red China	

REVIEW QUESTIONS TO CHAPTER 26—PAGES 286–289

1. 3	11. 3	21. F	31. Puerto Rico
2. 2	12. 1	22. T	32. Dust Bowl
3. 4	13. 1	23. F	John Steinbeck's
4. 1	14. 2	24. T	33. Suburbs
5. 2	15. 1	25. F	34. John Kenneth Galbraith
6. 2	16. T	26. F	35. Hoover Towns
7. 1	17. T	27. T	36. Fair Employment Practices
8. 3	18. F	28. T	Commission
9. 2	19. F	29. T	37. John Maynard Keynes
10. 4	20. T	30. F	38. Full Employment Act of 1946
			39. Sputnik

REVIEW QUESTIONS TO CHAPTER 27—PAGES 307–310

1. 1	11. 1	21. T	30. Missiles
2. 3	12. 3	22. T	31. Inspection
3. 2	13. 2	23. F	32. Steel
4. 1	14. 2	24. T	33. 1937
5. 3	15. T	25. T	34. Federal Reserve
6. 2	16. T	26. New Frontier	35. Mississippi
7. 3	17. T	27. 43	36. John Birch
8. 4	18. F	28. Dean Rusk	37. Khrushchev
9. 2	19. F	Robert Kennedy	38. Bay of Pigs
10. 2	20. F	29. John Glenn	39. Alliance for Progress
		Scott Carpenter	40. Peace Corps

REVIEW QUESTIONS TO CHAPTER 28—PAGES 321–322

1. 4	7. 3	12. Great Society	16. Vietcong
2. 3	8. 3	13. Housing and	17. Watts
3. 2	9. 5	Urban Development	Los Angeles
4. 1	10. 1	14. Vista	
5. 2	11. 3	15. Black Muslims	
6. 4			

REVIEW QUESTIONS TO CHAPTER 29—PAGES 337–338

1. 3	8. 2	15. Wounded Knee	22. h
2. 3	9. 2	16. 1973	23. d
3. 1,4	10. 1	17. Watergate	24. g
4. 4	11. Communism	18. b	25. i
5. 1	12. Southern	19. f	26. a
6. 4	13. Vietnam	20. c	27. k
7. 3	14. Inflation	21. j	

REVIEW QUESTIONS TO CHAPTER 30—PAGES 348–350

1. 2	10. Human Rights	19. k	27. j
2. 4	11. Helsinki Accord	20. a	28. c
3. 1	12. Panama	21. i	29. e
4. 1	13. PLO	22. d	
5. 4	14. Chicanos	23. h	
6. 1	15. BIA	24. b	
7. 4	16. Medicare	25. e	
8. Energy	17. Affirmative	26. g	
9. Inflation	18. a		

REVIEW QUESTIONS TO CHAPTER 31—PAGES 358–360

1. 3	11. New Federalism	21. d
2. 4	12. Lebanon	22. e
3. 3	13. Golan Heights	23. c
4. 4	14. Christians	24. i
5. 1	15. An oil-rich region bordering Iran	25. h
6. 1	16. k	
7. 1	17. j	
8. 3	18. g	
9. 3	19. b	
10. 1	20. a	

REVIEW QUESTIONS TO CHAPTER 32—PAGES 369–371

1. 3	11. F	21. b
2. 2	12. T	22. a
3. 4	13. F	23. e
4. 3	14. T	24. c
5. 1	15. T	25. d
6. 4	16. Drug Trafficking	
7. 2	17. Muammaral-Qaddafi	
8. 1	18. Nicaragua	
9. 1	19. Ferdinand Marcos	
10. 3	20. Corazon Aquino	

REVIEW QUESTIONS TO CHAPTER 33—PAGES 385–387

1. 2	11. F	21. c
2. 3	12. T	22. a
3. 1	13. T	23. e
4. 4	14. F	24. b
5. 4	15. F	25. d
6. 3	16. Germany	
7. 4	17. Bulgaria	
8. 2	18. Strategic nuclear arms	
9. 1	19. Air and naval	
10. 4	20. Operation Restore Hope	

REVIEW QUESTIONS TO CHAPTER 34—PAGES 398–399

1. 2	11. T	21. b
2. 1	12. T	22. c
3. 3	13. F	23. d
4. 4	14. F	24. a
5. 4	15. F	25. e
6. 1	16. Family Medical Leave	
7. 1	17. The World Trade Center	
8. 3	18. Economic	
9. 4	19. Ethnic Cleansing	
10. 2	20. North American Free Trade Act (NAFTA)	

APPENDICES

REVIEW QUESTIONS FOR ESSAY-TYPE EXAMINATIONS

1. Sketch the political, social, and economic changes the Civil War brought to the South.

2. Why did Andrew Johnson have so much trouble with Congress? Write a short essay upholding Johnson's views.

3. Evaluate the combination of cynical and idealistic motives of the Radicals.

4. Name and explain the provisions of the three Civil War amendments to the Constitution.

5. Evaluate the consequences of the carpetbag governments in the Southern states.

6. Why did the North eventually abandon reconstruction in the South?

7. What were Grant's shortcomings as President?

8. Explain the leading political repercussions of the depression in the 1870s.

9. Explain the disputed election of 1876 and how it was settled.

10. Enumerate political and economic factors that encouraged industrial growth after 1865.

11. Explain how insiders profited through the railroad construction companies. Name five leading transcontinental railroads in order from North to South.

12. List the leading new post-Civil War industries.

13. What were the main causes of the settlement of the West after the Civil War?

14. Sketch the evolution of government on the mineral frontiers.

15. Sketch the successive changes in transportation and communications in the Far West.

16. What factors promoted the rise of the range cattle industry? Its decline?

17. What unfavorable conditions delayed the settlement of the Great Plains area?

18. Explain the nature of the main economic problems of the 1870s and 1880s.

19. State the arguments for and against high tariffs.

20. Enumerate abuses of the railroads that led to their regulation.

21. What were the leading changes related to labor after 1865?

22. What demands of the Populists came to be enacted into law?

412

23. What economic problems did Cleveland have to contend with in his second administration?

24. State as many outcomes of the election of 1896 as you can. State the significance of the election.

25. Account for the renewal of American interest in overseas areas beginning about 1890.

26. Sketch causes and background of the Spanish-American War. What were its important consequences?

27. What changes related to immigration occurred about 1880?

28. What changes related to education occurred after the Civil War?

29. Discuss American response to Darwinism.

30. Evaluate T. Roosevelt as a leader of reform.

31. Enumerate political reforms won in the states by the Progressives.

32. Outline American relations with China and Japan from 1900 to 1950.

33. What political and other obstacles did the United States have to overcome to build the Panama Canal?

34. Trace the change in British-American relations after 1896 to about 1905.

35. Analyze the political weaknesses and legislative achievements of President Taft.

36. What was unique and significant about the election of 1912?

37. Enumerate the legislative achievements of the Democrats in Wilson's first term.

38. How do you think a Republican administration would have dealt with the various foreign problems encountered by the Wilson administration?

39. Evaluate the numerous causes and factors in American entry in World War I.

40. State fully why Wilson failed to win Senate ratification of the Treaty of Versailles.

41. Contrast Harding and his administration with Wilson and his administration.

42. What favoritism did Harding and Coolidge manifest toward business?

43. What is the significance of the Washington Conference?

44. Evaluate significant economic developments of the 1920s.

45. Why was prohibition enacted and repealed?

46. Characterize the changes in customs and morals of the 1920s.

47. Explain the causes of the Great Depression.

48. What were Hoover's remedies for the problems of the depression?

49. Characterize New Deal philosophy and action in response to the problems of the depression.

50. What three reform measures of the New Deal do you consider to be the most important? Why?

51. What great changes did the New Deal bring that affected labor?

52. Sketch aggressive acts of Japan, Italy, and Germany from 1931 to 1939.

53. During the early 1930s, how did America's response to foreign wars differ from the past?

54. What steps did Roosevelt take to lead America to the aid of the Allies?

55. Sketch the overall American military strategy employed to defeat Japan.

56. Trace main American military campaigns against Germany.

57. Evaluate the criticisms of various agreements made with Russia at Yalta.

58. How does the organizational machinery of the UNO compare with that of the League of Nations?

59. Why was the Taft-Hartley Act passed? How did it seek to regulate labor union abuses?

60. Identify the leading acts of Truman to meet the challenges of international Communism.

61. What various factors helped Eisenhower to become President in 1952?

62. What change did the Eisenhower administration introduce affecting each of these: choice of appointees to high office, agriculture, labor, public utilities, and tariff?

63. What steps did government take under Eisenhower to further racial equality?

64. What are the larger domestic consequences of the Russian challenge to American leadership in world affairs?

65. What was unique and significant in the election of 1960?

66. Enumerate population changes in America since the depression.

67. What changes in economic philosophy did the depression experience produce?

68. What economic changes did the Second World War bring?

69. Name some leading technological developments of the 1950s and 1960s.

70. What obstacles blocked the early fulfillment of the promises of the "New Frontier"?

71. Name leading problems Kennedy faced in the years following his election.

72. Characterize foreign policy changes from Roosevelt to Kennedy.

73. What were the accomplishments of Nixon in foreign relations? Why could he succeed as he did?

74. How do you account for Nixon's election victories in 1968 and 1972?

75. Enumerate some of the violations of law by zealous Nixon campaign leaders in relation to Watergate.

76. What problems did Ford face after he became President? How did he resolve them?

77. Why did Carter's attempt to be a Populist President fail?

78. What were Carter's greatest accomplishments and greatest failures in foreign policy?

79. Describe the economic situation in the United States under the Carter administration.

80. Compare Reagan's attitude and policies toward the Soviet Union in his two administrations.

81. Describe Reaganomics and explain how the policy contributed to Reagan's concept of a New Federalism.

82. What were the causes and outcome of the Persian Gulf War?

83. Describe what is meant by Bush's foreign policy doctrine labeled New World Order and give examples of how he applied it.

84. Why were the Democrats able to capture the presidency in the 1992 election?

85. How would you assess Clinton's first year in office?

GENERAL OR SURVEY FINAL EXAMINATION REVIEW QUESTIONS

1. What has been the pattern of Native American-white settler conflict and reconciliation in American history? What factors caused the renewal of Native American wars before and after the Civil War? Sketch the evolution of government policy toward the Native American tribes from the 1820s to the present.

2. Cite a few political and legislative changes following the Civil War that reflect the change from Southern agricultural to Northern industrial domination of the nation.

3. What similarities do you see in Populist, Progressive, and New Deal philosophies?

4. Characterize policies toward labor of the following administrations: Cleveland, T. Roosevelt, Wilson, Harding, F. D. Roosevelt, Kennedy. What have been the major changes in the organization of labor since 1866?

5. Which presidents brought substantial changes in tariffs from 1870 to 1960? Describe these changes.

6. Trace gains made by farmers through favorable legislation since 1914.

7. After 1900, what presidential elections brought a defeat to incumbent political parties? Why were they defeated?

8. Sketch milestones in the abandonment of isolationism by the United States from 1898 to 1940.

9. Describe the impact on American society of changes in transportation since 1860.

10. What enduring differences do you see between the two major parties as shown by their policies since 1865?

11. Describe the major cultural changes of U.S. life since 1920.

12. What have been the major developments in the struggle for racial equality in the nation since 1870?

13. What does history tell you about the position of the two major parties on the economic problems facing the U.S.? Give illustrations.

14. Sketch major changes in American policy toward Latin America.

15. How has the Supreme Court changed from the Warren to the Rehnquist Court?

16. Why has the Middle East remained a powderkeg from 1976 to the present?

17. What has been the impact of the fall of Communism on U.S. foreign policy?

18. How have voting patterns changed from 1960 to the present?

19. What have been the patterns of immigration and immigration legislation from 1870 to the present?

20. Describe the major themes of the New Deal, New Frontier, and Great Society.

STATES OF THE UNION

Original Thirteen States in Capitals

State	Capital	First Permanent Settlement	Date Entered Union[1]	Area in Square Miles
Alabama	Montgomery	1702	Dec. 14, 1819	51,609
Alaska	Juneau	1790	Jan. 3, 1959	590,884
Arizona	Phoenix	1848	Feb. 14, 1912	113,909
Arkansas	Little Rock	1785	June 15, 1836	53,104
California	Sacramento	1769	Sept. 9, 1850	158,693
Colorado	Denver	1858	Aug. 1, 1876	104,247
CONNECTICUT	Hartford	1635	Jan. 9, 1788	5,009
DELAWARE	Dover	1638	Dec. 7, 1787	2,057
Florida	Tallahassee	1565	Mar. 3, 1845	58,560
GEORGIA	Atlanta	1733	Jan. 2, 1788	58,876
Hawaii	Honolulu	—	Aug. 21, 1959	6,449
Idaho	Boise	1842	July 3, 1890	83,557
Illinois	Springfield	1720	Dec. 3, 1818	56,400
Indiana	Indianapolis	1733	Dec. 11, 1816	36,291
Iowa	Des Moines	1788	Dec. 28, 1846	56,290
Kansas	Topeka	1727	Jan. 29, 1861	82,276
Kentucky	Frankfort	1774	June 1, 1792	40,395
Louisiana	Baton Rouge	1699	Apr. 30, 1812	48,523
Maine	Augusta	1624	Mar. 15, 1820	33,215
MARYLAND	Annapolis	1634	Apr. 28, 1788	10,577
MASSACHUSETTS	Boston	1620	Feb. 6, 1788	8,257
Michigan	Lansing	1668	Jan. 26, 1837	58,216
Minnesota	St. Paul	1805	May 11, 1858	84,068
Mississippi	Jackson	1699	Dec. 10, 1817	47,716
Missouri	Jefferson City	1764	Aug. 10, 1821	69,674
Montana	Helena	1809	Nov. 8, 1889	147,138
Nebraska	Lincoln	1847	Mar. 1, 1867	77,227
Nevada	Carson City	1850	Oct. 31, 1864	110,540
NEW HAMPSHIRE	Concord	1623	June 21, 1788	9,304
NEW JERSEY	Trenton	1664	Dec. 18, 1787	7,836

[1]Date ratified Constitution, or date of admission to Union.

New Mexico	Santa Fe	1605	Jan. 6, 1912	121,666
NEW YORK	Albany	1614	July 26, 1788	49,576
NORTH CAROLINA	Raleigh	1650	Nov. 21, 1789	52,712
North Dakota	Bismarck	1766	Nov. 2, 1889	70,665
Ohio	Columbus	1788	Mar. 1, 1803	41,222
Oklahoma	Oklahoma City	1889	Nov. 16, 1907	69,919
Oregon	Salem	1811	Feb. 14, 1859	96,981
PENNSYLVANIA	Harrisburg	1682	Dec. 12, 1787	45,333
RHODE ISLAND	Providence	1636	May 29, 1790	1,214
SOUTH CAROLINA	Columbia	1670	May 23, 1788	31,055
South Dakota	Pierre	1856	Nov. 2, 1889	77,047
Tennessee	Nashville	1757	June 1, 1796	42,244
Texas	Austin	1691	Dec. 29, 1845	267,339
Utah	Salt Lake City	1847	Jan. 4, 1896	84,916
Vermont	Montpelier	1724	Mar. 4, 1791	9,609
VIRGINIA	Richmond	1607	June 26, 1788	40,815
Washington	Olympia	1811	Nov. 11, 1889	68,192
West Virginia	Charleston	1727	June 20, 1863	24,181
Wisconsin	Madison	1766	May 29, 1848	56,154
Wyoming	Cheyenne	1824	July 10, 1890	97,914

POPULATION OF THE UNITED STATES, 1790–1990

1790 3,929,214		1870 38,558,371	
1800 5,308,483		1880 50,155,783	
1810............ 7,239,881		1890 62,947,714	
1820 9,638,453		1900 75,994,575	
1830 12,860,692		1910 91,972,266	
1840 17,063,353		1920 105,710,620	
1850 23,191,876		1930 122,775,046	
1860 31,443,321		1940 131,669,275	

1950 150,697,361
1960 179,323,175
1970 203,302,031
1980 226,504,825
1990 248,709,873

PRESIDENTS AND VICE PRESIDENTS

Term	President	Vice President
1789–1793	George Washington	John Adams
1793–1797	George Washington	John Adams
1797–1801	John Adams	Thomas Jefferson
1801–1805	Thomas Jefferson	Aaron Burr
1805–1809	Thomas Jefferson	George Clinton
1809–1813	James Madison	George Clinton (d. 1812)
1813–1817	James Madison	Elbridge Gerry (d. 1814)
1817–1821	James Monroe	Daniel D. Tompkins
1821–1825	James Monroe	Daniel D. Tompkins
1825–1829	John Quincy Adams	John C. Calhoun
1829–1833	Andrew Jackson	John C. Calhoun (resigned 1832)
1833–1837	Andrew Jackson	Martin Van Buren
1837–1841	Martin Van Buren	Richard M. Johnson
1841–1845	William H. Harrison (d. 1841) John Tyler	John Tyler
1845–1849	James K. Polk	George M. Dallas
1849–1853	Zachary Taylor (d. 1850) Millard Fillmore	Millard Fillmore
1853–1857	Franklin Pierce	William R. D. King (d. 1853)
1857–1861	James Buchanan	John C. Breckinridge
1861–1865	Abraham Lincoln	Hannibal Hamlin
1865–1869	Abraham Lincoln (d. 1865) Andrew Johnson	Andrew Johnson
1869–1873	Ulysses S. Grant	Schuyler Colfax
1873–1877	Ulysses S. Grant	Henry Wilson (d. 1875)
1877–1881	Rutherford B. Hayes	William A. Wheeler
1881–1885	James A. Garfield (d. 1881) Chester A. Arthur	Chester A. Arthur
1885–1889	Grover Cleveland	Thomas A. Hendricks (d. 1885)
1889–1893	Benjamin Harrison	Levi P. Morton

1893–1897	Grover Cleveland	Adlai E. Stevenson
1897–1901	William McKinley	Garret A. Hobart (d. 1899)
1901–1905	William McKinley (d. 1901) Theodore Roosevelt	Theodore Roosevelt
1905–1909	Theodore Roosevelt	Charles W. Fairbanks
1909–1913	William H. Taft	James S. Sherman (d. 1912)
1913–1917	Woodrow Wilson	Thomas R. Marshall
1917–1921	Woodrow Wilson	Thomas R. Marshall
1921–1925	Warren G. Harding (d. 1923) Calvin Coolidge	Calvin Coolidge
1925–1929	Calvin Coolidge	Charles G. Dawes
1929–1933	Herbert C. Hoover	Charles Curtis
1933–1937	Franklin D. Roosevelt	John N. Garner
1937–1941	Franklin D. Roosevelt	John N. Garner
1941–1945	Franklin D. Roosevelt	Henry A. Wallace
1945–1949	Franklin D. Roosevelt (d. 1945) Harry S. Truman	Harry S. Truman
1949–1953	Harry S. Truman	Alben W. Barkley
1953–1957	Dwight D. Eisenhower	Richard M. Nixon
1957–1961	Dwight D. Eisenhower	Richard M. Nixon
1961–1965	John F. Kennedy (d. 1963) Lyndon B. Johnson	Lyndon B. Johnson
1965–1969	Lyndon B. Johnson	Hubert Humphrey
1969–1973	Richard M. Nixon	Spiro T. Agnew
1973–1974	Richard M. Nixon	Gerald R. Ford
1974–1977	Gerald R. Ford	Nelson Rockefeller
1977–1981	James E. Carter	Walter Mondale
1981–1985	Ronald W. Reagan	George H.W. Bush
1985–1989	Ronald W. Reagan	George H.W. Bush
1989–1993	George H.W. Bush	J. Danforth Quayle
1993–	William J.B. Clinton	Albert Gore

CHIEF JUSTICES OF THE SUPREME COURT

John Jay, New York	1789–1795
John Rutledge, South Carolina	1795
Oliver Ellsworth, Connecticut	1795–1799
John Marshall, Virginia	1801–1835
Roger B. Taney, Maryland	1836–1864
Salmon P. Chase, Ohio	1864–1873
Morrison R. Waite, Ohio	1874–1888
Melville W. Fuller, Illinois	1888–1910
Edward D. White, Louisiana	1910–1921
William H. Taft, Ohio	1921–1930
Charles E. Hughes, New York	1930–1941
Harlan F. Stone, New York	1941–1946
Fred M. Vinson, Kentucky	1946–1953
Earl Warren, California	1953–1969
Warren E. Burger, Virginia	1969–1986
William H. Rehnquist, Arizona	1986–

COMPREHENSIVE BOOKS IN AMERICAN HISTORY

Works listed in this bibliography have been carefully selected from authors generally recognized for reliability and readablity. The reader interested in a reliable listing of paperback books should check Bowker's *Paperbound Books in Print,* printed in quarterly editions and available in most libraries. Annotated and more extensive bibliographies may be found in most American history textbooks. Students who need a still more extensive, classified bibliography should consult the ***Harvard Guide to American History.***

Bailey, T.A. and Kennedy, D.M., *American Pageant: A History of the Republic* (1990).

Bailey, T.A., *The American Spirit: American History as Seen by Contemporaries* (1984).

Bailey, T.A., *Voices of America: The Nation's Story in Slogans, Sayings and Songs* (1976).

Baylin, B., *The Great Republic: A History of the American People* (1985).

Blum, J.M., et al., *The National Experience: A History of the United States from 1877* (1988).

Brogan, H., *The Pelican History of the U.S.A.* (1987).

Brugger, Robert J., *Ourselves, Our Past: Psychological Approaches to American History* (1981).

Burner, D., and Genovese, E.D., *An American Portrait: A History of the U.S.* (1983).

Burner, D., et al., *The American People Vol. II from 1860* (1980).

Carroll, P., and Noble, D.W., *The Free and the Unfree: A New History of the United States* (1988).

Conlin, J.R., *The American Past: A Survey of American History* (1987).

Crowly, H., *The Promise of American Life* (1989).

Current, R., et al., *Current History of the United States* (1984).

Current, R., *The Essentials of American History. Vol. II, from 1865* (1986).

Davis, J., *The American Presidency* (1986).

Garraty, J.A., *A Short History of the American Nation* (1988).

Grabner, W., and Richards, L., *The American Record: Images of the Nation's Past* (1987).

Graff, H.F., *America, The Glorious Republic from 1877* (1985).

Grob, B., *Interpretations of American History. Vol. II: since 1865* (1990).

Jordon, W.D. and Litwack, L.F., *The United States: A Brief Edition* (1990).

Legunn, J., *Highlights of American History* (1979).

Madaras, L., and Sorelli, J., *Clashing Views on Controversial Issues in American History* (1989).

Marcus, R.D., and Burner, D., *America Firsthand Vol. II: Reconstruction to the Present* (1989).

Mumford, R.L., *An American History Primer* (1989).

Nasaw, D., *Course of U.S. History Vol. II: from 1865* (1987).

Nash, G., *Private Side of American History: Readings in Everyday Life Vol. II: since 1865.*

Nevins, A. and Commager, H., *A Pocket History of the United States* (1989).

Norton, M., et al., *A People and a Nation; A History of the United States* (1986).

Risjord, N., *America: The Glorious Republic Vol. II: since 1865* (1988).

Wheeler, W., and Becker, S., *Discovering the American Past. Vol II: Since 1865.*

Wilson, R., et al., *The Pursuit of Liberty: A History of the American People. Vol. II, since 1860* (1990).

Young, W., *American Realities: Episodes in American History from Reconstruction to the Present.*

Zin, H., *A People's History of the United States* (1990).

DICTIONARY OF IMPORTANT AND DIFFICULT TERMS

Adamson Act, 1916—An act of Congress that established the eight-hour day for railroad workers on interstate railroads.

Affluent Society—Book by John Kenneth Galbraith dealing with the increased prosperity in American society.

Agricultural Adjustment Act (AAA), 1933—The first farm relief measure passed by the New Deal. It adopted the principle of restricting production by paying farmers to reduce crop acreages. When the act was declared unconstitutional crop restrictions were accomplished by the Soil Conservation and Domestic Allotment Act of 1936. This latter act in turn was superseded by a second Agricultural Adjustment Act in 1938.

Alabama Claims—Damage claims of the United States against Great Britain for destruction of American shipping during the Civil War by British-built commerce raiders released to the Confederacy.

Aldrich-Vreeland Act, 1908—Created the National Monetary Commission to study banking and currency systems; made recommendations to Congress that were embodied in the Federal Reserve Act of 1913. The Aldrich-Vreeland Act also provided for the issuance of emergency currency.

"Alliance for Progress," 1961—A program of economic assistance for Latin America begun by the Kennedy administration; had objectives of political and social reform as means of combating Communist influence among impoverished peoples of Latin America.

America First Committee—A pacifist organization begun in 1940 to prevent American entry in World War II; represented conservative and isolationist elements.

American Disabilities Act of 1990—A law that curbed discrimination against disabled Americans.

American Federation of Labor (AFL)—Organized in 1881 as a federation of craft unions; a relatively conservative movement among labor organizations.

American Indian Movement—Known as AIM, a group of Indian activists occupied the Bureau of Indian Affairs headquarters in Washington, DC and seized control of Wounded Knee in order to protest reservation conditions.

Americans for Democratic Action—A liberal organization, known as the ADA, it urged increased federal spending and blamed the Eisenhower administration for the economic slowdown the country was facing.

anarchism—A political philosophy opposed to organized government which it considers an instrument of oppression used by the ruling classes. Some anarchists advocated various forms of violence to achieve their goals.

ANZUS Pact, 1951—A mutual security pact between Australia, New Zealand, and the United States, signed to allay fears of the possible military resurgence of Japan.

Atlantic Charter, August 1941—A joint statement of war aims issued by Roosevelt and Churchill. Corresponded to the Fourteen Points in World War I but was not as specific.

Australian ballot—The secret ballot, first adopted in Australia.

baby boom—Increase in population immediately after soldiers returned from duty in World War II. It leveled off in the 1960s and zero population growth occurred in 1972, except for immigrants. The first "baby boomer" elected president was William Clinton in 1992.

Bakke decision—Supreme court decision that ruled that strict admission quotas to state funded colleges were unconstitutional.

balance of payments—The difference in the value of goods and services bought and those sold by a nation. An unfavorable balance represents payments in excess of receipts and ultimately may have to be settled by payments of gold.

Berlin Wall—Built in 1962 by East Germany to prevent their citizens from escaping to the West, it became the symbol of the Cold War. It was destroyed as part of the democratization of Eastern Europe in 1989.

Bessemer process—A method of producing steel cheaply; developed contemporaneously by Henry Bessemer in England and William Kelley in America during the 1850s.

Big Four—Term applied to the national leaders who first dominated the Versailles Conference after World War I. They were Woodrow Wilson (United States), Lloyd George (Britain), Clemenceau (France), and Orlando (Italy). The term is also used in reference to the Californians who built the Central Pacific Railroad: Leland Stanford, Mark Hopkins, Collis P. Huntington, and Charles Crocker.

bill of attainder—Punishment of an individual by legislative process used formerly in England for political reasons and used in the place of judicial processes requiring evidence of guilt; the Constitution denies this power to Congress.

bimetallism—The use of both gold and silver as standards of value in a monetary system; under bimetallism the standard unit of money, as the dollar, is defined as equal to fixed weights of both gold and silver.

"Black codes"—Laws passed by the Southern states immediately after the Civil War to regulate behavior of the former slaves.

"Black Friday"—Stock and gold market crisis, September 24, 1869, caused by attempt of the speculators Jay Gould and Jim Fisk to corner the national gold supply.

blacklist—A list of names or firms with which one refuses to do business; a weapon formerly used by management to prevent the employment of union organizers and members.

Black Muslims—militant black activist organization led by Malcolm X, who advocated a policy of black nationalism and separateness. "Black Power" became their slogan.

"blue laws"—Legislation to regulate individual conduct and morals, such as compulsory observance of the Sabbath and prohibition of certain kinds of recreation; enacted by colonial Puritans.

"Boomers"—Homeseekers who defied federal authorities and occupied land in Oklahoma during the 1880s. The term also is applied to those who made the "runs" legally to take up land. See "Sooners."

boondoggling—Practice of spending public funds to create unneeded jobs; term has implications of political motives.

Boxer Uprising, 1900—Nationalist uprising in China in which many foreigners were killed; led to intervention by an international expedition that included United States troops.

boycott—A concerted movement, as of labor or consumers, to refuse to buy, sell, or use certain goods.

brain trust—Term applied to a team of able advisers, including a large number of university professors, who helped Roosevelt formulate the New Deal reforms.

Brannan Plan—A change in agricultural policy offered in 1949 by Secretary of Agriculture Brannan under President Truman; essentially it proposed to subsidize farmers directly instead of through price supports and would have left prices of commodities to the determination of a free market.

Brown v. Board of Education—Landmark 1954 Supreme Court decision establishing integration of schools and overturning the separate but equal doctrine of *Plessy v. Ferguson.*

"Bull Moose" Party—Nickname given to the Progressive Republicans who nominated Theodore Roosevelt in 1912.

Burlingame Treaty, 1868—American treaty of friendship with China that permitted unrestricted immigration of Chinese to the United States.

Camp David Accords—negotiated by President Jimmy Carter, they led to peace between Israel and Egypt.

"Cannonism"—Term applied to the tactics of Joseph Cannon, leader of the Republican "Old Guard" and Speaker of the House, who used his power of appointing members of legislative committees to crush minority opposition. Insurgent Republicans and Democrats combined in 1910 to reduce the powers of the Speaker.

Carey Act, 1894—An act of Congress to encourage irrigation of desert lands in the West. It did not succeed because it made no provision for interstate cooperation.

carpetbaggers—Derogatory term applied to Northern politicians, businessmen, and others who migrated to the South during Reconstruction to take advantage of opportunities to advance their own fortunes.

Casablanca Conference, 1943—A meeting between Roosevelt and Churchill at Casablanca, Morocco, to plan military strategy for the conquest of Europe. From the meeting came the decision to demand an "unconditional surrender" of the Axis powers.

caucus—An informal political meeting; up until 1824 caucuses of members of Congress nominated presidential candidates.

Central Treaty Organization (CENTO)—Middle East defense pact against Russia initiated by the United States in 1955 and known as the Baghdad Pact until the name was changed in 1959. The United States did not become a full member until 1958.

Civil Rights Act of 1957—First major civil rights legislation since 1875, which created a civil rights commission and gave the Department of Justice powers of enforcement.

Civil Rights Act of 1964—The most far-reaching civil rights legislation since the Civil War, it authorized the Attorney General to send federal registrars to register black voters.

Civil Works Administration (CWA), 1933–1934—An emergency relief program to provide employment in make-work programs.

Civilian Conservation Corps (CCC), 1933—A relief agency organized by the New Deal and administered by the War Department. It provided employment for young men in conservation work projects; most of their wages were paid to their parents on relief.

Clayton Antitrust Act, 1914—A complex antitrust law passed under President Wilson to strengthen the Sherman Antitrust Act.

Clayton-Bulwer Treaty, 1850—A compromise between the United States and Great Britain by which it was agreed that neither power would take exclusive control over any isthmian canal.

Clean Air Act of 1990—Set overall sulfur dioxide standards and attempted to deal with the acid rain problems.

Cold War—A term widely used after 1947 in reference to the developing hostility between the United States and the Soviet Union.

Committee on Public Information—United States propaganda agency created by Congress in 1917 to mobilize public opinion behind the war effort; headed by the journalist George Creel.

common law—The unwritten law of England based on ancient customs and handed down in court decisions which became precedents for the settlement of similar, subsequent cases; differs from Roman law and statutory law.

Common Market—Created in 1958, it is officially known as the European Economic Community. Its purpose is to create a unified Europe, first economically, then politically.

compact theory—A term used to designate both John Locke's theory of government and the states' rights theory of the relationship of the states to the federal government.

Congress of Industrial Organizations (CIO)—Aggressive nationwide labor union led in early years by John L. Lewis. The initials "CIO" originally stood for the Committee for Industrial Organization, within the American Federation of Labor. In 1938 it became an independent labor union following the principle of industry-wide unionism rather than craft-based unionism.

Credit Mobilier—A scandal, exposed in 1872, named after the Credit Mobilier, the construction company of the Union Pacific Railroad. Wholesale bribery was practiced.

"Crime of '73"—Name given to an Act of Congress discontinuing the coinage and use of silver as money.

Cross of Gold speech, 1896—Name given to the speech by William J. Bryan at the Democratic National Convention in 1896. This speech opposing the gold standard won the presidential nomination for Bryan.

Dawes Act, 1887—Act of Congress providing for distribution of Native American tribal lands to individual ownership and conferring citizenship upon those who renounced tribal allegiance.

"Death Sentence Clause"—A provision of the Public Utility Holding Company Act of 1935 requiring ultimate elimination of most utility holding companies as unnecessary and monopolistic.

De Lome letter—A private letter written to a friend by the Spanish minister to the United States. De Lome wrote disparagingly of President McKinley; the letter was stolen from a post office in Havana and released by Cuban revolutionists in order to stir up American opinion against Spain in 1898.

direct primaries—Elections held to permit the voters to choose party candidates instead of leaving their nomination to political machines.

"Dixiecrats"—Nickname for the States' Rights Party made up of insurgent Democrats of the South who bolted the Democratic Party in 1948 and nominated Governor Strom Thurmond of South Carolina as their presidential candidate.

Dixon-Yates Contract, 1954—Federal agreement under President Eisenhower to purchase electric power from a private syndicate instead of expanding the TVA generating facilities. The contract was abandoned because of public protest against the large profits it would have given a private utility at the expense of taxpayers.

"Dollar Diplomacy"—Term describing the policy of using national diplomacy to promote business interests of American citizens in foreign countries. The policy was employed especially by the Taft administration in the Caribbean area and in China.

Drago Doctrine—A policy formulated by Luis M. Drago of Argentina in 1902; the policy stated that European powers should not be permitted to use force to collect defaulted debts owed them by American nations.

Dust Bowl—A semiarid high plains area subject to serious wind erosion in years of drought; the area straddles parts of Texas, Oklahoma, Colorado, and Kansas.

"eggheads"—A nickname for intellectuals, came to take on a derisive connotation as used by the opponents of Adlai Stevenson in the 1952 campaign.

Eisenhower Doctrine, 1957—A policy of the Eisenhower administration of using military and economic aid to support Middle Eastern nations in resisting aggression of "any nation controlled by international communism."

Elkins Act, 1903—An act of Congress secured by Theodore Roosevelt to increase the regulatory powers of the Interstate Commerce Commission and to stop the practice of railroad rebates.

enumerated powers—The principle that a government may exercise only those powers granted to it by its founders, as in the American Constitution.

Equal Rights Amendment—Known as the ERA, it is a proposed constitutional amendment guaranteeing women equal rights. It has not received the necessary votes for ratification.

Esch-Cummins Transportation Act, 1920—Act of Congress representing a change in the policies of regulating railroads from that of restrictive regulation to one of financial assistance. The act returned the railroads to private management after World War I, permitted consolidations, and sought to assure railroads a six percent return on invested capital.

established churches—Official, or government, churches in the colonies; tithes were collected from all citizens for their support during this time of union of church and state; the disestablishment of the churches brought the separation of church and state.

European Common Market—A customs union of six nations—France, Germany, Italy, the Netherlands, Belgium, and Luxembourg—officially known as the European Economic Community (EEC) and established by the Treaty of Rome (1957). Its ultimate goal is the economic and political unification of its present member nations and of others to be admitted later.

European Cooperation Administration—See Marshall Plan.

excise—An internal revenue tax; term usually applied to a sales tax upon selected commodities as distinguished from a general sales tax.

ex post facto—Any law or measure providing a penalty for an act not made illegal before it was committed. Such laws are forbidden by the Constitution.

Fair Deal—Label given to the New Deal policies as modified and promoted by President Truman after his election in 1948.

Fair Labor Standards Act, 1938—Also called the Wages and Hours Act. As applied to interstate commerce, it established the 40-hour maximum work week, fixed minimum wages, and prohibited child labor. Subsequent amendments have increased minimum hourly wage rates.

Farmers' Alliances—National and local farmers' organizations prominent in the 1880s; they took over the leadership of the farmers' protest movement begun by the Grangers. The Alliances disappeared as they were absorbed by the Populist Party in the early 1890s.

Federal Farm Board, 1939—This agency was created under the Agricultural Marketing Act passed by Congress under the Hoover Administration; it promoted the organization and lent money for agricultural marketing cooperatives as a means of price relief to distressed cotton and wheat farmers; it failed and was abolished in 1933.

Federal Farm Loan Act, 1916—The first federal law to provide agricultural credit; it created the twelve Federal Farm Loan Banks to lend money secured by land mortgages.

Federal Housing Administration (FHA), 1934—An agency established under the New Deal to guarantee private home mortgages and provide funds to promote housing construction.

Federal Trade Commission (FTC)—An agency created in 1914 to assist in enforcing the antitrust laws and to prevent unfair methods of competition in business; it issues "cease and desist" orders to businesses accused of unfair practices of competition.

Feminine Mystique—Book written by feminist Betty Friedan, urging women liberation from traditional values. An outgrowth of the book was the birth of NOW, the National Organization for Women.

Fenians—A secret organization of Irish-Americans during the Civil War period; invaded Canada in 1866 in a plan to exchange Canada for Irish independence.

filibuster—This term has two distinct meanings: (1) an unauthorized military expedition of adventurers against another country in time of peace; (2) obstructive parliamentary tactics employed by a minority to prevent passage of unwanted legislation, usually takes form of long pointless speech-making.

"Fire-eaters"—Southern extremists who favored secession in the decade preceding the Civil War.

Food and Agricultural Act of 1962—Provided direct government subsidies to wheat and grain farmers to maintain their incomes.

Fourteen Points—A statement of American war aims as announced by President Wilson in January 1918, and accepted by Germany as the basis of the Armistice in November 1918. The Fourteenth point called for the establishment of the League of Nations.

franchise—Any special right granted by a governing body, such as the individual right to vote or the right of a corporation to operate a public utility.

Frazier-Lemke Bankruptcy Act, 1934—An act of Congress to delay foreclosure of farm mortgages; replaced by a second and modified Frazier-Lemke Act when the first was declared unconstitutional in 1935.

freedom buses—Buses filled with white and African American activists from the North who headed South and began a campaign for civil rights using nonviolent tactics such as sit-ins.

Freedmen's Bureau—Controversial federal agency that provided relief for distressed freedmen in the South after the Civil War.

freemen—In colonial times those possessing the right to vote.

fundamentalism—The term is applied primarily to orthodox religious beliefs upholding the literal interpretation of the Bible—opposed to the modernists who accept the findings of science.

Fur Seal Controversy, 1889–1893—Also known as the Bering Sea Controversy. Quarrel between the United States and Great Britain over the killing of fur seals in the Bering Sea. The dispute was submitted to arbitration and the United States lost on every disputed point.

GAR, Grand Army of the Republic—Organized in 1865 among the Union veterans of the Civil War.

Gentlemen's Agreement, 1907–1908—An agreement reached between the United States and Japan by an exchange of notes; by the agreement Japan refused to issue passports to immigrants to the United States and the San Francisco School Board rescinded its order segregating Japanese children.

gerrymander—To organize legislative and congressional districts in such a way as to secure the greatest number of districts with a majority of voters favorable to the party doing the redistricting.

glasnost and peristroika—Russian terms which became popularized during the Reagan administration, indicating that Russia was striving for more open and peaceful relations at home and abroad.

Good Neighbor Policy—Foreign policy of friendship toward Latin America begun during the 1920s but given this name by Franklin D. Roosevelt who emphasized the policy.

GOP—Grand Old Party, nickname of the Republican Party.

"grandfather clauses"—Laws passed in Southern states to prevent African Americans from voting. So-called because they qualified persons to vote whose ancestors had voted before 1867 or other dates that excluded Negroes.

Granger laws—State laws enacted under the influence of the Farmers' Grange during the 1870s to provide for the regulation of public utilities, especially the railroads.

Grangers—Popular name for the post-Civil War farmers organization officially known as the Patrons of Husbandry.

Great Society—The name given to Lyndon Johnson's program of domestic and social reform. Such legislation as the Economic Opportunity Act and Medicare were passed.

Gulf of Tonkin Resolution—Passed by Congress in 1964, it gave President Lyndon Johnson authority to commit U.S. troops to Vietnam.

habeas corpus—A legal writ by which an arrested person may demand his freedom unless sufficient cause can be shown to justify holding him for trial.

"Half-Breeds"—A nickname given to Liberal Republicans by their "Stalwart" opponents about 1880. "Half-Breeds" included Hayes, Blaine, and Garfield; "Stalwarts" included Conkling, Platt, and Arthur.

Hatch Act, 1887—A federal law creating the state agricultural experiment stations.

Hatch Act, 1939—A federal law passed to prevent corrupt political practices; its main effect was to prevent political campaigning by federal civil service employees. As amended in 1940 it sought to limit campaign contributions and expenditures in federal election campaigns.

Havana Conference, 1940—A Pan-American Conference to prevent the transfer of Latin-American territories; prevented any attempt of the Axis powers to claim European colonies in America.

Haymarket Affair, 1886—The explosion of a bomb among police who attempted to disperse a mass meeting called by anarchists and labor leaders in Haymarket Square, Chicago. Afterwards, several anarchist leaders were convicted; four were hanged.

Hepburn Act, 1906—The first effective amendment to the Interstate Commerce Act of 1887; secured effective regulation of railroads by greatly increasing the powers of the ICC.

holding company—A corporation owning sufficient shares in other corporations to effectively control them; frequently used as a monopoly device.

Home Owners Loan Corporation (HOLC), 1933—An emergency home refinancing agency created to prevent loss of homes by foreclosure.

Hundred Days—Term applied to the flood of relief and recovery legislation passed by Congress during the first three months under Franklin D. Roosevelt.

implied powers—Powers of Congress not directly granted by the Constitution but permitted by the elastic clause which gives Congress the power "To make all laws...necessary and proper" for executing the powers expressly granted.

Income Tax Act of 1986—The first major overhaul of the tax codes, it compressed the number of tax brackets.

initiative and referendum—Processes by which voters may directly vote upon laws; intended to give law-making power to the voters since state and local legislative bodies are not always fully responsive to the popular will.

injunction—A court order forbidding some action; frequently used as a weapon against organized labor except as outlawed. Violation of an injunction may result in assessment of heavy penalties for "contempt of court."

Insular Cases—A series of Supreme Court decisions made after 1900 relating to the status of colonies and territories outside the United States mainland. These cases recognized liberal powers of Congress to apply or refuse provisions of the Constitution in these possessions.

Iran-Contra Affair—The arms-for-hostage deal negotiated by members of the Reagan administration. It resulted in a congressional hearing which laid the responsibility on the President.

Iron Curtain—A term first used by Winston Churchill in 1946 in an address in Fulton, Missouri; it called attention to Russian domination of the countries of Eastern Europe and to the threat of Soviet aggression.

"Irreconcilables"—Republican members of the Senate who opposed the Treaty of Versailles—even with the reservations added to it.

isolationism—The American policy of avoiding "entangling alliances" with European nations.

Johnson Act, 1934—Act of Congress against European nations that had defaulted debts arising out of World War I; prohibited such nations from marketing bond issues in the United States.

Kellogg-Briand Pact, 1928—Also known as the Pact of Paris. American Secretary of State Kellogg and Aristide Briand, French foreign minister, took the lead in negotiating treaties by which most of the nations of the world renounced war as an instrument of national policy.

Keynesian economics—The economic recommendations of the most influential economist in recent times, John Maynard Keynes of Britain. He dealt especially with the problem of depression; as countermeasures against depression he advised deficit spending, mild inflation, and liberal welfare payments.

Knights of Labor—Aggressive national labor union organized in 1869 by Uriah S. Stephens. Terence V. Powderly came to be its greatest leader. It declined in the late 1880s because of its loss of two railroad strikes, its mixed membership, and the effect of the Haymarket Affair.

La Follette Seaman's Act, 1915—Effectively regulated and improved conditions of seamen employed by the American merchant marine but increased costs of American ship operators in the face of foreign competition.

laissez-faire—Almost literally, "Let them do as they please"; economic philosophy associated with Adam Smith in his *Wealth of Nations;* calls for an economy free of government controls; the free enterprise system.

Landrum-Griffin Act, 1959—The most important federal labor legislation since the Taft-Hartley Act; contained various provisions to prevent abuses by labor union officers and enlarged the prohibition of secondary boycotts.

Lend-lease Act, 1941—A measure sought by President Roosevelt that permitted the President to lend or lease war materials to nations acting as American allies in World War II.

Liberal Republicans—A faction that left the Republican Party in 1872 to support the Democratic nominee Horace Greeley.

lobbying—Practice of individuals and pressure groups of seeking by various means to influence the vote of members of governmental bodies.

log-rolling—A practice of vote-trading by legislators in support of each other's favorite laws.

Lusitania—A British passenger liner, carrying troops and munitions as well as American civilians, sunk by German submarine attack in 1915. The sinking was used by pro-British propagandists to turn American opinion against Germany.

McCarthyism—A term designating ruthless, reckless, and unfair charges of Communism, like those used by Senator Joseph McCarthy, against one's enemies.

McNary-Haugen Bill—A farm relief measure defeated several times in Congress and by presidential vetoes during the 1920s; the bills sought to secure higher domestic prices for farm produce and to subsidize agricultural exports.

mandamus—A written order of a court ordering that a specific thing be done.

Manifest Destiny—A widely held belief among Americans that the United States was clearly destined to occupy all of North America.

Mann-Elkins Act, 1910—An Act of Congress extending the powers of the ICC to include telephone and telegraph lines and to further strengthen the regulation of railroads.

Marshall Plan—Also known as the European Recovery Program (ERP). An American plan to aid economic recovery in Europe; it was promoted by Secretary of State George C. Marshall and President Truman and went into effect in 1948; contributed much to Europe's attainment of higher levels of prosperity.

Merchant Marine Act, 1920—An extremely liberal measure to return control of shipping to private operators after World War I; it provided loans, subsidies, and regulations to aid American shipping companies.

merit system—The civil service system by which public employees are chosen upon a basis of qualifications rather than by political influence.

"missile gap"—Term much used in the early 1960s to refer to the alleged lag in American missile development and production as compared with that of Russia.

Molly Maguires—A secret, criminal labor organization operating in the anthracite coal fields of Pennsylvania in the 1870s; eventually suppressed.

Montevideo Conference, 1933—A Pan-American Conference at Montevideo, Uruguay, where President Roosevelt declared his opposition to armed intervention in inter-American affairs.

moratorium—A provision for delaying the repayment of debt.

Muckrakers—A nickname given by Theodore Roosevelt to journalists who actively exposed, after 1900, the wrongdoings of big business.

"Mugwumps"—Reform Republicans who supported Cleveland in the election of 1884.

Mulligan Letters—Letters written by James G. Blaine to James Mulligan; these letters which showed that Blaine had received and returned favors from a railroad company probably kept Blaine from becoming President.

Munich Conference—A meeting at Munich, Germany, in 1938, where the British and French signed a pact granting Hitler's demands against Czechoslovakia.

Muscle Shoals Bill—A measure introduced by Senator George Norris of Nebraska providing for federal operation of the dam at Muscle Shoals, Alabama, for the production of low-cost fertilizer; the project was finally realized in 1933 through the creation of the TVA.

National Labor Relations Board—The agency created in 1935 under the Wagner Act to administer laws affecting labor-management relations in interstate commerce. The two main functions of the Board are to prevent unfair labor practices and to determine employees representation in collective bargaining.

National Labor Union—The first national labor organization, founded in 1866 and lasted until 1871; it was a federation of other unions instead of being a single great union.

National Recovery Administration (NRA), 1933—New Deal agency established by the National Industrial Recovery Act to promote recovery by preventing cutthroat competition among the nation's businesses, both large and small. The NRA administered codes of fair competition, fixed minimum prices and wages, and maximum hours.

New Federalism—Reduction of spending by the federal government and a decrease in social and entitlement programs initiated by President Ronald Reagan.

New Frontier—The inauguration theme of the Kennedy administration representing his advocacy of dynamic change for the country.

Newlands Act, 1902—Also called the Reclamation Act of 1902. The law established a revolving fund to be used to finance irrigation projects and has been notably successful in its work in the West.

Nixon's New Economic Policy—A domestic policy established by President Nixon that set wage and price controls in order to combat inflation and high interest rates in 1971.

Norris-La Guardia Act, 1932—An Act of Congress outlawing the "yellow-dog" contract and the use of injunctions against labor unions in strikes.

North Atlantic Treaty Organization (NATO)—A national defense organization created by the Western nations in 1949 under the North Atlantic Treaty; the danger of Russian aggression motivated its organization.

Nuclear Proliferation Treaty—Signed by 63 nations in 1968, it outlawed further spread of nuclear armaments.

Nuclear Test Ban Treaty—Signed by the Soviet Union, England, and the United States in 1963, it prohibited atmospheric nuclear testing.

Office of Price Administration (OPA)—An agency created in 1942 to administer price controls after the outbreak of World War II. It had the power to place ceilings on all prices except farm commodities and to ration scarce supplies of such goods as auto tires, sugar, coffee, and gasoline; various food items were rationed later.

"Ohio Idea"—An inflationary proposal of paper money advocates to pay the Union Civil War debt with greenbacks instead of in gold.

Open Door Policy—The American foreign policy begun in 1899 under Secretary of State Hay to promote equal rights of foreign nations in China and to uphold the rights of China against aggressive imperialist powers.

Operation Restore Hope—The United States-led invasion of Somalia aimed at restoring peace and providing food in the civil war-torn country.

Organization of American States (OAS)—A collective defense system organized in 1947 at Rio de Janeiro by the United States and Latin America under the Rio Treaty.

Panama Canal Treaty—Authorized control of the Canal Zone by Panama in 1979 and a complete takeover of the canal by Panama in 1999.

Paris Agreement—Pact which in 1954 recognized the sovereignty of West Germany and integrated the country into NATO.

paternalism—The practice by a nation or employer of controlling and caring for people as dependents in the manner of a father toward his children.

Peace Corps—A foreign aid agency created in March 1961, to provide teachers and technicians to assist underdeveloped countries likely to come under Communist influence.

Pendleton Act, 1883—Act of Congress that created the Federal Civil Service Commission and instituted the merit system for federal employees.

Persian Gulf War—Conflict between the United States and its allies against Iraq. Began as Operation Desert Shield, after Iraq's leader Saddam Hussein invaded oil rich Kuwait. Ended as Operation Desert Storm, with complete Iraq defeat after the first 100 hours.

Platt Amendment, 1902—Certain clauses that the American Congress required Cuba to add to her constitution; they were designed to regulate Cuban foreign relations and made Cuba a protectorate of the United States.

Plessy v. Ferguson—Landmark 1896 Supreme Court decision establishing the separate but equal doctrine for access to public facilities.

plurality—The votes polled by the leading candidate, not necessarily a majority of all votes cast.

Point Four—A program of technical economic assistance to foreign countries announced by President Truman in 1950.

pool—A monopoly device adopted in the 1860s; agreements to avoid competition by dividing markets geographically or by percentage or by the payment of profits to a common treasury to be divided according to agreement.

Populism—A reform third party of the 1890s, especially active among farmers in the West and South; protested against big business domination of American economic and political life.

Potsdam Conference, 1945—A conference between Truman, Churchill, Attlee, and Stalin at Potsdam, Germany. The meeting called for the immediate surrender of Japan, but dealt mainly with the occupation of Germany and with other European problems.

primogeniture—Laws of inheritance providing descent of land to the oldest son.

Public Works Administration (PWA)—A federal agency established in 1935 under the National Industrial Recovery Act to provide for the construction of large public works projects; a "pump-priming" measure to stimulate business and increase employment.

Pujo Committee, 1912—House committee created to investigate the "money trust" and banking system; revealed evidence of monopoly in commercial and investment banking; it influenced provisions of the Federal Reserve Act.

Pullman strike, 1894—Nationwide railroad strike beginning with employees of the Pullman Company in Chicago. President Cleveland intervened by sending federal troops to permit trains to move in Chicago.

Rainbow Coalition—Jesse Jackson's minority coalition that advocated voter registration among minorities.

Reagan Democrats—A traditional Democratic party base that voted Republican in the 1980 presidential election.

Reaganomics—The program to limit federal spending that resulted in a deflationary economy for the country.

Reciprocal Trade Agreements—Treaties negotiated for mutual reduction of tariffs. In the Trade Agreements Act of 1934 the Democrats approached the problem of tariff reduction by reciprocity treaties rather than by revision of the Hawley-Smoot Tariff Act which remained in effect as the basic tariff law.

reciprocity—Mutual concessions to reduce tariff rates, trade agreements between two countries.

Reconstruction Finance Corporation (RFC)—A federal lending agency created in 1932 to alleviate the depression-born financial difficulties of corporations, the states, and local governments; abolished in 1954.

rediscount—A method employed by the Federal Reserve Banks of lending money on notes; the rediscount represents the advance payment of interest by the member bank doing the borrowing.

referendum—A form of direct legislation whereby certain measures are required to be submitted to the decision of voters, usually because of a failure to act by a legislative body.

refunding—The settlement of a debt by substitution of a new issue of bonds for an earlier issue.

reparations—Payments assessed usually against a defeated nation held responsible for war damage.

Resumption Act, 1875—An Act of Congress providing for the resumption of specie payment beginning January 1, 1879; it made greenbacks redeemable in gold and practically placed the nation on the gold standard.

Roosevelt Corollary—An interpretation and enlargement of the Monroe Doctrine by Theodore Roosevelt asserting the right of the United States to intervene in Latin-American nations to require them to meet their financial obligations to creditor nations.

Roe v. Wade—Landmark Supreme Court decision legalizing abortion with no restrictions within the first trimester of pregnancy.

Root-Takahira Agreement, 1908—An executive agreement reached between the United States and Japan recognizing the status quo in the Pacific and the Open Door in China.

"Rum, Romanism, and Rebellion"—A derogatory reference to the Democratic Party and slur at Catholicism made by a Republican campaign speaker in New York in 1884 in the presence of the presidential candidate James G. Blaine; it lost the presidency for Blaine.

S & L Bailout—Begun during the Reagan administration, it allocated money to over 350 savings and loan associations in order to prevent bankruptcy of those institutions.

Sacco-Vanzetti case—A much-publicized trial in Massachusetts of two anarchists on charges of robbery and murder. Reputable opinion holds that the two were convicted for their radical beliefs rather than upon sufficient evidence of crime. Both were executed in 1927.

Sackville-West letter, 1888—This incident is also referred to as the Murchison letter. A letter was written to the British minister to the United States, Sackville-West, during the presidential campaign, seeking his advice on how to vote. His reply implied a recommendation to vote for Cleveland and may have been responsible for Cleveland's defeat by turning the Irish-American vote against him.

sanctions—The application of economic or other measures against a nation to force it to obey international law.

Scopes trial, 1925—The trial in Dayton, Tennessee of the high school teacher John T. Scopes on charges of violating the Tennessee anti-evolution law; the case represented a conflict between fundamentalism and modernism in religion and was sensationalized by the press.

"Sea-dogs"—English sea captains under Queen Elizabeth acting as legalized pirates in conducting trade and raiding Spanish towns and ships in America and Europe.

Securities and Exchange Commission—A federal agency established in 1934 to administer the Securities Exchange Act. The Commission requires full disclosure of information regarding new issues of securities and regulates practices in securities markets.

Sherman Silver Purchase Act, 1890—A victory for the inflationists and advocates of the use of greater amounts of silver money; the law required the treasury to purchase and coin 4,500,000 ounces of silver per month and pay for it with legal tender treasury notes redeemable in gold.

sit-down strike—A labor weapon used by the CIO in 1937 and 1938; instead of maintaining pickets outside plants to prevent strikebreakers from replacing strikers, the strikers remained in possession of the plant.

"sixteen to one"—A political slogan used by silver money advocates to express the price to be paid for silver in terms of gold. One ounce of gold was to be paid for sixteen ounces of silver, a very favorable price for silver.

Soil Conservation and Domestic Allotment Act of 1936—Act of Congress to restrict farm production by making benefit payments to farmers to plant part of their land in soil-building crops.

"Solid South"—Term applied to the one-party (Democratic) system of the South following the Civil War; followed to preserve white supremacy.

"Sooners"—Term applied to landseekers around 1890 who tried to enter Oklahoma sooner than the deadline for the "runs" to begin.

Southeast Asia Treaty Organization (SEATO)—A weak mutual defense organization begun in 1954; was initiated by the United States and included Great Britain, France, Australia, New Zealand, Pakistan, Thailand, and the Philippines; does not commit members to go to war in case a member is attacked.

Sputnik—First man-made orbiting satellite launched by Russians in 1957. The U.S. responded by passing the National Defense Education Act providing for funds for states to aid individuals in the study of science.

"Stalwarts"—Nickname applied to the spoilsmen and conservatives in the Republican Party around 1880. See "Half-Breeds."

Stimson Doctrine, 1931—The American policy of opposition to Japanese invasion of Manchuria as stated by Secretary of State Stimson; it declared that the United States would not recognize Japanese seizure of Chinese territory.

St. Lawrence Seaway—In 1954 Congress authorized the St. Lawrence Seaway Project, after Canada had decided to proceed alone if necessary with the long-discussed project. The project has opened the Great Lakes to ocean-going ships.

Strategic Arms Limitation Treaties—Popularly known as SALT, these treaties reduced the nuclear arsenal of the United States and the Soviet Union.

Suez Crisis, 1956—Threat of international war begun with the Israeli invasion of Egypt in October, 1956. Britain and France joined Israel, but the United States and Russia, acting through the UN, secured a cease-fire.

syndicalism—Radical trade union movement and philosophy advocating use of violent, direct action such as sabotage and general strikes.

Taft-Hartley Act, 1947—A comprehensive labor law that modified the labor policies established by the Wagner Act. While the Wagner Act strengthened unionism vis-a-vis management, the Taft-Hartley law included various provisions intended to regulate union practices.

Tariff Commission—This advisory body was established as a permanent agency in 1916 to assist the president in tariff rate-making.

Teapot Dome Scandal—A case of corruption in the Harding administration. Secretary of the Interior Fall was tried for bribery for leasing lands of the Teapot Dome reserves in Wyoming to the Doheny oil interests.

Teller Amendment, 1898—A clause in the war resolution against Spain disclaiming any American intention to rule Cuba.

Tennessee Valley Authority (TVA)—The TVA was created in 1933 to achieve various purposes. One of the main purposes was to create a "yardstick" to determine the cost of producing electric power to aid in public utility regulation over the nation.

Trade Expansion Act of 1962—Passed in response to the Common Market, it granted the president increased authority to reduce tariff duties in return for concessions by other nations and gave federal aid to industries hurt by foreign competition.

triangular trade—The predominant patterns of foreign trade by the thirteen colonies with Europe, Africa, and the West Indies.

Triple Entente—The alliance between France, Great Britain, and Russia preceding World War.

Truman Doctrine, 1947—Policy begun by President Truman of giving military and economic aid to countries threatened by Communist subversion;

first put in effect by congressional appropriations to aid Greece and Turkey.

trust—A device used to create business monopolies. Under it competing corporations surrender voting stock to a board of trustees in return for trust certificates. The trustees then operate the separate companies as a unit for purposes of price-fixing and other policies.

Tweed Ring—A grossly corrupt political machine in New York City around 1870, led by "Boss" Tweed.

Union League—A propaganda agency of the Radical Republicans in the South worked to assure the loyalty of the Freedmen to the Republican Party.

United Nations Relief and Rehabilitation Administration (UNRRA)—Agency created in 1945 to aid liberated countries.

Venezuela Boundary Dispute—A long-standing dispute between Great Britain and Venezuela over the boundary between Venezuela and British Guiana. President Cleveland forced Britain to submit the dispute to an arbitration tribunal.

Venezuela Intervention, 1902—Britain, Germany, and Italy were seeking to collect debts owed them by Venezuela when the United States intervened to support arbitration. President Roosevelt upheld the Monroe Doctrine against Germany in this incident.

Vietnamization—Nixon's foreign policy doctrine which stated that South Vietnam must assume the greater part of the defense burden against Communist aggression.

Volstead Act, 1919—Act of Congress implementing the Eighteenth Amendment. It prohibited the manufacture, transportation, and sale of alcoholic beverages and provided penalties for violations.

Wade-Davis Bill, 1864—Reconstruction program introduced by the Radical Republicans but pocket-vetoed by Lincoln.

Wagner Act—See National Labor Relations Board.

War Powers Act—Passed in 1973 in response to the Vietnam War, it limited the president's ability as commander in chief to commit U.S. troops to combat.

War Production Board—The agency created by executive order in 1942 to oversee the production of war equipment and allocate materials between war and civilian needs.

Washington Naval Conference, 1921–1922—A conference of the leading naval powers leading to the Four-Power Treaty, the Five-Power Treaty, and the Nine-Power Pact.

watered stock—Stock issued with a nominal value in excess of capital actually invested in earning assets of an operating corporation.

Watergate—The greatest political scandal in U.S. history, ultimately forcing the resignation of President Richard Nixon.

wildcat banks—state-chartered banks that followed unsound banking practices by issuing paper money not sufficiently backed up by reserves of specie.

Womens Christian Temperance Union (WCTU)—Founded in 1874 to curb liquor consumption and promote prohibition laws.

Workers' Compensation Laws—Also called employer's liability laws. State and federal laws that make employers liable for injuries sustained on the job by employees. Employers protect themselves by insurance against accidents.

Works Progress Administration (WPA)—The largest and most comprehensive of the New Deal relief agencies. It promoted a great variety of programs to provide jobs and incomes for the unemployed.

Yalta Conference, 1945—The most publicized wartime conference of the Allied leaders. They met at Yalta in Russia where many important decisions were made relating to ending the war against Japan and the disposition of territories won from the defeated powers.

"yellow-dog" contract—An agreement required by employers that an employee promise not to join any union during his employment.

"yellow" journalism—Newspapers made sensational to attract readers; associated originally with the use of yellow ink, particularly in the first comic strip, "The Yellow Kid."

Zimmermann Note, 1917—A message revealing the plan of Germany to urge Mexico to attack the United States and also urge Japan to switch from the Allies to the Central Powers in World War I.

See index for persons or terms not listed above.

INDEX